WHITE CAP
AND BAILS

WHITE CAP AND BAILS

ADVENTURES OF A MUCH TRAVELLED UMPIRE

Dickie Bird

with
Keith Lodge

Illustrations by Bill Gregory

Hodder & Stoughton

First published in Great Britain in 1999
by Hodder and Stoughton
A division of Hodder Headline PLC

A CIP catalogue record for this book is available
from the British Library

ISBN 0 340 75087 1

Typeset by Palimpsest Book Production Limited,
Polmont, Stirlingshire
Printed and bound in Great Britain by
Clays Ltd, Bungay, Suffolk

Hodder and Stoughton
A division of Hodder Headline PLC
338 Euston Road
London NW1 3BH

CONTENTS

PHOTOGRAPHIC ACKNOWLEDGEMENTS

The author and publisher would like to thank the following for permission to reproduce photographs:

Allsport, Richard Binns, Gerry Cranham, Patrick Eagar, Glamorgan County Cricket Club, Gloucestershire County Cricket Club, Hampshire County Cricket Club, Nottingham Post Group, PA News, Popperfoto, Reuters, Sport & General, Jan Traylen, Worcestershire County Cricket Club.

All other photographs are from private collections.

INTRODUCTION

AFTER writing my autobiography I thought at first that there was nothing else left to say. That was it. The end. Then, early last year, Hodder and Stoughton editor Roddy Bloomfield, who had been such an invaluable help in the production of my best-seller, suggested over lunch one day that I ought to write another book – and he had an idea about what to put in it. He proposed that I should focus primarily on my experiences around the county championship grounds, with references also to incidents on the international circuit which I may not have covered before.

I must admit I was sceptical at first, but the more I thought about it the more the idea appealed to me, and I was further encouraged by the reaction of friends and well-wishers who had read my autobiography and were delighted at the prospect of more of the same. When Keith Lodge, the Sports Editor of the *Barnsley Chronicle* and my trusted friend from childhood days, agreed to help me with the manuscript I readily decided to go ahead. It was Keith who did such a magnificent job recording my words so accurately in my autobiography.

It has been hard work, but I have also had so much pleasure taking a wander down memory lane, county by county, recalling so many humorous occasions, some of which were only hazy recollections until my memory was given a timely jog. In this respect I am indebted to many people for countless reminders of half-forgotten incidents, especially my old friend Don Mosey, who turned up trumps by recalling a fund of stories from my cricketing life. He very sadly died this month. It was so good to visit all those grounds again, even though it was mainly only in my mind's eye, because they have all been like second homes to me during my long career as player and umpire.

I am well aware that some of the stories in this book and my previous one have been given a little poetic licence along the way. It's the way I tell 'em, you see. However, there is always someone keen to point out that maybe the facts were marginally different from my recollection. That being so, there is a statistical section at the back of this book which I can assure you is totally accurate.

It really has been a labour of love, re-living so many incidents which have made me laugh – and cry, too. I have always said that the main thing in cricket – indeed, in any sport – is to enjoy the game. I hope that you find enjoyment in this book by sharing these recollections.

Dickie Bird
August 1999

WHITE CAP AND BAILS

ADVENTURES OF A MUCH TRAVELLED UMPIRE

Chesterfield

DERBYSHIRE

1

I NDIA'S master batsman Sachin Tendulkar stood at the side of me in the middle during a tourists' match at Queen's Park, Chesterfield in Derbyshire, and reflected, 'Do you know, Dickie, I don't think I have ever seen a more beautiful cricket setting than this.'

As we looked out past the flowers in full bloom, through the archway of trees in all their greenery, to the famous crooked spire of All Saints' Church, I had to agree with him. In its pomp, in the middle of summer, there is no more picturesque ground in the world, with the possible exception of Newlands, in South Africa.

In future, however, Derbyshire will stage all their matches at their Derby headquarters. It is a shame that such out-grounds as Buxton, Burton-on-Trent, Heanor, and especially Queen's Park, have been lost to county cricket. They all had an appeal and an atmosphere of their own.

Don't get me wrong. I have nothing against Derby, and tremendous improvements have been made there. As a player I remember the Racecourse Ground being very bleak and open, and having to use the old dressing rooms where the jockeys used to change before the races. It was not very inviting. These days there are imposing stands, a magnificent pavilion, excellent changing accommodation, banqueting suites and all the trimmings. The facilities are probably better than those at Chesterfield, but the setting does not compare, and I do not think they will get better support than they did at Queen's Park.

The Chesterfield ground always had a lovely atmosphere, probably because it is so steeped in history. One of my earliest memories is of a Yorkshire and Derbyshire match in 1946, when Bowes and Smailes were having a lot of trouble with both length and line. Eventually Hutton, fielding down at third man, became so perplexed by it all that he insisted on the pitch being checked. Imagine the colour of the groundsman's face when the pitch was found to be twenty-four yards long instead of the statutory twenty-two!

Derbyshire started as a first-class county in 1882, and in their long history have won the county championship on just one occasion, in 1936, when they were led to their solitary success by their captain, A. W. Richardson. They were, however, the first winners of the NatWest Trophy in 1981, and they won the Sunday League in 1990 and the Benson and Hedges Cup in 1993.

There have been quite a few characters connected with Derbyshire through the years, one of them being Major Douglas Carr, who was Secretary for a long time. He took great pains to keep the spectators informed, and he just loved to go on the public address system. Unfortunately, he had a bit of a prissy delivery and there was always some merriment among the Derbyshire following when they heard the familiar, 'Attention plee-ase.'

I was umpiring at Chesterfield on one occasion and having arrived at the ground early, as I always do, I found that torrential rain had flooded it. The beautiful lake which lies adjacent to the cricket field had spilled over, and some areas were ankle deep. Borrowing the groundsman's Wellington boots, I strode out into the middle, to be greeted by several ducks who were happily exploring waters new.

Major Carr emerged from the pavilion, also Wellington booted, and carrying an enormous umbrella. He came up to me and moaned, 'Dickie, for goodness' sake tell me what's happening. I would like to go on the Tannoy and tell the public exactly what the situation is.'

I looked at the Major. I looked round the deserted ground. And I looked at the ducks. 'Major,' I said, 'there's only me, thee and t' ducks here. What is there to tell?'

The cries of those Chesterfield ducks can be very apt at the fall of certain wickets. In fact, I am told that when West Indian Laurie Johnson once bagged a pair there in a match against Sussex, two ducks from the lake walked off with him!

Quackers, I call it.

The Major's brother, Donald, became captain of Derbyshire. He was a splendid batsman, bowled slow left-arm googlies and chinamen, and was a fine slip fielder. Batting at number three or four, he got a stack of runs and still holds the record for one season, scoring 2,165 in 1959. He went on to become my boss at the Test and County Cricket Board, and I have a lot of respect for him. He was great to work for, and a marvellous help. If ever I had any problems – and I had a few in my time – he used to say, 'Stop wittering, Dickie. Come into my office, and we'll sort it out. Now, how about a nice drop of whisky?'

Another name that always springs to mind in association with Derbyshire, and Queen's Park in particular, is that of George Henry Pope. He was a magnificent all-rounder who played for England once or twice before being cast aside after he upset the selectors: George was once so annoyed at being made twelfth man that he made his feelings known in no uncertain manner. That was the end of his international career, which was very sad, because he was a great bowler, a good batsman, and a terrific fielder. The story goes that it was George who taught Alec Bedser, the legendary Surrey and England bowler, how to bowl the leg-cutter. George had a brother, Alf, who was a similar type of bowler and a more than useful player. Both of them, along with several other Derbyshire players, including Tommy Mitchell and Bill Copson, played wartime cricket in the Bradford League. Tommy, incidentally, was a rarity at the time – a leg-spin bowler who spun the ball an awful lot.

Cliff Gladwin was another fine bowler with Derbyshire just before and after the war, and opened the attack with George. They were a formidable pairing, although both acknowledged the debt they owed to Alan Revill for many of their wickets.

Alan used to field close to the wicket for both Pope and Gladwin, and he was one of the best short-leggers there has ever been. He used to snap them up just like catching pigeons, despite the fact that he had a bit of a squint. You used to wonder whether he was looking at you or someone just behind your shoulder. It was weird. He could certainly see the ball, however, no matter how quickly it came to him, and no matter how little time he had to react.

Les Jackson carried on the tradition of great fast bowlers, just as the careers of Pope and Gladwin were coming to an end, and for me he was possibly the best of them all. I played against Jacko, and he was a bowler I always used to face in fear and trembling. Many's the time I'd get my pads across to let one of his deliveries go by, and suddenly it would pitch, nip back, and hit me between the legs. In the real soft spot. And I'd be in agony.

At the end of the day Les always bought me a pint, and I would think he wasn't such a bad bloke after all. Until the next day. Then he'd be at it again. No mercy. I used to say to him, 'Nay, Les, don't be like that. Just back off a bit and I'll buy *you* a pint tonight.' Maybe he didn't believe me, because the next ball always came down even quicker and nipped back more smartly than ever.

Then there was Harold Rhodes, an England player who was no-balled out of the game by the great umpire, Syd Buller. Syd called him for throwing in a match at Chesterfield, and Harold was never the same again. It virtually ended his career.

Strangely enough, one or two Derbyshire pacemen have been caught up in controversies. Alan Ward was sent off by his own captain in one game in 1973: Brian Bolus, who had taken over the captaincy on his arrival from Nottinghamshire, sent Ward for an early bath for refusing to bowl against Yorkshire. 'Right,' said Bolus, 'if that's your attitude, you can get off the field and send out the twelfth man. You're no use to me.' There had never been anything like it in the modern game, and I am told it was only the third known case of its kind in history.

Television summoned F. S. Trueman to the studios for his opinion on the matter. In his usual blunt, straight-to-the-point way, Fred said, 'To be a great fast bowler you 'ave to 'ave a big 'eart and a big arse. Wardy's nivver 'ad eether.' Needless to say, the interview was curtailed at that point. Derbyshire went through fourteen captains in thirty-two years. Not bad going by any standards. But there were some very interesting characters among them. Charlie Lee, for instance. He was a lovely chap, but he took himself and his duties very seriously. In the middle 'sixties Charlie was captain of the side for a pre-season practice match, and in the team was a young man called David Smith who was a good Bradford League player and anxious to be offered a county contract.

Charlie told him, 'Listen, lad, if you make a century in this game you stand a very good chance of being given at least a three-match run with us.'

Young Smith could hardly wait to get out to the middle to show what he could do. Then he caught sight of the batting order. He was down at number seven. What odds a century going in then?

Derek Morgan was a good all-round cricketer and a sound enough captain, but he was hardly renowned for his sense of humour. Playing against Somerset, Derbyshire were having to put up with the usual barrage of 'chat' from Bill Alley, who never shut up, whether batting, bowling or fielding. On this occasion he was doing a fair amount of damage to the opposition with the ball. Morgan got on his high horse. As captain he issued an instruction to his players that on no account should they get involved in a war of words with the big Australian. Realising what was happening, Alley goaded the remaining batsmen even more mercilessly. And in the end Morgan ordered his players to 'stop LISTENING to Alley!'

In the early 1960s, a young man called George William Richardson joined the county. He was a left-arm fast bowler and middle-order right-hand batsman. His father, Arthur, had captained Derbyshire in the early 1930s, and both were products of Winchester School. They therefore seemed rather out of place among the miners, steelworkers and suchlike who formed the greater part of the Derbyshire team.

Richardson the younger made his first appearance at Chesterfield, and after the first day's play the newspapers carried reports referring to debutant 'Bill' Richardson. The following day a formidable female stormed into the press box in a fury.

'My son's name,' she informed the startled gathering, 'is William. And I would be very much obliged if you did not call him Bill.'

The pressmen, who had heard on the grapevine that there was a very strong possibility that the young Mr Richardson would eventually be appointed captain of the county, persuaded their respective Sports Editors to use the more formal 'William' in future reports.

The *Daily Mail*, however, took the bull by the horns. Their correspondent, having noted that G. W. Richardson sprayed his deliveries all over the shop when bowling the following day, tagged him 'Wild Bill'.

There was relief all round when Mrs Richardson failed to put in a feared reappearance.

In more recent times Derbyshire has boasted two other fine fast-bowling internationals in the shape of Devon Malcolm and Dominic Cork.

Now, although Devon is a lovely man, I have to report that he once struck me. With the ball, I hasten to add. And quite unintentionally, or so he says. He claims that he thought I was the stumps. I was umpiring at square leg, and glorious Devon, who normally wears glasses but opts for contact lenses when playing, was fielding on the fine-leg boundary. The ball was played down towards him and he raced round – well, ambled is probably a better description, because he's no Linford Christie – in order to field it. He threw it in and it hit me smack between the shoulder blades. I wondered what the hell had happened. I went down like a pricked balloon.

Devon ran up to me, concern written all over his face. He picked me up, dusted me down, and muttered, 'Sorry, Dickie, I thought you were the stumps.'

'Dev,' I said, 'I know your eyesight isn't brilliant, mate, but I can't believe that. Whenever did you come across stumps wearing a white cap?'

From that day to this I'm convinced that he had forgotten to put his contact lenses in.

Devon was also a big appealer for lbws, but he bowled so wide of the return crease that he did not stand a cat in hell's chance of getting a decision. Not from me, anyway. He could shout and bawl as much as he liked, but it would always be 'not out'.

Corky has a gift whereby he can swing the ball away late

when he's really on song, so he always has a chance of getting even the great players out. He is a marvellous competitor, both for county and country, and he certainly makes himself heard, not to mention seen. I've had no problems with him, despite his histrionics. He's not a bad appealer: he really lets it rip. Gets down on his hands and knees, praying for you to give him an lbw decision.

I used to tell him, 'Get off thy knees, Corky, tha'll be wearing 'em out one of these days an' then tha'll not be able to bowl at all.'

Corky always argued that he was in with a shout, quite literally, of an lbw – even from me – because he bowled wicket to wicket, and he would never let me forget it. He would constantly remind me of it out there in the middle. I had it all damned day. In the end I'd turn to him and say, 'All right, Corky, I've got the message. Now for goodness' sake put a sock in it.'

He was right, though: if a bowler bowls wicket to wicket, keeps it straight, and the ball holds up, then he is in with a great chance if ball raps pad.

Derbyshire had another fine bowler in Dallas Moir, a big, slow left-armer from Scotland. It pains me every time I think about him.

Moir was the chap who bowled a long hop to South African Ken McEwan, batting for Essex at the time. McEwan was one of the hardest strikers of the ball in the game, and he pulled it towards me at square leg. It struck me on the shin, and I thought I'd broken my leg. As I went down clutching it, my leg came up like a football before my eyes, which were watering ever so slightly. Moir came over, stooped down, picked me up in his great big arms as if I were no more than a little baby, carried me off to the physio's room, and laid me ever so gently down on the treatment table.

At the time I wasn't sure whether my shin bone was connected to my thigh bone or my ankle bone, or if it was still connected to anything at all.

There was another sorry tale of someone being hit by the ball, though thankfully not me this time, when Glamorgan visited Chesterfield in 1978. Glamorgan batsman Malcolm Nash received a long hop and hit the ball, off the full blade of the bat, straight at Phil Russell, who was crouched down at short leg. The ball lodged in Russell's protective helmet, and there was blood all over the place, as well as the odd bit of bone. It was nasty. The poor lad's cheekbone was shattered.

There was, of course, a great deal of immediate anxiety about the state of Russell's health, but once he had recovered sufficiently to be taken to hospital, we umpires had to decide whether it was a catch or not. Was the batsman therefore out? No one knew. Nothing like this had ever happened before. Eventually I decided the best course of action was to declare a dead ball. It seemed the fairest and most logical thing to do. When my colleague, Eddie Phillipson, and I later consulted Lord's, they agreed, saying that we had handled the situation correctly and had made the right decision. Our ruling was incorporated into the Laws of the Game, making me instrumental in writing a little bit of cricketing history.

I always enjoyed umpiring at the out-grounds, although one game between Derbyshire and Gloucestershire at Ilkeston was not very appealing. Or, to be more strictly accurate, none of the players was. Stevenson, of Derbyshire, was bowling to David Shepherd, who is now a very fine first-class umpire and my Test match colleague for many years. Shep played down the leg-side, and from my square-leg position it looked as though the ball had flicked his glove. I waited for the appeal, but none came. Not from Bob Taylor, who took the ball behind the stumps. Not the bowler. Not the close-to-the-wicket fielders.

No one appealed. I couldn't understand it. Had I dreamt it? Was I seeing and hearing things? Was that a squadron of pink elephants that had just flown by?

At the end of the over I strolled across to Shep and looked at him accusingly. 'You gloved that, you bugger,' I said.

He smiled. Sheepishly. As a Shepherd might well. 'I know I gloved it, Dickie. You know I gloved it. But nobody else does. There was no appeal. So I'm not going to walk, am I?'

The situation was Taylor-made for me to have a little chat with wicketkeeper Bob, so I made a beeline for him. 'He gloved that, Bob,' I said.

'Get away,' he replied. 'You're having me on.'

'You ask him, then,' I retorted. So he did.

Shep admitted, ''Course I gloved it, but nobody appealed, so I'm staying put.'

I have often wondered if he would have walked had someone appealed. Or would he have waited for the umpire's decision? And what does David Shepherd the umpire now think of the actions of David Shepherd the batsman that day?

Another non-walker was that great South African all-rounder Eddie Barlow, who did a tremendous job captaining Derbyshire between 1976 and 1978. He lifted spirits to sky-high proportions, injected steel into the side, and made keen competitors of the players. Barlow was such a competitor himself, that he would never give an inch to the opposition, which is why he never walked. He believed it was the umpire's job to give him out, and he would always wait for the decision.

He once told me, 'I've got away with a lot, Dickie. I've been given not out when I should have been out. But, then again, I've been given out when I knew I wasn't. It's swings and roundabouts. Either way I never complain. I go back to the dressing room, take off my pads and gloves, and say nothing.

I accept decisions, good or bad, because they even themselves out in the long run. But I never walk.'

I admired Barlow for that honesty, and respected him for being prepared to accept decisions, rough or smooth, without the slightest complaint.

Ashley Harvey-Walker was also quite a character and no mean batsman. He was the player who once handed me his teeth for safe keeping while he went out to bat on a brute of a pitch at Buxton, which had been badly affected by a sudden snowstorm on 1 June, 1975, right in the middle of one of the hottest summers on record. And there I was, hoping they wouldn't bite.

It is the only time in my life that I could have been tempted to utter that famous 'Yorkshire' expression, which no self-respecting Yorkie ever does utter, 'Eeh, by gum, Ashley lad.'

Through the years Derbyshire have recruited some of the top foreign players, the first being South African Chris Wilkins. Fellow South African Peter Kirsten holds the Derbyshire record for the most centuries in a season – eight in 1982. The greatest overseas player to join Derbyshire was the West Indian fast bowler Michael Holding, whom I included in my World Squad in my autobiography. While with Derbyshire he opened the bowling with Ole Mortensen, one of the few Danish players to have been successful in the English game. To his amusement, we used to call him 'Stan' after the great Blackpool and England footballer. He was also christened 'Erik Bloodaxe' by Mike Hendrick.

New Zealander John Wright was with Derbyshire for quite a few years. He was a fine left-handed opening batsman who went on to captain his country, and I would like to have seen him take over as Derbyshire coach. He would have done an excellent job.

Current Indian captain, Mohammad Azharuddin, skippered

Derbyshire in 1991 and scored a lot of runs for them, and a former Indian captain, Venkataraghavan – we called him Venkat for the simple reason that we couldn't get our tongues round the rest of his name – turned out for them for a while before going on to become a well-respected international umpire.

Aussie Dean Jones took Derbyshire to second place in the championship in his first season as captain, and they could have won the title with a bit of luck. It went right to the last three matches, when a draw at Taunton and defeat by Warwickshire at Derby ended their chances.

Home-grown stars who have made a name for themselves include batsmen Denis Smith, Chris Adams, John Morris, Peter Bowler and Kim Barnett, who is now playing for Gloucestershire. Fast bowlers Mike Hendrick, who now coaches the Irish team, and Fred Rumsey, both played for England, as did off-spinner Geoff Miller. Edwin Smith and Bob Berry were also fine spin bowlers.

Of the current crop of players Karl Krikken is following in the tradition of such outstanding wicketkeepers as Harry Elliott, Bob Taylor and George Dawkes, and medium-pacer Andrew Harris is also a very good prospect.

I could not leave Derbyshire without making reference to their most humiliating season, in 1920 – even before my time, that! – when they lost seventeen out of their eighteen matches. The other was abandoned without a ball being bowled!

After that, things could only get better.

Durham University Ground

DURHAM

2

TIM LAMB, now Chief Executive of the England and Wales Cricket Board, had been invited up to Durham to have a look at the site for a new cricket ground. He stood on that god-forsaken piece of bog-like wasteland on an icy-cold afternoon at the wrong time of the year, listening to groundsman Tom Flintoft describing the state-of-the-art stadium of his dreams.

Tom showed his VIP visitor where the square would be laid, walked him round the imaginary boundary, and pointed to where there would be practice areas. He had it all pictured in his mind's eye. He knew exactly what he wanted. It must have been difficult for Tim to visualise the same exciting scene, however.

Today the Riverside Stadium at Chester-le-Street is the realisation of Tom's vision as much as anyone else's, and full credit to him.

Much careful planning, thought and foresight went into the construction of the beautiful ground – and it shows. For example, three sides of the arena have covered stands, but the fourth side has been left open so that nothing restricts one of county cricket's most magnificent views. Spectators can gaze out from the other seating areas on to the breathtaking backdrop of Lumley Castle, with the River Wear winding its way to the sea, alongside the lush green grass and sandy-bunkered oases of the golf course. Marvellous.

The facilities are also first class, car parking is excellent, and you could hardly have a better access, with the A1 motorway close at hand.

There were a lot of setbacks along the way, and because Durham wanted to set the wheels in motion they played too soon on the pitch. Tom Flintoft knew that better than anybody, but he cheerfully worked to ease any difficulties, and by the time he retired, although it had not fully settled, the pitch was almost right. It was certainly a lot better than it had been at the outset, when there was a lot of uneven bounce.

I stood at a match at Chester-le-Street in 1992 when Pakistan won by 107 runs, despite three Durham centuries, two of them by Australian Dean Jones.

Replying to Pakistan's opening knock of 308 for 7 declared, Durham totalled 341 for 4 declared, with Jones making a superb unbeaten 134 and opener Wayne Larkins hitting 118 in a second-wicket partnership of 162. A fine 90 by Aamir Sohail gave the visitors the impetus to run up 338 for 6 declared in their second innings. Waqar Younis and Wasim Akram, who took 5 for 22 and 3 for 65 respectively, then bowled Durham out for 198, with Jones, defiant to the last, battling away for 105.

I umpired that game with Pasty Harris, who had me in a real old tizzy after lunch on one of the days. On leaving the field, I always write down who has been bowling to whom, and at which end, just so there is no argument when play resumes. Pasty was supposed to do the same, and because the Pakistanis were due to reopen the bowling from his end after the break, Pasty had the job of looking after the match ball.

We arrived in the middle for the afternoon session, and after a couple of deliveries Salim Malik sidled up to me and said, 'Are you sure this is the right match ball, Dickie?'

I looked at it, gave it a couple of twirls, and looked at it again. 'Now you come to mention it,' I admitted, 'no, I'm not at all sure.'

I strolled over to Pasty, who was shuffling about uneasily from one foot to the other. 'Did you put the match ball in your pocket when we came out of the dressing room?' I asked him.

His eyes went to the ball, then to Salim Malik, and back to me. 'I did, Dickie, honest I did. But it rather looks as though I've picked up the wrong one, doesn't it? I dare say the right one is still lying on the table.'

My first county championship match in Durham was on 2 June, 1992, when I stood at their game with Somerset at Feethams, a nice little ground in the centre of Darlington which is shared by Darlington Football Club. I have fond memories of the place, since it is where I scored my first century for Yorkshire Seconds in the Minor Counties League. Before they were elected to the county championship, Durham also used to play at Stockton and Gateshead.

The newest first-class county, having become the eighteenth side to join the championship, as recently as 1992, Durham had a long and distinguished history as a minor county for 110 years before that. It was as a minor county that they pulled off their most memorable victory in 1973, when they defeated Yorkshire by five wickets in a Gillette Cup match. They also knocked out Derbyshire in 1985, and in their first season as a county championship side, they reached the quarter-finals of the same competition.

As a first-class county they have, however, failed to reach the knock-out stages of the Benson and Hedges Cup, and their best Sunday League finish was in 1993, when they were seventh. As for the championship, their highest position, prior to 1999, was fourteenth in 1998.

The first Durham fixture at the Riverside was a second eleven game against Middlesex. Graeme Fowler was captain, and a crowd of two or three thousand had turned out for what was, after all, an historic occasion. Even so, Fowler and his colleagues were amazed at the number of spectators – and the players had to get changed in the scorebox!

On winning the toss, Fowler decided to put Middlesex in to bat, which gave Franklyn Rose, who played Test cricket for the West Indies, the honour of bowling the first ball at the ground.

The following day witnessed one of the worst thunderstorms you are ever likely to see. It became so dark and threatening that umpire John Hampshire had the players off the field before the first few drops of rain fell – he could see what was coming. The heavens opened, and play was abandoned for the day.

Tom Flintoft and his staff did a great job covering the square, but it was all to no avail. Next day Durham had little option but to call the game off, hardly an auspicious start to cricket at the Riverside.

It was still a memorable occasion for Fowler, however. His wife gave birth to their first child that very night. Amid all the thunder and lightning.

Tom has just retired after doing an absolutely magnificent

job at the Riverside, and he was one of the best groundsmen I have known. He used to be at Middlesbrough's Acklam Park, where Yorkshire sometimes played, and I was so impressed with his work there that I recommended him for the job of head groundsman at Lord's. He nearly got it, too, but they decided to appoint Mike Hunt, who had been on the Lord's groundstaff since he was a young lad.

Tom later applied for the job at Southampton. He wrote a very impressive letter, and club Secretary Jimmy James was instructed to invite him down for an interview. Charles Knott, who was Chairman of the Hampshire committee at the time, was not all that sure about Tom, but Jimmy contacted me for an opinion.

'He's the best,' I said. 'Clearly the man for the job.' And he got it. He went on to produce the best pitches in the country at Southampton.

Not all groundsmen are quite in Tom's league, however, as Durham's Simon Hughes discovered when he once wintered in Sydney, captaining a local club side. Simon went to inspect the pitch before play one Saturday, and as it looked a bit patchy, he thought it might not be a bad track to bowl on. Having won the toss, he put the opposition in, reasoning that with a bit of luck and a following wind his lot could knock over four or five batsmen with the new ball.

After half an hour the score was 50 for none and the batsmen were going like express trains. Hughes's opening bowlers, on the other hand, could not stop dropping the ball short, as if the pitch had been suddenly and secretly lengthened overnight. Which, in effect, it had.

It transpired that the club had just employed a new grounds-man – a Vietnamese council gardener with little or no know-ledge of cricket. They discovered at lunch after a wearying morning session chasing leather that he had marked out a strip twenty-three yards long. 'A Saigon Special,' muttered Hughes.

Nor was that all. During the following week the guy was seen rolling the pitch crossways instead of lengthways – a Vietnamese Roll? – and he later started to cut the grass diagonally across the square. An Oriental Snip?

Wayne Larkins, who featured in my first umpiring appointment at the Riverside, had rather better fortune as a result of a visit to Australia. He and Peter Willey received 2,016 pints of beer – seven barrels in all – from a brewery in Northampton for their efforts with England Down Under in 1979–80. I just hope they didn't sup it all at once.

I had been on my way to umpire a match in Durham when I was called to the Yorkshire Television studios to record a programme of funny cricketing stories. Or so I thought. Instead they sprang a *This is Your Life* on me.

I told them straight: 'Well, I suppose it's all right, so long as it doesn't take too long. I'm umpiring in Durham tomorrow, you know. I've booked in a hotel up there and I want to get there before dark.'

Out came the famous red book, with Michael Aspel as cool, courteous and professional as ever, and I was escorted into the big studio where all the guests were already waiting to make the recording. Afterwards there was a bit of a party, with a few drinks, and everyone had a good natter – there were people I had not seen for years.

It was soon pretty obvious that I had no chance of making it to Durham that night, so they booked me in at the Queen's Hotel in Leeds.

Well, I couldn't sleep. Whether it was the excitement of the day, or the worry that I might not make it in time for the eleven o'clock start the following morning, I don't know. When I stole a look at my watch for the umpteenth time it was five o'clock.

'Right, that's it,' I said to myself, 'pot it. This tossing and turning is not a bit of good. I'm going to pack up my bags and drive up to Durham now.'

I arrived with the milk.

That game was the second team fixture at Sellafield, right beside the nuclear power station. It was bitterly cold. It was windy. Not long after the game started, so did the rain. There was some sleet in the air, too. Finally we had to admit defeat and come off.

It was not quite as bad, however, as the first day of the 1999 season, when there were three inches of snow at Riverside, and David Boon, that excellent Australian batsman, was photographed with a great big snowball in each hand. Being an Aussie, he had not seen much of the stuff, and certainly not in the cricket season. He could not pin the blame on me this time: I wasn't even there.

Lancashire were the visitors for a one-day match in the 1998 season and they revelled in the glorious weather, winning by an absolutely massive margin. Ironically, however, there were two stoppages during the day – and one of them was because of the sun. It was so bright that the reflections from the cars in the car park were blinding the players. So the spectators were asked to go and cover up their cars with blankets, newspapers, or whatever they could lay their hands on, in order to stop the glare.

I also remember umpiring Durham against Lancashire at Gateshead in September, 1992, when I gave Michael Atherton out, caught behind by Fothergill off Bainbridge, for 199. As he trudged off he gave me a rueful smile and said, 'I didn't think you'd pick that one, Dickie. It was only a very faint nick.'

'Aye, well, I'm sorry, Athers, you being only one run off your double ton an' all that,' I replied, 'but a nick's a nick, no matter how faint it is.'

Lancashire went on to total 562, with Peter Martin hitting

133, and they eventually won by ten wickets, so Athers would not have been too disappointed.

One fellow who surely was, during a match against Warwickshire at Edgbaston, was Durham wicketkeeper Chris Scott. After dropping West Indian batting star Brian Lara on two, he turned to the slip cordon and remarked, 'I hope he doesn't go on to make a century.' The record books tell us that Lara finished on 501 not out!

Graham 'Budgie' Burgess and I decided to add to the entertainment when we umpired a Sunday League match at Chester-le-Street towards the end of my career. Jockey Willie Carson, whom I knew very well, had popped into the dressing room for a chat before play. When the time came for me and 'Budgie' to go out into the middle Willie sighed and said, 'I wish I was walking out with you.'

I said, 'Well, why not? Come on, we'll get you togged up. I'm sure there must be a spare umpire's jacket lying about somewhere.'

So we put a jacket on him, stuck one of my caps on his head, and the three of us walked down the pavilion steps together. The crowd erupted, and Willie cackled away in that peculiar way of his. He was having the time of his life. He did look comical, though: as you are well aware, Willie is not the biggest fella in the world, and the umpire's jacket simply smothered him. What with that, the cap and his jockey-strap, it was not a pretty sight.

Chelmsford

ESSEX

3

I HAVE often thought that it is just like Billy Smart's Circus on the move when Essex stage matches away from the county ground at Chelmsford. Instead of the big top, the performing animals, the clowns and the trapeze artists, it is the players, advertising boards, scoreboards, office equipment, extra seating, and goodness knows what else, that are whisked away in convoy to the out-grounds at Colchester, Southend or Ilford. Chief Executive Peter Edwards is the ringmaster on such occasions. He gathers all his troops together, lines up the vans and lorries, and off they go. When the match is over, all the trappings are transported back to Chelmsford. It is quite an operation – the only one of its kind in county cricket – and very well organised.

Chelmsford itself is a lovely, compact ground, but I always used to enjoy matches at the out-grounds, where you are so much closer to the crowd and can have a natter to them during the interval and at close of play.

We umpires had to change in a caravan at the out-grounds, although that is not quite as basic as it sounds. It had all the mod cons, including a toilet, although I do remember having to fill a bucket with water for some reason. The caravan was very comfortable and I've often had a bit of a nap there during the lunch and tea intervals. Some players – and spectators, too

– have suggested I sometimes still had my eyes shut when play resumed, but that's just a malicious rumour.

There was, however, one match at Southend when I was really dog-tired at the end of the day's play – we didn't come off the field until half past eight in the evening. It had recently been introduced into the playing conditions that 118 overs should be bowled a day, and we were finding it very difficult getting through them all.

I was so shattered when we eventually came off that I walked through what I thought was the gate leading to the pavilion, realising in the nick of time that it led to the adjoining lake. I only just managed to stop myself going head over heels into the water. In my early years working down the pit the miners used to have 'laik' days, when they had unofficial time off work – that was very nearly another one for me.

I had a similar experience when Essex entertained Surrey at Colchester some years later. It was twenty-five minutes to nine when we walked off that day. It was mid-August, and the nights were drawing in, so it was nearly pitch black by the time we had to abandon play because of 'bad light'. Believe me, it was almost cricket by the light of the silvery moon. Surrey bowlers Martin Bicknell and Cameron Cuffy, the big West Indian, both trundled all the way back to the sightscreen to start their run-up. I had tried all day to chivvy them on, but my pleas fell on deaf ears. The pair of them must have walked and run many a mile that day, and I was knackered just standing there watching them.

On the last day of the county championship match between Essex and Sussex at Valentine's Park, Ilford, in June, 1988, I suffered a clotting of the blood in my right leg and had to be rushed off to hospital. Poor old Chris Balderstone was left standing at the other end with no fellow umpire – that was until George Clark stepped into the breach to save the day.

George was the attendant who looked after the players and umpires – getting them drinks and seeing to all their creature comforts. Fortunately, he was also a second eleven umpire, and although not on the county championship list, was able to do a good job at square leg, while Chris took both ends behind the stumps until reinforcements arrived in the shape of Don Oslear after lunch.

It turned out all right in the end, but I did feel a bit of a clot at the time, by George!

The Essex physio in those days was Ray Cole, and it was he who attended to me on the field. He was also the physio for Colchester United Football Club and he told me a tale that caused him a great deal of embarrassment. Apparently one of the Colchester players went down with a bad leg injury and Ray dashed out on to the pitch to administer his medical expertise, which by now had progressed beyond the famous 'magic sponge' cure-all. Ray hurriedly strapped and bandaged the leg, and it was not until he tried to turn to pack all his equipment back into the bag that he realised he had also bandaged his tie to the player's leg.

Clacton was another venue which was very popular with visiting sides in the 1960s – largely because there was usually an invitation to spend an evening or two at Butlin's Holiday Camp.

There was one instance in 1963, when a group of Yorkshire players ventured into the camp and, on arriving at the 'Crazy Horse Saloon' were somewhat taken aback to find it crammed to the rafters with holidaymakers enjoying the spectacle of two of their number – no doubt as a result of the large amount of liquid refreshment they had consumed – having a right old ding-dong, no-holds-barred, in the middle of the floor.

The noise was deafening as the crowd urged on their respective favourites. Suddenly there was a brief pause in the din. And it was then that Richard Hutton inquired, 'Do you mean to tell me that people actually come to this sort of place to *enjoy* themselves?' He was quickly and forcibly ushered out.

It was not one of Richard's better fixtures, at least off the pitch. He had just graduated from Cambridge and had not been able to acquire a car of his own, so he arranged to drive to the next game at Scarborough with Ray Illingworth. Richard volunteered to take the first stint of driving and Raymond settled back for a kip. He was woken up sometime later by Hutton, complaining, 'I say, Illy, your brakes aren't very good.'

As it was a brand new car, Illy was most concerned. And he shot bolt upright when he saw they were approaching a roundabout at close on eighty miles an hour. It turned out that Hutton had driven seventy or eighty miles from Clacton with the hand-brake on!

It took them a long time to find a garage which was open. Even longer to find one which was open and also willing to set about repairing a ruined braking system so late at night. It was nearly four in the morning when the two players reached Scarborough.

There was still little rest for the wicked. After only a few hours' sleep they arrived bleary-eyed at the North Marine Road ground just in time for Yorkshire to lose the toss, upon which they were invited to field!

I was only a bit of a whippersnapper when my dad took me to see the great Australian side of Bradman, Lindwall and Miller at Bramall Lane in 1948, the same year that Miller was involved in a bizarre incident when the tourists met Essex. He told me the story himself when I visited him at his home in Sydney many years later, by which time we had become close friends.

Keith was a great one for the horses. Loved to have a flutter on the gee-gees. He asked Bradman if he could have time off to go to the races instead of playing in the Essex game, which

31

was scheduled for the Whitsuntide holiday period. His skipper refused, insisting that Miller turned out.

By the time Keith trudged out to bat, Bradman had put on 219 in ninety minutes with Brown, and the capacity crowd waited in eager anticipation for the great all-rounder to continue the onslaught. However, Miller was in no mood for a crowd-pleasing exhibition of strokeplay that day. Instead he played no shot at all to a straight ball from Bailey and allowed himself to be bowled for a duck. He had made his point, but he still didn't get to the races!

Miller's action did not affect the result: Bradman went on to make 187 not out in two hours and five minutes, the Aussies totalled a massive 721, which remains the most runs scored in a day, and Essex were bowled out twice on the second day, to leave the Aussies winners by the amazing margin of an innings and 451 runs. What a team that was.

England batsman Doug Insole played a big part in my career. He was chairman of the sub-committee which brought me on to the Test match panel as an umpire in 1972. He was a very good cricketer, and captained Essex for eleven years until Trevor 'Barnacle' Bailey, another Essex stalwart, took over in 1961.

Trevor gave sterling service to England and went on to make a name for himself as a summariser, along with Brian Johnston and co., on *Test Match Special*. He was known as 'Barnacle' Bailey because of his ability to stick at the crease for hours on end and bore everybody silly. At least, that is what some critics used to say. Not me, of course.

Trevor batted for four and a quarter hours at Lord's in 1953 to save England from defeat against the Australians, and put that little effort into the shade five years later when he took more than seven hours to score forty-eight, with the Aussies again on the receiving end.

He could hit out if necessary, though, something he proved

at Brisbane in 1954 when he clouted a mighty six which went right out of the ground, to the astonishment of all and sundry. Mind you, a local businessman had offered a hundred pounds to the first player to clear the boundary ropes!

Trevor was also known as 'Boil'. And there are two explanations for this. In those days it was possible to play both cricket and football professionally, and Trevor turned out in the winter for Walthamstow, with whom he won an FA Amateur Cup-winners' medal. The story goes that supporters yelled out to him in the broadest cockney, 'Come on, Boily!' Brian Johnston, however, claimed that the nickname originated when Trevor was on a tour of Switzerland with Cambridge University and the public address system announcer had great difficulty with the pronunciation of his name, which came out as 'Boiley.' Whatever the true source, it was very often 'Boil'-ing in the commentary box when Trevor was around.

In 1955 Doug Insole was playing for the Rest against Surrey at the Oval, and facing Tony Lock, one of the most aggressive of all cricketers, who bowled his left-arm stuff as if his very life depended on it. His action had been viewed with great suspicion for some time, and when he dismissed Insole in that match, Lock looked questioningly down the wicket at his adversary, who was standing his ground and declining to walk.

'That's out,' snarled Lock.

'Oh, I know that,' admitted Insole. 'I just wondered if I'd been bowled or run out.'

That story always reminds me of another bowler whose action caused concern to one of my umpiring colleagues. The umpire decided to have a quiet word with the player's captain during the lunch interval. 'I have to say I think he throws,' he said.

'Oh, aye,' admitted the captain, 'but he throws 'em so quick and so straight we decided to keep him in the side.'

Four years later I had firsthand experience of Insole when I played for Yorkshire against Essex at Scarborough. I had gone in to partner Brian Close, and Closey, taking me under his wing, as always, said to me, 'Nar, look 'ere, lad.' He always called me lad. 'Nar, look 'ere. I'm going to 'elp thee. I'll tek leg-spinner, 'cos I know you're not too happy facing 'em. You can play t' seamer.'

Insole, who was Essex captain at the time, overheard the conversation and immediately chipped in, 'I hate to tell you this, Closey, but I think you've got a bit of a problem, my old son. Because we've got not one leg-spinner, but two.' He promptly put Bill Greensmith at one end and Bertie Clarke at the other, so Closey's advice to me wasn't worth tuppence.

There was I, left with not just one, but two leg-spinners to deal with. I remembered the advice that Maurice Leyland had always given me. 'When playing leg-spin always push for the googly. If it turns out to be the googly you'll play it. If it's the leg-spin you'll miss it, and with a bit of luck it'll go through to the wicketkeeper.' That's what I tried to do, but without much success. I didn't last long. I was in a heap of trouble, thanks to Closey's big mouth.

Dickie Dodds was another popular player around at that time. I first met up with him when Don Wilson and I were called up to Middlesbrough from Scarborough, where we were with the second eleven, at the same time Johnny Wardle was sacked from Yorkshire. Wilson was drafted into the team in Wardle's place and I was made twelfth man.

Dickie was a big churchman, and before he went out to open the innings he said to me, 'The good Lord has told me that I should play my shots today. The message has come to me to get after the ball.'

I took it all with a pinch of salt, but Dickie must have had a good line of communication with the Big Boss upstairs that day, because he hit the first ball out of the ground for six and rattled up fifty-odd in next to no time. He smashed the bowling all over the place before finally getting out.

In 1961 I played for Leicestershire against Essex at Ilford when we crashed to defeat by 207 runs on a bone-hard, alarmingly fast track, the seamers operating right the way through the match. Trevor Bailey and Barry Knight hit me all over my body that day. There was not one single part of me that escaped unscathed, or so it seemed at the time. I took a fearful battering on the first evening. In the second innings, when we were left with an impossible target of 347, I ended up black and blue and could hardly walk out of the ground at the end of the game.

Still, I consoled myself, I had done the right thing. I had been brave. I had got in line. And I had defied all efforts to get the ball past me, even if it meant that I ended up feeling as though I had been on the wrong end of a coconut shy.

Bailey came up to me afterwards and remarked, 'That was a magnificent effort of yours.'

In some ways I suppose it was, but I had scored 32 runs over the two innings, whereas Maurice Hallam, my captain and opening partner, had scored 69. I turned to Bailey and replied, 'That's as maybe. But Maurice backed away, slashed at nearly every ball – and got twice as many runs as me.' It still rankles to this day.

Keith Fletcher also played in that match. He was a fine captain who led Essex to all their successes in the 'seventies and 'eighties. He had a great knowledge of the game and was aware of all the weaknesses of the opposition. He would soon sort them out, would Fletch. His players thought the world of him – they would jump over the pavilion for him if necessary. He also had the knack of changing his bowlers at just the right time, too, although he always had difficulty getting the ball out of John Lever's hands. John would bowl all day if you let him.

Fletch is a big fisherman – well, more of a little fisherman, really. That's all he does in his spare time. Yorkshire folk say he's better at catching fish than catching cricket balls, which stems from the time he was selected ahead of Yorkshire's slip-catching wizard Phil Sharpe for his Test debut at Headingley. Fletch dropped three catches and the Headingley crowd never let him forget it. They gave him an ear-bashing whenever he returned to the ground. To be fair, though, Fletch made the best catch of all in the Broad Acres: he married a Yorkshire lass.

Fletch was nicknamed 'the Gnome': at a time when pointed shoes had almost gone out of fashion, Fletch still wore a scuffed old pair on which the toes actually turned up. When he strode into the changing room wearing them one day, someone remarked that he looked like a gnome who'd just fallen off a toadstool, and the nickname stuck. So if you see a group of garden gnomes on your travels, Fletch will be the one with the fishing line.

I have mentioned John Lever, and he was a fine bowler. No doubt about that. However, he found himself in trouble in 1976 when he toured India with England, and was unfairly accused of using Brylcreem – or some kind of Vaseline – on the ball to make it swing more. John would never do anything so underhand. He was not that type. He was a natural swinger of the ball and could make it go both ways. In the right conditions he was capable of bowling any team out. Perhaps the Indians were just a little bit miffed that he had taken 10 for 70 in his first Test in New Delhi.

There can hardly have been a more endearing character at Essex than Brian 'Tonker' Taylor. They called him that because he loved to give the ball an almighty tonk. He was both captain and wicketkeeper, and he has never been allowed to forget a match at Colchester when he dropped Geoff Boycott off the first ball – and Boycs went on to make a double hundred.

Tonker was the one who brought on all the top Essex youngsters, such as Graham Gooch, John Lever, Neil Foster, David Acfield, and Ray and David East and such like. He was a strict disciplinarian. Under him the Essex lads always wore their blazers for lunch and tea. Collar and tie, too. No slouching around in slovenly attire when he was around. Look smart, play smart, was his philosophy, and there is a lot in it.

When the team took to the field he would line them all up and march them out, army style. 'Right, lads,' he would say. 'Altogether now. Snap to it. Look lively, the lot of you. I shall say "left right, left right" and off we will go. I don't want anyone out of step. Follow me . . .'

One day he went through all his usual rigmarole and marched proudly out to the middle at the head of his team. Or so he thought. When he arrived, he turned round and was startled to find that he was completely on his own. The players were still on the other side of the fence, having a good laugh. They never did it again, though. Oh, dear me, no.

Under Tonker, Essex were never short of ideas for getting batsmen out. He tried all sorts. He would have had a go at the liquorice variety given half the chance.

There was one time when he set out to trick a compulsive hooker into playing the shot that would most likely prove his undoing. In the course of one over he moved square leg a little deeper after each ball. The fourth delivery was the inevitable bouncer, and as it was on its way towards the batsman, the fielder set off running towards the boundary in gleeful anticipation of what was to come. Sure enough, the batsman, unable to resist the temptation, hooked the ball high and hard and was brilliantly caught just inside the ropes. Tonker and his team were ecstatic. Until they realised that the umpire had called 'no-ball'.

All eyes turned accusingly towards the bowler, and his frustrated colleagues tore him off a strip until the umpire explained that he had not called the bowler for overstepping. He turned to Tonker. 'It was your fault, skipper,' he said to him. 'You've three men behind square leg.' The laws allowed for only two.

Tonker looked round in disbelief. He counted once. He counted twice. And he counted again. Then the penny dropped. 'Don't tell me you were counting that chap right on the boundary edge,' he muttered menacingly.

'Of course,' replied the umpire.

Exploded Tonker, 'That's not a fielder, you fool, that's the bloody ice-cream man.'

I have mentioned Ray East, the left-arm spinner under Tonker's captaincy. He was responsible for one of the funniest things I have ever seen on a cricket field. He was given out lbw by umpire Jack van Geloven off the last ball before the tea interval, and all the way back to the pavilion he chuntered on at Jack, trying to get him to change his mind.

'You didn't really give me out, did you?' Ray pleaded. 'You're just kidding me, aren't you? I mean, that ball would have hit another set of stumps, it was that wide.'

But Jack persisted. 'Ray, stop moaning. You're out, and that's an end of the matter.'

When play resumed after tea, a 'new' batsman came in to bat, unfamiliar to most of the opposition players. And to the crowd. He had a droopy moustache and a beard and wore an old-fashioned ringed cap. The bowler was just about into his delivery stride when the batsman stepped back from the crease, pulled off his moustache and beard and took off his cap – to reveal Ray East!

The place was in uproar. Jack yelled at him, 'East, I've told you once and I shan't tell you again, you're out. Now bugger off.'

Off he went, stopping every few steps to look pleadingly over his shoulder at the umpire, who kept pointing him in the direction of the dressing rooms.

Easty was renowned for being a bit of a prankster. For example, if a car backfired in the distance, he would suddenly fall to the ground clutching his heart, as if he'd been shot. I've even seen him come up and bowl with a piece of fruit he'd picked up from the lunch table. First delivery of the afternoon and out it would come. Sometimes the future was bright. And orange. Sometimes it would be a peach of a ball.

Ray would sometimes go down on his knees, a bit like Dominic Cork at Derbyshire, and pray for me to give him an lbw decision. I used to tell him, 'In order to get an lbw decision out of me, lad, you've got to straighten the ball.'

One day at Chelmsford he was at it all the time. Never shut up. Finally, I actually raised my finger and barked, 'That's out.'

Easty looked at me in disbelief. It was the first time I'd known him lost for words. Then he exclaimed, 'Oh, Dickie, Dickie, thank you, thank you so very much. I never thought I'd live to see the day.'

I said to him, 'Look, lad, I've been tellin' thee for ages that if you'd only straighten one, I'd give it. And that straightened.' I do like to think that, in my own way, I helped keep Easty on the straight and narrow.

In another match at Chelmsford, when Sussex were the visitors in June, 1977, Ken McEwan scored a magnificent double century before eventually being caught by Javed Miandad off Tony Greig, and he was presented with a magnum of champagne. During the drinks break the twelfth man took it out on a tray with glasses for the players. Easty popped the cork, and up it went, bubbling all over the place. He turned to me and offered me the first glass. I had a little sip – couldn't drink too much on duty, you see, otherwise I might have ended up seeing double.

There are a few houses well within striking distance of a straight drive over the sightscreen at Chelmsford, and when balls landed in the gardens, the club sent members of the groundstaff to retrieve them. Very often, however, the residents refused to give them back. There was one famous occasion, in 1979, during a match against Kent, when in the course of a morning's play eight sixes were deposited in the gardens, resulting in four lost balls. A search party was duly despatched during the lunch interval – they came back with not four, but five balls!

In a match against Middlesex at Valentine's Park in 1981 I asked Essex all-rounder Stuart Turner if I could inspect the ball, and my suspicions were aroused when I saw that the seam appeared to be raised. I looked at Turner accusingly. 'Stewy, you're not picking this seam by any chance, are you?'

He returned my gaze, all hurt and innocence. 'How could you even think such a thing, Dickie? Of course not. Would I do anything like that?' He then took one of those old-fashioned half-crowns out of his pocket and began tossing it in the air and catching it.

I gasped, 'You are, aren't you? You're using that half-crown.'

'No, Dickie, honestly. Just having a bit of fun. I wouldn't dare do such a thing. Not with you around,' he laughed. I always wondered, though.

By that time Essex had put together a very good side, including a number of players who could bat and bowl, which is why they won so many one-day trophies. The big breakthrough came in 1979 when they won the county championship and the Benson and Hedges Cup. In 1981 they won the John Player League, and the county championship again in 1983, as well as reaching the Benson and Hedges final. The following year they became the first county to win both the championship and the John Player League. In 1985 they won the NatWest Trophy and the John Player League, and were again beaten finalists in the Benson and Hedges competition.

Finally, after a season in which, with a NatWest final victory, he became the only captain to win all four trophies in a career, Keith Fletcher stepped down to be replaced by Graham Gooch.

Goochy went on to become an England selector, and, remarkably, had more hair than when he was playing. That, of course, was due to a famous transplant – he probably made more money for those ads than he ever did playing cricket – which has kept him looking more youthful than ever. Still, he was never one to let success go to his head.

In my mind Gooch has to go down as one of the greatest batsmen England has ever had, yet he made a dreadful start to his Test career. I stood at his debut match in 1975 when he collected two ducks. I keep reminding him of that, and he doesn't thank me for it.

What I admired about him that day was the way he walked for one down the leg-side. Had he stood his ground it would have been very difficult to have given him out, but he walked straight off, which was tremendous for a young player in his first Test, with so much at stake. It showed the character of the man.

That pair held him back for a few years, but he eventually returned to the Test arena better than ever, and went on to captain his country.

Goochy also bowled gentle medium-pace stuff which got him quite a few wickets, but he was best with the ball when imitating other bowlers. That was his party piece. His Bob Willis impersonation was brilliant. Not as quick, mind, but all the characteristics were there, and there was no doubt at all who he was taking off. It was a toss-up as to whether he bowled better as Gooch or as Willis. He did a fair Geoff Boycott as well, with cap turned back to front and sleeves buttoned around his wrists.

He also livened up a dreadfully dull series in India when five drawn Tests followed a win for the home team in the opener in Bombay. During the match in Calcutta he went through his repertoire and, to add authenticity to his impression of India's star left-armer, Dilip Doshi, he borrowed a pair of spectacles from a spectator. Another instance of Goochy making a spectacle of himself!

One knock by Aussie batsman Stuart Law, the county's overseas player, at Chelmsford in 1996 will always stick in my mind. Essex were playing India and the pitch was very green, with a lot of moisture on it. The ball was seaming about all over the place, and Robinson, Grayson and Hussain had already gone – for 1, 2 and 7 respectively – when Law came out to try to avert a total collapse. He said to me, 'Only one way to play on here, Dickie. I'm just going to give it an almighty thrash.'

And boy, did he thrash. He thrashed his way to 153 before being caught by Venkatesh off leg-spin googly bowler Hirwani. It was an amazing effort. He turned things round just by throwing bat at ball, although to be fair the pitch did ease out to become a good, flat track later in the day, and he took full advantage of the improvement in the conditions. One spectacular six was hit over the sightscreen, clearing the trees, and ending up in one of the gardens of the houses beyond. Another lost ball.

During that match they were doing some building work on the hospital just outside the ground, and a massive mechanical hammer made a terrible noise throughout play. Boom, boom, boom, boom, it went. Nonstop. It was driving me crackers. You would think I could have coped, having umpired in India, where the noise from the crowd is unbelievable, but this was something else. It went right through you, all day long. The only time we had a break from it was when the builders had their cup of tea and sarnies. You could always tell when it was snack-time: silence. And it was certainly golden. But then the row would start up again. Thump, thump, thump. It was murder.

Finally I could stand it no longer, and I sent a message to the workmen asking if it would be possible for them not to make any noise during the hours of play. They could use the hammer from hell, I suggested, during our lunch and tea intervals and in the evening after play had stopped for the day. Either that or put a muffler on the damn thing.

I hardly dare tell you the message I received back, but it began with an F and ended in off.

Gooch retired in 1997. The following year Essex won the Benson and Hedges and finished third in the Sunday League, yet bottom of the county championship table, leaving the club with a lot of rebuilding to do. They are concentrating on bringing their own youngsters through, but that will take time, and people will have to be patient.

St Helen's, Swansea

GLAMORGAN

4

THE record books say there are 'more than' seventy steps to the pavilion at Glamorgan's ground at St Helen's, Swansea. The last time I walked up them I counted eighty-nine. It is, however, just possible that I may have been seeing double by the time I got to the last dozen or so, because my blood pressure had shot up so high.

It is no laughing matter for the batsman, who, after making that long, long trek to the middle, gets a duck and is faced with an immediate return journey all the way back again. Not only is it the steepest climb in county cricket, it is also the longest walk, because it is such a big ground. Should you stroll right round the boundary's edge you will cover a third of a mile.

I remember Ken Taylor getting a first-ball duck for Yorkshire, and that walk must have seemed even longer and steeper for him. It was the one thing you worried about more than anything else when you batted at Swansea – being done first ball.

That apart, it is a lovely ground, with a terrific view over the beautiful Mumbles Bay to the sea and ships, with families relaxing on the beach, and the Devon cliffs in the distance. The ground is virtually on the sea front and, possibly because of this, has a special character of its own.

Openers Roy Fredericks and Alan Jones have good cause to look upon the Swansea ground with affection, for in 1972 they put on a record 330 for the first wicket in a county championship match there against Northamptonshire.

It is also the ground where Gary Sobers famously hit his record-breaking six sixes in an over off Glamorgan fast bowler Malcolm Nash. Even to this day people still talk about that onslaught, and Nash has become almost as legendary as Sobers himself.

I have a feeling that after Sobers had clobbered him for four of those sixes, Malcolm was secretly hoping that his last two would suffer the same fate, because then his name would go in the record books along with the brilliant West Indian all-rounder – the best I have ever seen. That feeling is confirmed whenever I see Malcolm. He'll say, 'Dickie, they'll never forget, will they? I'm in the history books. Whenever people in this part of the world meet to chat about cricket, that is one occasion they will always talk about. It's made me famous.'

One of those Sobers sixes ended up in the middle of Swansea, and Ossie Wheatley, who was fielding at the time, remembers each ball vividly – as if it happened only yesterday, rather than in 1968. Let him describe that over for you.

'The first six, over long-on, cleared the wall and smacked against a pub in Gorse Lane; the second went to mid-wicket and connected with another pub a little bit further down the road; the third landed among the spectators at long-on; the fourth did likewise at mid-wicket; the fifth was caught by Roger Davis at long-off before he fell backwards over the boundary ropes; and the last one went sailing over mid-wicket down a side street towards the Town Hall and was not recovered until the next day.'

In fact, that sixth six went all the way past Bill Edwards' sports shop. Bill was on the committee at Glamorgan, and when I paid him a visit at his shop, we looked up towards the ground and marvelled again at the length of that enormous hit as we sat there recalling that memorable day.

Ossie Wheatley, incidentally, captained the Glamorgan side, and a very good job he did, too. He liked to make a game of it and was renowned for his bold declarations. He was also a good bowler, with the ability to leave the bat late.

Although he was not particularly elegant with the bat, he did, however, cut a dashing figure when he dressed up for one of the many social occasions he attended. He led a very busy life off the pitch, and on one occasion arrived at Colchester on the morning of a match against Essex still clad in the dinner jacket he had worn the previous evening. He was particularly pleased to win the toss that day. He opted to bat, which gave him the opportunity to relax in the pavilion while his players did him proud in the middle with a total of 322 for 7 – one of their better efforts of that particular year. Ossie went on to become chairman of Glamorgan County Cricket Club, and a very respected figure.

I always used to enjoy playing and umpiring at St Helen's – despite those damned steps. The pitch there has always taken spin, going right back to my playing days with Yorkshire and Leicestershire, and there were some great spinners in the Glamorgan side in those days, such as Jim McConnon, Peter Walker, Jimmy Pressdee and Don Shepherd. Pressdee took 9 for 43 against Yorkshire in 1965, while Shepherd, the backbone of the Glamorgan bowling for twenty years, is the only man from the county to have taken more than 2,000 first-class wickets.

St Helen's still takes spin, as witnessed in my last season on the county list, when Surrey beat Glamorgan inside three days, Ian Salisbury and Pakistan's Saqlain Mushtaq combining to bowl the home team out twice.

It is a shame that county cricket will not be played at Swansea any more. It is steeped in history and has a store of happy memories for a lot of people – including myself.

I have also played and umpired at Neath, a small, compact ground more famous for stirring Rugby deeds than cricketing romance. I travelled from there through the valleys to Llanelli to umpire a Sunday League match between Glamorgan and Leicestershire on a day when it teemed down with rain. When I arrived the ground was waterlogged, and David Gower, captain of Leicestershire at the time, said to me, 'Right, Dickie, it's down to you. You can call it off now. There's no chance we'll play on that.' I could tell David was not too keen on turning out, and I could hardly blame him – conditions were awful.

However, it had stopped raining by this time, and the groundstaff did a tremendous job mopping up so that we were able to play a match of 13 overs a side.

Conditions were still far from pleasant, and the mud was ankle deep in places, but David was happy enough when his side knocked off the 78 runs to win in 12.1 overs. My old county were certainly no stick-in-the-muds that day.

We had been duty bound, really, to try our best to put on a game of cricket for the sake of the spectators, who had come from Welsh villages, valleys, towns and cities for the day, despite the rain, packing the small ground to capacity and spilling over into the friendly bars. I am happy to say that everyone enjoyed what little cricket there was.

Glamorgan also used to play the occasional game at Colwyn Bay, again a fixture which attracted big crowds. It was usually against Lancashire, the neighbouring county, and a lot of Lancastrians would book their holidays for that week. It is another nice little club ground. There used to be a bank behind one end, a smaller version of the famous hill at Sydney, although that has gone now, replaced by a large stand seating a fair few thousand people.

It was at Colwyn Bay one day that my umpiring colleague Barrie Leadbeater went missing, and not for the first time. I was ready to walk out after the tea interval when I realised that Ledders was nowhere to be seen. The players were already out in the middle waiting for us, so I shouted, 'You'll have to hold on a minute until I find my mate.' Eventually I did find him – telling the tale round the back of the pavilion.

I said, 'What do you think you're doing, Ledders? You should be out there in the middle with me.'

He looked at me in some surprise. 'Oh, sorry, Dickie, I didn't realise what time it was.'

Abergavenny is another of Glamorgan's out-grounds, in more senses than one. It is not even in Glamorgan, but Gwent. It is neat, efficient, and framed by a backdrop of tree-clad hills. The facilities are as good as any club ground – and the homemade teas are delicious.

There was one highly unusual game played there in 1985 when Glamorgan openers Hopkins and Holmes scored 114 not out and 106 not out respectively, enabling their side to declare at 250 without loss in reply to Worcestershire's 294, the idea being to try to bring about a result other than a draw. The visitors were looking set for a good total in their second innings when six of their players were struck down with a stomach bug, joining two more, who were injured, on the sidelines. The openers were therefore faced with the task of batting on for as long as they possibly could, because Worcestershire were unable to declare, having only three fit men to take the field. They were finally rescued from their predicament by rain!

Glamorgan also used to play at Cardiff Arms Park, the famous national stadium associated, like some of the smaller Welsh grounds, more with Rugby than cricket. I used to enjoy going there. It is a venue with a lot of character, and my fellow Yorkshireman John Hampshire, who went on to join me on the first-class umpires' list, has particularly fond memories of the ground.

He started life as a schoolboy cricketer who bowled leg-breaks and batted at number eleven. He quickly realised that leg-break bowlers were treated by Yorkshire much as pork at a vegetarian party, so he set about improving his batting, and did so well that he earned a place in the county team early in the 1960s, his bowling a forgotten relic of his youth.

In 1963 he opened the batting regularly with Dougie Padgett, and was called upon to bowl only five overs – one at Taunton and four at Bristol – in games that were petering out into a draw. Then, on the afternoon of 25 July that year, when Yorkshire had enforced the follow-on against Glamorgan at the Arms Park, Ray Illingworth, who was captaining the side in the absence of Brian Close and Fred Trueman, tossed the ball to John and asked him to bowl leg-spin.

You could have knocked him down with the proverbial feather. But it made sense in a way, because Illy and Don Wilson, the other main spinner, were a bit jaded after bowling Glamorgan out once and attempting to do it for a second time.

John took two wickets, and, as they left the field, Illy informed him that he would be opening the bowling the following morning. This he did – and claimed another five wickets to finish with 7 for 52. You might think his leg-break talents would be called upon more often after that, but over the next eighteen years in first-class cricket he was given the opportunity to take just twenty-three more wickets!

It is a pity that Glamorgan left Cardiff Arms Park – the Cardiff club now play their Rugby on what was once the cricket square – to move across the city to Sophia Gardens, which has now become the county headquarters, but it was thought at the time that the size of the crowds did not merit such a big venue.

The early days at Sophia Gardens brought quite a few problems. It was a pleasant enough parkland setting, protected by trees, and with the River Taff flowing alongside, but the square was far from ideal. When a new drainage system was installed, one of the channels caused a ridge halfway down the pitch, which fast bowlers were able to hit with unerring accuracy, making batting quite a hazardous occupation.

In the early 1980s the square was finally relaid, and although this rectified the flying ball and the uneven bounce, it has now provided a pitch of the opposite extreme – slow and low.

One 'perk' for umpires at Sophia Gardens is a beautiful flat in the pavilion where we can stay at a special rate, although a lot of umpires who have stayed there have had their cars broken into. Not me. I continued to stay in Cathedral Road. No problems there.

Glamorgan have won the county championship three times – in 1948 under Wilf Wooller; in 1969, when Tony Lewis was captain; and in 1997, with Matthew Maynard at the helm. Their only success in the limited-overs game came in 1993 when they won the Sunday League title, the whole of Wales, or so it seemed, descending on Canterbury to roar their side on to victory.

They have reached only one final at Lord's, in 1977, when they lost by five wickets to Middlesex in the final of the Gillette Cup – a match noted for the huge six hit almost to the top of the pavilion by Mike Llewellyn. Their best performance in the Benson and Hedges Cup was a semi-final place in 1988.

The umpire at Glamorgan's decisive match in 1948, their first championship-winning season, was a Welshman, Dai Davies, and when he gave the final decision in favour of Glamorgan's John Clay, he cried, 'He's out – and we've won the championship.'

Wilf Wooller, the captain of that side, was a tremendous

competitor. I had a lot of admiration and respect for him, and we became very friendly. Whenever I umpired in Wales, he always came to the umpires' room to see how I was. I was very sad when he died, and I missed him on the county scene.

Wilf was great character. For example, Glamorgan were playing Gloucestershire on a brilliant red-hot summer's day at Bristol. There was not a cloud in the sky and the visiting bowlers had been made to toil in the field for six hours while Gloucestershire piled up more than 400 for 4 in the day.

Gloucestershire captain George Emmett had made 50 when the first wicket fell, heralding the arrival of Wally Hammond. At tea Emmett was still only in the 60s, while Hammond was way past 100 and showing no signs of giving his partner a piece of the bowling. Emmett got a bit fed up, thinking he might just as well go back to the dressing room and watch from there in comfort.

The weather changed dramatically during the evening, and, remember, the pitches were uncovered in those days. Wooller was having a drink in the bar with Emmett and suggested the two of them go for a meal. George declined, saying, rather mischievously, that he preferred to sit and listen to the lovely sound of the rain drumming on the roof, and think of what his spin bowlers would be able to do on that beautiful sticky dog they would have at their disposal the following day. 'Better than any food, that,' said George. It certainly gave some food for thought for poor old Wilf.

Arriving at the ground the following morning, Wooller was met by a grinning Emmett, who announced brightly, 'We have declared at our overnight score.'

'I rather thought you might,' said Wilf, and retired to rally his troops.

'This is our plan of campaign,' Wilf told them. 'It's a difficult pitch, it has to be said. A lot different to the one we had to bowl on yesterday. But it will get worse. So if we can somehow manage a lead of 120 or so it will become unplayable. Then we can really get at 'em. We could win by an innings.'

The batsmen clearly did not share his optimism. To top 400 on a good pitch would be asking a lot. On this one it was asking the impossible. However, no one dared challenge Wilf, or he would drop on them like a ton of bricks.

Just over an hour later Glamorgan were all out for 38. Dear old Sam Cook, who became a colleague of mine on the umpires' list, but is dead and gone now, bless his soul, took six wickets with his slow left-armers.

Said Emmett to Wooller, 'I'd like you to follow on.'

'Thought you might,' said Wilf, who then went back to the dressing room for another Churchillian rallying speech.

'Right then, lads,' he said, 'It's a different story now. We have to follow on. That makes it more difficult, I know, but we can still win. The top will have completely gone by the time they have to bat again. A lead of even 90 will be enough to give us a chance.'

No one dared so much as look at him. They must have thought he was barmy. There was not a cat in hell's chance of doing anything other than lose. Unless, of course, it started to pour down again.

Someone mumbled, 'We'll do our best, skip.'

'You'd better,' snapped Wooller, 'otherwise you'll not be playing in the next game.'

The second innings started, and developed in much the same way as the first, so that when Wooller went out to bat the scoreboard was showing 26 for 6. On his way to the wicket he passed Cook, who was looking quietly confident, to say the least. Wooller paused. 'I suppose you'd like to bowl at this circus of mine every day of your life, wouldn't you Sam?'

With ten wickets in the match under his belt already, Sam was prepared to let the question answer itself.

Wooller marched on to the crease, slammed his bat down and took his guard. 'Come on, Cookie, now let's see what you're really made of,' he challenged Sam.

Sam trotted up, flighting the ball on a good length. It pitched, bounced, turned, hit Wilf on the glove and short-leg took the catch: 26 for 7.

As Wooller walked away past the bowler, head bowed, Sam enjoyed his moment of triumph. 'Cheerio, ringmaster,' he grinned.

Incidentally, Sam was buried in his local cemetery, right in the corner of the graveyard, and two of his colleagues, John Mortimore and Arthur Milton, mused, 'Well, at least Sam will be a happy man now. He's down there at third man, where he always used to field.'

Wilf, who also played for Wales at Rugby, was not one for half measures. Once, when Brian Close was captaining Somerset and refused to declare to make a game of it, Wilf went on to the public address and told the spectators that if they wished to ask for their money back he was prepared to consider their applications. Closey batted on into the second day, forcing Glamorgan to follow on, and he smiled when he heard Wilf's announcement. Somerset won by an innings!

Then there was the time when, fielding at wide mid-off, he questioned a decision by umpire Frank Lee in a championship match. Lee had turned down a big lbw shout and Wilf had a real go at him. Frank took it all in his stride. However, when Wooller came in to bat for Glamorgan later in the day and asked for his guard, Frank turned and walked slowly and deliberately to wide mid-off.

'I'll give you your guard from here, Wilf, in view of the fact that you obviously feel this is a much better position than behind the wicket to see whether anything's in line with the stumps.'

In later years, when he was chairman, Wilf marched into the Glamorgan dressing room just after lunch on the third day of a county championship match with Northamptonshire at Swansea. John Steele had seen him coming, and hid, knowing that Wooller was coming to give him some earache: the pitch was turning and Steele was the only spinner in the side.

Said Wooller, 'It's no good that bugger Steele hiding himself away. I know he's there. And if he doesn't go out this afternoon and take five wickets on a pitch that's made to measure for him, then he'd better be prepared to face the sack.'

John duly took his five wickets, Glamorgan won, John's job was safe, and Wilf was happy.

John is the brother of David Steele, the Northamptonshire, Derbyshire and England batsman, and I was umpire at another championship match when the two brothers were on opposite sides. To my amazement, as David prepared to bowl to John, I saw him picking the seam. I said, 'Just a minute, David, old lad, what the hell do you think you're doing? I'm surprised at you, really I am. Picking at the seam like that. Especially when you're bowling to your own brother.'

'Don't you worry about it, Dickie,' he replied. 'This is a family matter.'

'Oh, but I do worry about it,' I said. 'It's just not on. You'll get us all into bother. You've got to put a stop to it right now.'

David had really ripped away at the seam to try to gain an advantage. Not an ounce of brotherly love there at all. Mind you, I should have known. It was always the same when they came up against each other. For example, David would trample all over the pitch, bowling as close to the stumps as possible, and then following through virtually in line with the wickets. On one occasion I had to warn him twice.

'Look here, David,' I told him, 'I'm sorry to have to say this, because you're really not such a bad chap, but if you do that again I'm going to give you a third warning and you'll be off. Simple as that. So come on, be a good lad.'

And then, blow me, he went and got John out. He turned to me with a smile of triumph. 'I'll come off now, Dickie. I've done what I wanted to do. I've got the bugger.'

David finished with 5 for 30 that day. As for John, he later joined me on the first-class umpires' list.

During my umpiring days, Glamorgan had a good fast bowler called Allan Jones, another to make the switch from player to umpire, although a little later than me. He was hurling them down when Ray Illingworth took over as captain at Leicestershire, and one day Illy went out to bat against him.

Allan had a habit of letting out a big grunt at the point of delivery, and on this particular occasion it totally confused Illy. Untypically, he played an almighty cow-shot at one ball, completely missed it and saw his off-stump go cartwheeling merrily towards the boundary. 'You wouldn't believe it,' Illy muttered, 'I thought the umpire had called no-ball. That's the reason I played a shot like that.'

The other players just grunted. A bit like Allan, but not quite as noisily.

Bernie Hedges opened the innings with Gilbert Parkhouse for Glamorgan at the time I was playing, and both did a fine job for the county. Bernie is one of the nicest men I have ever come across in county cricket. I have seen him walk off, without waiting for the umpire's decision, to be met by colleagues in the dressing room questioning whether or not he had got a nick.

'Didn't think you touched that one, Bernie,' they would say.

'Neither did I,' would come the startling reply, 'but somebody

appealed, so I must have done.' With the massive appealing
that has crept into the game since then, I doubt that he would
ever score a run these days.

Tony Lewis, who captained Glamorgan to their second
championship success in 1969, also played for England, and
once, on a tour of the West Indies, he popped into the
dressing room at Barbados to find all the players clustered
round the radio. He heard a voice say, 'A hundred and
twenty-seven.'

'Hey, that's not a bad score, who made that?' he asked.

No one looked up, but someone muttered, 'Not runs, old
boy, gold. That's the highest price it's been. It's a record.'

Tony first showed his leadership qualities at Cambridge,
and went on to captain his country in India and Pakistan.
He was a quiet captain, with a keen eye for detail, while as
a batsman he was a pleasure to watch, showing a high degree
of technical ability.

In that championship-winning season Glamorgan were undefeated in twenty-four games. They were really a team of
well-equipped all-rounders, with a magnificent batting spearhead in Pakistan's Majid Jahangir Khan.

One day, when I was umpiring at Cambridge University, I
was chatting to groundsman Cyril Coote, who has produced
some of the best pitches in the country through the years,
and I asked him who was the best batsman he had ever seen
at Fenner's. Bearing in mind he could go right back to great
players like Peter May, Doug Insole and Ted Dexter, he said,
'I don't have to think about that, Dickie. The best for me was
Majid Khan.'

For Cyril to put Majid Khan ahead of Peter May, whom I have
always rated as the best England batsman I have seen since the
war, was a tremendous compliment to the Pakistani, who went
on to captain his country. He really was a wonderful batsman,

one of the most exciting in the game, as well as being a good fielder and a useful bowler.

Majid used to have digs at Cambridge, and one day I asked where they were. 'See that house there, Dickie?' he said, pointing to a building just outside the ground. 'That's the one. I just walked through the gates from the back garden on to the field of play.'

He was a good captain of both county and country, doing it in his own quiet way, although some said that he was perhaps a little too nice to lead a Glamorgan side that needed tough discipline and restructuring.

There was, however, at least one occasion when he lost his cool. Annoyed by his dismissal in a match against Derbyshire he asked the groundsman for a saw, took it to the dressing room and did not rest until his bat lay in two pieces on the floor, with enough sawdust to cover any damp spots for the remainder of the season!

It was during the last home game of the 1969 campaign, against Worcestershire early in September, that Sophia Gardens became part of the county's history. In front of a crowd of 16,000, Glamorgan won by 147 runs. Majid Khan scored a hundred before lunch and went on to make 156, Don Shepherd took his 2,000th first-class wicket, and pandemonium reigned when victory clinched the championship. Such excitement has never been witnessed at the ground since.

Two years later there was drama of a different kind when Roger Davis was hit on the head by the ball while fielding at short leg and had to be revived by the kiss of life from a doctor who just happened to be in the crowd. Davis was rushed to hospital, but thankfully made a complete recovery.

Majid Khan scored another century before lunch – 147 to be precise – in 1967, only this time it was for Pakistan and against the county he served with such distinction.

59

Another very good Glamorgan captain was Hugh Morris. It is tradition that the captain has a room on his own when playing away, so when Hugh resigned the captaincy he had to find a room-mate. He certainly did not want to share with 'Baz' Barwick, who was a very heavy smoker, and all the other players appeared to be paired up. Robert Croft and Tony Cottey, for example, were 'as good as married'.

Whoever it was needed to keep sociable hours. 'In other words,' said Hugh, 'a boring old bugger who goes to bed early after a nice meal and a bottle of wine.'

There was really only one candidate: fast bowler Steve Watkin, who was an incredibly nice lad. He had played with Hugh at schoolboy level and they had come through the system together. They were an ideal pair. Watkin, who played once or twice for England, also had a Welsh cap, so I am told – for eating!

Tony Cottey, incidentally, lists his relaxations as marathon running – he has run the New York and Athens events – and lager-tasting. Presumably in that order. He is another cricketer/footballer, having played for Swansea City. He also won a Welsh Youth cap for soccer.

The Glamorgan scorer, Byron Denning, is a very witty man and a good friend of mine. As well as scoring, he introduces the players over the public address system, and they came to look forward to some of his gaffes. In 1997 Waqar Younis was announced as Waqar Hussain, Darren Thomas became Dean Thomas, while Dean Cosker became Darren, and so on. I could never understand him mistaking Darren Thomas for Gary Butcher, though – they don't even have the same colour skin!

Glamorgan's best ever partnership was produced in 1993, when Adrian Dale and Viv Richards put on 425 against Middlesex at Cardiff. South African-born Dale has always been a good all-round cricketer and has played for England A. Many people believed Dale would go on to make the senior England team, but he is now thirty, and perhaps time has run out for him.

I have had a soft spot for Glamorgan ever since that day in May, 1959, when I made my highest score in county cricket against them – 181 not out at Bradford Park Avenue.

I was recalled to the team only because Ken Taylor was on England duty. The pitch was poor, turning a lot against one of the best spin attacks in the country – Jim McConnon, Don Shepherd, Peter Walker and Jimmy Pressdee – and I was not too confident of making many runs.

Although conditions should have suited those four to a tee, we won by an innings, and I felt marvellous after my big century. However, I was soon brought back down to earth, as I was dropped for the next match.

Cheltenham College Ground

GLOUCESTERSHIRE

5

I ALWAYS felt on top of the world at Bristol. The ground is very high up, and you can look out over the city, spread out below. Yet it is far from being a bleak and isolated place, as that description might suggest, and although it is a massive ground, you are never overwhelmed by the sheer size of it.

Ashley Down has a character of its own, and standing there in the peace and quiet after a match, it is easy to picture, in your mind's eye, all those famous players of the past. You can hear the roars of the crowd in the remarkable tie with the Australians in 1930; the grudging applause of appreciation when the tourists gained revenge on that invincible tour of 1948, when they scored 774 for 7; the delight in Tom Goddard's 17 for 106 in one day against Kent in 1939 and his 5 for 4 against Somerset in 1947; the admiration for Sadiq Mohammad as he made 163 not out and 150 in the 1976 Derbyshire match. I could go on. Such a lot has happened at Ashley Down.

It was there that I was due to umpire a county match, after a day standing at the Oval. I packed my bags and took them out to the car ready for the drive down to Bristol. When I went to get my bags out of the car on arriving at my Bristol hotel, I could hardly believe my eyes. The boot was empty. It dawned on me that I had left them on the car park tarmac back at the Oval. I didn't know what to do. I was umpiring the next day, and I had no gear. I had no overnight stuff either, and had to sleep in my shirt and underpants.

I was standing with David Shepherd, and ended up borrowing some of his gear. Shep is eighteen stone if he's an ounce, and I'm slim and trim by comparison. His jacket buried me. No way could I wear that. I managed to find another one, but I had to wear Shep's spare trousers – held up by a tie fastened round my waist. The players gave me some monumental stick. I must have looked the scruffiest, worst-dressed umpire who had ever appeared in first-class cricket, especially as I had not been able to shave because my razor was still in my bag back at the Oval.

The ground at Bristol has been improved dramatically, as television viewers saw during the 1999 World Cup matches. It was also on this ground that the tossing of a coin first decided a limited-overs game after Gloucestershire and Middlesex had been unable to make a start because of the weather.

My most memorable Gloucestershire match, however, was the famous televised Gillette Cup semi-final at Old Trafford in 1971, which lasted until ten to nine.

Tony Brown, the Gloucestershire captain, who went on to become the administrative manager for the England and Wales Cricket Board, put on spinner John Mortimore to bowl, with Lancashire chasing the runs and falling further behind the required rate as darkness fell. I could not believe it. Why didn't Brown recall one of his fast bowlers? Mike Procter, for example, still had two overs left. Lancashire captain Jack Bond would not have appealed, having already said he would play to a finish. As it was, David Hughes hit Mortimore for 24 in one over to win the match for Lancashire – but more of that when we come to the Red Rose county.

Despite his error of judgment on that occasion, Brown was a good captain and led Gloucestershire in their most successful decade, when they were runners-up in the championship, third three times, and twice in with a shout until the last gasp.

Many great players, both from home and overseas, have boosted the Gloucestershire ranks through the years, which makes it all the more surprising that they have never won the county championship, although they have finished runners-up six times – in 1930, 1931, 1947, 1959, 1969 and 1986. Always the bridesmaid, never the bride. They have also had a second place in the Sunday League in 1988, but their first trophy came in 1973 under Tony Brown, when they won the Gillette Cup, following it up by carrying off the Benson and Hedges Cup four years later with Mike Procter as captain.

The Grace family was largely responsible for the formation of the county club in 1870, and three brothers, W. G., E. M. and G. F., all played that year. It was W. G., however, who went on to become the legendary figure. He may not have scored the majority of his runs for Gloucestershire, or played the majority of his games for them, but such was his personality that John Arlott once wrote of him, 'In the public mind W. G. *was* Gloucestershire.'

W. G. once advised a young player who was due to face Yorkshire, 'Make sure you bring a box tomorrow, because we are playing against George Hirst, and you will need one.'

That particular protector was not as common an item of cricket wear as it is today, but the youngster dared not disobey the great man. He was, however, a little embarrassed when venturing into a Bristol sports shop to be confronted by a lady sales assistant. Eventually he came away with a metal device, having been assured that it was 'the very latest model and what all the best batsmen are wearing'.

Next day he found himself facing Hirst, with his captain looking on from the other end. He managed to get bat on ball to a couple of deliveries that were well pitched up, but the next nipped back off the pitch and thudded into his nether regions – to the accompaniment of a tuneful clang.

This happened again in Hirst's next over, and Grace strolled down the pitch and said to the youngster, 'I know I told you to get a box, but I didn't mean a musical box.'

The good doctor was so feared by the umpires of his day that some hardly dared give him out, and he bent the rules quite unashamedly on more than one occasion. During one innings in a county match he lofted the ball skywards into the outfield, ran one, and, as he turned for the second, noticed a fielder nicely positioned for the catch. He immediately declared the innings – with the ball still in the air – to avoid being given out and having his average spoiled. He claimed that the catch had been taken after close of play.

The influence of W. G. spread to league cricket. At Alveston, near Thornbury, a visiting batsman hit the ball high over the bowler's head, and seemed certain to add six more to his total of 70. The ball landed on the sloping roof of a cowshed, the wall of which doubled as a sightscreen, bounced back into the field of play and was caught by a fielder. The umpire gave the batsman out.

Naturally, he questioned the decision, but the umpire told him, 'You be out, zur, no argument. W. G. Grace caught a ball off that roof in 1886 and he said it were out, so out it has been ever since, and out it will always be.'

Wally Hammond arrived on the scene between the wars and hit an amazing thirty-six double hundreds. No other Englishman has ever come close, and that figure is only one less than the record total of the great Don Bradman.

Hammond was probably the greatest batsman on all kinds of pitches. I remember one occasion when he captained the side against Somerset, and after Gloucestershire had totalled around the 360 mark, Hammond making a century, Tom Goddard bowled Somerset out twice for a few. The story goes that after the game Hammond led the full Gloucestershire team back out to the middle, told Goddard to set his field on a pitch that had been turning dramatically, and proceeded to play the bowler with the edge of his bat! Unplayable? Not for Hammond. That was a remarkable example of his excellent technique.

For the first five years of his career Goddard was a fast bowler, but he then developed into a fine off-spinner and his career record of 2,979 wickets speaks for itself. However, he was sometimes left to toil rather than spin if the pitch was not quite to his liking, something that happened with a vengeance during one county match.

B. O. Allen, who came close to leading his side to the title in 1947, was captain that day, and he had to leave the field, handing over the captaincy to Goddard, who was in the middle of a bowling stint at the time.

Goddard continued to send down over after over, although it was not a pitch for spinners and he was having no success. Finally, completely knackered – he had been clouted to all corners of the ground – he turned to a colleague and groaned, 'Why doesn't the bugger take me off?' He had completely forgotten he had been left in charge, by which time he had bowled forty-two consecutive overs!

Tom Goddard's benefit game provided probably the most memorable match ever to be staged at the Wagon Works ground, another Gloucestershire venue. Nottinghamshire were the visitors in that last fixture of the 1936 season, and on the first day everything went right for the home team, Goddard fittingly taking 4 for 49 as Notts were bowled out before tea.

Gloucestershire, however, lost two quick wickets after the interval, and Tom started to worry. Hammond was next in, and Tom knew that if he was out before the close, there was little chance of a big crowd when play resumed on the Monday.

As he walked out, Hammond predicted, 'Don't worry, Tom. I'll bat out tonight and I'll bat all day on Monday as well.'

So he did. A crowd of 7,000 turned up that day – a record for the ground – and by the end of it Hammond had scored 317, his highest score in England.

One of the features of that ground is a railway carriage, which now forms part of the neighbouring bowls club pavilion. It was made at the wagon works in 1915 on order from the Argentine Railway, but unfortunately the ship carrying it sank. Eventually it was salvaged and brought back to Gloucester to become the changing room of the bowls club.

Bomber Wells was another fine Gloucestershire spin bowler. He had a very short run-up and could easily catch you unprepared. He did exactly that to Brian Close one day. The Yorkshireman was just looking up from his guard when the ball rapped him on the pad and he was out lbw. He was not amused.

I could sympathise: Bomber did me too. I yelled to him, 'Hey, Bomber, that's not reight, I weren't ready.'

'Ever been a scout, Dickie?' he barked back down the pitch. 'You know what they say – be prepared.'

After that, Closey and I used to take guard immediately after

Bomber had bowled one ball, so that we would be ready for the next. Bomber wasn't going to catch us out again. But Bomber still put one over on Closey after moving from Gloucestershire to Nottinghamshire. Playing at Scarborough, he saw Closey approaching 200 – a feat he never achieved throughout his career – when the batsman pulled the ball to deep square leg. Mervyn Winfield raced miles, or so it seemed at the time, round the boundary's edge, and brought off a stunning running catch. As Closey departed, cursing, Bomber grinned at him. 'You never change, Brian. You always were a sucker for my leg trap.'

I have already mentioned Mike Procter, the best overseas professional I have ever seen, along with Malcolm Marshall. Proccy gave everything to Gloucestershire County Cricket Club. Towards the end of his career, the South African would come in and bowl with bad knees showing the wear and tear of the years, on the low, slow pitches that were a feature of Bristol, never complaining, and giving everything he had, despite the obvious pain.

He was a great all-rounder, and game for a laugh, too. At one match I umpired at Bristol in the Sunday League, torrential rain overnight had continued early in the morning, and we did not think there would be any play. Proccy had been out on the tiles the previous night, having a beer or seven, and someone rang to tell him he need not bother rushing to the ground because the odds were that the game would not be played.

However, the rain cleared, the groundstaff did some magnificent work on the pitch, and we decided to play a reduced game of thirty-two overs.

Proccy arrived in the nick of time, looking distinctly worse for wear. He opened the bowling from my end, and his first three deliveries were wides. He looked at me apologetically and said, 'Sorry about this, Dickie, I'll go round the wicket to see if I can get one straight from there.' No joy. Another wide. So he reverted to over the wicket. And produced yet another wide. That was five in a row to start the game off.

He eventually managed to get through the over, much to the relief of all and sundry. 'Thank goodness for that, Proccy', I said to him. 'I thought we were heading for the record books – the only Sunday League game in history to last all day without getting through one over.'

Proccy had the last laugh, though: Gloucestershire went on to win by virtue of a faster scoring rate.

I did have one run-in with him during a Gloucestershire v. Essex game at Cheltenham in 1976. I was just debating with myself whether to intervene and warn him about the over-use of short-pitched deliveries, when he fizzed another down. It clipped Ray East's nose as it went past and blood spurted on to the pitch. It was red-nose day for Ray, although I doubt he felt any comic relief. He was a right old mess. The physio had a hard job stopping the bleeding.

'Right, I've had enough,' I said to Proccy. 'I'm giving you an official warning for intimidatory bowling.'

I called the captain, Tony Brown, over, and explained the situation to him. He was not happy, but I have always been a big believer in stamping down hard on intimidatory bowling, and I felt Proccy had overstepped the mark on this occasion, so, mate or no mate, he felt the sharp end of my tongue.

As well as Mike Procter, Gloucestershire have been fortunate in having two more outstanding overseas players in their ranks in the 1970s and '80s – the brilliant Pakistan pair of Zaheer Abbas and Sadiq Mohammad.

An elegant batsman, whose classic style brought constant delight to the Gloucestershire supporters, Zaheer made his mark at Cheltenham in 1977 when he became the only batsman to score a double hundred and a hundred in a match three times, hitting 205 not out and 108 not out against Sussex.

Sadiq, a stubborn opener who could also bowl left-arm spin, comes from a cricketing family. He is the youngest of five brothers who have all played first-class cricket: Hanif, the little master, a legendary figure in Pakistan cricket, Wazir, the first to gain a Test cap and who inspired his brothers, Mushtaq, Raees and Sadiq. Mushtaq, Hanif and Sadiq created history in Karachi in 1969–70, when they became the first three brothers to appear in a Test match together.

Gloucestershire have had quite a few players who have doubled up as professional footballers: Ron Nicholls, Bob Etheridge, Barrie Meyer, who went on to become one of my umpiring colleagues at Test match level, and Harold Jarman all played for either Bristol Rovers or Bristol City.

The greatest of them all was Arthur Milton, a double international. What made Arthur so remarkable was that he played for England against Austria at Wembley in 1951 after playing only twelve league games for Arsenal. He admits that he has lived off that ever since.

Barrie Meyer, incidentally, was in the Bristol Rovers side which took on the famous Busby Babes of Manchester United, and he still takes great delight in telling me about the team talk of Rovers' manager Bert Tann, who simply said, 'Listen, lads, don't worry about that lot. We have eleven players, they have eleven players. They are just another team. Now go out there and enjoy yourselves.'

Rovers obviously did just that. They won 4–0.

Peter Rochford, another umpire, who used to keep wicket for Gloucestershire in the 1950s, was also one for the odd tale or two as we chatted during lunch or tea intervals, or stoppages for rain, bad light or whatever, and he once told me about a match against Middlesex at Bristol.

Middlesex had lost a wicket very quickly, and Bill Edrich went out to bat at number three. Bill liked a drink, and the previous night he had had a very, very heavy session. When he got to the middle he obviously had great difficulty standing up straight and keeping still while taking his guard off the umpire. He turned to Peter and muttered, 'If I can just get through this first over I should be okay. Just one over. That's all I need. I'll get a hundred if I can survive that.'

Said Peter, 'Poor Bill was a bit wibbly-wobbly, to say the least. In that first over he played and missed, played and missed. He simply could not lay bat on ball. But he somehow survived, more by luck than management. And he went on to score a magnificent century. Just as he said he would.'

Another of my umpiring colleagues was Jack Crapp, a former Gloucestershire batsman, who won seven caps for England. When I was placed on the first-class list, I went to Jack for advice, as did all new umpires, because they respected him. He told me, 'Find another job, Dickie lad, that's my advice. It's not worth the worry.' Thank goodness I took no notice of him!

The Graveney family have served Gloucestershire well, three of them having captained the county. Tom was one of the most handsome batsmen of post-war years, both for his county and England, and it was sad when he left to join Worcestershire after the captaincy was taken from him and given to C. T. Pugh after the 1960 season. Brother Ken had a spell as captain in 1963 and 1964, and Ken's son, David, led the side for seven seasons between 1982 and 1988.

During one match against Sussex at Hove, David tried to play throat-high deliveries from John Snow off the front foot, and at the end of one particularly torrid over, Snowy sauntered down the track and said, 'I think, young man, that you are going to have to learn to play off the back foot.'

David, of course, is now chairman of the England selectors!

Tom Pugh was out of the game for months after terrible injuries in a game against the West Indies. He ducked into a really fast delivery that he thought was going to be a bouncer, and was hit on the face, his jaw broken in two places. He had ducked so low that the West Indies appealed for lbw!

Former Manchester United, Sheffield Wednesday, Aston Villa and Nottingham Forest manager Ron Atkinson had his proudest cricketing moment when he survived a spell from Gloucestershire's left-arm fast bowler Jack Davey in a benefit match. Ron thought that Jack was lightning quick, and he had therefore done exceptionally well against him. Next day he was a bit miffed to hear Brian Johnston describe Davey as 'slow medium pace'.

Said Big Ron, 'If he's slow medium, what the hell must it be like against a real tearaway?'

That experience taught him a far greater appreciation of how batsmen handle the really quick bowlers.

Daily Telegraph cricket writer David Green played for Gloucestershire after a spell with Lancashire, and I enjoy reading his reports and comments. He has played the game and knows what it is all about. His period at Old Trafford ended on a sour note when he was sacked. On hearing the news, he immediately took off his Lancashire blazer and set fire to it. Years later, when he returned to do a match report for the *Telegraph*, the Lancashire hierarchy presented him with a new one. As far as I know it is still intact.

Fast bowler David Lawrence, who was Young Cricketer of the Year in 1985 and went on to play for England, was nicknamed 'Syd' after the bandleader 'Syd' Lawrence. He was also known as 'Hissing Syd', stemming from the fact that when he used to bowl from my end, I always knew when he was on his way in because I could hear him hissing. He ran many a mile, and the hissing grew louder as he approached. 'Hey up, here he comes,' I used to say to myself. 'He's on his way. Hissing Syd.' Sssss, sssss, *sssss*, SSSSSSS.

Sadly he was forced to retire from cricket because of a nasty knee injury sustained in a Test match in Wellington, New Zealand. He tried to make a comeback, but his knee could not take the strain, which was a great shame.

Cheltenham provides another beautiful setting for cricket, especially during the famous Festival week, when the white tents dotted about provide a lovely complement to the imposing chapel, the school tower, and the lush green of the pitch itself. The air of tradition is also very apparent, reinforcing, yet again, what a perfect place England can be for playing this great game – given the weather!

Gloucestershire have also played at Stroud. There are railway lines at one end of the ground, and it has been known for a train to stop behind the bowler's arm, putting the batsman off. He would crouch there at the crease wondering if the train would move off any minute. Some umpires have even tried to wave the train on, despite the fact that it was waiting for the signal to change, and sometimes there was no option but to hold up play for a little while until it steamed off. Train stopped play. It makes a change from t' rain stopped play, I suppose.

Moreton-in-Marsh, a pretty ground in the middle of the lovely Gloucestershire countryside, has staged Sunday League matches, and during one match Gloucestershire scored 243 off 50 overs batting first, Phil Tufnell taking 4 for 44 for Middlesex. During the tea interval there was a tremendous thunderstorm. It rained cats and dogs. The ground was awash, and it was an impossible task for a small club, without the big squeegees that are available at county grounds, to get the pitch fit for play again. Volunteers did their best with mops and mats and buckets, but they were fighting a losing battle.

The Middlesex players decided there was no chance of any further play, so they showered, changed, got in their cars, and drove off. Apart from their captain, Mike Gatting, who was still in the middle, arguing the toss with me and the other umpire, Roy Palmer, along with all those workers who had sweated blood trying to make play possible. Gatt was playing hell up, while his lads were all waving goodbye. At least, I believe that's what they were doing.

Gloucestershire have also played at Swindon, in neighbouring Wiltshire, in the Sunday League. Unfortunately it proved a bit of a disaster as instead of treating the pitch with fertiliser, the groundsman accidentally doused it with weedkiller.

In Jack Russell Gloucestershire had one of the best wicket-keepers I have ever come across. He should have played more for England than he did, but the selectors preferred to play a batsman/wicketkeeper. I disagreed with that: you should always select the best man for the job, especially in such a specialist position. In any case, Jack was a far better batsman than people give him credit for, and scored a lot of runs.

I have seen Jack get England out of some very ticklish

situations. What about his magnificent century against India at Lord's in 1996; the Old Trafford Test against the West Indies in 1995, when he played a crucial part in England's victory; and, best of all, that memorable occasion on the winter tour of South Africa in 1995–6, when he stuck there with Michael Atherton to save the second Test, against all the odds?

Jack is probably one of the most psyched-up players you will ever see. At six thirty in the morning – hangover time for most cricketers – you will find Jack pounding the hotel floor tucking into the Jaffa Cakes that he lives on, and knocking a ball against his bat, waking everybody else up.

Jack treasures that floppy white hat of his. I'm sure he used to take it to bed with him. Probably he slept in it – the state of it suggested he did. He's frightened to death someone will pinch it one day.

He is a superb artist, both with gloves and the paintbrush. He has done several drawings of me, and I treasure them. He also provided me with my last decision in Test cricket when England played India at Lord's in 1996 – lbw at that. Sourav Ganguly was the bowler.

Jack came up to me afterwards and said, 'That's a present for you, Dickie. With best wishes, from me.'

'Present?' I spluttered. 'It were nowt of the sort. Tha were plumb.'

I hope Mark Alleyne is given more chances to play for England. Since they made him captain, Gloucestershire have done very well, coming very close to winning the championship for the first time, something which reflects on Boo-Boo's leadership qualities. I was delighted when he was selected for the one-day internationals in Australia last winter, and it was a tragedy that he had to return home early because of the death of his father, who was killed in a car crash in Barbados.

The line of outstanding overseas stars was continued by

Mark's predecessor as captain, Courtney Walsh. The big West Indian paceman and I have become good friends, and he agreed to come over and help me with my 1998 video, *A Bird's Eye View of Cricket*, which became a bestseller.

We had arranged for Courtney to bowl to me at Headingley, the scene of that famous 'You don't need me, you need a plumber' incident in the Test between England and West Indies, when a burst water pipe flooded the ground. There I stood, at the age of sixty-five, with helmet – never had those in my playing days – thigh-pads, chest protector, padding down the inside and outside of both legs, elbow guard, not forgetting box, pads and gloves. Every part of me, I prayed to the good Lord, was protected from the fearsome menace about to be unleashed on me.

Courtney steamed in off a full run. I never saw the first ball. Goodness knows where it went. The second whistled past in similar fashion. The third and fourth likewise. Then he let rip a bouncer, which hit me on the helmet. I did finally manage to lay bat on ball a couple of times, while nonchalantly waving other deliveries past.

Eventually, however, the inevitable happened. All three stumps were flattened, with barely two overs gone. I had wondered if my eyesight was not quite what it once was, and that proved it.

In April 1999 I was due to speak at the Everyman Theatre in Cheltenham in front of a packed audience, including 140 people from Gloucestershire County Cricket Club. I was scheduled to go on stage at seven thirty in the evening, so I arranged for my driver, Joe Palmer, to pick me up from my home at one o'clock.

We arrived in Cheltenham at three thirty, and Joe looked for somewhere to park while we went for a bite to eat. He said, 'I'm not going to risk parking on the streets. Ten-to-one we'll get clamped, and we don't want that, do we? Apart from anything else it's a fifty-quid fine.'

Joe decided to park up at the big Debenham's store. Although it was Sunday afternoon, it was open and there was plenty of room in the car park, which was one of those where you get a ticket as you go in and pay the required amount on leaving.

We went and had a lovely meal and strolled back to the car at about twenty minutes to six. When we got to the car park we saw a woman with three kids, and she was crying her heart out. 'What's up, luv?' I said.

She sobbed, 'I can't get in for my car. It's all locked up, and I can't get home.'

Only then did it dawn on me that the iron gates across the car park entrance were locked. We rattled those gates until our hands hurt, but no one came. We were in a terrible predicament.

Joe spotted a notice which said, 'In case of emergency ring this number,' and rang it. The chap who answered said, 'I'm only the bloke who clamps cars parked outside. Nothing to do

with me, mate. Can't help you.' And put the phone down.

Joe then rang the police. They were not interested either. 'Sorry, nothing we can do. It's locked for the night. If you want your car, you'll have to come back at eight o'clock in the morning when everything opens up again.'

What a mess. I had to be back in Barnsley for an important meeting at eleven o'clock the following morning.

Joe said, 'Can't waste any more time, Dickie, you've got to get to the theatre. There's nothing for it but to leave the car here and walk.'

Luckily it was not too far away, and I arrived in plenty of time to do my show, *An Evening with Dickie Bird* – but without my *Test Match Special* music which I use as an introduction. The tape was still in the car, along with all my books and videos. I didn't sell a sausage that night.

The first thing I said when I walked on stage was, 'If there are any security guards from Debenham's in here, will you come round during the interval and bale me out, because you've locked my car in your damn car park.'

There was no response, so Joe had to ring a local hotel and book us in for the night. At a hundred pounds for a single room, it was extortion. And what about my eleven o'clock appointment in Barnsley the following day? Said Joe, 'If we get away as soon after eight as possible, we'll have to gamble that we get a traffic-free run. Then you might just make it.' Traffic free? On the M42 and M1 on a Monday morning? Fat chance.

When I finally came off stage at a quarter to ten, the manager of the theatre was waiting for me. His own security people had contacted their counterparts at Debenham's, and he had been able to speak to the chap in charge, who at first had said, 'No way. Once that car park's locked we don't open it for anyone. Tell them to come back tomorrow at eight o'clock.'

The theatre manager had said, 'Oh, very well, but I hope you know that the bloke you've locked in is Dickie Bird.'

'You're joking,' said the security guy.

'No, I'm not. He's on stage now. You can have a word with him yourself when he's finished speaking.'

'No need for that,' came the reply. 'If it's Dickie Bird, we'll come and let him out straight away. Wouldn't do it for anyone else, mind.'

By the time I came off stage, the car was at the theatre waiting for me.

I got home tired, but relieved, in the early hours of Monday morning. On my birthday.

So my advice is this: if you ever go to Cheltenham, don't, for goodness' sake, park your car in Debenham's. Park it on the street and risk being clamped.

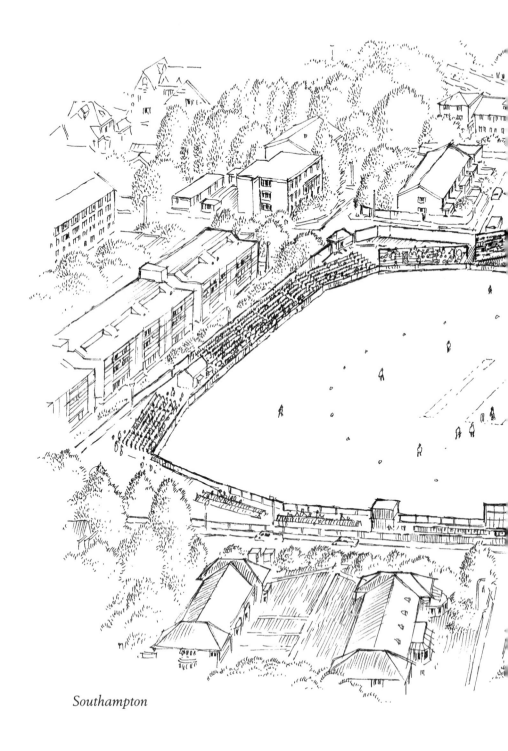

Southampton

HAMPSHIRE

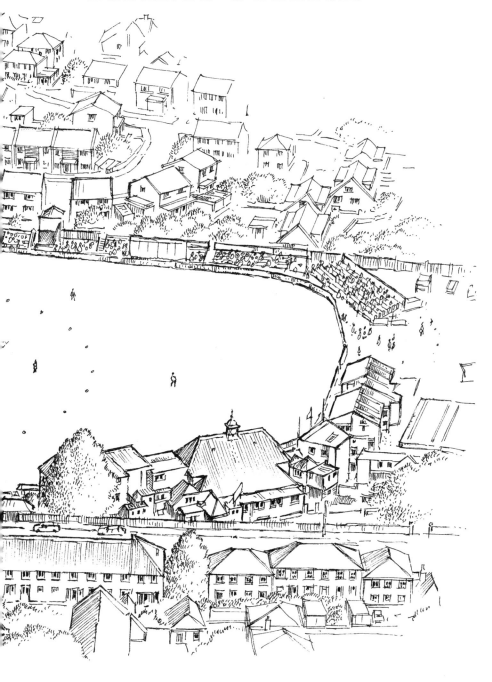

6

H AMPSHIRE are on the move. But not very far. Their headquarters in Southampton are being transferred to the outskirts of the town, where a magnificent new stadium is in the process of being built to provide a county ground more in keeping with the twenty-first century.

I just hope that the atmosphere I have always found at Southampton can also be transported to the new surroundings, because although in appearance the ground in Northlands Road is not a particularly inspiring place, I have always found it one of the friendliest venues on the county circuit – and certainly one of the sunniest.

As for the pitch, my old friend Colin Cowdrey always used to say that it was ideal for strokemakers – and he should know.

There have been quite a few colourful characters down the years, none more so that Lionel Tennyson, grandson of the famous poet. His swashbuckling approach to the game gave Hampshire a reputation for cavalier cricket which has been associated with them since. Tennyson was at his best in 1928 when he scored the only double hundred of his career against the West Indies. Learie Constantine had bamboozled the early Hampshire batting before His Lordship went in with the score at 86 for 5. Four hours later he had made 217.

For a modern-day equivalent you need look no further than

Colin Ingleby-Mackenzie, the flamboyant mastermind behind Hampshire's first county championship success in 1961, after nearly a century of trying. They clinched the title on the first day of September when Danny Livingstone, a West Indian from Antigua, caught Derbyshire's Bob Taylor in the deep at Dean Park, Bournemouth.

A three-cornered fight had developed between Hampshire, Middlesex and Yorkshire, with Ingleby-Mackenzie's side taking over at the top on the first day of August and never being caught. They won nineteen of their thirty-two matches, including five in a row during the last few crucial weeks. Ten of their wins came from declarations, which tells you something of their captain's approach.

Colin was one of the greatest characters I have ever come across. On top of that, he was a gentleman, and it was nice to see such a genuinely good bloke go on to become President of the MCC, a tremendous honour. The thing I liked about him was that he so obviously enjoyed the game to the full. It is said that he used to go out all night partying and then arrive at the ground the following morning still dressed in his top hat and tails. How true those stories are, I don't know. I never saw him attired like that in any match. He certainly never batted in a top hat. Although, come to think of it, he was a tail-ender.

I would not have been surprised, though, if Colin had taken the field in his gladrags. He was that kind of personality. I've known him to have a transistor radio in his pocket, listening in to the racing commentary during the afternoon while he was out there fielding. You could hear it: 'Now here we come to the three o'clock at Kempton and the runners and riders are just approaching the tape. And they're off. Into the lead goes Dickie's Delight, closely followed by Not Out and That's A No-Ball . . .' And so it went on. He used to have a flutter, and would want to know if he'd made a bob or two.

He once stopped a game between the MCC and Yorkshire at Lord's while he moved to the boundary fence to tune in to the BBC's live commentary of the St Leger. He wasn't a happy chappie at the end of it, though: his horse came nowhere. Started at ten to one and was still running at five past four.

It was Ingleby-Mackenzie who described the spirit of his successful side as originating from wine, women and song. When questioned about discipline, he once replied, 'Oh, well, of course I always insist that my men are tucked up in bed by ten o'clock. After all, play starts at half past eleven.'

That summed up his attitude to cricket. A glorious mixture of flair and enjoyment, and largely because of that, Hampshire's championship success was universally popular.

Colin would, of course, be the first to acknowledge that he had some very talented players under him, such as Derek Shackleton and Roy Marshall.

I remember playing for Yorkshire against Hampshire at Dean Park in 1959 and facing up to Shack on a rain-affected pitch – bearing in mind pitches were uncovered in those days. I got to 68, but it took me nearly all day to do it. I simply could not hit Shack off the square. He was deadly accurate with his medium-pacers. I went out after close of play to look at the pitch, and there was a dark patch, eighteen inches or so square, where he had pitched everything with remarkable accuracy, right on a length. All around, the track was still quite grassy.

Shack's bowling brought him a county record of 2,669 wickets, and the combination of Shack, White and Cottam – sounds like a firm of solicitors, doesn't it? – bowled Yorkshire out for 23 at Middlesbrough, the lowest total in White Rose history. Incidentally, I could not be even partly blamed for that, having moved to Leicestershire by then.

Shack was such a key part of the Hampshire team, that when

ve Three Test captains, Richie Benaud (Australia), John Reid (New Zealand) and
 Dexter (England).

w Former Test cricketers pictured at Lord's in 1972. *Back row* (left to right):
 Simpson (Nottinghamshire), W. J. Edrich (Middlesex), J. D. Robertson (Middlesex),
 . P. Wright (Kent), T. G. Evans (Kent), H. Gimblett (Somerset).
t row (left to right): C. J. Barnett (Gloucestershire), N. W. D. Yardley (Yorkshire),
 . S. Wyatt (Warwickshire and Worcestershire), P. B. H. May (Surrey), L. Hutton
 kshire), C. Washbrook (Lancashire).

Left Freddie Brown, who instilled a new spirit and sense of purpose when he took over as captain of Northamptonshire in 1949. He was also recalled to the England team as captain and later became President of the MCC.

Below left Gloucestershire and England batsman Wally Hammond, who was the greatest player on all types of pitches.

Below right Gilbert Parkhouse and Wilf Wooller emerging to open the batting for Glamorgan after coming down all those steps at St Helen's, Swansea. Eighty-nine made it.

ree famous sportsmen who all became Test cricketers and famous footballers:
ve left Arthur Milton (Gloucestershire, Arsenal and Bristol City).
ve right Willie Watson (Yorkshire, Leicestershire, Huddersfield Town, Sunderland
 Halifax).
_ow_ Patsy Hendren (Middlesex, Brentford, Queen's Park Rangers, Manchester City
 Coventry).

Above The scoreboard at the Parks, Oxford
– a little bit different from the computer-
operated constructions in use at the big
grounds today, but very efficient nevertheless.

Above Any idea where this leads? Two o
my colleagues make their escape from th
umpires' room during a Hampshire coun
game.

Above The scoring tent in all its glory at
Heanor, Derbyshire, on what was obviously
a very hot summer's day.

Right Frank Chester, one of the greatest
umpires of all time, who also had a
promising future in the game as a player
until he lost his right arm in the war.

ove Tom Graveney, one of the most
ndsome of strokemakers who also graced
· international arena. His test career
ssomed after he left Gloucestershire –
·r a disagreement concerning the
ptaincy – and became a major force in
· Worcestershire side.

Above Two more members of the
Graveney clan, Tom's brother Ken and
nephew David, who is now chairman of
the England Selectors, and is consequently
not seen smiling quite as much as in this
photograph. All three Graveneys captained
Gloucestershire.

ove Tom Graveney (*third right*) celebrates his hundredth hundred in the
orcestershire dressing room, along with (*left to right*): Ray Booth, Norman Gifford, Ron
·adley, Jack Flavell, Martin Horton, Alan Ormrod, Dick Richardson and Don Kenyon.

Above Tony Lock (Surrey and England), who was a magnificent bowler and brilliant close-to-the-wicket fielder. He would dive under a bus to get a caught and bowled.

Above Peter May, also of Surrey and England, who, for me, was the greatest English batsman since the war, as well as becoming a very able administrator.

left Alec Bedser, that
⸍at Surrey and England
⸍wler, who bowled me in
⸍th innings when I first
⸍yed against Surrey for
⸍cestershire.

⸍*t* Apartheid dogged the
⸍eer of Cape Coloured
⸍sil D'Oliveira, who
⸍owed great courage to
⸍me through it all to play
⸍ Worcestershire and
⸍gland. He is a man I
⸍e always admired and
⸍ who talks a lot of sense
⸍h regard to coaching.

⸍*ht* Freddie Trueman, of
⸍rkshire and England,
⸍doubtedly one of the
⸍ne's greatest characters, a
⸍mendous competitor and
⸍ruly magnificent fast
⸍wler.

⸍*ove* With my umpiring colleague Bill
⸍ey, an extrovert Aussie who created a
⸍merset county record of 2,761 runs in a
⸍son at the age of at least 42. No one is
⸍te sure how old Bill is – and he'll not
⸍.

Above Yorkshire legend Len Hutton, the
outstanding batsman in the world of his
time. Australian fast bowler Ray Lindwall
once said he was sick of the sight of him.
Len is shown here chatting to Joe Hardstaff
(jnr) of Nottinghamshire and England.

Above It's Geoff Boycott, but not as we know him. The dedicated Yorkshire and England batsman as he was in his bespectacled days in my home town of Barnsley, where he played with me at Shaw Lane.

Above You don't scare me. The fearless Brian Close (Yorkshire, Somerset and England) sways out of the way of a short pitched delivery from Michael Holding, with my mate Bill Alley keeping a watch eye on things.

Above David Bairstow, sadly missed, who emerged in the 1970s as an excellent wicketkeeper for Yorkshire and a bubbling personality. Bluey also played for England.

Above Brian Close in one of his quieter moments. He was another of the game's most colourful characters. The only proble with him was that nothing was ever his fau

he retired *Wisden* commented, 'Hampshire without Shackleton will be like Blackpool without its tower.' There was a lot in that.

He went on to become a first-class umpire, but did not enjoy the success he had enjoyed as a player. His marks were not up to par and he was eventually sacked. He was very disappointed, but sadly we umpires live and die by those marks.

Born in Barbados, Roy Marshall was a fine batsman who played a few Tests for the West Indies, and enjoyed a short spell as captain. He produced a lot of exciting knocks for Hampshire, but the best of all was probably when he made the highest score of his career – 228 not out against Pakistan in 1962. He threw the bat at the ball with a refreshing gusto that made him a popular figure wherever he appeared. There is no doubt that he played a big part in Hampshire's success.

I was once playing for Yorkshire at Dean Park when Don Wilson was bowling to Marshall. Don was an excellent left-arm spin bowler who played for England and could really turn the ball, yet that day Marshall kept cutting him backward of square for four after four. Finally, our skipper, Ronnie Burnet, not only had two fielders backward of square, he had two square at cover point, plus an orthodox cover point, and Marshall still got the ball through for fours. He cut Wilson to ribbons.

Marshall passed the 2,000-run milestone in that title-winning season, as did another batsman, Henry Horton, who had been recruited from Worcestershire in 1953, the same year that Marshall signed up for the county. Horton had an ungainly crouch at the crease, and one of the funniest things I have ever heard came from Brian Johnston, that doyen of broadcasters, when he tried to describe the stance as looking like someone sitting on a shooting stick. After three attempts, it finally came out as, 'It looks as though he's shitting on a shooting stick.'

Another in the cavalier tradition was Gordon Greenidge,

who went on to form a great opening partnership for the West Indies with Des Haynes. Gordon actually came over to this country from Barbados at a very early age and went to school in London before joining the groundstaff at Southampton. He seemed only a tot when I chatted to him at the ground one day as he was sweeping out the stands, and he said to me, 'I won't be doing this much longer, Mr Bird.' How right he was. What a run-scoring machine he proved to be.

One of his more memorable knocks for Hampshire was 177 out of a total of 371 for 4, in a Gillette Cup match with Glamorgan in 1975.

Then there was Barry Richards, who also played for Hampshire for a while in the late 'sixties and early 'seventies. Without a shadow of doubt he was the greatest batsman I have seen. Sir Donald Bradman said the same about him, and that will do for me. Barry played under Richard Gilliat in the team which regained the championship in 1973, and got stacks of runs. His greatest shot was the cover drive, which was marvellous to see, but he had the lot. He played all his strokes with that special arrogance that is the trademark of the highest class. He was simply magnificent.

Sadly, because of apartheid and South Africa's ban from international cricket, he was lost to the Test arena for the vast majority of his career, which was a tragedy for the game in general and Richards in particular.

Richards eventually became bored with the county game in England. I have watched him score a superb hundred and then turn to me and say, 'That's it, Dickie. Time I had a rest now and gave someone else a chance.' Then he would hit one in the air quite deliberately to get out, and off he would go.

Finally, he went even further than that, telling me one day, 'Dickie, do you know, I feel there is nothing left for me to play for. There is nothing more to achieve. I find it difficult to get out of bed in the morning to go and play for Hampshire.'

I replied, 'Well, if you feel like that, Barry, you'd better pack it in. Once the enjoyment has gone, that's it as far as I am concerned.'

He looked me straight in the eye and said, 'That's exactly what I'm going to do.' And he did.

He could have played for quite a few more years, and I always wondered what he would have achieved had he been able to play international cricket today. He would, I am sure, have broken all records. Sadly, he was born at the wrong time, and had to be content with just four Test appearances. In those four games he averaged 75, and only four other batsmen in history have topped 60 – Sir Donald Bradman, Graeme Pollock, George Headley (the Black Bradman) and Herbert Sutcliffe.

The latest in the line of Hampshire crowd-pleasers is South African-born Robin Smith. He is a fine batsman. You have only to look at his record for England, for whom he averages 47. He has a habit of blinking his eyes as he is waiting for the next delivery, which has led to suggestions that he is of a nervous nature, but he never showed that in his batting, especially when taking on the quickest of bowlers, a challenge he still relishes.

Robin's brother, Chris, who has played for England, once said of him, 'Robin only ever pulls his head out of the way at the last split second. He loves looking down the gun barrel. He does it just for the buzz. He is one of the bravest people I have ever met. Probably the only batsman in the world who loves fast bowling. The faster the better. Some are very good at playing it, but Robin is actually turned on by it.'

People have said that Robin has a weakness against spin, but I don't go along with that. He came up against some of the top spinners in the world at Test level and still got runs.

He took over the captaincy of Hampshire in 1998 and did a

tremendous job. John 'Stanley' Stephenson had been captain before him, but the responsibilities affected his all-round play and in the end he resigned, though some said that he was asked to do so. Smith brought on some of the youngsters and now Hampshire have some new exciting talent coming through.

One of the brightest prospects is a lad from my home town of Barnsley, Alex Morris, who played some of his early cricket at Shaw Lane, where I started my career. He is a strapping twenty-two-year-old who is 6ft 4ins tall, and I have always rated him, even though he was released by Yorkshire before joining Hampshire last season. He is a very good all-rounder. Watch out for him.

Then there is Dimitri Mascarenhas, who was born in London but is of Sri Lankan extraction. He is only twenty-one, and, although he can also bowl, he is primarily a batsman. He started at number six, but moved up the order in 1998 after getting a stack of runs, he and Robin Smith carrying the batting to a large extent. He's another big lad, standing 6ft 2ins.

According to Tim Tremlett, a former medium-pacer who is now on the coaching staff, Robin Smith has always been the fittest man at the club. During the pre-season training sessions he would be the one doing one-handed press-ups, and the one leading the cross-country run – after jogging to the ground from his home ten miles away. Afterwards he would 'warm down' with a game of squash before having a quick shower, followed by lunch.

The other players dreaded the health and fitness routine imposed on them by physio David 'Adolf' Newman. He would get on his racing bike and expect the players to follow him – on foot. That 'little trip up the avenue to the common and back' was far from as simple as it sounded: apart from the odd triallist, wanting to impress, the 'field' would be gradually whittled down as one or two of the more experienced participants would have a pitstop at one of the hostelries *en route*, while another would pop into the golf club, presumably to play a round.

As for Tremlett himself, he admits to being persuaded by Chris Smith to catch the number 47 bus back to the flat where the latter's mother lived, just in time for morning sherry. From the top of the double decker they would inevitably see Cardigan Connor chatting up the local lovelies. After an hour or so Tim and Chris would then be chauffeured back to the ground by Chris's mum, sprinting the final fifty yards or so to arrive looking suitably knackered.

Meanwhile, Gordon Greenidge and Malcolm Marshall, fresh and fighting fit after twelve Tests and thirty-five one-day internationals during the winter, and having just flown in from the West Indies, would be huddled up like Michelin men, attired in umpteen sweaters, with thermals underneath, trying their best to keep warm in the groundsman's hut. Happy days.

Marshall, of course, was one of the two magnificent West Indian bowlers who served Hampshire so well, the other being Andy Roberts. I umpired Roberts at Oxford University's Parks ground when he played his first game for the county and I thought to myself, then, 'Crikey, this fella's a bit quick.' He really fizzed them into the wicketkeeper's gloves.

Roberts was ineligible to play in county championship matches that season, yet amazingly Hampshire went on to win the title without him. The bookies laid odds of 50–1 against that happening as the season started, and I always wondered if Ingleby-Mackenzie had a flutter.

The captain of that side, Richard Gilliat, was a good number-four left-hand batsman, but it was as a leader that he excelled. Tactically he was very clued up, and he did a magnificent job as Hampshire took the county crown for the second time.

With Roberts available for 1974 hopes were high that Hampshire could retain the title, but despite his 111 wickets, the weather prevented that happening. Hampshire lost five whole days' play in their last three matches, otherwise they would surely have been successful. Instead, Worcestershire, with the sun shining on them in more ways than one, finished two points better off.

Hampshire also took an awfully long time to reach a Lord's final, having to suffer a string of semi-final defeats until they finally managed to carry off the Benson and Hedges Cup in 1988, and then again in 1992. In between they also won the NatWest Trophy in 1991, and they have also come top of the Sunday League three times, in 1975, 1978 and 1986.

Allan Lamb once said that if Malcolm Marshall had played for Northamptonshire, they would have won the championship for the first time. Yet Hampshire never won it while Marshall played for them – NatWest, Benson and Hedges, Sunday League, yes, but never the big one.

Along with Michael Procter, of Gloucestershire, I would rate Marshall as the best overseas professional to have played county cricket, because they both always gave a hundred per cent.

Somerset's Peter Roebuck also paid Marshall the compliment of admitting that one ball bowled to him by the West Indian was the fastest he had ever faced. He could not believe that such a small man could generate that amount of pace. It was at Bournemouth in 1982 on a pitch that was not the best – as some batsmen had already pointed out, there was a sizeable hole in it, a foot wide of the off-stump. Marshall hit that spot with an absolute snorter of a delivery and the ball flew past Roebuck before he could blink. It was taken by Bobby Parks standing thirty yards back, and even then the wicketkeeper had to leap high into the air to catch it.

Peter told me, 'Of all the great bowlers, Marshall stands alone as a man of his age who never bowed to the conditions and never gave second best to any batsman.' How right he was.

I did have a bit of a dispute with Malcolm in a Test match at Edgbaston, however, and gave him an official warning for bowling too many short-pitched deliveries. He was not at all pleased, I can tell you. He muttered, 'If I can't bowl short, they won't be needing helmets.'

He was a good lad after that, though: he pitched them up – and finished with five wickets. He came up to me at the end of the innings, put his arm round me, and said, 'No hard feelings, Dickie. You were right. I did a lot better when I started bowling a full length.' Then he added, mischievously, 'But they didn't need the helmets anyway, did they?'

Marshall and Geoff Boycott had a special ritual whenever they came face to face in the middle. Marshall, about to open the bowling, would say, 'Morning Boycs.'

'Morning, Macca,' would come the reply.

'You hooking today, Boycs?'

'Not when you're bowling, Macca.'

'Okay, man.'

In the first over, Boycs would inevitably get a bouncer and duck out of the way. There would be a stare from Marshall. Followed by a big grin.

'Okay, Boycs, let's get on with it.'

It was a bit of by-play that stemmed from mutual respect.

Marshall's closest friend was probably Des Haynes. They were brought up together in Barbados and played at school level. However, when they faced each other on opposite sides they were always very competitive. Marshall was once bowling to Haynes, who hit him arrogantly for four, much to the bowler's obvious annoyance. Haynes, however, hardly had time to savour the moment. The next ball split his protective box!

They roomed together all over the world when playing for the West Indies, and even then Marshall would usually get the better of his colleague. Whenever they booked into a hotel

Marshall would always make sure that he entered the room first so that he could take the bed furthest away from the door. Then, when anybody knocked, Marshall would shout to Des, 'You answer it, you're nearest.' Des never learned.

Marshall, incidentally, is now coach at Hampshire, and is doing as good a job as ever, with the same total commitment he always showed when playing.

One of the homegrown Hampshire fast bowlers who made quite an impression on me was David 'Butch' White, who played in the 1960s. I played against him for Leicestershire at Hinckley in the days when we did not have helmets. Or big chest protectors. Or thigh-pads. Nothing like that. My thigh-pad was my handkerchief, which I used to slip over my jockstrap.

On this particular occasion I did not need the chest protector. Or the thigh-pad. But the helmet would certainly have come in handy. Butch hit me smack on the head with a bouncer and the ball ricocheted over the sightscreen. Unbelievable. I have to confess I felt a bit groggy and sank to my knees, but I got up and carried on. The next day I had a lump on my head the size of an ostrich egg, and a bit of a headache.

After that, Butch always tried to knock my block off. He never bowled at the stumps. Now when I see him on the county circuit I always duck first before opening the conversation.

We umpires often have difficult decisions to make, and I feel a lot of sympathy for my colleague Peter Wight. In 1969 he went out to inspect the pitch after a long hold-up in a game involving Hampshire, and he declared it fit for play. At half past five on the third day! He then discovered that all the Hampshire players, scorers, press and just about everybody else, had gone home, including the spectators, who had long since given up hope of any further play.

The visiting Glamorgan team, however, were still on the

premises, so Wight went out into the middle, called play, and, with no Hampshire players present, awarded the game to Glamorgan.

More recently, David Constant and Alan Whitehead refused to leave the field in the tea interval during Hampshire's John Player League match with Essex in 1984. They sat out on the square and had a pot of tea taken out to them as their way of making the point that it was impossible for them to have a cuppa in their dressing rooms, quite apart from anything else they might need to do, in the reduced fifteen-minute break.

I was umpiring in 1997 when Hampshire were entertaining the touring Australians at Southampton, and it just so happened that Matthew Hayden, an Aussie from Queensland, was Hampshire's overseas player. In the second innings he took guard off my colleague Barrie Leadbeater as Jason Gillespie prepared to bowl. With his first ball Gillespie knocked his countryman's off stump many a mile. It went cartwheeling past the wicketkeeper.

As he made his way back to the pavilion, Hayden hissed at Leadbeater, 'It's all your fault.'

'How do you mean, my fault?' queried an astonished umpire.

'You must have given me the wrong guard,' retorted Hayden.

Another umpire, Nigel Cowley, who is on the reserve list, got out in a bizarre way when he was batting for Hampshire seconds. The ball hit him on the front leg and ricocheted away for an easy leg-bye. He set off, but had gone only a couple of yards when he suddenly felt a pain in his leg, which gave way beneath him. He was run out while still lying prostrate in the middle of the pitch. It was a sad end to his debut innings. Hardly got off on the right foot, did he?

I always enjoyed umpiring at Dean Park, Bournemouth, and I'm very sad that they do not play there any longer. It is a lovely ground, surrounded by trees. There are usually a lot of holiday-makers there, with their beach bags, picnic lunches and deckchairs, and the marquees add to the atmosphere of a typical cricketing scene on an English summer's day.

The one eyesore at Dean Park is a modern building which towers above the sightscreen from the centre of town. It is an ugly monstrosity and former groundsman Fred Kingston always used to say that someone should put a bomb under it.

Hampshire also play at the United Services ground at Portsmouth, the only military ground now used for county cricket. Although it has a magnificent gate leading into it, the ground itself is rather spartan. There is an old concrete terrace for spectators, the scorers will, likely as not, sit out in the open at a table, and the press are housed in a caravan. There is also a railway line running across the back, and the trains can be a distraction when you are batting.

The thing I remember most about Portsmouth is the enormous heavy roller. And I do mean heavy. It is massive. It weighs five and a half tons and I feel sorry for the poor old horse, or more likely team of horses, which had to drag it up and down during the pre-war years. Today it has a 350hp V8 cylinder engine, and it's a wonder it doesn't make a huge dint in the pitch, let alone flatten it.

Sad to say, United Services is not noted for the high standard of its catering. When Yorkshire once played there, the lunch of mackerel and salad was so unappetising that the players sent for one of their travelling supporters and asked him to find a fish-and-chip shop. He returned with twelve portions, much to the delight of umpire Paul Gibb, who subsequently asked for all the spare 'official' lunches to be passed on to him. A legendary trougher – he could eat for England any time – Gibb got through most of them before the end of the interval.

Hampshire's other out-ground is at Basingstoke, which has quite a slope. In the early years of the country's visits there, the pitch was often reported as being of suspect bounce, and that appeared to be the case in 1974 when Kent's Colin Cowdrey, no longer at his most mobile – if he could ever be so described – was felled by the ball when mistiming a hook off Andy Roberts and was given out after falling on to his stumps. He had to retire from the match. In recent seasons, however, the present groundsman, Bill Hiscock, has been commended for his pitches.

Whenever I umpired at Southampton I stayed with the Hampshire scorer, Vic Isaacs, a man for whom I have a lot of respect. He is now in his twenty-fifth year as Hampshire scorer, and it would have been nice had he received recognition by being appointed as England scorer on an overseas tour, something he would have loved. He would have deserved it. Vic has been a tremendous help providing statistical material for this book.

I always enjoyed staying with Vic and his good lady, Brenda. After close of play, a shower and quick change, I would dash over to their house, where Brenda used to make sure that I had my roast beef and Yorkshire puddings. And believe me, her Yorkshire puddings were excellent – for a Hampshire lass! I do miss them now I've retired. Vic's son, Richard, helps with the scoring from time to time, although he works for the tax office, and the couple also have a daughter, Rachael.

Vic, incidentally, used to support Southampton Town in the winter, but he's been so disappointed in recent seasons that he's stopped going.

Former Hampshire captain, Nick Pocock, once played in a benefit match for Kenny Barrington in Amsterdam on a very hot day. He got quite a few runs, and when he came off the field, sweat was pouring out of him. His shirt was wet through. He wasn't too sure where the showers were, never having played on the ground before, but Surrey's Ron

Tindall, who also played football for Chelsea, was quick to help.

'We've made arrangements,' Ron said, 'to shower in that house on the other side of the road. If you don't fancy a shower, you can have a bath.'

So Nick made his way over, undressed, helped himself to a whisky and settled down to soak in the bath. He had been luxuriating in the tub for a few minutes when, to his amazement, a woman walked in. She was just as shocked as he was, and Nick didn't know how to cover his embarrassment.

'What on earth do you think you are doing in my bath?' she demanded.

Nick stuttered, 'I'm playing in the cricket match across the road and we've been given permission to shower and bath here.'

The woman shouted for her husband, who stormed in red faced. 'Who are you? I've given no one permission to shower, bath, drink my whisky or anything else. Now clear off before I call the police.'

When Nick returned to the pavilion, Tindall popped his head round the door and asked, 'Enjoy your shower, Nick?'

Another Hampshire story that also tickles me concerns a village team who once imported several members of the county side for their annual fixture with the Club President's XI. Not surprisingly they won the match convincingly.

The following year they fielded their more usual line-up, without the big-name celebrities, but they did wonder if the President would retaliate by bringing in outside help. They were relieved when they saw that the opposition consisted of a few good club players and an elderly chap who looked so dithery that they readily granted him a runner when he went out to bat. He was obviously stone deaf, and couldn't hear the umpire at all when he took guard. However, he proved remarkably sprightly, and the village team were amazed when he played a match-winning innings.

The following year the village captain asked the President if he had brought along the old man who had done so well twelve months earlier. 'As a matter of fact,' said the President, 'I have.' The captain was astonished when he was introduced to a young man of about thirty. He had heard of the elixir of youth, but this was ridiculous.

It turned out that the 'old man' was, in fact, a very fit and sprightly Ronny Aird, of Cambridge and Hampshire, who was secretary of the MCC for many years and President in 1969–70. The disguise had been so good that he had completely fooled the entire opposition team throughout an afternoon's cricket.

Canterbury

KENT

7

MENTION Canterbury to me and I always think about the lime tree that stands within the playing area, and as such is unique on county grounds. It has been there donkey's years, and it is recorded that a certain Colonel A. C. Watson, of Sussex, hit a six clean over the top of it in the 1920s.

Another story is told of a chap called K. L. Hutchings, who thought he had scored a certain six, only to see the ball hit the top of the tree, drop from branch to branch, and eventually into the gleeful hands of a fielder waiting patiently below.

Formed in 1859, Kent had been crowned champions for the first time in 1906, and they also won the title in 1909 and 1910 before their 1913 triumph. They then had to wait fifty-seven years before Colin Cowdrey led them to the top spot in 1970. Since then, they have shared the honours with Middlesex in 1977 and won it outright in 1978. They have proved very successful in the limited-overs game, winning the Gillette Cup in 1967 and 1974, the Benson and Hedges in 1973, 1976 and 1978, and the Sunday League in 1972, 1973, 1976 and 1995.

One of Kent's smaller grounds, at Folkestone, provided me with my most memorable umpiring occasion in the hop county. The year was 1970, and Kent, under Colin Cowdrey's captaincy, were preparing to take on Nottinghamshire and Leicestershire in their last two home games of the season, on the back of a

102

remarkable run which had lifted them from the bottom of the championship table at the beginning of July, to a title-winning position.

In the first game against Notts, Kent won by three wickets, with just eight balls remaining, despite 123 not out from the great Gary Sobers, Brian Luckhurst topping that for the home team with 156 not out.

Folkestone always took spin, and in the second match of that dramatic 1970 finale, when Leicestershire were the visitors, I remember saying to Kent spinner Derek Underwood, 'You know, Derek, I think you're bowling from the wrong end.'

'Do you think so, Dickie?' he replied.

'I don't think, Derek, I know. This end's not for you. You want to be at the other end. It will be a lot more help.'

'Well, thanks for the advice,' he acknowledged, and ambled over to have a word in the captain's shell-like.

His captain was a bit miffed. 'What's the matter with the end you're bowling from?'

'Nothing really, skipper, but a little Bird told me I might have better luck from the other end.'

'Well, I suppose we've got nothing to lose,' said his captain. 'Have it your way. We'll give it a go.'

Derek went on to take 6 wickets for 58 runs from the end where my colleague, Arthur Fagg, himself a Kent man, was

standing. Kent, having scored 421 for 7 in their opening knock, went on to win by an innings and 40 runs, which left them needing only a few points against Surrey in their final match at the Oval to clinch the championship for the first time since 1913 – with a little help from yours truly.

Folkestone is a lovely ground, very picturesque, with a glorious panoramic view from the pavilion; Tunbridge Wells saw a remarkable innings by Kapil Dev when the World Cup was played in England in 1983; there have been some interesting encounters at the Bat and Ball ground at Gillingham; and Dover will almost certainly remain in Ray Illingworth's mind as a favourite ground.

It was there, in August, 1964, that Yorkshire arrived for the last game of their southern tour. They were immediately suspicious when they learned that there was not one bowler of any kind of pace in the Kent squad. There were, however, two slow left-armers, an off-spinner and a leg-break/googly bowler, while the batting line-up had Alan Knott at number eight and Alan Dixon at number ten.

Yorkshire sensed that there was some dirty work afoot, but it was too late to send for either reinforcements or replacements.

It was a pitch on which a batsman never knew what was going to happen next. The ball sometimes shot along the ground. At other times it lifted. And all the time it turned. Yorkshire lost three wickets in quicksticks and they looked to be heading for disaster. It was then that Illy produced one of his greatest knocks, leading his side to a total of 256 with a marvellous 135, which, on that pitch, was nothing short of magical.

Kent were made to follow on after being bowled out for 97, and they fared little better in their second innings, finishing on 146 all out. This, despite the fact that they had in their ranks such distinguished batsmen as Colin Cowdrey, Brian Luckhurst, Mike Denness and Alan Knott.

Illy followed up his 135 runs by taking 7 for 49 in Kent's first innings and 7 for 52 in the second. Oh, yes, upon my soul, our Raymond will always have a soft spot for Dover.

However, it is Canterbury, with its tree, the famous cathedral rising majestically in the background, and, during Canterbury Week, row upon row of white tents with brightly coloured flags flying above them and deckchairs dotted about in front, which has always been the jewel in the crown of Kent grounds.

When I stand there, gazing out over such a spell-binding scene, I recall some of the county's great heroes of the past. Leslie Ames, Frank Woolley and Colin Cowdrey, for example, form a tremendous trio of outstanding players who have spanned this century. Woolley made 270, his highest innings for the county, against Middlesex at Canterbury in 1923; Ames scored his hundredth hundred on the last day of Canterbury Week in 1950; and Cowdrey recorded a hundred in each innings against the Australians in 1961.

Both Ames and Woolley have had stands named after them at Canterbury. The 'Iron Stand' bears the name of Ames, and the concrete stand is known as 'the Woolley'.

The latter erection featured in a juicy duel one year when Yorkshire paid a visit. Alan Brown, who always looked as if he was scything grass when he batted, swiped 33 agricultural runs off Fred Trueman in next to no time, including a barrage of 4, 6, 6, 6 in successive deliveries. Not even the greatest batsman in the world, never mind a cross-batted tailender, was allowed to do that to Fred, and he was absolutely livid. He got his revenge, though: when Yorkshire replied he made exactly the same score as Brown in round about the same time. And, as if to prove a point, the biggest hit of all came off his adversary, a real steeper which landed in the top storey of the Woolley Stand.

Ames, who also played for England, was a manager/coach at the club when a young cricketer called David Constant was emerging through the ranks. Ames saw Constant as an obvious choice as a future captain, but sadly the player failed to fulfil his early promise and fell by the wayside. However, Conny did go on to become one of the top Test umpires, and I had the privilege of standing with him at international level.

Incidentally, Ames was one of a remarkable number of top-class wicketkeepers produced by Kent, including Godfrey Evans, Paul Downton, Derek Ufton – who also played centre-half for Charlton Athletic and England and is now Chairman of Cricket at Kent CCC – Alan Knott and Howard Levett.

Levett was a chap who quite liked a drink, and after having been out on the tiles one night, reported at the ground next morning a little bit worse for wear, to put it mildly. The captain took one look at him and told him he was in no fit state to play. Unfortunately there was no other wicketkeeper available, so he had to turn out. His colleagues dressed him in all his gear, and somehow managed to propel him out to the middle without him falling down.

Incredibly, once the game got underway he proceeded to give one of the finest wicketkeeping exhibitions his team-mates had ever seen. He caught everything. He dived to his left, he dived to his right, he snapped the ball up in front of the startled slip cordon, and nothing got past him. It was as if he had a magnet in his gloves, attracting the ball.

His nickname was 'Hopper', and he certainly hopped about to remarkable effect that day. Just possibly it was the hops in all the beer he had drunk which did the trick.

Although small of stature, 'Tich' Freeman was another giant of the past. Between the wars he claimed 3,776 wickets – a total bettered only by the great Wilfred Rhodes – and he was the only player to take more than 300 wickets in a season. He had figures of 17 for 92 against Warwickshire at Folkestone in

1932, to become the first bowler to take 17 wickets in a match on two occasions.

When 'Tich' retired from county cricket he christened his house Dunbowlin'. His wife was reputedly a bit of a dragon, and the story goes that when Freeman's funeral cortège was late arriving at the church, one friend was heard to whisper, 'She probably hasn't let him come.'

Dartford is the kind of ground that could be said to be the backbone of club cricket all over the country. There is nothing grand about the place, but it always developed a special atmosphere of its own as the temporary stand was erected, advertising boards sprang up round the perimeter, refreshment tents appeared, car park areas were roped off, and a whole battalion of gatemen, attendants and stewards descended from out of nowhere.

In 1970 the ground witnessed one of the most fearsome onslaughts ever seen in the county, when Lancashire's Clive Lloyd produced one of those effortless big-hitting innings of his. It is quite a small ground, and the Kent attack was not at its most potent. You could tell Clive was really beginning to enjoy himself, from the way his beaming smile grew broader and broader as the ball was sent hurtling to all parts of the ground – and way out of it at times.

One local old lady became so alarmed as she heard the thuds on her roof and saw slates hurtling off into the street below, that she called the local police. A sergeant duly arrived to investigate and, in keeping with his position, sized up the situation in quicksticks. He sauntered across to the ground and approached the Kent twelfth man in pursuance of his enquiries.

''Ello, 'ello, 'ello,' he said, 'and just what's been going on here, then? You'll have to put a stop to all this missile-throwing, you know. There's a little old lady across the road who's scared out of her wits.'

'Quite right, officer,' said the player. 'I cannot tell a lie, it's that man out there with the bat. You should lock him up right now before he does any more damage.'

Dartford was also the scene forty years ago of one of the most remarkably brave – either that or plain foolish – acts of defiance ever witnessed on a cricket field. Glamorgan had batted well in their opening knock, and had Kent in a spot of bother in reply. What is more, the home team had lost David Halfyard, who had just returned from a visit to Dartford hospital, a broken ankle having left him with his leg in plaster and hopping about as best he could on crutches.

Unbelievably, when the ninth Kent wicket fell, Halfyard, having removed the plaster and thrown away his crutches, went out to bat. Even more incredibly, he then opened the bowling when Glamorgan started their second innings! Dave was hard as nails: once he had the bit between his teeth you couldn't get him off. He'd go on churning out over after over after over. Give him the ball first thing in the morning and he'd still be bowling last thing at night if you let him.

He was a well-built chap, which made it all the more remarkable the way he somehow managed to squeeze himself

into one of those little 'bubble cars' which were popular in the 1950s and 1960s. Remember them? He also used to astonish teammates by leaving a ground last but yet arriving at the next venue before everyone else. No one ever found out how he managed to achieve such a miraculous feat. The blooming thing must have sprouted wings.

Dave retired in 1967, when he gained a place on the first-class umpires' list, but, after one year, he returned to play for three seasons with Nottinghamshire, before resuming as an umpire in 1977.

Another brave performance came from Colin Cowdrey in a Test match against the West Indies at Lord's in 1963. Having returned to captain the team, he broke his left arm facing up to a fearful barrage of fast bowling from Wes Hall and Charlie Griffith, yet he went out as the last man to try to salvage a draw, rather than allow the tourists to claim victory. There were just two balls remaining, and Gloucestershire off-spinner David Allen managed to block them, so that Cowdrey's capabilities as an enforced left-hander were not tested.

Colin's son, Christopher, also went on to play for England, and Colin told me of the time he was driving to work in 1984 listening to the ball-by-ball commentary on *Test Match Special*. He really sat up and took notice when it was announced that Christopher was being brought on to bowl his first over in Test cricket, and he became so engrossed in what was happening thousands of miles away in India that he turned his car the wrong way up a oneway street.

Now, there is never a bobby when you want one, but if you turn your car the wrong way up a oneway street . . . Colin was flagged down and had to try to talk himself out of a possible fine. As he was doing so, there was a roar from the car radio. Christopher had bowled Kapil Dev for 42 with his fourth ball. When the bobby realised what the circumstances were, he did not have the heart to book the proud father, and Colin escaped with a caution.

If Canterbury is renowned for its tree, then Tunbridge Wells can boast the most magnificent display of rhododendrons you could wish to see. It is a lovely ground whatever the time of year, but when the rhododendrons are in full bloom it is an absolute picture, although cricketing hayfever sufferers of my acquaintance have not always appreciated the beauty of it.

There was a most unusual affair at the ground in June 1963 when Kent's match with Middlesex was delayed because only three members of the visiting team turned up on the Monday morning. The rest had been held up in traffic. The umpires declared Middlesex's first innings closed, and Colin Cowdrey, who was Kent captain at the time, loaned out eight players to the visitors to make up their numbers.

Of course, if the Middlesex players had followed my example and set off at the crack of dawn to make sure of not being late, the problem would never have arisen.

In 1976 Kent suffered more than most when Kerry Packer tempted players from all over the world to take part in his 'Cricket Circus' in Australia. Derek Underwood, Alan Knott, Asif Iqbal, Bernard Julien and Bob Woolmer all teamed up with Packer, and when the Kent committee decided at the end of 1978 to dispense with the services of these 'rebels', Alan Ealham was left with the unenviable job of captaining a team shorn of all its best players.

It is to Alan's credit that he led his new-look side to another championship success, as well as victory in the final of the Benson and Hedges Cup. Alan is as straight and honest as they come, and he deserved that reward. He has done a lot for Kent and is still looking after the second eleven, bringing the young players through. They could have no better man for the job. His son, Mark, is maintaining the proud family tradition, having played for England on the 1998–99 tour of Australia.

Kerry Packer, incidentally, was the first to introduce floodlit cricket on a big scale, and Kent's Asif Iqbal was the first to score a century under lights. The ball that was used on that night has become one of his most treasured possessions.

There is no doubt that night cricket revolutionised the game. My first experience of it came in the early 1970s when I umpired a match at Stamford Bridge, home of Chelsea Football Club. We put matting down in the centre circle area, but otherwise the pitch was just as it was for football, and the very short boundaries made it a bit of a farce. The unevenness of the surface also caused a few problems. I was running backwards to square leg to judge a run-out when I fell down a crater which I swear was six inches deep, and had to hobble about like a stork on one leg for the rest of the game.

I am not too keen on day–night cricket myself. Even with the best floodlights in the world it is still a problem seeing the ball at dusk, for players, umpires and spectators alike, and the side batting second is at a big disadvantage. In all the floodlit matches I have umpired in England, the team taking second knock has been rolled over quickly. Wickets tumble – they go down like skittles.

I have to say that the lights were excellent when I was in Australia for the last two Test matches and the one-day series in the winter of 1998–9, but there was still that problem as day turned into night. For me, the only time to play cricket is during daylight hours. You can't argue with the big crowds they get at floodlit matches, however. They prove a very big attraction, and there is certainly a special atmosphere about them.

Asif Iqbal is one of several stars from other countries who have played with distinction for Kent, including Australian pace bowler Terry Alderman, West Indian Carl Hooper, and

Sri Lankan Aravinda de Silva, who Kent players reckon is the best overseas star they have ever had.

It was Iqbal, however, who was responsible for an innings which Derek Underwood always claimed was the one he would never forget as long as he lived. On one of the worst pitches Derek had ever seen at county level, Iqbal made 152 against Glamorgan at Cardiff in 1979, and to put that knock into context, Kent bowled Glamorgan out for only 46 to win the game.

Iqbal once used his head to help dismiss Australian Ross Edwards in a World Series match in Perth. The latter belted a short-pitched delivery straight at Iqbal, who was fielding fearlessly at silly point. The ball bounced off the fielder's head, spun away and was caught by Andy Roberts in the covers.

As for Underwood, he was always one of the top-class bowlers in the Kent side. He was a lot quicker than other left-arm spinners, and he was unplayable if the conditions suited him. He would run through a side if there was any help at all in the pitch. If it was rain-affected or dusty, you had no chance against him. He was a brilliant attacking spin bowler. However, the decision to cover wickets made him a much less potent force. He still remained a good bowler, but became more defensive on the better batting wickets and was never as effective.

Talking about defence, I have rarely seen a more defensive batsman than Chris Tavaré, who opened the innings and was Kent captain for a spell. He showed rich promise early in his career after arriving from Oxford, but he flattered to deceive. He never took the bowling by the scruff of the neck, as all the best batsmen do. I have to say, if he was batting in my back garden I would draw the curtains.

I have already mentioned the many terrific wicketkeepers Kent has produced, and there has been none greater than Alan Knott. I regard him as the doyen of them all, and in my autobiography I chose him in my World Squad. For ten years he was the undisputed number one for England.

One of his most embarrassing moments came in the fifth Test against Australia at Old Trafford in 1981, when he had just caught Martin Kent off John Emburey and was having a bit of a natter with a colleague while new batsman Dennis Lillee strode to the crease. There was an announcement over the public address system, and, assuming it was something to do with the great Australian fast bowler, he joined in the applause.

Ian Botham called out to him. 'For goodness' sake, stop showing off, Knotty.'

'How do you mean?' queried Knotty, a bit perplexed.

'Well,' retorted Both, 'they've just announced that you've broken the record for wicketkeeping dismissals against Australia.'

There was another red-faced occasion when a dog wandered on to the pitch during a Sunday League game against Warwickshire at Edgbaston. Knotty didn't notice when the dog cocked its leg up on one of the stumps, giving it a drenching, and had no idea why the Kent players fell about laughing every time he crouched down behind the stumps. It was not until he saw the television highlights that night that he realised what had caused their merriment.

Playing against Middlesex one day, Knotty was being peppered by a very fired-up Wayne Daniel, the big West Indian paceman who was in his benefit year. Knotty told me that the first two balls he received were bouncers that moved with the speed of light. Like tracer bullets, they were, whistling past his ears. It was a great relief when he found himself at the non-striker's end for the next over, bowled by Norman Cowans, although he knew that if they failed to make a single, there would be more to come.

He feared the worst, after Cowans had bowled a maiden,

when he saw Daniel striding menacingly towards him before picking up the ball on his way back to his mark. 'Can you play in a benefit match for me at the end of the season?' Daniel enquired.

Knotty was so surprised, not to say relieved, that he could answer neither yes nor no. 'I'll have to check my diary,' he stammered.

The next over contained three bouncers. At the end of it Knotty called Daniel over and said, 'I'd love to play in your benefit, Wayne.'

It worked. It was back to two bouncers in the next over.

Knotty also tells the tale of when he was wearing a helmet for the first time as a batsman, against the West Indies in a World Series Cricket game. With the visor pulled down, the poor lad could hardly see. Not only that, but because the helmet covered his ears, he couldn't hear, either.

He somehow survived one ball, then, more by good luck than management, turned the next down the leg-side. Unfortunately, he failed to hear Tony Greig's call for a single, and was run out by half the length of the pitch. When asked in a radio interview whether he had heard Greig's call, he replied, 'Pardon?'

Although it was rare, Knotty did occasionally turn his arm over as a bowler himself. In fact, he bowled in a Test match in Pakistan to none other than Majid Khan. He sent down a long hop, and Majid hit it many a mile. It went so high and so far that Knotty swears Pat Pocock caught it somewhere near the India and Pakistan border. On the Indian side.

Knotty, incidentally, was the one who commented, after a streaker had interrupted a Test match at Lord's in 1975, 'It's the first time I've ever seen two balls coming down the pitch at the same time.'

I was once umpiring at Canterbury when John Shepherd was bowling to A. C. Smith, the Warwickshire captain who became Secretary of Warwickshire CCC and then Chief Executive of the Test and County Cricket Board. Alan was all arms and legs when he was batting, and a little bit knock-kneed to boot, so when Shep came in from my end and hit him between the knees everyone burst out laughing. It looked comical.

Shep went down in front of me, tears streaming down his face, and he was only just able to splutter, 'How was that, then, Dickie?'

In between fits of giggles, I replied, 'That's out, Shep. Twice. One for each knee.'

During a triangular one-day series in Australia in the winter of 1998–9, all hell broke loose when Sri Lankan bowler Muttiah Muralitharan was called by Australian umpire Ross Emerson for 'throwing'. It caused a lot of controversy, with the entire Sri Lankan team walking off.

It reminded me of an incident in 1998 when I was in the

process of buying my pride and joy – an XK8 Jaguar. A sales rep from London was due to bring a demonstration model for me to have a test drive, and he asked if a friend of his could come with him. Apparently this friend played local league cricket in Kent and had been labelled a chucker by all and sundry, and he would value my opinion.

So the chap took a day off work and we all met at the Turnpike Garage on the main Barnsley to Wakefield A61 road just round the corner from my cottage.

'Look here,' I said to the alleged thrower, 'I'm only too willing to help, but we do seem to have a bit of a problem. We've no stumps and no ball. I would like both if I'm to make a proper judgment.'

'Not to worry, Dickie, I've brought my own,' he said, and took three stumps out of the boot of the car, leaning them up against the carwash. Then he took a ball out of his bag and proceeded to mark out his run-up. I assumed he would take just a few steps and trundle one down, while I toddled over to somewhere near the petrol pumps, where square leg might be, to have a gander.

But no. He went on walking. Off the forecourt and up the A61, before putting down a handkerchief to mark the start of his run. Well, all the traffic came to a standstill, horns blaring, wondering what the hell was happening. Then he set off back down the road, on to the forecourt, and fizzed in a delivery towards the stumps at the carwash end.

The garage owner, Geoff Grundy, went purple when he saw the ball smack into the building and ricochet desperately close to the office window, and I thought he was going to have a heart attack. Enough was enough, and I had reached a decision.

'Go back to Kent,' I said to the would-be Freddie Trueman, 'and tell everybody down there that Dickie Bird says you don't throw. A slinger, yes. But not a chucker.'

'Dickie,' he said, 'you've made my day,' and he put the ball in his pocket, collected his three stumps, went to pick his hanky off the A61, and went back to Kent as happy as a sandboy.

I bet that's one Canterbury tale you've never heard before.

Old Trafford, Manchester

LANCASHIRE

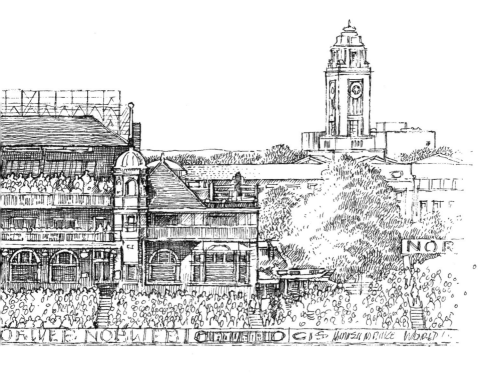

8

'OLD TRAFFORD is a ground of delight in its playing characteristics and splendour in its accommodation; a place of cricket, scarred by war and enshrined by tradition; a name to be respected and an experience to be enjoyed.'

If anything is needed to persuade you that the Lancashire county ground in Manchester is one of the finest in the country, then consider the fact that such glowing praise was written by a Yorshireman, Jim Kilburn.

I echo his sentiments. It is a magnificent Test match ground, with excellent visibility for umpires, players and spectators alike, and its facilities and standards are absolutely first class. It is almost unbelievable to think that this wonderful venue was left with huge craters across the turf, and devastating damage to the pavilion, stands and groundsman's house as a result of bombing during the Second World War. The transformation through the years has been quite remarkable.

It is also a ground which provided me with one of my most memorable county experiences.

Picture the scene. Darkness was fast approaching in the one-day game, but Lancashire captain Jack Bond was so certain that his side could not possibly win, that he declined the offer of bad light from Arthur Jepson and me. 'There is no point going off,' he said. 'We can't possibly win, so we might as well see it through to a finish tonight.'

And see it through to a finish we did – by the light of the moon at nearly ten minutes to nine in what has become known as 'the Lamplight Match'. It was so dark that some players declared they were being blinded by the lights on Warwick Road Station.

That match was, of course, the incredible 1971 Gillette Cup semi-final between Lancashire and Gloucestershire which has gone down in cricketing legend. And Bond was wrong: Lancashire could win. They did win. In sensational fashion.

In front of a full house of more than 23,000 with people spilling over on to the grass – another good reason for wanting to reach a result on the day – Lancashire were apparently on their way out of the competition. Desperately chasing the runs, they fell further and further behind the required scoring rate as darkness began to fall and Gloucestershire supporters were already preparing to celebrate.

However, we had all reckoned without the extraordinary big-hitting talents of Lancashire all-rounder David Hughes, aided and abetted by a puzzling decision by Gloucestershire captain Tony Brown, which I have never been able to understand to this day. Instead of recalling one of his fast bowlers – Bond would not have objected, having already said he was prepared to play to a finish, come what may – Brown unbelievably put on off-spinner John Mortimore. It was like meat and drink to Hughes.

Hughes said to his skipper, 'If I can see 'em, I think I can hit 'em.' And, boy, did he hit 'em. He hammered 24 runs – two sixes, two fours and two twos – in the 56th over, leaving Bond himself to score the winning single off the fifth ball of the next over, with the clock showing nearly ten minutes to nine. That signalled a crowd invasion by the jubilant Lancashire

121

supporters, who had just about written off their team's chances of a place in the final.

I have umpired some remarkable matches in my time, but no one-dayer at county level can compare with that one. The dramatic assault by Hughes was almost beyond belief in the gathering gloom.

Nor was it a one-off as far as Hughes was concerned: he repeated that match-winning spree when Lancashire beat Kent in the Gillette Cup final that year, slamming 4, 6, 2, 2, 4 and 6 off one over.

Hughes was also responsible for a one-man demolition of that fine Indian slow left-arm bowler Bishen Bedi in the 1976 final. He hit Bedi, who was playing for Northamptonshire, for 4, 6, 2, 2, 6 and 6 – 26 runs – in the 60th over to lift the Lancashire total to 195 for 7. This time not even such a savage onslaught was enough to win the match, but it certainly made for a far more interesting contest.

David was also quite useful as a slow left-arm bowler himself, and in one county match against Glamorgan he bowled 13 consecutive maidens, finishing with figures of 18 overs, 14 maidens, 11 runs, 1 wicket. At one point it looked as though he might beat Somerset bowler Horace Hazell's record of 105 balls without conceding a run.

Big-hitting was in the family, as you will gather from the story about David's dad, Lloyd, who played for Newton-le-Willows. One of the regular spectators at the time was a young lad by the name of Colin Welland, who went on to become a well-known actor, first coming to the fore in Z-Cars, the police series on television, and later starring in the film Kes, which was based in my home town of Barnsley.

Colin had been bought a bat as a birthday present, and one day he took it with him to the ground. Lloyd Hughes was practising in the nets when he broke his bat. He was due to open the innings in a few minutes and was desperate for a replacement. His eyes fell on Colin, and his brand new 'three-springer'.

'Excuse me, young man, would you mind if I borrowed your bat?'

Colin eyed him up and down. 'Oh no, Mr Hughes, I daren't do that. It's a birthday present, you see.'

Lloyd was very persuasive, though, and eventually he sweet-talked Colin into it. The young lad's chin dropped and his bottom lip trembled, but he reluctantly handed over his pride and joy.

Lloyd strode purposefully to the crease and hit the first ball over the bowler's head and clean out of the ground, the longest hit they had ever seen in that neck of the woods. He went on to make a big score, and afterwards he went up to Colin and said, 'Do you know, that's the best bat I've used in years. Could I buy it off you?'

Colin replied, 'No fear. I've let you borrow it, but I've got to have it back now. I know it's still a bit big for me, but it's a birthday present. Me mam and dad'd kill me if I sold it.'

Colin treasured that bat for a long time, oiling it, cleaning it, rubbing it down, and thinking back to that memorable occasion when 'his bat' became the talk of Newton-le-Willows Cricket Club.

Lancashire have had a good number of other players who have been able to put bat to ball in the same way as the Hughes father-and-son combination, so it is little wonder that they have become specialists in the limited-overs game. They have an outstanding record in that format, winning the Gillette/NatWest seven times – in 1970, 1971, 1972, 1975, 1990, 1996 and 1998; the Benson and Hedges Cup four times – 1984, 1990, 1995 and 1996 – and the Sunday League four times – 1969, 1970, 1989 and 1998.

They would, however, swap quite a number of those successes for just one county championship. Although they have won that title seven times, they have not done so since the Second World War, and that really rankles. Their winning years were 1897, 1904, 1926, 1927, 1928, 1930 and 1934.

The last championship-winning Lancashire side included such great players as Eddie Paynter, Ernest Tyldesley and Cyril Washbrook.

Paynter played 293 innings for Lancashire, and two of them assured his place in folklore. At Bradford in 1932 he hit five sixes and seventeen fours in an innings of 152 against Yorkshire, and at Hove in 1937 he needed only five hours to run up a massive 322 against Sussex, with three sixes and thirty-nine fours flowing from his bat.

Tyldesley was remarkable in that he played in not one, but five of Lancashire's championship-winning sides, scoring 34,222 runs and hitting ninety hundreds. He topped 2,000 runs in a season five times and 1,000 nineteen times. What a player!

The Second World War virtually ended Paynter's career and made a large hole in the developing career of Washbrook, who was on the fringe of international cricket in 1939. However, Cyril did go on to play for England, and he also captained his county.

Cyril often opened the innings with Alan Wharton, who played with me at Leicestershire before serving Lancashire for many years. On one occasion Alan had reached 99 not out when Cyril pushed the ball just wide of cover point and set off for a single. Alan stubbornly stood his ground. Cyril failed to scramble back to the safety of his crease when he realised that his partner was not going to budge an inch, and was run out, which was a rarity in itself.

Alan went on to complete his century, but when he returned

to the dressing room he found a very irate Washbrook waiting for him. Said the England opener, 'It is a well-known fact, Alan, that I am the best judge of a single in the country.'

To which Alan replied, 'When I'm on 99, I'm the best judge of a single in the whole bloody world.'

Cyril was a superb batsman, and as a young member of the Yorkshire side, I was thrilled to come up against him in a match at Aigburth. Prior to the start of play on the first day he called over our spin bowler, Jack Birkenshaw, and invited him to bowl at him in the nets. Cyril could not lay bat on ball: Birky kept bowling him, had him beaten all ends up.

I perked up when I saw this, and said to the Yorkshire lads, 'Cyril Washbrook looks in terrible nick. Jack's got him taped. Nowt to worry about today.'

Lancashire batted first and scored well over 300, of which Washbrook made 135. Do you imagine that perhaps he was kidding us with that bit of net practice?

Wharton was involved in another controversial run-out when he was batting with Jack Dyson, who also played football, being a member of the Manchester City team which won the FA Cup in 1956. Both players ended up running towards the 'safe' end after a terrible mix-up in the middle. Wharton appeared to be winning the race when Dyson stretched out his bat, put it between his colleague's legs, and tripped him up. Alan went full length, and, as he scampered past, Jack chirruped, 'You've had it now, sunshine. Out you go.'

Alan called his partner all the names under the sun. The air was blue. He still had to go, though, muttering darkly under his breath as he did so.

Phil King, a Yorkshireman who had played with Worcester-shire, also joined Lancashire just after the war. He was batting against Kent at Old Trafford when a vicious delivery from one of the visitors' fast bowlers rose off a length and hit him full on the box. He collapsed in agony on the pitch, let out a stream of foul language and rapidly unbuttoned his flies to check the damage.

His batting partner fairly flew down the track to him and warned, 'Phil, you can't do that there here. Thousands of people are watching.'

'Blow the thousands,' replied Phil with feeling. 'I've only got one of these.'

Phil, incidentally, also played Rugby league and went on to become a very good journalist.

Two other great bowlers of that era were Dick Pollard, the old workhorse who would keep going for ever, and Eddie Phillipson, who later became another of my colleagues on the Test match panel.

From 1950 through to his retirement in 1968, Brian Statham dominated the Lancashire bowling. He was a magnificent bowler, and he and Freddie Trueman in tandem were as good an opening pair as England could wish to find. What England would give for a partnership like that today.

The two of them had the same philosophy when it came to getting fit for the season. In April, when they reported back, they would bowl off just a couple of paces, gradually building up until they were off a full run by the end of the month. They were very rarely injured: no pulls, no strains, nothing.

'George' was so accurate it was uncanny. No one could keep count of the number of times he just missed the stumps or the edge of the bat, and he was dreadfully unlucky in that respect. He could have had a lot more wickets had fate smiled a little more kindly. Even so, in nineteen seasons he took a record 1,816 wickets for the county. He got me out a few times in that total. I could never hit him off the square.

When Statham teamed up with Ken Higgs, a bowler who really hit the deck hard, Lancashire came close to getting back on the championship-winning trail, but they eventually had to be content with second place in 1960.

It was around about that time that Lancashire produced another England opening batsman in Geoff Pullar. His nickname was 'Noddy', because he could nod off anywhere. He could sleep on a clothes line, and even had a nap before going out to bat. It seemed as if he had no nerves whatsoever. In 1959 he became the first Lancastrian to score a Test hundred at Old Trafford when he made 131 against India. Noddy also played for England at table tennis.

Lancashire emerged as the dominant force in limited-overs cricket under the captaincy of Jack Bond, who took over the reins in 1968. It was a great one-day side which included the likes of Jack Simmons, David Lloyd, David Hughes, Harry Pilling, Ken Shuttleworth, Peter Lever, and overseas stars Farokh Engineer and Clive Lloyd. With their great talent and Bond's supreme knowledge of the game, Lancashire became the kings of one-day cricket.

Simmons was renowned as a typical born and bred Lancashire man with a love of meat pies and mushy peas. He knew all the best meat pie shops in the county. In fact, it is said that if ever Jack goes sightseeing, it is round the butchers' shops.

To many of his fans throughout England he is known as 'Jolly Jack', but to his Lancashire team-mates he became known as 'Friar Tuck'. He is one of the few people who puts on weight while dieting. On one occasion, on yet another diet, he could bear the hunger pains no longer while batting, and as the tea interval approached, he was seen to beckon for the twelfth man, leaving all his colleagues to wonder what he wanted. It couldn't be a sweater, surely: the sun was cracking the causeway flags. Then they heard him telling the young man he was feeling a bit peckish, so could he ask the chef to save a few chicken legs for his tea? On another occasion he took a lunch order for fish and chips between overs for players who felt like a change of menu.

Jack also fancied himself as a footballer in his slimmer days – whenever they were. He played for Great Harwood, but not all that often, since he broke his leg four times, surely a world record.

He believed he had blown his chance of getting his county cap in July 1971 when Lancashire played Somerset at Old Trafford. In those days the committee would gather on the balcony in preparation for such an event, without revealing in advance that the cap was to be awarded. Jack knew he was tipped as the next in line, and he was fielding in the slips that day when Clive Lloyd spotted the group gathering together.

'Hey, Jack,' Clive said, 'look up there on the balcony. Must be your day.'

A few minutes later Jack spilled a straightforward catch and Clive remarked, 'Look, Jack, up there on the balcony. They've buggered off.'

Jack still got his cap, though, and deservedly so.

He was also known as 'Flat Jack', because he was an off-spinner who never flighted the ball. He didn't give it any air at all, despite the pleas of that great West Indian Clyde Walcott, and my good self. As far back as the early 1950s, when a young Jack was playing in the Lancashire League at the same time as Walcott, he had been told to give the ball some air. Clyde used to tell him, 'Line and length, and give it air. That's the way to bowl, Jack.' Jack didn't take a blind bit of notice, however, and went his own sweet way.

Many's the time, when he has been bowling from my end, I've pleaded with him, 'For goodness' sake, Jack, give it some air. Let it bite, man. If there is anything in the pitch, it gives the ball a chance to turn.'

He would reply, 'Thanks for the advice, Dickie. I'll try it.'

The next ball would be speared down almost as quick as a Michael Holding delivery. It fairly flew towards the batsman. Zoom. Flatter than ever.

Despite that, Jack should have played for England in one-day matches, because he was an extremely good bowler in limited-overs cricket, and always played a key role in the Red Rose successes in one-day competitions. His style suited that kind of game. Because he bowled it in so flat at the leg and middle stump, batsmen found it extremely difficult to get him away, which is how he made his name, and it kept his career going as long as it did.

Unfortunately, he bowled just the same in county championship matches, so never got the spin – or the number of wickets – he might have done had he taken notice of me and Clyde.

Jack used to complain that I never gave him any lbws. Other bowlers felt the same, but Jack thought he was particularly hard done by. He used to moan, 'I bowl wicket to wicket, yet whenever I appeal for lbw you always say not out. Why's that? Come on, tell me.'

So I told him. 'The reason is, Jack, that you always get in front of me in your follow through. I just can't see. Simple as that. After all, you're hardly the smallest player in the side, are you?'

One winter, when we were both coaching out in South Africa, I promised Jack I would help him iron out the problem. I got him running off the pitch after delivery so that I could have a good view of the batsman's position. We worked on it for hours on end.

Eventually I was satisfied. I told him, 'That's marvellous, Jack.

You've finally got it right. I can see. I've got a great view. There will be no problem from now on. Next season, when I've got you with Lancashire, just remember what I've taught you, and you'll be in with a chance. If it's plumb, that old finger will go up for you, Jack, you just see if it doesn't.'

When my fixtures arrived for the following season my first match was Lancashire at Old Trafford: I knew Jack would be waiting for me, and he was. I arrived early, as usual, and had not been there ten minutes when there was a knock at the door. It was Jack. He chortled, 'Right, Dickie, this is it. The day I've been waiting for. I've kept practising what you told me in pre-season, and I've got it down to a fine art. Don't forget, get that finger ready.'

Lancashire won the toss and fielded. The batsmen saw off the quickies and the captain called Jack over. 'Here you are, Jack, you have a go. Which end would you like?'

Jack's eyes gleamed. 'There's only one end I want. And that's Dickie's.'

The first ball rapped the batsman on the pad. And Jack was up there in front of me, blocking out the sun. There was a tremendous appeal, full of absolute confidence. 'HOWZAAAAAAT!'

I looked at him in despair. 'I'm sorry, Jack,' I said, 'but I'm going to have to give it not out. I couldn't see the damned stumps. You got in front of me again.'

He could not believe it, and nor could I. All those hours of practising, and with the first ball of a competitive match, he'd forgotten everything I had told him. He was so upset after that, he did not even bother to appeal when he hit the pads again that match, so he still did not get any lbws from me. It did not stop us from being great friends, though.

Jack was a very popular figure all round, if you see what I mean. He enjoyed a record benefit of £128,000 in 1980, and as a result became known in some quarters as 'the shy millionaire'.

Seven years later I was umpiring another Lancashire match and noticed that Jack, fielding at mid-on and mid-off, was not bending to stop the ball. If it came close to him he would just shove out a boot and kick it, soccer style, for someone else to pick up.

I wandered across to him between overs and asked, 'Nar then, Jack lad, you can tell your uncle Dickie, what on earth's the matter? Have you gone on strike or summat?'

He said, 'No, I'm just a bit stiff today. My back's playing me up something terrible.'

'If it's that bad,' I replied, 'you'll have to call it a day and retire.'

He stared at me in disbelief. 'Not bloody likely. I'm playing on till I get another benefit.'

I lost my voice in that same match. Pat Patterson had difficulty with his front foot and I had to call him time after time for overstepping. It went on so long that eventually I could hardly talk, never mind yell 'no-ball' in my usual ear-bashing fashion. Sign language had to suffice, although it hardly helped the batsmen, who did not realise it was a no-ball until they had hit it.

Finally I went up to Pat and whispered hoarsely, 'Look, mate,

131

you can see what a state I'm in. For goodness' sake cut out the no-balls.' There must have been about sixteen in one over, and I thought we would never get through it.

Jack is now Chairman of Lancashire County Cricket Club and is very proud to hold that position. We are still good friends, and as soon as he was made Chairman he wrote to me to say that I would always be welcome at Old Trafford as his guest, a nice gesture which I appreciated very much.

One of Jack's predecessors was Cedric Rhoades, who also did a lot for Lancashire cricket. It was he who once asked Farokh Engineer if, in view of the continued hostilities between India and Pakistan, there was any likelihood that he would be going home to fight for his country.

'Only if the fighting reaches my village,' replied Farokh. 'Then, of course, I will have to go to protect my wife and children.'

Rhoades asked, 'Which village is that?'

'Altrincham,' came the reply.

Farokh was a fantastic wicketkeeper-batsman, who always insisted that he was too quick for the umpires with his leg-side stumpings. The double-shuffle of the feet. In and out. Like lightning. It is very difficult for an umpire to make a judgment. He quite made my day when he once told me, 'Do you know, Dickie, you are the only one who can pick them out on the leg-side. That takes some doing.'

David Lloyd's nickname is 'Bumble' – he is just like a giant bee, always buzzing around. Never stops, from when he gets up in the morning until bedtime. As a player he was always a bit of a prankster, and I remember once when England were playing Australia in Melbourne in the winter of 1974–5 he and Mike Hendrick went into a toy shop just round the corner from the hotel where they were staying, to buy some tricks to liven up a party.

They came away armed with stink bombs, invisible ink, cigars and cigarettes that went bang, and a whoopee cushion to put under the chair of some unsuspecting victim. It always brought a laugh when, as bottom perched on cushion, the cushion would send out a sound that suggested the poor chap was having trouble with wind.

Lloydy was also to the forefront on plane journeys. As the air hostesses demonstrated the life-jacket procedure, he and Hendrick would lead the players in repeating the words in unison and going through all the actions. Then the two of them would bury their heads between their knees, and when the air hostess came up to ask what was wrong, they would sit bolt upright with hideous masks on their faces. Luckily the girls always saw the funny side of it in the end.

It was not so funny for Lloydy out there in the middle on that Australian tour, though. Like everyone else, he took a tremendous battering from Lillee and Thomson and was quite shellshocked when he returned home.

In the first innings of one of those Tests, Lloydy was caught off his glove fending the ball away from his face, and the lads told me that when he entered the dressing room his eyes were staring. He was completely dazed, and couldn't believe what had happened. He did not speak for a long time. Anyone who watched that tour will know what I am talking about. Many of our batsmen took an awfully long time to recover from it, and some never did.

Lloydy had a similar experience in a county match between Lancashire and Northants at Northampton. When the home team batted first, David Steele pulled a hamstring and was unable to take the field when Lancashire replied, so he watched the game among the spectators in the pavilion.

In the second over Bob Cottam bowled one short to Lloydy, who completely misjudged a hook shot, pulling the ball into his face. There was concern all around the ground as the unfortunate batsman was carried off on a stretcher, but one old chap, puffing away at his pipe in the seat next to Steele, muttered, 'Well, what do you expect, playing a terrible shot like that?'

It was a bit like the gladiators in the Colosseum in Rome. Carry one off, bring another one on, and the old fella had obviously given the thumbs-down to poor old Lloydy.

Back in Australia, the late Lord Vic Feather was once guest at a Lord Mayor's reception in Brisbane, and David had a laugh and a joke with His Lordship before eventually asking him for his autograph. Lord Feather was quite chuffed, so he took the pencil offered him by Lloydy and began to write his name. As he did so, the pencil collapsed. It was made of rubber.

Lord Feather looked at 'Bumble' murderously, but soon laughed as he saw the funny side of it, and he grinned, 'You've done me, haven't you, you little bugger?'

David has always been very outspoken, and his biggest gaffe was probably his infamous 'we flippin' murdered 'em' outburst after an inglorious failure by England in Zimbabwe in 1996–7. That really did get him into hot water. He was told to mind his Ps and Qs – or else.

There is certainly never a dull moment when 'Bumble' is buzzing around, but he more than met his match when he tangled with umpire Bill Alley, who accused him of ball-tampering. When David protested his innocence Bill quipped, 'Don't tell me this ball has chapped lips.'

Both as player and coach, Lloydy has the ability to keep morale high with his infectious enthusiasm, as well as his japes. He can also laugh at himself, as he showed when I chatted to him during England's unsuccessful Test series in Australia in 1998–9. He asked me, 'Do you know if there are any good jobs going, Dickie?'

Incidentally, he made his county debut in a Roses match at Sheffield's Bramall Lane. I have to tell you it was not an auspicious occasion. He bagged a pair.

Barry Wood was a Yorkshireman who went over the Pennines to play for the 'old enemy'. He was a good all-round cricketer who did a great job for Lancashire and was a player I always admired.

Woody's nickname is 'Sawdust', but that has nothing to do with his surname as most people suppose. The truth is that when his new bats arrived before the start of the season, he used to saw off one and a half inches from the handle, because he preferred a very short-handled bat. There would be sawdust all over the floor, hence the nickname.

During one match in which he was twelfth man, the captain was shouting instructions to the groundsman to cover the wet ends with sawdust. As he did so, Woody strode out to gales of laughter.

Like me, Woody spent a period coaching in South Africa, and in his first year out there he played for the Eastern Province against Transvaal. Most of the Transvaal players had never heard of him, but he soon made himself known with six brilliant catches in the gully off the bowling of Peter Pollock.

The South Africans noticed that Barry stood deeper than a normal gully, and they were so impressed with his success, that ever since then everyone in South Africa has adopted the 'Wood' position when fielding in that area.

Woody, who has a strong Yorkshire accent, could also be a bit abrasive, and his Lancashire colleague, Harry Pilling, once said of him, 'If I had the choice of being bitten by an alligator or Sawdust, I would have to pick the alligator.'

Harry was the shortest cricketer in the first-class game, and he was once asked if he did not feel at a disadvantage when batting with the tall and gangly West Indian, Clive

Lloyd. 'Not so long as he doesn't tread on me,' little Harry replied.

Despite these fine players, so masterful in the one-day game, Lancashire could not translate that success into the county championship, although they did finish third in 1970 and 1971, and when Bond retired in 1972 he left behind a very good side which included the likes of Wood, David Lloyd, Peter Lever, Ken Shuttleworth and Frank Hayes, who all played for England.

When I first saw Frank, he was a young lad playing for Sheffield University against Paignton Cricket Club, when I was player and coach there. After the match I sought him out to have a chat, because I had been so impressed with him. I told him then that I thought he had a great future and there was no reason why he should not go on to play for England.

Hayes had tremendous ability, and although he probably did not quite fulfil the rich promise he showed, he certainly had his moments. There was the match at Swansea, for example, when he scored 119 for Lancashire against Glamorgan and almost equalled Garfield Sobers' record of six successive sixes in an over off the same hapless bowler, Malcolm Nash. Frank clouted five sixes, but the second ball of the over had gone for four.

He was also the unluckiest batsman I have ever come across with regard to getting out in the 90s. When he played his first match against Middlesex at Old Trafford in June 1970, he would have become only the fifth Lancashire batsman to have scored a century on his debut had he managed just six more runs. He was out on 94, brilliantly caught at mid-on by K. V. Jones off the bowling of Peter Parfitt, having hit two sixes and fifteen fours. Then, a few days later, in the next match at Southampton, it was Hayes, stumped Stephenson, bowled Sainsbury 99.

Frank did, however, record a century in his first Test against the West Indies, although that proved a millstone round his neck for the rest of his career. Not many players achieve such a feat, and from then on too much was expected of him. Frank was a very nervous character, and it preyed on his mind.

Lancashire have had some excellent wicketkeepers through the years. I have mentioned Engineer, and there was also Geoff Clayton, nicknamed Chimp because of the way he walked, which I always thought was a bit unkind.

Then, in the 1960s, there was Keith Goodwin. I was umpiring Lancashire and Hampshire at Southampton, and Keith set off for what I considered to be an impossible second run. I was so caught up in the game that for a moment I forgot I was an impartial umpire and shouted, 'No, Goody, get back, get back.' He took not a blind bit of notice, carried on running, and I had to give him out.

There was also the time when Lancashire played Cambridge University at Fenner's. The players were invited by the students to a party, and after a wonderful evening, someone asked, 'Where's Goody?' They heard a shout, and when they looked up he was prancing about on top of a high wall doing a balancing act. Next thing he disappeared: he fell off, Humpty Dumpty style. Thankfully nothing was cracked and it was not necessary to put him together again. He had fallen on a grass verge and emerged with hardly a scratch. In fact, he played next day, none the worse for his escapade.

George Duckworth was another magnificent wicketkeeper between the wars. He toured Australia three times with the MCC in 1928–9, 1932–3 and 1936–7, and played in all five Tests over here in 1930. He was a true Lancastrian, and no doubt he could have let rip his longest, loudest and most heartfelt appeal if he had been around in 1977, when, for the first time in sixty-seven years, there was no Lancashire player in the England squad to go to Australia.

There have been some stirring performances at Southport since it had its first taste of bigtime cricket in 1969, when Lancashire entertained Glamorgan there in the first year of the John Player League.

In 1979, for example, David Lloyd scored a hundred in each innings of the match against Worcestershire at Southport – 116 and 104 not out – to give Lancashire victory, and three years later Graeme Fowler performed the same feat, against Warwickshire, in one of the most extraordinary county championship matches I ever umpired.

Warwickshire batted first and ran up a massive total of 523 for 4 declared, thanks mainly to a remarkable fourth-wicket stand of 470 between Alvin Kallicharran and Geoff Humpage, who scored 230 not out and 254 respectively. Needless to say, the records tumbled. Their partnership was the highest for the fourth wicket in England; the highest for any wicket except the first; and the record for any partnership for Warwickshire.

In his career-best 254, Humpage hit thirteen sixes, the most by an Englishman in an innings, and equalled then in England only by Majid Khan and Gordon Greenidge.

The second day brought another, rather unusual record. Warwickshire manager David Brown became the first substitute in county cricket to take a wicket, when he replaced Gladstone Small, who was put on standby for England. Small eventually returned to resume in the county match for the afternoon session.

Incredibly, Lancashire replied with 414 for 6 declared, and then bowled Warwickshire out for only 111, opening bowler Leslie McFarlane taking 6 for 59.

I could then hardly believe what I was seeing, as Lancashire scored 226 runs for victory without losing a wicket, to complete one of the most remarkable turnarounds I have ever seen. Lancashire's batting hero was Graeme Fowler, who set up a unique record of his own: having been injured in the field on the first day, he batted with a runner during both his innings of 126 and 128 not out.

What a match it was; there had seemed no way that Warwickshire could lose after their first-innings run riot, but they did. It was an amazing game of cricket, one of the best I have ever had the pleasure of umpiring.

During that game I went for a shower, leaving my wallet in the safety of the dressing room. So I thought. I said to Jack van Geloven, who was standing with me, 'Just keep an eye on my wallet, Jack, while I go for a shower. Whatever you do, don't leave the dressing room.'

The next thing I knew Jack was standing next to me in the shower. I said, 'Hey, Jack, what about my wallet? You've surely not left it in there on its own, have you?'

He said, 'Well, I thought it best, Dickie. It would have got wet had I brought it in here with me.'

I didn't think that was at all funny. I fumed, 'I thought I told you not to leave the room. There's no one there now to keep an eye on my money.'

I dried off as quick as I could and raced into the dressing room, but my wallet had gone. With all my money in it. Did I give Jack some pain for the rest of that game.

There was another memorable piece of quick scoring when Leicestershire visited Old Trafford in September, 1983. Batting in the second innings, when Lancashire were going for a declaration, Steve O'Shaughnessy scored 105, including a century in thirty-five minutes, which equalled the record of Percy Fender set in 1920.

It has to be said, though, that Leicestershire were just tossing the ball up, trying to force a result: David Gower bowled nine overs for 102 runs and James Whitaker, who had never bowled at all before, was hit for 87 in eight overs.

Lancashire eventually got enough runs to leave the visitors a declaration target – but then it rained, so they didn't get a result after all.

David Hughes always said that the pitch at Aigburth, Liverpool, was the best in England. I am sure Gordon Greenidge would agree: in 1983 he scored 104 and 100 not out in a county championship match there, and also scored 162 not out on the Sunday, giving him an aggregate for the four days of 366 runs. He would have loved to have been able to take that pitch round with him.

The ground belongs to Liverpool Cricket Club, and has its own groundsman and groundstaff, who do a marvellous job. The enormous dressing rooms have to be seen to be believed. It provides a nice setting, too: you can look down over the field, across to the green benches and the beds of roses, and then out still further to the River Mersey beyond.

Neil Fairbrother is the current one-day specialist in the Lancashire side. He was named Neil Harvey after the great Australian left-hander. Fairbrother is the type of player I would want to play an innings for my life, but only if I wanted to know my fate sooner rather than later.

He went out to bat in a one-day Texaco Trophy clash between England and the West Indies at Lord's in May 1991, with 15 overs gone and his side struggling at 48 for 2 in reply to the West Indies' 264 for 9 in their 55 overs. Neil believed that this would be his last chance to play for his country if he failed.

Against the strongest possible West Indies attack of the time, with Ambrose, Patterson, Walsh and Marshall forming a formidable four-pronged attack, Fairbrother hit a dazzling 113 out of a third-wicket stand of 213 in 31 overs with Graeme Hick, who made 86 not out, to lead England home by seven wickets with 8.5 overs remaining. It was a record partnership for any wicket in one-day internationals in England. Fairbrother hit two sixes and ten fours in 109 balls, demonstrating just what a brilliant one-day cricketer he is.

I umpired Neil when Lancashire played Worcestershire at Lytham St Anne's in my last year. He was fielding at fine leg when the ball was nicked in his direction, and he raced round, preparing to pick up and throw it back. Unfortunately he trod on the ball, did a spectacular somersault, and disappeared behind the sightscreen. Next thing we knew, he was being stretchered away by the physio, and the ambulance was called out to cart the poor lad off to hospital with a broken ankle. We couldn't help laughing at the time, because it looked so comical, but it was not at all funny for Neil.

Paul Allott, who played in the 1970s and '80s, was a massive appealer. He used to go up for anything. It didn't matter where the ball hit the batsman, he'd be up for it. It must surely have been tongue in cheek when Michael Atherton once said of his

colleague, 'He has never been known to swear at umpires or opposition batmen.' Don't you believe it!

I have always been a tremendous admirer of Athers. I rated him a very good captain of England, and it was a shame that he resigned when he did.

It was Athers who was responsible for arranging for the Indian and England teams to line up in front of the pavilion at Lord's when I made my final Test match appearance. I walked through the Long Room and the members' enclosure and out on to the pitch, and was surprised to see both teams forming a guard of honour, with the crowd on their feet clapping and cheering. It was marvellous, and a wonderful thought from Athers.

Athers went out to bat, and I gave him out lbw in the first over! He said, with a rueful smile as he made his way past me back to the pavilion, 'After all I've done for you, you give me out lbw of all things. How could you?'

I said, 'Sorry, mate, but it were plumb.'

John Crawley took over the captaincy of Lancashire for the 1999 season from Wasim Akram – a good choice. I'm a big fan of Creepy's, although he had not quite hit it off at Test level going into the new campaign. Athers is also still there, along with the fine all-rounder Ian Austin, who excels in the one-day game – they call him 'Bully' because he is built like a bull. Lancashire have a very promising youngster, Andrew Flintoff, who went on the 1998–9 tour of Zimbabwe and South Africa with the England A team, and was selected for England's World Cup squad in the summer.

Akram's place as the overseas professional has been taken by the controversial Sri Lankan spin bowler Muttiah Muralitharan, who was called for throwing in the triangular series in Australia in 1998–9, and I believe he will do well on the Lancashire pitches, providing he can steer clear of umpire trouble.

It is just another part of the difficult job an umpire has to do, and sometimes it is necessary to take unusual action to solve a particular problem. There was one occasion when Lancashire were playing Middlesex at Old Trafford and I stopped play to allow a Boeing 707 to fly over. It was making a heck of a racket. I thought to myself, 'Dickie, lad, if someone gets a faint nick, you're not going to be able to hear it,' so I suspended play, and we all sat down for a breather until the plane flew over.

The crowd was in uproar. 'Get on with it, Bird,' they were shouting. 'It's enough for you to take them off for rain and bad light, but this is ridiculous. It's a bright sunny day. There isn't a cloud in the sky.'

'It's not my fault,' I yelled back, pointing to the fast-disappearing plane. 'It's that other big bird up there. It's far too noisy. I can't hear myself think.'

Grace Road, Leicester

LEICESTERSHIRE

9

FEW people in the old days relished a visit to Grace Road. Not only was the ground difficult to find, it was also a very depressing place when you eventually arrived there.

The attitude of many players with regard to this most unattractive of venues was summed up by the late, great Jim Laker on one of his appearances there, when he remarked, 'It looks its usual broken-down shambles, and it seems quite incredible that those rickety, worn-out old steps which lead in darkness to the leaky, spasmodic, cold shower, have not yet completely disappeared.'

I have similar memories from my playing days. The changing room and shower facilities were unbelievable. You used to get spells in your feet going to the shower, and it was just like the Black Hole of Calcutta down there. If there was water at all, you were lucky, if it was hot, then that was a real bonus.

I had to spend more time there than most, as a Leicestershire player, and the fact that we were bottom of the table did not exactly help morale. It was not easy playing for that county in those days.

When I left Yorkshire to go to Grace Road, I had the chance to join quite a number of other counties, but I chose Leicestershire mainly because Willie Watson was there: he was a fellow Yorkshireman; I had played with him for the White Rose county; and he was captain.

Bill was a double international, playing for England at both cricket and football, and was one of the last to do so. It is simply not possible these days, with the greater demands on both sports. He was a great cricketer, and one of the best left-hand batsmen I have ever seen, especially on a bad pitch. Bill learned his trade in the old school, on uncovered pitches in Yorkshire, which is what made him so good.

One of the things I remember about Bill was that he was a chain-smoker. He told me that he had started the habit at the age of fifteen and could not give it up. He smoked one after the other in the dressing room before he went out to bat, and as soon as he was dismissed he was back in there puffing his way through another packet or three.

As a non-smoker, I am not too keen on people smoking while I am within choking distance, and it is even worse in the confines of a dressing room. There was a terrible fog in there most days.

It seems remarkable that he was still such a brilliant sportsman. Smoking certainly did not seem to do him any harm. He is still going strong in his seventies, and looks just the same as ever. Although he now lives in Johannesburg, Bill has visited England several times in recent years, and I always greet him by saying, 'See you've still got a fag in your mouth, Bill.'

Many's the time, when batting with him at Leicestershire, I've gone down the pitch and taunted him, 'Bet you fancy a fag right now, don't you, captain?'

He'd reply, 'I could eat one, Dickie. I could eat one.'

Talking of eating, Bill never had much breakfast. A cup of tea, two half slices of toast, a fag, and a cough. First thing every morning, without fail.

Bill was a very quiet man, didn't say much at all, so I

was a bit surprised one day when he asked, 'Are you doing anything tonight, Dickie? I've got a couple of tickets to watch Leicester City at Filbert Street, and I'd like you to come along with me.'

We sat there in the stand that evening, and Bill didn't speak for quite a while. Then, just before kick-off, he turned to me and said, 'I've been relieved of the captaincy, Dickie.' Just like that. No warning. Right out of the blue. I could not believe it.

'Never, Bill, never,' I said. 'You're having me on.'

'It's true right enough, Dickie. That's why I've brought you here tonight. To let you know just what's happening. Maurice Hallam is taking over. And I'll tell you something else. This will be my last season as a player. They will try to get shot of me at the end of it.'

And they did.

Born in Bolton-on-Dearne, not far from my home town of Barnsley, Bill married Barbara, a lovely lass from Huddersfield, and they are still together after all these years. When he stopped playing he was offered a job at the Wanderers Club in Johannesburg, advising and coaching, and he chose to remain in South Africa after he retired.

Another player I remember well from my playing days at Leicestershire was Terry Spencer, a fine fast bowler. There were England trials in those days – an England XI would play the Rest, for instance – and Terry was invited to play in one of these matches. Nothing came of it, though, and I am convinced that it was because Leicestershire were then an unfashionable county and bottom of the championship table.

Just to give you some idea of what things were like at the club, I was talking to one of the committee men, Mr Jimson, one day, and he asked me, 'Who is that man there, Bird?' He pointed out a chap a few yards away.

'That's Peter Broughton, sir,' I answered.

'Broughton? Broughton? Never heard of him. Is he with you?'

'No, sir,' I told him. 'He's a fast bowler who used to play with Yorkshire.' After a brief pause, I added, 'And you've just signed him on a three-year contract.'

He looked a bit sheepish, then stammered, 'Oh, that Broughton.'

The Leicestershire committee had a very offhand way of dealing with players, as Alan Wharton will testify. After he had played his last match for the county in the 1960s he went to the committee room, where he found a meeting in progress. He politely waited until the members had concluded their debate, and finally, realising that the player was not going to leave without being heard, the chairman snapped, 'Yes, Wharton, what is it?'

'Well, sir,' replied Wharton, 'as my contract is up and I have played my last game for Leicestershire I just thought I would come to say goodbye.'

After a moment's silence the chairman replied witheringly, 'Oh, I see. Well, I must say you haven't done very well for us, Wharton, but thank you all the same.'

It was the only time in his entire career that Alan was lost for words.

Another great character I played with at Leicestershire was Ray Smith, a slow left-arm bowler and a laugh a minute. He really enjoyed his cricket, but even he felt he should not be expected to play for next to nowt, as we say in Yorkshire. An uncapped player, he was on three pounds a week, and was spending a hundred quid a year on cricket gear!

Ray went to the committee to ask for a rise, and they generously made his weekly salary up to £4 10s. He was not exactly over the moon about it, but it was better than nothing.

Ray eventually asked to be released from his contract because he very rarely featured in the first team and was keen to try his luck elsewhere.

Willie Watson told him, 'You take wickets in the second team, and I'll play you in the first. It's up to you.'

Thus encouraged, Ray redoubled his efforts, and halfway through the season he had 60-odd wickets to his name. However, he still wasn't called up for the first eleven, and he decided that, if they wouldn't pick him now, they never would. This time he would not take no for an answer, and his request to be allowed to leave was granted.

When Maurice Hallam was made captain in 1963, Ray was brought back on to the staff, with the idea that he would play a vital part in a great masterplan. Maurice's brainwave was to have the pitch roughed up at both ends and sanded, in order that it would favour the spin bowlers, and he twinned Ray with off-spinner John Savage.

What Maurice failed to take into account, however, was the fact that other counties had even better spinners, England players, who could roll us over in next to no time. A case in point was when Essex arrived with Jim Laker, who was not a bad bowler, as older cricket fans and the Australians, in particular, will remember. We were skittled out for a meagre total and Jim took 7 for 89.

Before that match I remember Essex captain Trevor Bailey going out and sitting in the middle on a deckchair. He settled himself down, looked round, and chuckled, 'Well, here we are, then. I'm on the beach now.'

Trevor knew what the job was – sand all over the damned place – and he knew that Jim would have a field day.

It went on match after match. We always seemed to get the worst end of the stick, so eventually Maurice's big idea went up in smoke. Boom. No more sand-dance to put us all in a spin.

...ve Colin Ingleby-Mackenzie at the ...s, where he was frequently found. ...flamboyant mastermind behind ...pshire's first county championship ...ess in 1961, he thought nothing of ...ning to the racing commentary on a ...sistor radio, which he kept in his ...et, while he was fielding.

Above A welcome cup of tea to steady my nerves at Headingley before going out to umpire my final match between Yorkshire and Warwickshire in September 1998. *Below* The tea ladies, bless 'em. One car park attendant at New Road, Worcester, told a newspaper reporter that they were far more important than he was.

Left Tony Lewis acknowledges the che[er] of the supporters afte[r] leading Glamorgan to county championship 1969.

Below left Garfield Sobers, the best all-rounder the world ha[s] ever seen, whose mos[t] famous feat in county cricket was hitting six sixes off one over whe[n] batting for Nottinghamshire agai[nst] Glamorgan's Malcolm Nash at Swansea in 1[9].

Below right Ossie Wheatley, who was fielding for Glamorga[n] that day and vividly remembers every sing[le] hit.

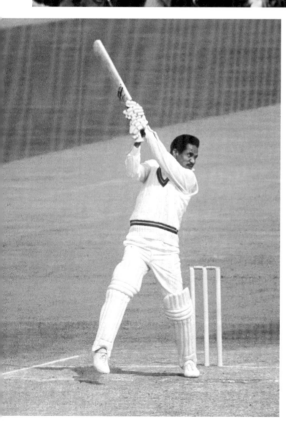

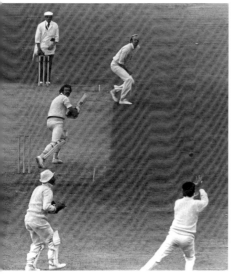

ve Tony Greig, the South African-born
ounder who did a very good job as
ain of both Sussex and England,
ured bowling against Australia in 1977.

t Michael Brearley, captain of England
Middlesex, the master tactician at
k.

ve The Nawab of Pataudi, another
ex captain, who also captained India in
ests.

Above Ray Illingworth holds aloft the
Benson and Hedges Cup after captaining
Leicestershire to victory. Beside him is Billy
Griffith, Secretary of the MCC.

Above Ian Botham and Viv Richards, as happy as sandboys at Somerset, where they continued the big-hitting bonanza. Even umpire John Langridge seems amused.

Right Mike Procter and Tony Brown raise the Gillette Cup in triumph after Gloucestershire's success in 1973.

Above A close call. John Edrich, of Middlesex and England, just makes his ground as India and Lancashire wicketkeeper Farokh Engineer prepares to whip off the bails.

ve England bowler Derek Underwood,
o had me to thank for a spot of advice
en Kent won the county championship
dramatic finale to the 1970 season.

Above Dennis Amiss (Warwickshire and
England) whose suggestion it first was that
protective helmets should be brought into
the game.

ve Sussex and England fast bowler
n Snow, who produced a bit of a soap
ra performance when bowling to
cestershire's Peter Marner at Grace Road.

Above An excellent leader of men, John
'The Trout' Barclay proudly displays the
John Player League trophy after captaining
Sussex to success in 1982.

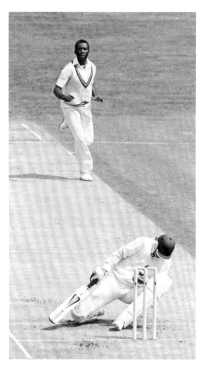

Above Andy Lloyd is struck a terrible blow as he ducks into a ball from West Indian Malcolm Marshall in the Edgbaston Test of 1984. He was badly shaken and never pla for England again, although he did go on to captain Warwickshire.

Left I have a close-up view of Jeff Thom: one half of that magnificent Australian 7 pairing of Lillee and Thomson.

Below Another superb fast bowler, Richard Hadlee of New Zealand. 'Paddl developed into one of the best all-round in the world and was instrumental in bringing success to Nottinghamshire.

ve Chris Broad, of Gloucestershire, ttinghamshire and England, blots his ybook on a tour of Australia in 1987–8 knocking the stumps over with a swipe his bat after getting out to Steve Waugh. was severely criticised by the media. w he is a media man himself!

Above Hello, hello, hello, and what's going on here then? England captain Michael Atherton caught in the middle of the 'dust-in-the-pocket' ball-tampering affair which caused such a fuss when England met South Africa at Lord's in 1994.

w Mike Gatting (Middlesex) in confrontation with umpire Shakoor Rana when he tained England on the tour of Pakistan in 1987–8. Tour manager Peter Lush is the rmediary. Gatting was to come face to face with his adversary again in unexpected umstances during the following season in England.

We have a streaker! Or
two of them to be prec
Batsman Alan Knott of
England and Kent, Aus
Alan Turner and umpir
Tommy Spencer obvio
find it amusing as a bra
chap clad only in traine
and socks leaps the
stumps at Lord's in 19
while the police provic
cover-up job for the
young lady who cause
me some embarrassme
at Edgbaston.

Ray Smith was also in the side when we played the West Indies at Leicester in 1963. They had just come from the Test match at Edgbaston. Frank Worrell, their captain, was batting, Ray was bowling, and I was fielding at gully. Worrell played forward, the ball held its line, and he got a thick edge. Ray Julian snapped up the catch behind and we all went up.

We could not believe it when umpire Laurie Gray gave him not out, although we did wonder afterwards whether it might possibly have had something to do with the fact that Worrell had been the victim of a very dodgy decision in the Edgbaston Test, when he had been given out off his arm. The umpire on that occasion just happened to be a certain Laurie Gray.

Ray also likes to tell the story of the flood. We were due to play Surrey at Ashby-de-la-Zouch, but we arrived on the morning of the match to find that some water pipes had burst – it was a bit like the scene that greeted me when I umpired a Test between England and the West Indies at Headingley some years later. There was water all over the place and the ground was virtually flooded. We didn't bowl a ball all three days.

On the Friday night we flew out to play Ireland. When we arrived it was raining. And it didn't stop. They hadn't seen anything like it since Noah was a lad. Another flooded ground. Another three days kicking our heels. At least there was no sand this time. None to be seen, anyway: the tide was well and truly in.

Ashby-de-la-Zouch, incidentally, is the place where birds nest in the dressing rooms. The feathered variety, I should add. Nothing to do with me. Or the opposite sex. It is such a picturesque ground, with an old pavilion surrounded by marquees and smaller tents. Very olde worlde.

There was one occasion, round about that time, when quite a few of the first eleven members were instructed to go to play with the second team at Lutterworth. Gerry Lester, who played for the county for many years and went on to become coach, was captain of the seconds then, and, with the visitors batting on a featherbed of a pitch, he informed his own players, 'We shall attack them.'

They thought he was mad, but he was the skipper, so they did as they were told, and gathered round the bat in close-catching positions ready to snap up the chances that they were pretty certain would never come. You can imagine what happened. As anticipated, the batsmen simply hit the bowlers over the top, and before you could say Jack Birkenshaw, the total had reached 300 without loss.

The aforementioned Jack the lad had to do a tremendous amount of bowling that day, and he was not a happy chappie. None for a lot, he had.

These days Manager and Coach at the club, Jack was only a young lad when I was there and at one stage he became so depressed that he said he was going to pack the game up. When I told him not to be so daft and give it at least one more season, he said there was not much point because he would never be good enough. That's how low he was.

However, Tony Lock then arrived on the scene to give him hope and encouragement, man to man, spinner to spinner. Locky persuaded him to stay on and give it a go. The two of them took a stack of wickets as Leicestershire made their way up the county championship table, and both played for England. Birky had even greater success when Ray Illingworth took over as captain at Grace Road. That's when it all changed and they went on to win the title.

By that time I was the one who had left. I had decided to call it a day as a player – mainly due to my dodgy knee, which was giving me more and more pain. If I had known what was just about to happen, though, with the many vast improvements on and off the pitch, and championships and cups and trophies to come, I might have given it that little bit longer.

Lock did the groundwork, but it was Illingworth and Mike Turner between them who brought about the remarkable transformation that has made Leicestershire one of the finest cricket clubs in the world, with a ground fit to grace such talent. The change has been unbelievable.

Turner was on the staff when I arrived there. He was not a bad bowler, with his leg-spinners and googlies, but nothing special. When he was offered the Secretary's job, he took to it like a duck to water. He has a lot of drive, a good brain, and loads of common sense. Having played the game, he also knows what is best for the playing staff. Born in Leicester, he has the good of his home-town club at heart, and, with the help of an excellent committee, he has moulded a magnificent set-up.

In the splendid long room and members' hall there are wonderful displays of memorabilia – bats, balls, blazers, and a pair of boots once worn by one of the county's great bowlers, George Geary. No one else has worn bigger boots than George, but he was never too big for them. He was modest and very well respected. A fine all-rounder, he played for England, but not as often as he should have done.

One of my old Leicestershire colleagues remembers visiting George at Charterhouse, when he was coach there, and George said to him, 'See that lad over there? That's an England cricketer of the future.' He pointed to a fourteen-year-old by the name of Peter May. P. B. H., of course, went on to captain England, and always said that George was a tremendous influence on his career.

In that hall of fame, incidentally, there is a big cardboard cut-out of one Dickie Bird. They shoved me in there some time in 1997, so I'm a complete newcomer compared to Joey the fox, who met his fate way back in 1899 and has hung there in all his stuffed glory ever since.

There have been some fine players at Leicestershire down the years, particularly under Illingworth, who brought the best out of everybody. Players such as those two outstanding Ceylonese, Stanley Jayasinghe and Clive Inman; Andy Roberts, of the West Indies; Ken Higgs, who arrived from Lancashire; and Graham McKenzie, the great Australian fast bowler.

Graham is one of the nicest men I have ever met, and whenever I go to Perth I always look him up. They used to call him 'Garth' because he had such a fine physique, but for me he was always the gentle giant.

When he bowled from my end he used to get batsmen so plumb lbw that even I had no hesitation in giving them out. Graham hardly ever appealed. Everyone else would go up – wicketkeeper, slips, close-to-the-wicket fielders – but not Graham. Just occasionally, as he walked back past me, he might casually enquire, 'How was that, Dickie?' He is the only bowler I have ever come across who just got on with the job and left all the yelling, shouting and bawling to others.

One of the younger players emerging at the time was David Gower, and the others who played in that 1975 team – the best in the club's history – included wicketkeeper/batsman Roger Tolchard, Barry Dudleston, Chris Balderstone (who also played football for Doncaster Rovers, Huddersfield Town and Carlisle United), Rhodesian Brian Davison, who was a very fine batsman, John Steele and Jack Birkenshaw.

Graham Cross had been around a little earlier, but he packed in cricket to concentrate on football, and went on to play for Leicester City in the FA Cup final of 1969, when the Foxes went down 1–0 to Manchester City – after beating my team, Barnsley, 2–1 after a replay in the third round.

With Illy as captain, that 1975 team won both the county

championship and the Benson and Hedges Cup. They also beat the Aussies for the first time since 1888.

It is quite remarkable, incidentally, how many former Leicestershire players have gone on to become umpires. As well as myself, there have been van Geloven, Dudleston, Balderstone, Steele, Birkenshaw and Julian, and, going back further into history, the great Alec Skelding.

In between his playing and umpiring careers, Alec also had a spell as county scorer, and the story goes that one day the batsmen hit so many runs that the scorebox had great difficulty keeping up with them. At the end of the day they could not balance the books, and neither scorer could agree who was right. Eventually, in desperation, Skelding stuck his head out of the box, called a young lad over, gave him some coppers and said, 'Here, son, go and buy an evening paper. We'll get the score from there.'

Alec also devised a neat little trick of his own for easing the tension after a run-out appeal which was so close that it was impossible to give a definite decision with the naked eye. In those days there was no third umpire and video replay to get you out of a tight spot. Alec used to wait patiently for all the yells of the fielding side to die down and then tell them, 'Gentlemen, it's a photo finish, and, as I have neither the time nor the equipment, I declare the batsman to be not out.'

Skelding was the first umpire to wear white boots. In those days umpires all wore traditional black or brown shoes. Alec bought some white ones, just to be different. Very heavy, they were, like colliers' clogs. He used to take them to the ground carefully wrapped up in brown paper. Those white boots soon became part of every umpire's attire. I may have been responsible for the white cap, but Alec put the white boot in.

Another of the old Leicestershire stalwarts was Jack van

Geloven, who was capped in 1959, the year before me. He was a fine all-round cricketer and another of the many Yorkshiremen who have gone on to play for Leicestershire. He was with the county for nine years and did well, with 60 or 70 wickets every season, as well as a stack of runs. Indeed, one year he did the double – 100 wickets and 1,000 runs. At the end of his tenth year, however, they sacked him. Jack was due for a benefit the following season, so why didn't they keep him on to reward him for all his loyal service? It was sheer petty-mindedness, and I've always had a lot of sympathy for him.

Jack was also known as a very 'tight' Yorkshireman. It was virtually impossible to persuade him to buy a beer. Gerry Lester, at his retirement, said he would die happy if he managed to get a pint out of Jack. But he had as much chance of getting a pint of blood.

Jack has now retired as coach and groundsman at a public school in Edinburgh, and one of his last contributions to his native Yorkshire was to recommend the promising Gavin Hamilton to the county.

Another recruit from Yorkshire was Jack Firth, who kept wicket. He was a lovable character, and generous with it, although sometimes he had to pay dearly for it. For example, when he held his benefit year, he treated everyone so well at every event he attended, that when he went to collect his cheque at the end of the year the committee told him, 'Sorry, Jack, but you've given away so much money at all your benefit bashes, that you owe us!'

Another benefit match, this time for Aussie bowler Jack Walsh, who bowled googlies and chinamen, produced one of the most amazing bowling performances of all time. Visitors Surrey were 42 for 2 in their first innings, with P. B. H. May on 28 not out, when Charles Palmer took the ball with the intention of bowling only one over, to enable Vic Jackson,

156

another Aussie off-spinner, to change ends. Palmer's second ball bowled May, and, with his off-cutters finding a slightly worn patch with deadly precision, he captured eight wickets, seven of them clean bowled, in 64 balls, without a single run being scored off him. That is still a world record.

Jim Laker then came in, and off the 23rd delivery edged two to end the spell, leaving Palmer with final figures of 14 overs, 12 maidens, 7 runs and 8 wickets.

The Surrey captain, Stuart Surridge, sportingly went on to the field to congratulate his rival captain, who, with his usual modesty, apologised for the inconvenience he had caused. In fact, he had been advised by the doctor not to bowl, and had not previously turned his arm over at all, in practice or matches, throughout that season.

Although Surrey eventually won the match by seven wickets, Palmer had another remarkable analysis in the second innings, this time bowling 13 overs, 12 maidens, for one run and no wickets.

I talked to Charlie afterwards, and I don't know whether he was kidding me or not, but he claimed that he had bowled them out with donkey drops!

At a famous match between Leicestershire and Nottingham-shire in 1981 – the year Notts won the title – Balderstone, Steele and Davison all scored centuries in Leicestershire's first innings of 431 for 8 declared.

Notts, forced to follow on, appeared to have saved the game when Derek Randall and Neil Weightman – in only his second first-class game – scored 101 and 105 respectively. Leicestershire, however, eventually bowled them out and went on to score the winning leg-bye off the next-to-last ball of the game. It couldn't have happened in my day!

That match was played at Hinckley, a good club ground, with excellent facilities, where you could usually guarantee a lot of runs being scored on a very good pitch. These days Leicestershire play only second eleven matches there.

I have made brief reference to David Gower already, and he was, of course, one of the greatest batsmen to play for Leicestershire. His dress sense, however, often left something to be desired, and it caused quite a bit of merriment on occasions.

There was one time, when he came to the ground wearing a white sock on one foot and a pink sock on the other. No doubt he was left feeling suitably in the pink, having put something red in the washing machine along with the white load. At least, that was the theory. On another occasion he turned up at Trent Bridge with one black shoe and one brown after dressing hastily in the dark before setting out from Leicester.

Ray Illingworth was not best pleased, so on the next away trip David tried to make up for it. He attempted to impress his captain by arriving at breakfast on the Sunday of the match with Somerset at Taunton in full dinner suit, complete with a pair of gleaming black shoes which had received such generous spit and polish that you could see your face in them.

Ignoring the highly unusual occurrence of Gower having made it down for breakfast in the first place, Illy was totally deadpan in his response. 'Aye, well, see you've just got in, then, lad,' he remarked, scarcely batting an eyelid.

Gower was a fine fielder as well as a master batsman, but he got his come-uppance one day when Leicestershire entertained Derbyshire. Illy had gone on to bowl his allotted spell, and Ashley Harvey-Walker, my old toothless friend, was batting.

Gower was sent down to field at deep mid-wicket, and Ashley clouted Illy many a mile up in the air in David's direction. Eventually the ball came down with snow on it, and mercifully stuck in Gower's hands. It was a well-taken catch and the delighted fielder decided to celebrate in time-honoured fashion by throwing the ball back high in the air and catching it again for an encore.

All he got for his trouble was an enraged cry in an unmistakable Yorkshire accent, 'Throw it back, you daft bugger, it's a no-ball.'

While the golden boy was tossing the ball around, the Derbyshire batsmen had decided to run a second. When Gower eventually recovered his composure sufficiently to throw the ball in, he hit the stumps. The ricochet took it away from his colleagues – and the batsmen gleefully ran another one. So they took three off a no-ball.

Illy was not amused.

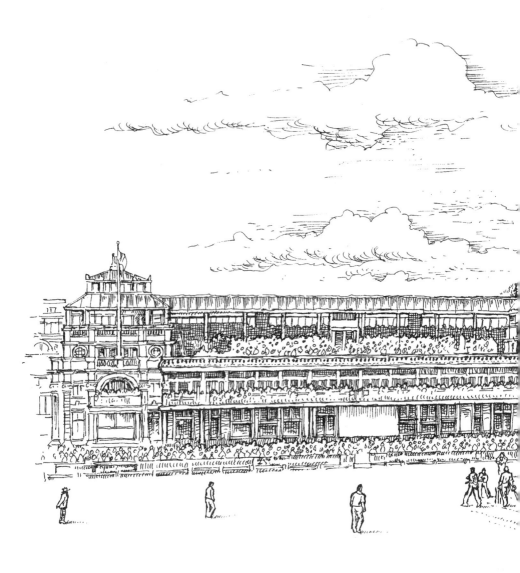

Lord's

MIDDLESEX

10

L ORD'S, headquarters of the MCC and Middlesex's county
ground, is my second home.

Maybe there are more picturesque grounds – Queen's Park,
Chesterfield, and New Road, Worcester, for example – but
there is something special about Lord's. It has a magic of
its own. For me it is the finest ground in the world, and it
holds many happy memories which I will treasure for the rest
of my life. From the minute you walk through the Grace Gates,
you can sense the atmosphere. It is a wonderful, wonderful
feeling.

The facilities at Lord's are excellent, yet are still being
improved, the marvellous new stands being an example. The
practice facilities at the Nursery End are first class, and at the
back of the stands is another practice ground where matches are
also played. Lord's has one of the best indoor cricket schools in
the world, and the pitch is in the top bracket. I could go on.
Everything about it is simply magnificent.

There are bigger grounds – Melbourne and Calcutta have
capacities of around 120,000 – but big does not necessarily
mean best. Ask any player, from any cricketing nation, and
he will say the same: Lord's is the Mecca. You simply cannot
beat it.

If I had to choose to do another match anywhere, it would

be at Lord's, although I am happy enough that my final Test match against India was at the headquarters of cricket. I would not have wanted it any other way.

That is not to say players have never complained about Lord's: behind the stands at the Nursery End there are some trees, and during an England versus Australia Test, Greg Chappell, who was batting, said to me, 'I'm finding it difficult picking up the ball at the Nursery End, Dickie.'

'What's the problem?' I asked him.

He replied, 'It's those trees. Any chance of having them chopped down?'

'Shouldn't think so, mate,' I answered. 'Not today anyway. Not in the middle of a Test match. No way. Not a cat in hell's chance. I could see about tomorrow if you could hold out that long. Now for goodness' sake, get on with the game and stop nattering.'

Middlesex also play at Uxbridge, a lovely little ground with an excellent pitch. Because it has a small playing area and a fast outfield, it is renowned for quick scoring.

Mike Gatting made what was then his highest score of 169 against Surrey there – and then ran himself out off a no-ball! In 1982 Leicestershire's Brian Davison cast a rare question mark against Mike Brearley's captaincy, taking advantage of the decision to put the visitors in by scoring a hundred before lunch.

The only time I can remember a bowler having great success on that ground was in the first county game ever played there, when fast bowler Vintcent van der Bijl took 10 for 60 in the match, which was a superb effort on that pitch.

Middlesex have won the county championship ten times – in 1903, 1920, 1921, 1947, 1976, 1980, 1982, 1985, 1990 and 1993 – and they have been successful four times in the Gillette/NatWest Trophy, in 1977, 1980, 1984 and 1988.

The Benson and Hedges Cup has been theirs twice – 1983 and 1986 – and they have won the Sunday League just once, in 1992.

One of the most famous players from the 1920s, when two of those championships were won, was Patsy Hendren, a very smart operator, as he proved one day in 1929 when Surrey were the visitors to Lord's.

Before the start of play on the first day he took opposition new boy Alf Gover to one side for a few friendly words of advice. Patsy said he hoped that Alf would enjoy his game at the headquarters of cricket, and would he mind not pitching anything too short at him because he could not pick the ball up too well, his eyesight not being as good as it once was.

Later in the day Hendren went in to bat, and Gover knew exactly the right ball that would soon send him on his way back to the pavilion. He bowled him a series of bouncers, which, to his amazement, were all duly despatched to the boundary with the minimum of fuss. After watching a second over on similar lines, Surrey's Jack Hobbs went up to Gover and asked him what the hell he thought he was playing at.

Alf replied, 'Well, Mr Hendren doesn't like short-pitched bowling these days. He told me so himself.'

Patsy, incidentally, was one of the pioneers of protective headgear. In 1933 he took to wearing a kind of deerstalker hat. A report at the time described it as 'having the side-effect of converting his appearance from that of an amiable but hungry bull mastiff into that of an amiable but hungry bloodhound.'

Hendren still holds the record for most runs in a career – 40,302 between 1907 and 1937.

When Hampshire visited on one occasion, their captain, Lord Lionel Tennyson, became more and more frustrated at the slow rate at which Peter Mead was scoring runs. Finally he could stand it no longer. He wrote out a telegram which he had delivered to the batsman at the crease. It read, 'Too slow. Get out at once.'

Gubby Allen was also to the fore at that time, and in 1929, against Lancashire, he became the only bowler to take all ten wickets in an innings in a county match at Lord's. He served Middlesex for many years as player, captain and committeeman, as well as playing for England. I used to talk to him a lot, and he was a tremendous help to me. He knew the game inside out.

Gubby had the unique privilege of a private gate from the garden of his house which led directly into Lord's. He almost lived at the ground. Like me, he never married. Cricket was his life, and he gave an awful lot to the game.

In the 1940s it was Bill Edrich and Denis Compton who hit the headlines. They played key roles in the county championship success of 1947, and enjoyed another golden year the following season, the highlight being an unbeaten third-wicket stand of 424 against Somerset at Lord's.

Denis once told me that his doctor had advised him to have a couple of glasses of red wine a day because it was good for

the circulation. Denis took the advice, and developed quite a taste for the drink. So much so, that instead of two glasses a day, it became two bottles. Or three. I also drink red wine, for the same very good reason, but three bottles a day is going just a little bit far. You can have too much of a good thing.

Captain of that 1947 championship-winning side was Walter Robins, who also captained England and later became a leading administrator at Lord's. He was known as 'Cock' Robins, a nickname which stemmed from his far from retiring nature.

Robins once had a bit of a do with umpire Bill Reeve. A good leg-spin bowler, he strutted about, doing his stuff and appealing for a variety of dismissals, all met with a shake of the head from Bill. Robins stuck at it. First one end, then the other. From lunch through to tea. Still nothing doing.

After the last over before the tea interval, Reeve handed Walter his Middlesex sweater, which, as cricket lovers will know, has three scimitars proudly displayed on the front. Walter refused to take it. He told the poor old umpire, 'You can stick that up your backside, swords an' all.'

Eyebrows were raised in 1952 when Arsenal's Highbury stadium played host to one of the first games played under floodlights. An 8,000 crowd turned up for a benefit in aid of Middlesex's Jack Young, played on a matting pitch. The opposition was provided by a team of Arsenal footballers, including Leslie Compton, who was also eligible for Middlesex. Arsenal totalled 189 all out before Middlesex replied with an innings played under lights. An ordinary red ball was painted white, and had to be replaced at intervals because the paint kept chipping off. In the end Middlesex shaded a win, with Young, the beneficiary, taking the crease with a miner's lamp on his helmet to provide further illumination.

In the 1950s and '60s there were no trophies for the Middlesex mantelpiece, but there were still some interesting characters around, including Tim Lamb, who now does a tremendous job as Chief Executive of the England and Wales Cricket Board.

It has to be said that Tim was never a great batsman, although Derek Randall did call him Wally Hammond when, going in at number eleven, he drove one through extra cover. But then, Derek always was a bit of a joker. Tim never instilled any great confidence in his team-mates when he went out to bat. When the ninth wicket fell, they all rushed for their fielding boots as he left the pavilion: they knew it wouldn't be long now. As Tim himself once said, the groundsman never ran out of petrol as his heavy roller idled in anticipation of the tenth wicket to fall. He also joked, 'Even opponents mustn't feel I look quite right at the crease. I was asked on one occasion if I had all my own tackle.'

Tim once borrowed some red pepper ointment from John Price, who swore by it. He had kept his muscles warm and loose throughout his career by using it. Tim got a bit carried away, however. He did not realise that a very little of the stuff went a long way, and he had not been out in the field long before he felt himself burning up all over. His back was worst: it was on fire, and he could hardly bear to stand still. The only way he could get a bit of ventilation was continually to lift the tail of his shirt and flap it about like a white flag of surrender. Goodness knows what the crowd made of it all.

John Warr was captain of the side between 1958 and 1960. During that period Middlesex had a game at home to Sussex which was being covered by BBC radio. At one stage in the afternoon the chap in the studio told listeners, 'And now back to Brian Johnston at Lord's for another progress report.'

Said Jonners, picking up the link, 'The latest news from Lord's is that Warr's declared.'

And an old lady rang up to ask who the war was against.

It was Warr, incidentally, who first interested me in becoming an umpire, in 1969. When he initially mentioned it, I laughed it off. 'You've got to be joking,' I said.

'No, seriously,' insisted John. 'You go home and think about it.'

I did, and that's when I applied. JJ said he thought I would make a good umpire, although not many people agreed with him at the time. I like to think I've proved him right.

Peter Parfitt was given a fiery introduction to Fred Trueman when they came face to face for the first time at Lord's. Fred had got wind of the fact that the Middlesex batsman, who later played for England, rather fancied himself as a good hooker, and before the game he went up to him and snarled, 'Hear tha not a bad hooker, kid. Well, tha'll get plenty o' practice today, sunshine.'

Sure enough, Parfitt's arrival at the crease prompted a barrage of short-pitched deliveries from Fred. The batsman took an immediate blow in a part of the anatomy that is guaranteed to make your eyes water, and it brought a further warning from a highly unsympathetic Trueman. 'That's one in t' box for starters,' he growled.

Poor old Peter then gloved one on to his face and had to retire to have the wound dressed. Although still feeling groggy, he decided to resume his innings at the fall of the next wicket, just to show Fred that he wasn't scared of him.

As he made his way to the middle, with appreciative applause ringing in his ears, he was met by Trueman, mildly impressed by the fact that this young man was coming out for more punishment. 'Well,' said Fred, 'I'ave to say tha's got something, sunshine, 'cos the' don't usually come back when 'ave felled 'em.'

There was also rather an amusing report in the *Daily Telegraph* around about the same time, concerning an encounter between Middlesex and Essex. It read, 'With the score at six, Knight had Dale lbw, and eight runs later Preston clipped one of Russell's balls about fifty yards.'

Ouch!

In 1975 it was a case of 'Hello, sailor' as Michael Angelow, a twenty-five-year-old cook on the oil tanker *Explorer*, streaked on to the field and jumped over both sets of stumps during the England v. Australia Test at Lord's.

John Arlott was commentating live on radio at the time, and he described the incident as follows: 'We have a streaker – it's masculine, and not very shapely, and I should think it has seen the last of its cricket for the day.'

Angelow told the magistrate's court, 'I didn't think anyone would object. The woman in the next seat actually held my clothes for me.' He had done it for a bet, but lost all his winnings to the court, which fined him £20.

By that time the good days were starting to return, due in no small measure to the inspirational captaincy of Mike Brearley, who led the side from 1971 to 1982.

Mike complained that I was neurotic: he said that I was the kind of man who had to keep going back to the front door to make certain he had locked it. I don't know what he was getting at – everyone knows I'm not a bit like that. He also said to me once, 'Dickie, there is no such thing as an absolute certainty, only the certainty that befits the subject. What is certain or accurate for a carpenter is not certain or accurate for a geometer.'

I told him straight: 'I don't know what the hell you're talking about, captain, but I'll tell you one thing for sure. When it comes to giving lbw decisions, I have to be absolutely certain, whatever you might think, and there have been times, my old lad, that you've had cause to thank me for that.'

Mike was a brilliant captain. He has a keen mind and sharp

brain and, as I said in my autobiography, if he could be persuaded to come back to the game, he would be the ideal man as supremo of English cricket. With Brearley at the helm, we would soon give the Aussies a real run for their money.

Another key part in the Middlesex revival was played by Clive Radley, an excellent batsman with whom I built up a very close friendship through the years.

He was the kind of player who just seemed to accumulate runs without you noticing it. If you watched him in the nets, you would wonder what the hell anybody saw in him – how could this fella ever get runs? – but he was one of the most effective players there have been in the game, simply through making the most of his strong points.

Clive knew what he could and could not do, and concentrated on what he was good at, which was more or less push and run. He would shove the ball towards mid-off at just the right pace and command, 'One.' Sometimes it would be 'Come two,' and off he would charge. He just knocked the ball into space, and Bob's your uncle. Another run. Or two. Or three. He was one of the best judges of a run I have ever seen. If the opposing captain moved the fielders around, he would infuriatingly start to nudge the ball in the space they had left. On top of all that, he had a tremendous temperament.

When Clive first went to Middlesex for a trial, the coaches wondered why he had bothered. Jack Robertson was going to send him back where he had come from. However, no less a judge than Bill Edrich felt he could see something in the youngster, and he persuaded them all that this fellow from his native Norfolk was destined to be a fine player. 'He is not particularly attractive to watch, I grant you,' he said, 'but he will score some runs.'

Bill managed to convince others to give the young man a chance, and, no doubt, in later years, he would have raised a glass in that great pavilion in the sky, looked down with a beaming smile on his face, and uttered, 'Told you so.'

Radders went on to score thousands of runs for Middlesex, and also played for England. He made his debut in Christchurch in the second Test of the series against New Zealand in 1977–8, and in his second England appearance – the third Test in Auckland – he scored 158. It was, however, the slowest 150 in Test-match history. It took him 594 minutes!

Radders had been called up from Australia, where he was spending the winter, to join the England party as a replacement for Mike Brearley, who had broken his arm in Pakistan.

The Middlesex players wrote to him, asking if he could persuade BBC commentator Don Mosey to describe, in one of his broadcasts, what Mike Gatting had for breakfast in New Zealand. Don obliged with a one-word answer. 'Everything.'

At times, Clive really got my dander up, however. He had a habit of running full pelt straight down the middle of the pitch as he made a bee-line for the other end when chasing one of his quick singles. He was a devil for the shortest route from A to B.

'If you don't get off that damn pitch, I'm going to have to tell you to take those spikes off and put crêpes on,' I would warn him. Trouble was, I knew full well that crêpes would probably be worse: they scuff up the surface and do more damage than spikes, and Clive would slip and slide all over the place.

In the 1984 NatWest Trophy final at Lord's, Radders and Paul Downton restored the flagging run rate with a fifth-wicket stand to ensure a Middlesex victory, John Emburey scoring the winning run off the last ball. And I got the man of the match award.

On closer inspection I discovered that my umpire's medal had Radders' name on it. He, meanwhile, was going bananas in the dressing room, having suddenly realised that he had my umpire's medal. We did a swap, of course, but I still hold the record of being the only umpire to have been presented with a man of the match award in a Lord's final.

It was in the middle of that match-winning innings, having hit Kent's Derek Underwood for three successive fours, that Radders sauntered up to the bowler and asked, 'Can you do me an article for my benefit year, Deadly?' What a time to ask, I thought, but Deadly did.

Radders must have had a winning way with him in that respect, because he did exactly the same to Peter Roebuck in another Lord's final. Roebuck was fielding so close that he could see Radders' striped underpants through his flannels. 'Benefit next year, Robey. Can you do something for my brochure?' Radders asked just as the bowler started his run-up.

Radders was with Middlesex so long that he had two or three benefits. Even he lost count. He was still going strong at forty-three years old.

Not a lot of people realise that Radders, who is now head coach at the indoor school at Lord's, took eight wickets in his career at an average of 20. From what I can make out, the only bowlers of his time with a more impressive average than that were Joel Garner, Richard Hadlee, Malcolm Marshall and Derek Underwood. These four, plus donkey-drop Radders. What an attack, eh?

Philippe Edmonds was a very good spin bowler, but something of a rebel, and he often got the wrong side of captains, managers and England selectors. Although he bowled slows, he once sent down a very quick bouncer in a Test match. He was warned by the umpire not to intimidate the batsman, so he promptly bowled another the very next ball. Good job I was not umpiring that game.

He was also suspended from a Middlesex match in 1984 having been seen lying in the outfield soaking up the sun at a tense moment in play. Later, during a quiet spell in Calcutta, he picked up a newspaper and started to read it while fielding on the boundary edge.

What a character he was. But a fine bowler, make no mistake about that.

Fred Titmus was another magnificent spin bowler who played for Middlesex and England. Unfortunately he was deaf in one ear, and on many occasions he was not too sure whether the batsman had got a nick or not. He would turn to me and ask my opinion. I have to be honest and admit that there were instances when I knew very well that the ball had found the edge, only for wicketkeeper John Murray to fluff the catching opportunity, and on those occasions I simply dared not tell Fred the truth, or JM would have throttled me.

When Graham Rose was at Middlesex, his best friend was Colin Metson, who went on to play for Glamorgan. One evening, after a second eleven match, they were enjoying a game of football with some of the other Middlesex youngsters when Colin slipped the ball past Rosie and prepared to continue his dazzling run. Next thing he knew he had been flattened by fourteen stones of muscle and sinew in a tackle that took all the breath out of his body. He was so badly hurt that he had to be taken to hospital.

Rosie was obviously concerned for the welfare of his friend, even more so when he saw what was written on the hospital record card. 'A separation of the left distal tibial epiphysis.'

He looked anxiously at his mate, lying there pale and suffering in the hospital bed. 'I say, Colin, that sounds serious.'

'Serious? Too right it's serious,' moaned Metson. 'That says it all. I've busted my bloody ankle.'

On the subject of healing, the curator at Lord's sent the following letter to *The Times* in June, 1983. 'Sir, I do not know whether Cardinal Hume's election to membership of the MCC has any bearing on the matter, but I have just had a letter from Trinidad. It was addressed to Lourdes Cricket Ground.'

Mike Gatting has dominated more recent years with the bat, scoring 28,411 runs in 412 matches for Middlesex during a career that has run parallel with mine. We even reached the retirement stage together. In my final year on the county circuit I came across him playing against Cambridge University at Fenner's. He made 160, and I said to him, 'Why don't you pack it in, Gatt, and give some of the youngsters a chance?'

'Not bloody likely,' he said. 'I'm after my hundredth hundred.'

He did not quite make it. Ended up in the nervous nineties. But he was still a very good batsman, even in those later years, as he proved in 1998, when he and Justin Langer put on 372 in a record first-wicket partnership against Essex in the one game played at Southgate while building work was going on at Lord's.

Gatt also captained England, and when he led the squad abroad he used to take charge of the food, making out his own shopping list for the tour so that his players ate the right things. If he was heading for India or Pakistan he was particularly keen that the diet should be safe – no Delhi bellies if he could help it. Whereas I used to take gingerbread men from the local baker in my home village of Staincross, Gatt used to order two dozen large jars of Branston pickle to take with him. Get Jack Russell on board with his Jaffa Cakes and we could have a real feast: gingerbread men, Jaffa Cakes and Branston pickle.

Gatt, of course, famously got himself in a bit of a pickle with a certain umpire called Shakoor Rana when he captained England on the 1987–8 tour of Pakistan. He felt he was getting the rough end of the stick, and ended up giving Shakoor a finger-jabbing lecture, for which he was later forced to apologise.

At the start of the following season in England, Middlesex

were due to visit New Road, Worcester. On the first day of the match Gatt arrived at the ground, pulled up by the attendant at the players' car park, wound down his car window and barked, 'Michael Gatting, captain of Middlesex.'

The attendant took off his white cap, bent down, smiled, and said, 'Shakoor Rana, Pakistani Test umpire.'

Arrangements had been made for Shakoor to come over, dress up and play a trick on his old adversary. It worked a treat. You should have seen Gatt's face! Talk about bearding the lion in his den.

Northampton

NORTHAMPTONSHIRE

11

N o one in his right mind would describe the county ground at Wantage Road, Northampton as beautiful. Functional, workmanlike, and practical, yes, but there has never been anything remotely picturesque about it. However, major improvements are in progress, and it is being developed into an impressive stadium more in keeping with its status.

One of the big problems is the fact that the ground has been shared with Northampton Town Football Club. This is never an ideal arrangement, and the overlap of the two pitches has created a rough area on the cricket outfield which has always made fielding a hazardous occupation. In addition, the football season has made it impossible for cricket to be played in April and September, so the county has had either to play away or use one of the out-grounds at the beginning and end of the season.

The Football Club has moved to another site now, though, and the County Cricket Club has been able to go ahead with ambitious plans to provide a very fine ground indeed when all the work is completed.

Maybe then Northamptonshire will be able to make their county championship dream come true at last. Although they entered that competition in 1905, they have never managed to claim the title, despite being runners-up in 1912, 1957, 1965 and 1976.

They have not had much success in one-day cricket, either, victories in the Gillette/NatWest in 1976 and 1992, and the Benson and Hedges Cup in 1980 being their only triumphs. It is the same story in the Sunday League, their best effort third place in 1991.

Mind you, Northants have had their share of bad luck in the one-dayers. For example, they were beaten in the 1981 NatWest final when the scores finished level, but Derbyshire came out on top because they had lost fewer wickets. Six years later they lost the Benson and Hedges Cup final to Yorkshire on the same ruling, and in 1990 they were pipped in the NatWest final again. In that same season they also faded in the championship run-in, when it had looked as though they were finally going to break their duck.

Northamptonshire first came into prominence in 1949, when Freddie Brown took over the captaincy. He was a strong captain, as well as a capable all-rounder, and brought a new spirit and a sense of purpose to the county. No one could have foreseen the tremendous change he was to bring, especially as he was thirty-eight years old and right at the end of his career when he was appointed. The way he pulled the side up by their bootlaces showed the strength and character of a man who was never afraid to speak his mind.

Such was the impact he made, that he was also recalled to captain England against New Zealand twelve years after he had last played in a Test match. He later used his leadership qualities to great effect with the Test and County Cricket Board and as President of the MCC.

A personal friend of mine, Freddie played in the Yorkshire Council with Hickleton Cricket Club, not far from my home town of Barnsley, during the war.

Freddie was a plain-speaking man who would not suffer fools gladly, and he upset a lot of people in his time. In 1951

Freddie Jakeman, another Yorkshireman who called a spade a spade, shared a record third-wicket partnership of 320 with Jock Livingston against the South Africans at Northampton. When he was finally out, Jakeman marched into the dressing room and said to Brown, 'There, that's how you bat.'

Said Brown, 'Aye, well, that's as maybe. But after all that time out there, I think you deserve a rest. You can play in the second team for the next three matches.'

That same season Jakeman scored 258 not out against Essex, again at Northampton, which tells you what a good batsman he was – and what a nerve Brown had, to treat him like that!

Another Yorkshireman with the county around about that time was Des Barrick, a big practical joker who was born in the same row of terraced houses as Geoff Boycott, Peter and Cyril Knowles, the footballing brothers, and Eric Batten, the Bradford and England Rugby league star.

The legendary Frank Tyson was one of Des's team-mates. Frank had joined the county from Lancashire, and although some people said he was a bit restricted by the pitch at Northampton, his meteoric England career certainly raised the prestige of his new county no end.

Frank did not care much for the ground at Derby. He always thought it was cold and bleak, at the back of beyond. There was one consolation, however: the enormous antique baths, ideal for a post-match soak when the old bones were aching like mad and the biting wind had reached the parts that other winds could not reach.

One typically freezing day, he had jumped straight in the huge bath and was just beginning to get some feeling back into his fingers and toes when Des 'Roly-Poly' Barrick tiptoed in and poured a bucket of ice-cold water over him.

Frank almost hit the ceiling. Not to mention Des, although he just restrained himself from the latter. In any case, the cackling Des was off like a shot.

Frank decided on revenge. He wrapped his towel round him, filled another bucket of ice-cold water, marched into the adjoining room where Des was, and poured it over his colleague's head.

Des was fully dressed by this time, and he stood there, as if in a state of shock, the water soaking into his clothes. A wicked grin slowly spread across his face, and Frank was a bit taken aback. He didn't quite know what to make of such a reaction. Then came the punchline.

Chortled Des: 'I've got news for thee, Frank, old lad. I rather thought you might try summat like that, so I've put thy clothes on.'

There was a similar incident when I was on umpiring duty with Jack van Geloven in a match between Yorkshire and Northamptonshire at Middlesbrough. In between the dressing rooms there is a massive communal bath, where everybody dives in together. Players from both teams were having a bit of a lark at the end of the day's play and Jack was enjoying some banter while walking round the edge of the bath. I could see what was coming; Jack obviously could not. The next thing he knew, he was gasping for air as he went under. Fully clothed. Somebody had given him a playful nudge when he least expected it, and he found himself pooling his resources with the rest of them.

Although Des may have been a bit of a prankster, that did not prevent him from being a very good batsman, as he showed only too well when putting on 299 for the second wicket with Jock Livingston against Sussex in 1953, and setting a fifth-wicket record partnership of 347 with Dennis Brookes against Essex in 1952, both those matches being played at Northampton.

Livingston was a left-hand bat who revelled in hitting

leg-spinners into the adjoining bowls club, while Brookes, yet another Yorkshireman, became not only the batsman to score most runs in a season for the county – 2,198 in 1952 – but also in a career, with a total of 28,980 in the years spanning 1934–59.

Brookes also had a successful spell as captain from 1954 to 1957, and in his last year in charge Northants twice beat eventual champions Surrey, only, as in 1912, to finish runners-up.

I have always admired Dennis. Not only was he a tremendous batsman, he was a good bloke. He is a big churchman – a Methodist, like me – and he is still a very respected figure at the club, where he is now an honorary life member. He is always around, and his advice is still sought and appreciated. He still lives in the same house, near the main entrance to the ground. Travelling to home matches was never a problem for him.

Dennis still recalls the first game played by the county at Wellingborough School, which shared with Cheltenham College the distinction of being the only school grounds to stage first-class cricket. It is a ground where facilities are limited, but there is always a good atmosphere about the place, and that inaugural match proved quite an occasion.

The great Len Hutton hit 269 not out when Yorkshire totalled 523, but in Northamptonshire's second innings Brookes and Norman Oldfield saved the game with an unbroken opening stand of 208. In the three days of the match 1,000 runs were scored, although the relatively short boundaries contributed to that.

As for Tyson, the other player involved in that watery escapade at Derby, Richie Benaud described the impression the fast bowler made on him in 1953, when the Australians visited Northampton, having been denied a second Test victory at Lord's by Trevor Bailey and Willie Watson, who had batted all day to save the game for England.

The Aussies looked at the Northants team sheet and started asking who this new chap Tyson was. Some said he had just come down from Durham University, so they did not reckon he would give them too much trouble. Richie, who was twelfth man, settled back to watch Tyson bowl the opening over, but he was soon sitting up and taking notice. The university chappie had walked right back to the sightscreen to start his run, then accelerated in to bowl a ball that was just a blur as it flew from his hand, finding the edge of Colin McDonald's bat, ricocheting over the slips, and careering first bounce into the crowd for four.

The second ball struck McDonald on the pad while the batsman still had his bat in the air preparing to make his shot; the third whistled past the nose of Graeme Hole, the batsmen having scampered for a leg-bye; and the fourth was a rip-snorting yorker which sent the leg stump cartwheeling to wicketkeeper Keith Andrew, who had stationed himself halfway between the stumps and the boundary.

It was all rather unnerving for the rest of the Australian batsmen, waiting to come in, but Richie could rest comparatively easy in the knowledge that he did not have to face Tyson himself. At least, not in that game. That dubious pleasure was to come eighteen months later, when Tyson terrorised the Aussies in the 1954–5 season Down Under.

Most players who took part in the third Test in Melbourne noted his bowling in the second innings as the fastest they had ever seen. He took 7 for 27 and England won by 128 runs.

He was certainly the quickest bowler I have ever seen through the air, and on one occasion he was the quickest bowler I never saw through the air. I made the mistake of hitting him for three successive fours when I opened the innings

for Yorkshire against the MCC at Scarborough. The fourth
ball was pitched short, reared up and hit me flush on the
chin. The next thing I knew, I was being whisked away by
ambulance.

Frank is now settled in Australia, and I paid him a visit when
I was there last winter. He looked me up and down. 'You're
looking well, Dickie. See you've still got the scars, though.' We
had a good laugh about it then, although it wasn't terribly funny
at the time.

It is strange that Frank did not last all that long at the top.
He seemed to blow himself out, rather like the Typhoon that
became his nickname, but at his peak he was the quickest
around. No doubt about that.

In 1958 Raman Subba Row took over the captaincy from
Brookes, and in that same year made Northamptonshire's then
record score of 300 against his former county, Surrey, at the
Oval. He went on to top the batting averages, and received great
support from Brookes and Peter Arnold, who both reached
1,000 runs for the season. Two other players who had come
through the ranks, Brian Reynolds and Albert Lightfoot, were
not far off that milestone, either, and it seemed at one stage
that Northants might claim the title at last, but yet again their
challenge fell away.

Subba Row also played for England, and had a better Test
average than Geoff Boycott, although, of course, he did not
appear in nearly as many matches for his country as Sir Geoffrey.
He later became Chairman of the Test and County Cricket
Board and is now a respected Test match referee, officiating
at matches all over the world.

Throughout their history, Northants have had a succession
of Australians in their ranks. Three in particular spring to
mind from the 1950s – left-arm bowler Jack Manning, Jock
Livingston, whom I have already mentioned, and George Tribe,

who was an outstanding all-rounder, but was best known for his left-arm googlies and chinamen.

I remember once watching him from behind the nets while he was practising prior to a game between Yorkshire and Northants at Northampton. I thought to myself, 'Dickie, lad, I reckon you can pick him.' I went out to bat in confident mood, and was bowled first ball, playing down the wrong line to a googly.

I recalled that occasion when I saw George in Melbourne last winter, and we got to nattering about the old days. He had never realised that I had been watching him practise before going out to bat, and I had to admit, 'I thought I'd got you sussed, George, but you were far too clever for me.'

George had not changed a bit. It was just like when we were opposing each other in the county championship: he never stopped talking. Talk the hind leg off an elephant, could George.

George was a fine bowler, and when Geoff Boycott was playing in Australia, he always used to seek George out to give him some practice against that type of bowling. Geoff travelled a long way to be with George and spent hours trying to tell his chinaman from his googly, but it was well worth it.

George would surely have played for Australia but for the fact that he signed a long contract with Northants when he came over here. Australia's loss was very much Northamptonshire's gain.

Jim Laker used to tell a lovely story about George. They played together in a Commonwealth team which toured India in the 1950s, and during a game against one of the princely states of Jajputana, the home side were captained by the Maharajah, who was the Head of State. George kept rapping him on the pads and appealing, but to no avail. The umpire was a member of the palace staff, you see.

Finally, George's patience snapped after yet another appeal

185

had been turned down and he grabbed the umpire by the front of his jacket and instructed him to 'have another look, you stupid bugger.'

The startled umpire, much alarmed, gasped, 'Oh, goodness gracious me, Mr Tribe, sir. You are indeed quite right.'

He then turned apologetically to the Maharajah. 'Your Serene Highness, I very much regret to be having to tell you that you are out!'

That game, incidentally, was the only one in which Jim Laker saw the heavy roller being pulled by an elephant!

One of the most colourful characters to arrive at Northampton in my days as a player was Colin Milburn, who thrilled spectators with his big-hitting, both for the county and his country. If ever there was a batsman guaranteed to pull in the crowds it was 'Ollie'.

He bludgeoned his way to the fastest century of both the 1966 and 1967 seasons, and was reaching the pinnacle of his powers when he lost an eye in a road accident. He was only twenty-seven, and although he made a brave attempt to return as a middle-order batsman and medium-pace bowler – he had also been a great slip-catcher – he was never the same again. It was the end of the 'Burnham Basher' as we had known him, a tragedy for both Northamptonshire and England.

By this time the club had been revitalised, largely due to the efforts of Secretary Ken Turner, who was responsible for bringing in such magnificent overseas stars as Mushtaq Mohammad, Bishen Bedi, and Sarfraz Nawaz. Ken also thought nothing of running discos and rock concerts in the indoor school in order to raise money. His infectious enthusiasm rubbed off on everybody.

There were times when players would knock on his door to ask for a rise, and he would say to them, 'Rise? What do you want a rise for? If you're not happy, the door's behind you. Pack your bags and off you go. Now good day.' But no one left.

One person who could always get the better of him, however, was Mrs Jellyman. Whenever I was umpiring at Northampton I would stay with her and her husband just across the road from the ground. It was very homely there, and it was so handy: I could roll out of bed, have my breakfast and walk straight into the ground with no need to bother about traffic and parking problems.

Mrs Jellyman was a member of the club, and she used to pop across the road regularly to see Ken, complaining about one thing or another. Ken used to say to me, 'That woman's been in again, Dickie. She's driving me mad. Can't you keep her away from me on a morning? Nag, nag, nag. She never stops. There's always something wrong, according to her.'

There was not much I could do about it, and in any case, I didn't want to upset her: she was such a good cook.

Mushtaq Mohammad spent thirteen seasons with the club and was captain between 1975 and 1977. He scored nearly 16,000 runs and took 550 wickets with his leg-breaks and googlies. His fielding was also top class. Under his leadership Northamptonshire gained their first success in any competition, winning the Gillette Cup by beating Lancashire in the final of 1976, and that same year they again came so very close to taking the county championship, finishing second to Middlesex.

Bishen Bedi enjoyed a successful swansong at the Wellingborough School ground against Middlesex in 1977. It was a spinners' pitch and Bedi revelled in the conditions to take 5 for 24 and 6 for 83 in Middlesex's two innings, he and Peter Willey being the only wicket-takers.

David Steele was a member of that Gillette Cup-winning side of '76, just a year after England had successfully turned to him to help resist the fiery challenge of the West Indies' pacemen.

With his grey hair and glasses, the thirty-four-year-old was far removed from the traditional picture of a sporting hero, but he did a marvellous job. His proudest moments were when he played for his country. He would point to the three lions on his chest and say, 'You can't take that away.'

He did, however, make the most embarrassing of entrances to his Test debut at Lord's. He was so used to going out to bat with Northants from the visitors' dressing room, that he got completely lost on his way to the middle from the home dressing room. Instead of going down two flights of stairs and through the Long Room, he went down three and ended up in the members' toilets. Above the doors are the signs 'In' and 'Out'. He went in. And came out. But he still had to go in before he was out in cricketing terms – and they were all waiting for him on the field, wondering where on earth he had got to.

His colleagues were just as bewildered as everybody else. They had seen him set off. So where could he be?

David managed to make it to the crease eventually, and went on to rescue his side, who were 10 for 1 at the time, with a gutsy half century.

At the end of the summer David was top of the England batting averages, and was also voted BBC Sports Personality of the Year, for the way he had bravely stood up to the West Indian pace barrage, yet he never played for his country again. The selectors decided not to take him on the winter tour of India, so his international career was over after only one very successful series. Because he had made his name playing against the quicks of the West Indies and Australia – Holding, Marshall, Roberts, Croft, Garner, Lillee and Thomson – the selectors believed that he was only happy facing fast bowling. Nothing could be further from the truth: David was one of the best players around against spin, and I always thought it a mistake that he was discarded like that, especially after the heroics he had performed. He was a fine all-round batsman, could bowl useful slow left-armers, and was a brilliant close-to-the-wicket fielder.

One thing David did not like was spending his money. Once, when I was umpiring a game in which he was playing, we had a bit of a natter between overs, and he told me, 'I went to the fair last night, Dickie, and I'm not very happy.'

'Why's that, then, David? What happened?'

'Well,' he replied, 'I spent sixpence on the hoop-la and didn't win a thing. I'm so disappointed.'

He did count his pennies, did David.

In 1980 Northants won the Benson and Hedges Cup for the first time, under the captaincy of Jim Watts. His successor, Geoff Cook, took them to the NatWest Trophy final in his first season, when both teams scored 235, but Derbyshire, losing only six wickets to Northants' nine, took the trophy.

An opening batsman and occasional slow left-arm bowler, Geoff Cook played seven times in Tests for England. He had the loudest voice in the Northants dressing room, and you always knew when he was around – especially if Leicester City had won, or his racehorse, Jungle Knife, had galloped in first past the post. Once you managed to prise him away from the *Sporting Life*, however, Geoff was a great team man and full of very shrewd advice.

On one occasion when Northants were playing Yorkshire, who were struggling at 50 for 4, Cook signalled Wayne Larkins to come on and have a bowl because the ball was seaming about all over the place and he thought the conditions would suit Larkins' little medium pacers.

David Bairstow was at the crease and Yorkshire were badly in need of some inspiration. The sturdy wicketkeeper was just the chap to provide it. However, Larkins' fourth ball struck him on the front pad and ballooned high in the air. To Bluey's horror, he realised that it was dropping straight back on to his stumps, so, without thought for his own safety, he did the first thing that came into his mind in a bid to save his wicket. He headed the ball away! Without the protection of a helmet. Unfortunately, in doing so, he flattened all three stumps and was given out hit wicket.

There was a Bluey tinge to the language that greeted that particular dismissal, I can tell you.

Another Yorkshire v. Northants battle took place at Scarborough in 1981. Ray Illingworth had recently suspended Geoff Boycott for remarks made to the press, and the natives were distinctly restless, ready and willing to have a pop at anybody and everybody at the drop of a hat.

As Cook led his team through the crowds on to the field, one fan rounded on Lamb and shouted, 'As for you, you've no right to be here at all. Bugger off back to South Africa.' The player he was bawling at was Lamb, true enough. But it was Tim, younger son of Lord Rochester, not Allan, who was not even playing that day.

Mention of Lamby's name has me twitching more than ever. I have always been very highly strung, but I am even more nervous when Lamby is around. I never know when he's going to set fire to my dressing room, lock me in, call me on a mobile phone out there in the middle of a game, take the wheels off my car, or order a firing squad to put me out of my misery . . . I could go on. He has been responsible for all those, and for putting me in a flap more times than I care to recall.

I still regard him as a friend, however, though he doesn't really deserve it. He was a great player, too, for both Northants and England. He was the first Northants batsman for twenty-six years to reach 2,000 runs in a season, and he went on to captain the side. It was his burning ambition to lead them to the championship for the first time, which would have been a fitting finale to a wonderful career. Sadly, it was not to be.

The first county championship match to be played at Luton's Wardown Park in neighbouring Bedfordshire in 1986 could not have been better. Yorkshire were the visitors – and that was a good enough start. In Northamptonshire's first innings Robert Bailey scored his maiden double hundred. Not to be outdone, Yorkshire's Ashley Metcalfe replied with 151, his second hundred in consecutive matches, and, although the match did not produce a result, the runs continued to flow, well over a thousand in all, giving both players – well, the batsmen at least – and spectators a great deal of enjoyment.

Bailey was a great competitor, a very good batsman who could also bowl off-spin. He turned down the chance of a rebel tour to South Africa and is still serving his county club with distinction. He captained Northants for two seasons in 1996 and 1997, before resigning.

Bailey should have played more for England; he had one or two games, but that is all. He played in the West Indies, when the ball was flying around the batsmen's ears from Roberts, Garner, Croft, Walsh and Ambrose, and he appeared to be judged on that one difficult tour. He had stuck by the Establishment by turning down a lot of money to go to South Africa: they did not exactly stand by him.

Rob is a good man, and good for the game. I have a lot of respect for him. He was a dream to umpire. If he got a faint nick, or the ball feathered the glove, he'd walk. He did not wait for my decision. That takes a lot of pressure off an umpire.

Rob was also one of the biggest eaters in the game. He maybe dropped the odd catch, but he would never drop a meat pie if you threw one to him. He loves his food and he does not have many rivals in the eating stakes – or even steaks. His knowledge of restaurants around the circuit is second to none, and I reckon he could write a best-food guide one day. His nickname is 'Nosebag', for obvious reasons. His relaxations are walking – to burn off all the calories he's just consumed, no doubt – and drinking at his local pub, where he puts them all back on again.

That great West Indian fast bowler, Curtly Ambrose, played for a few years with Northants, and he became big friends with all-rounder David Capel. They travelled and roomed together, although all the driving was done by David. He had a sponsored car, and it was very nearly taken away from him at one stage, all because of Curtly.

You see, Curtly just about lived on chocolate. He would eat bar after bar after bar. One particular day it was so hot in the car that the chocolate melted. It went all over the seats, the doors, the floor – there was even some on the roof – and when they saw the state the car was in, the sponsors went bananas. It took some smooth-talking by David to calm them down.

David actually started his first-class career on 18 July, 1981, on what would have been W. G. Grace's 133rd birthday. Previously he had played with Roade in the Northampton Town League, along with his father, who later became the team's umpire. David decided it was time to move on when dear old Dad kept giving him out lbw!

Capel played for England a few times, but his international career was cut short by Abdul Qadir on a tour of Pakistan. He had the greatest difficulty playing Qadir, which is not surprising, because, for me, he is the greatest spin bowler of his type – leg-spin, googlies, top-spinners. However, the selectors came to the conclusion that David could not deal with any spin bowling, and he hardly played again.

Capel was a good all-rounder who suffered, as many others have done, in comparison with Ian Botham. He lived in the great man's shadow. It is wrong to expect anyone to be like Both: he was a one-off, and we have to accept that there will never be another quite like him.

Ironically, David went on charity walks with Both in aid of leukaemia, as did I. He walked over the Sussex Downs with him, and complained about his feet. He said that it felt as if they were on fire. I can sympathise: Both really does go at a rare old lick. It is impossible to keep up with him – unless you hop on a bus, like I did in Devon.

Both turned to David and said, 'Stop moaning, Capes, you're a wimp.'

Next day, after struggling up yet another hill, and praying for a stretch of flat road, Capes tapped Both on the shoulder and declared that, whatever the torture in store, he was determined to complete a further thirty miles, just to prove that he was not the wimp Both thought he was. And he did.

Said Both, 'Capes, you'll do for me.' But David suffered for it. His feet were so swollen, he could not get his shoes off at the end of the day, and they had to be cut off. However, he had done it: he had shown Both that he was no wimp.

Another all-rounder of recent years is Kevin Curran, who was born in Zimbabwe and previously played for Gloucestershire. He was captain in 1998, but was replaced for the 1999 season by Matthew Hayden, an Australian left-hand opening bat who had never captained a side before, although the Queenslander had played in a few Tests. It was probably player power that brought Curren down, having upset a few of them.

At the moment Northants have some fine young players coming through, and if they can get the confidence they need, and believe in themselves, they should do well.

One young lad, Graeme Swann, has already played for England A, and is a tremendous prospect. A right-hand batsman, he is also an off-spin bowler. Northampton-born, he is still only twenty. His father played Minor Counties cricket for Bedfordshire and Northumberland and also for England Amateurs. His brother, Alec, also plays for Northampton.

Another youngster with lots of promise is David Sales, a right-hand batsman who has played for Young England. If people around him give him the right advice and proper encouragement, so that he can build up his confidence, he could go a long way in the game. At twenty-one, he has not yet fulfilled his rich potential. Having said that, he was the youngest batsman to score 50 in the Sunday League; he was also the first Englishman to score a double century on his championship debut, and the youngest since W. G. Grace to score a double century in England, when he made 210 not out against Worcestershire at Kidderminster in 1996. He has great ability.

One player who seems destined to go on and play for the full England side is Mal Loye, who scored a lot of runs in the unofficial Tests on the tour of Zimbabwe and South Africa in 1998–9. He holds the Northants record for the highest individual innings of 322 not out against Glamorgan at Northampton in 1998. Right-handed, he usually goes in at number three, but has also opened the innings.

Cricketer of the Year in 1998, Loye also holds the first-wicket partnership record, with wicketkeeper and Yorkshire lad Richard Montgomerie, of 372 against Yorkshire at Northampton in 1996, and the joint fifth-wicket partnership record with David Ripley – another Yorkie and now at Sussex – of 401, made against Glamorgan, again at Northampton, in 1998.

Yet another exile from the White Rose county is Chief Executive Steve Coverdale, who was with Yorkshire Seconds as wicketkeeper before moving to Northamptonshire. He is very efficient and does a marvellous job, although there is the odd occasion when he has a panic attack. He was in the dressing room at Lord's for a one-day final and was worrying because he thought he had forgotten the county flag. When teams play at Lord's, their county flag is always flown, and Steve moaned to all and sundry, 'I've forgotten the bloomin' flag. What'll I do?'

They let him stew for a while before someone took pity on him and pointed out that the flag was already flying high from the pole just behind where he was standing.

Another great character is Jack Mercer, the former Glamorgan and Northants wicketkeeper, who was scorer for the county for many years. If there was a stoppage for rain or bad light, Jack used to come into the dressing rooms to amuse the players and umpires with the magic tricks which he performed with cards and dice. He was good, too. It was amazing how Jack used to make the time fly during those stoppages. He used to look forward to my visits in particular, because he knew he would get plenty of opportunities to show off. 'Dickie's here, Jack. Bad light and rain. Time for the magic show.'

But then, cricket has a magic of its own, hasn't it?

Trent Bridge, Nottingham

NOTTINGHAMSHIRE

12

THE new stand at the Radcliffe Road End was opened by Sir Garfield Sobers in the summer of 1998, and Trent Bridge is now a wonderful arena. It has everything: magnificent stands; good viewing; excellent facilities for spectators and players; an indoor school; a clinic for sports injuries, including wards with beds where you can stay overnight if you are injured or sick; hotel rooms which can be booked for Test matches, with windows overlooking the ground; a beautiful outfield; and one of the best Test pitches in the country. What more could you want?

Trent Bridge has also led the way in the development of scoreboard techniques in this country. In 1951 the Nottinghamshire scoreboard became such a feature that they used to take sightseers on a tour round it. It showed virtually everything you could wish to know about the current state of play, including a flashing light to indicate which player had fielded the ball. Sometimes spectators were more interested in watching the scoreboard in operation than the play. Now it has been taken another step forward, and is fully computerised, a far, far cry from the scoreboard at Essex, which is trundled round on wheels.

Another feature of Trent Bridge used to be Parr's tree, which was named after a former county captain, George Parr, the greatest batsman of his generation, so I am told, and a famous leg-hitter, who despatched the ball into the tree with monotonous regularity.

Sadly, the tree was blown down in the January storms of 1976, and is no longer there. The late Leslie Crowther, a great comedian, cricket fanatic, and hard-working member of the Lord's Taverners, was appearing in pantomime at Nottingham Theatre Royal at the time, and he borrowed a handsaw from the night porter in order to sneak into the ground and saw off one of the branches as a keepsake.

He quipped afterwards, 'I had to do it. Trees have always been a feature of the history of Nottingham. Robin Hood's longbow was made of yew, and he hid it in the major oak in Sherwood Forest; Boots, who have their headquarters in the city, have branches everywhere – and then there was Parr's elm tree.'

Nottinghamshire also play at Worksop, a small arena right in the middle of the town centre. It is the ground of the Bassetlaw League Club, who share it with Worksop Town Football Club.

Curiously, my outstanding memories of Nottinghamshire are of individuals rather than matches and performances. There have always been characters at the county club, and one of the first I came across was Charlie Harris, among the funniest men ever to play cricket.

My sides ached with laughing the first time I heard the tale of when he ended up in hospital after dislocating his shoulder while fielding. He was moaning and groaning as they tried to put the shoulder back in place, and finally the nurse could stand it no longer. 'Mr Harris, I'm surprised at you,' she scolded. 'You're making a dreadful fuss about having your shoulder put back. There's a woman downstairs who has just had twins and she's making far less fuss than you.'

To which Charlie replied, 'That's as maybe, but you try putting them back and see what she says.'

When Charlie was batting he had an infuriating habit of teasing the bowlers, causing them, on occasion, to blow a fuse. He would stare down the pitch and declare, 'Right, young man, I'm going to play the ball back to you this over. You'll be glad of a maiden, no doubt.' An over later he would say, 'Okay, you've had your maiden, now I'm going to hit you for a few fours.' Then he'd decide, 'Time to block the next three balls. I'll push them back to you, so get ready.' Next over it would be, 'I quite fancy a six now.' And he would hit one. Just like that. Unbelievable, although he did come unstuck on the odd occasion.

Another Trent Bridge character was groundsman Ron Allsopp, who for many years was responsible for some of those excellent pitches.

Traditionally, Trent Bridge pitches had been featherbeds, graveyards for bowlers, with match after match ending in a high-scoring draw, and Ron always used to say he wanted to transform them into the fast, bouncy type that the Test and County Cricket Board were asking groundsmen to produce. Ron succeeded, while at the same time proving what a master of his craft he was, by providing different pitches to suit the Nottinghamshire attack for championship matches.

Ron was not quite sure whether to take it as a compliment or not when he read a newspaper article one day about the problems of facing Richard Hadlee, Clive Rice and Ron Allsopp at Trent Bridge. He told me, 'Well, Dickie, if the experts view the situation in that light, then my mission has been accomplished.'

The thing about Ron was that he never worried about what people said about his pitches. It didn't bother him. He would have a laugh and a joke about it and then get on with the job.

The only time I saw him nearly lose his cool was when some of the players decided to take the mickey out of him a few days before a Test match at Trent Bridge. He had worked all day out there in the middle, carefully preparing and tending his pitch so that it was as near perfect as he could make it. Finally he decided to call it a day.

That was the moment the players had been waiting for. As soon as Ron's back was turned, they carried mounds of soil and placed them at intervals, starting in the outfield and leading to the Test strip. They left a dead mole beside the covers.

When Ron arrived next morning and saw the scene of apparent devastation, he was in a state of panic. Closer inspection made him realise that there had been some monkey business afoot, however, and his panic turned to anger. He vowed to turn the tables on whoever had been responsible, if ever he got the chance. He soon cooled down, though, and almost saw the funny side of it. He did not make a big issue of the incident – he never was one to make a mountain out of a molehill.

The biggest county celebrations that I can recall at Trent Bridge came in 1981 when Nottinghamshire claimed their first championship success for fifty-two years, after a crushing defeat of Glamorgan. Although formed as long ago as 1841, the county had never enjoyed much success. They had won the title only twice previously, in 1907 and 1929, and they have won it only once since, in 1987. That same year they also carried off the NatWest Trophy. They won the Benson and Hedges Cup in 1989, and they topped the Sunday League in 1991.

That 1981 triumph and subsequent successes were largely down to two of the most outstanding personalities to have represented the club – Clive Rice, a brilliant captain and talented all-rounder, and that magnificent New Zealander Richard Hadlee, who developed into one of the best all-rounders in the world.

Rice was brought in as an overseas replacement for Garfield Sobers in 1975, and it was he who was responsible for the change in attitude with regard to the pitches when he succeeded Yorkshireman Mike Smedley as captain in 1979. Smedley was probably too nice a bloke to have been given the captaincy in the first place, but Rice was ideally equipped for the job. And where Smedley had instructed Allsopp to prepare the best pitches humanly possible, Rice told him to prepare pitches that would suit the Nottinghamshire attack. The old pitches were too good, and it was impossible to get results on them, so Rice insisted on pitches that would get the county winning matches. He and Ron combined to do just that.

Rice was one of the best county captains I have ever come across. As well as being a magnificent player, and a strong leader, he was also incredibly fair and honest. All the first-class umpires respected him so much that when he retired we wrote him a letter thanking him for all the support he had given us.

Clive did a wonderful job at Nottinghamshire, turning them from a very ordinary outfit into a championship-winning side. They carried off the title twice under his leadership, as well as lifting the NatWest Trophy.

When he retired he went back to South Africa and became a selector for the international team. Since he left, Notts had not done too well, so he was invited back to Nottinghamshire for the 1999 season as head coach and manager, in a bid to recapture some of the former glories enjoyed under his captaincy.

I was not sure whether it would work. Rice's previous successes had been achieved while he was on the field, leading from the front, and I believe you have to be out there in the thick of the battle to have the best influence. He was a great motivator and knew how to bring the best out of his players. That was his forte. He never asked anyone to do what he was not prepared to do himself, so the players always respected him. Could he do the same from the sidelines, though, with Jason Gallian, imported from Lancashire, as his captain on the field?

As for Hadlee, among other things he was the perfect guinea pig, Ron Allsopp told me, for his experiments in providing the kind of track that was required. Sometimes Ron got it right, sometimes not. And Richard did not take long to let him know. Ron always used to watch the first few overs of a match to see how the pitch was playing. If he saw Hadlee kicking the ball away in a sulk, the message was clear: it was not good enough.

There was a time, Ron confided to me, when the press was having a dig at his pitches, that he wished Hadlee would catch the next flight back to New Zealand and leave him to enjoy the quiet life. 'It never seems to occur to them, Dickie,' he said, 'that invariably there is nothing in the pitch to trouble the batsmen until Hadlee arrives on the scene with his size twelve boots. Paddles makes things happen when no other bowler can.'

Hadlee went on to develop into a magnificent attacking batsman as well, and he performed one of the most phenomenal cricketing feats of modern times, when he scored 1,000 runs and claimed 100 wickets in the 1984 season. That is mind-boggling, and I do not believe there is anyone around today capable of doing that.

That same season Notts had been racing neck and neck with Essex right through to the closing weeks, and when Mike Bore faced the penultimate ball of the final over in the final match against Somerset at Taunton, Notts needed four runs to regain the title they had won three years earlier. In the long history of the competition there had never been such a dramatic climax. Bore struck the ball cleanly and it sped towards the boundary. Had it continued on its flight it would have been a championship-winning six, but it was caught by the substitute just inside the ropes at long-on, and Notts had to be content with the runners-up spot.

That was tough enough to take, but they suffered a similar fate the following season, this time in the final of the NatWest Trophy against Essex at Lord's. Notts needed eighteen from the last over, and some typically brilliant improvisation from Derek Randall brought sixteen of them, so that they needed two off the last ball. Randall misjudged his shot and was caught. More last-ball agony.

There is no doubt that Randall was Trent Bridge's favourite player for many years. A born fidget, thrilling batsman and magnificent fielder, he produced one of the greatest batting displays of his illustrious career in 1979, when he scored 209 and 146 in his two innings against Middlesex.

Derek started out with Retford Cricket Club. He was very shy, they say, but he gradually developed into an impish character who attracted crowds wherever he went. He generated excitement, either at the crease batting, or lurking in the field waiting to pounce with a piece of magic that would lead to the downfall of some unsuspecting batsman.

People first began to sit up and take notice of his legendary fielding skills when he ran out Barry Richards by yards after sprinting in from cover and hitting the stumps with an underarm throw delivered as he slithered in on his backside. He ended up straddling the broken stumps with his legs, and grinning mischievously up at a bemused Richards, who gazed down in amazement at such an impudent dismissal from what he had assumed would be a comfortable single.

Derek was one of the best cover point and mid-wicket fielders I have ever seen. He is right up there alongside Viv Richards, Clive Lloyd, Colin Bland, Jonty Rhodes, David Gower and Neil Harvey.

Even he, however, was guilty of the occasional wild throw, and during the 1981–2 tour of Australia with England, he created overthrows in the match at Adelaide with a particularly wayward return which caused Chris Tavaré in the slips to remark to Eddie Hemmings, 'Do you realise, he's just thrown the ball for more runs than we've made in the whole match?'

It was also in Adelaide that poor old Derek was made to feel a bit of a drip.

He was sharing a room with Allan Lamb, and one evening he decided to have a bath while Lamby nipped downstairs to the bar. Just after Lamby had left, Derek thought he heard a knock on the door, so, wrapped only in a towel which he hurriedly fastened around his waist, he went to see who was there. When he opened the door he could see no one, so he stepped outside to look down the corridor. As he did so, the door closed and locked behind him.

Lamby, meanwhile, was chatting with a group of people, including the hotel manager, and enjoying his beer, when a member of staff, looking just a trifle harassed, sidled up to the manager and whispered, 'Excuse me, sir, but we appear to have a bit of a problem in the restaurant. Some guests have just complained that water is leaking through the ceiling and dripping on to their table.'

Just at that moment Randall walked in. Dressed only in a towel. Lamby did a double take. 'Good lord, now what's up?' he asked.

'I've been locked out of my bloody room, that's what's up, mate. And I haven't got a damned key to get back in,' retorted the embarrassed Randall.

The penny dropped immediately with the hotel manager. 'You didn't happen to leave the bath running as well, did you, sir?' he queried, ever so politely.

Derek could be absentminded at times. For example, after playing a great innings against the West Indies at Lord's, he left the ground in high spirits, reflecting with immense satisfaction on a magnificent knock. He went through the Grace Gates with a contented smile on his face, like the cat who had scoffed the cream, and swaggered his way to the Clarendon Court Hotel, where the players usually stayed. He picked up the key for room 405, took the lift, and was just about to put the key in the lock when it dawned on him that there had been a change in the arrangements. He should be in room 405 at the Westmoreland Hotel on the other side of St John's Wood!

Not everyone realised how competitive Derek could be. He and John Birch were once fighting it out for a place in the team, and before the eleven was announced they went for a game of squash. Randall buzzed about the court in his usual quicksilver fashion, and his racket somehow managed to connect with Birch's eye. The result was a black eye for John, and no selection problem for the skipper.

Birchy ended up the worse for wear on another occasion. He was one of several Nottinghamshire players who had taken part in a benefit match with Somerset. Clive Rice and Richard Hadlee, driving back on the M4 after the match, noticed the 'slow down' signs as the motorway went into one lane. They eventually saw that the hold-up was caused by a badly battered car, its luggage spread all over the tarmac.

'Hey,' said Hadlee to Rice, 'that's one of our club cars.' And so it was. John Birch's. The police told them that the occupants had been taken to Reading Hospital, so they picked up what luggage was left and sped off. Fortunately no one was seriously injured, but it did make me think. With all that travelling up and down motorways in the height of the busy summer, season after season, it is amazing that so few cricketers have been involved in serious accidents.

Birchy, incidentally, was a football fanatic. A big Nottingham Forest supporter. One day he got into conversation with Forest manager Brian Clough, a regular visitor to Trent Bridge and who played squash at the county ground. John was delighted when Cloughie invited him over for Forest's next match. They had a chat in Cloughie's office before the game and Birchy was then asked if he would like to sit in the dug-out. He was over the moon, as they say in football circles.

Everything went swimmingly for a while as Forest built up a 3–1 lead against visitors Southampton, but when the Saints hit back to draw 3–3, an expletive-deleted Cloughie turned to Birchy and snapped, 'It's all your damn fault. I knew I shouldn't have let you sit in the dug-out.'

Birchy survived to tell the tale, but only just.

Cricket was Cloughie's first love. He would gladly have swapped the dream of a winning goal at Wembley for a century against the Australians at Lord's. He had the greatest respect for Geoff Boycott and could not contain himself when he once got the great man out, caught and bowled, in a charity match. Boycs always maintained that he spooned the ball back deliberately, but Cloughie tells it differently. 'Don't you believe anything Boycott says, young man,' he insists. 'He couldn't read my wrong 'un.'

Trent Bridge, of course, had seen some magnificent bowling long before Richard Hadlee arrived on the scene, particularly by that deadly duo, Harold Larwood and Bill Voce, who both took more than a thousand wickets and were in the side that won the championship in 1929, Larwood right-arm over the wicket, Voce left-arm over the wicket. The ideal opening attack.

Larwood became the focal point of that infamous Bodyline tour of Australia, yet when he retired he chose to live Down Under. Whenever I went over there I used to have a chat and a drink with him at his home not far from the Sydney Oval Test ground.

For seventy years, between 1880 and 1950, there was always at least one Gunn playing for Nottinghamshire. There was William, his two nephews, George and John, and finally came G. V.

George was a law unto himself. He was something of a hypochondriac, and was particularly concerned about his digestive system. Half past one was lunchtime, and nothing could interfere with that. One day at Cardiff, where Notts were playing Glamorgan, George, having scored 80-odd not out, turned to make his way to the pavilion after what he believed was the final ball before lunch.

He was less than pleased when the umpire called him back and told him that it had been specially agreed to take lunch at two o'clock that day. George was going to change his lunchtime for no one, however. He raised his bat to the next ball, a straight delivery, and allowed it to hit the stumps, then off he strode.

His captain, A. W. Carr, was furious, and when Gunn reached the pavilion steps he demanded of his batsman what on earth he thought he was playing at.

'Well, Mr Carr,' replied Gunn, 'me digestion expects its vittles at half past one, and I don't see why today should be any different.'

George was also no mug when it came to driving a hard bargain, as illustrated one day when all the Nottinghamshire bowlers were slightly injured in a car accident on their way to play Yorkshire at Headingley. Luckily Carr won the toss and chose to bat first, giving his bowlers more time to recover. He then instructed Gunn to stay at the crease until teatime.

Gunn, who was no longer a youngster, thought this was asking rather too much of him, so he said he would try his best to follow his captain's instructions, only if he was paid a pound an hour above his usual wages. Carr eventually gave in to this demand, but there was more to come. At half past three, still going strong, George held another Gunn to his captain's head – time and a half for staying there until half past five. Again Carr agreed, and George continued on his untroubled way, scoring a steady thirty runs an hour until the day was saved.

Rice and Gallian may be quite relieved that there is no son of a Gunn around Nottinghamshire these days!

Then there were the Hardstaffs, father and son, Joe senior and Joe junior, the latter acknowledged as one of the best English batsmen either side of the Second World War. In 1937 he scored more than 2,500 runs in a season, including an innings of 243 at Trent Bridge against Middlesex.

William Arnold Sime is notable in that he went on to become a High Court Judge in 1972. A notable Rugby player with Bedford, Notts and East Midlands – he also had an England trial – he served on the Nottinghamshire CCC committee and became President of the club.

Arthur Jepson opened the bowling for Nottinghamshire for many years, and he was a real workhorse on those flat, unresponsive pitches. He had to be. He also played football for Stoke City, part of a great side with Stanley Matthews, Neil Franklin and Frank Soo. When we umpired together in later years, at both county and Test level, Arthur told me of the time he played for Stoke against Middlesbrough in the sixth round of the FA Cup at Ayresome Park.

Apparently the team talk in the Middlesbrough dressing room focused on the need to 'rile Jepson', because Arthur had a tendency to become over-excited, and when he did, his game suffered. They planned it out, and Wilf Mannion – what a great player he was – was given the job of riling Arthur. He didn't manage it until the dying seconds of the game, when, with the score still at 0–0, he elbowed Arthur in the ribs at a corner. Well, Arthur went potty. He raced after his opponent, calling him all the names under the sun, and while he was busy doing so, Middlesbrough lobbed the ball into the net to win 1–0 and clinch a place in the semi-final.

Another of my umpiring colleagues who played for Nottinghamshire was Bob White, an off-spin bowler and good left-hand batsman. Normally we do not make a big issue of which end we stand on the opening day of a match, but Bob always used to decide by rolling dice. High number one end, low number the other. To my knowledge he never rolled them to make an umpiring decision!

Reg Simpson and Cyril Poole were two other famous postwar batsmen, who shared an astonishing match-winning unbroken second-wicket stand of 251 against Leicestershire in 1949. The remarkable thing about that partnership was the short time it took them to rattle up those runs: the 100 came up in forty minutes, the 200 in seventy-five minutes and the 251 in ninety-seven minutes.

Simpson, who is now a committee member and a Vice-President, was captain when I first played against Notts in 1960, but he relinquished the position at the end of the season.

Three years later Brian Bolus, the former Yorkshire opener, made a real impact for Nottinghamshire, scoring 2,190 runs, including five centuries, one of them against Yorkshire. That kind of form earned him a call-up to the England team for the fourth and fifth Tests against the West Indies, and also for the MCC tour of India.

Bolus, who also played for Derbyshire, had a reputation for playing more with his pads than his bat, and Essex captain 'Tonker' Taylor never let him forget it. Whenever Bolus went out to open the innings, 'Tonker' was waiting for him. He would get the new ball and start ramming it into Brian's pads. 'Just giving you a bit of practice,' he would say.

In 1968, Notts signed up that great West Indian captain and all-rounder Garfield Sobers, and in his first season he scored 1,570 runs and took 83 wickets to send the county soaring to the dizzy heights of fourth in the table. Test calls, however, continued to restrict Sobers' appearances, and not even his inspirational play could maintain that improvement. While outstanding individual performances were maintained, team success still eluded the county.

In 1974 Notts turned to Jack Bond, who had enjoyed extra-ordinary success with Lancashire, particularly on the one-day scene. His reign was short lived, however, and he failed to repeat the triumphs of his Old Trafford days, probably because he did not have the same quality of players to work with. No Clive Lloyd, Farokh Engineer, David Lloyd, Jack Simmons, Barry Wood or Frank Hayes to call on now.

That was when Clive Rice was brought in, and 1975 saw the start of better things.

I have mentioned Richard Hadlee and Derek Randall from that era, but other outstanding performers during Rice's mag-nificent eight-year spell in charge were Bruce French, Chris Broad, Tim Robinson and Mike Hendrick.

French was an outstanding wicketkeeper, and played for England. He became the youngest player to play for the county, at the age of sixteen years and ten months, and holds the record for the number of wicketkeeping dismissals in a match at ten – seven caught and three stumped. He holds the record number in a season, eighty-seven in 1984, the same season he was voted Wicketkeeper of the Year.

The one big handicap of this former warehouseman, window cleaner and brickies' labourer, is that he has always been a bit accident prone. Consider the following catalogue of misfortune.

Bruce was hit in the chest by the ball, when touring Australia, and later contracted a chest infection. On a tour of Pakistan he needed stitches to a cut eye after being hit by a spectator's throw during a practice session. On his way to hospital for the stitches, he was struck on the leg by a car; and after treatment for that injury he banged his head on a light fitting. He missed another Test against Pakistan because of chicken pox. In the West Indies he was bitten by a dog while jogging, and in that same year, during the second Test at Lord's he was carried off with concussion after being hit by a short-pitched delivery from Richard Hadlee – his county colleague! He missed most of the 1988 season following an operation in May on the index finger of his left hand, having broken the same finger two years previously. It had been giving him a lot of trouble in the pre-season nets and he was advised to have immediate surgery to fuse a split bone in the top joint.

The next year he broke the same finger again!

Can you believe that such a person should list his other sporting interests as rock climbing, fell walking and all aspects of mountaineering?

Broad was signed from Gloucestershire in 1984 to form a new opening partnership with Tim Robinson, a very good player who had developed through the old cricket nursery at Sutton-in-Ashfield. Tim was a very private man. Really quiet. He captained the side for eight years between 1988 and

1995 and became very close friends with Yorkshire's Martyn Moxon.

Broad opened for England, but he blotted his copybook on a tour of Australia when he knocked the stumps over with a swipe of his bat after getting out. Chris always maintained that it was purely an immediate reaction to a bad mistake. He knew it was wrong, but he did not believe he should have been hauled over the coals for it. Some members of the press even called for him to be sent home, which infuriated him.

At the next Test, in Christchurch, New Zealand, he made a century and was forced, by the terms of the contract, to talk to the same press who had wanted him banished from the team. His rapport with certain members of that press corps was 'tarnished beyond repair', as he put it.

These days, however, Chris works for television and the press! His philosophy is, 'We all have a job to do. We should help each other.' That is exactly how it should be.

Hendrick spent most of his career at Derbyshire, joining Notts in 1982 and eventually becoming coach for a while. He

caused a chuckle on BBC TV one day when he said, 'I thought he was going to dive and decapitate himself – badly.'

These days Nottinghamshire have several young players coming through who could go on to make a name for themselves.

They have a very good wicketkeeper in twenty-four-year-old Chris Read, a Northampton lad who represented his country at schoolboy through to Under-19 level, went on tour with England A to South Africa and Zimbabwe in the winter of 1998–9, and made his Test debut against New Zealand in 1999.

Also on the South Africa/Zimbabwe tour was Paul Franks, a twenty-year-old left-hand batsman and right-arm fast-medium bowler who is another candidate for the full England side. He played for Young England when they won the World Cup and was the youngest Nottinghamshire player to score a hat-trick, at the age of 18 years 163 days against Warwickshire in 1997.

The third player who caught my eye in my last season umpiring was opening bowler Andy Oram. I was very impressed in the first innings against Surrey at Trent Bridge when he took 4 for 37 in 21 overs.

It was also during my last season on the first-class list that I met Stephen King, the American thriller writer. He had read my autobiography, and although he did not have a clue about cricket, enjoyed the book so much that he decided he would like to know more about this strange game.

Arrangements were made for him to come over and meet me at Trent Bridge, where I was umpiring the Sunday League game between Notts and Surrey. It turned into a bit of a horror story, however, as it chucked it down with rain all day and we didn't bowl a ball. Trent Bridge was awash.

I ended up taking Stephen into the dressing rooms to meet the players of both teams, who, of course, were all waiting with their copies of his latest book for him to sign. Then I walked out to the middle with him. In the pouring rain. Under a big brolly. Trying to explain to him about this great game of cricket which he had never seen played. I honestly don't know what he made of it. He had come all the way from America to watch, and he went back home still not having seen a ball bowled.

Maybe now that I have retired he will come back and try again. If I am not umpiring, he obviously stands a much better chance of avoiding the rain.

Taunton

SOMERSET

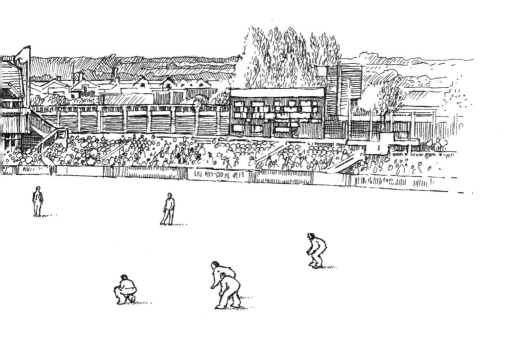

13

THE first thing I always did when I arrived at eight thirty for the opening day of a match at Taunton was to call the groundsman over and ask, 'Nar then, mate, where's t' owd cockerel's backside today?'

The fowl in question was perched on top of one of the neighbouring church spires, and I knew that if its backside faced towards the ground, then I would have to beware. Bad light. Rain. Floods. Storms. If the head was looking out over the cricket field, however, then I could relax. It was going to be beautiful. Sun. Blue skies. Warm breezes. Ideal conditions.

It is such a lovely setting at Taunton: church spires at one end, Quantock Hills visibile in the distance at the other, with the River Tone meandering on its way round the back of the pavilion. A typical rural scene, all adding up to one of the most pleasant grounds in the country. Just a pity that it is such a long, long drive from Barnsley!

The pitch has always been good at Taunton, going right back into history. There have been some real belters. One day, when I was playing for Leicestershire, I came across a batsman's dream. It was one of the flattest pitches I had ever seen, and I looked forward eagerly to a really big score, maybe even putting my record 181 for Yorkshire against Glamorgan at Bradford into the shade.

I had nudged a couple of singles, just to get my eye in, when I played forward to a ball from Ken Palmer, a fine all-rounder who later became a colleague of mine on the first-class umpires' list. It was in line with the middle stump, but I played forward confidently. Just before it should have hit the bat, the ball moved away off the seam and knocked my off-stump out of the ground. It was a magnificent delivery, I had to admit, but how had Ken managed it on such a flat track? Willie Watson and Alan Wharton both got big hundreds after I'd departed, and I don't think Ken managed another wicket.

Whenever we umpired together I used to ask him, 'Tell me the truth, Kenny, did you pick the seam that day to get me out like that?' He always used to smile – and say nowt. I still don't know. He'll not let on.

Despite my bitter disappointment that day, Taunton was always a good place to visit, particularly if you were a batsman. Somerset were not one of the strongest championship sides, so they were unlikely to turn you over, yet you could always be assured of a friendly welcome.

A big upheaval came about in the 1970s and '80s, with the advent of Brian Close, Ian Botham, Viv Richards and Joel Garner, who combined to bring a much more competitive edge

to Somerset's play – and with it the county's first successes. In five seasons they won all the limited-overs titles – the Gillette/NatWest in 1979 and 1983, the Benson and Hedges Cup in 1981 and 1982, and the Sunday League in 1979.

The county championship, however, has continued to elude them, although they have finished third on five occasions – 1892, 1958, 1963, 1966 and 1981.

Botham, of course, attracted a great deal of publicity during his years with the club, and some of his big-hitting exploits have gone down in Somerset folklore, but he was by no means the first batsman of that cavalier style to thrill the Taunton crowds.

Talk to any of the locals and they will regale you with stories of some of the heroes of the past. Tales of Sammy Woods are recounted with a certain amount of awe. In 1891, for example, when Somerset beat the champions, Surrey, at Taunton, it was Woods, the captain, who bowled John Sharpe, Surrey's one-eyed number eleven, to win the match, proving that he could also bowl a bit, as well as smash the ball to all parts of the ground.

Since Sammy there have been a lot of the long-handle experts. Between the wars there were few batsmen who could hit the ball harder than Guy Earle, according to the old-timers, who were of the opinion that when Earle batted, his sole purpose was to knock the ball clean out of the ground as often as possible.

He was followed by Arthur Wellard, who, like Woods, could also turn his arm over to good effect. He made a quarter of his career's total of runs in sixes. About five hundred of them. He very nearly beat Garfield Sobers to the six sixes in an over record by a fair few years, hitting five, one after the other, against Derbyshire in 1936 and then against Kent in 1938.

On the second occasion the bowler was Frank Woolley, and off the sixth ball Wellard was dropped in front of the pavilion. Woolley's comments, I am reliably informed, were unprintable.

Wellard also held the county record of sixty-six sixes in a season, until I. T. Botham came along in 1985 and rattled up eighty.

In the period from 1935 to 1954, just before I appeared on the county scene, there was no more exciting a batsman than Harold Gimblett, who achieved legendary status in his first appearance for the county at Frome, which is no longer a venue for the Somerset side.

As a twenty-year-old, Harold had been for a trial at Taunton, but had been rejected, and he was really down in the dumps when he returned to his father's farm near Watchet. He perked up, however, when the county sent for him to play against Essex.

Unfortunately, he missed the only bus available, and had to walk it to the ground. How far he did actually walk that day I'm not sure, but it was a long, long way and he only just made it in time for the start of the game.

When Gimblett eventually took his place at the crease, Somerset were 107 for 6 and in all sorts of trouble. Nobody believed that this young whippersnapper of a farmer's boy would be able to stop the rot. He was, after all, a raw novice, with no previous county experience, and he would surely be absolutely exhausted after his marathon walk.

Spectators could not credit what they saw with their own eyes. Gimblett scored 50 in 28 minutes, 100 in 63 minutes, and ended up with 123 in 80 minutes. It was the most sensational county debut of all time, and he continued in that vein throughout a remarkable career. He still holds the record for the most runs for Somerset – a grand total of 21,142.

Another memorable occasion, this time at Taunton in 1925, saw Jack Hobbs equalling W. G. Grace's record of 126 centuries, in a great season during which he scored 3,000 runs and topped the batting averages. Somerset were on the receiving end of that particular century onslaught.

Among the early big-hitters was Leonard Crawley, who, it is said, cleared not only the kiddies' play area and the pines, but also the church at Clarence Park, Weston-Super-Mare, with a massive straight six. Although it is hard to believe that, it was just about possible for Crawley, who was also an accomplished golfer, having won the England Amateur Championship and represented his country in the Walker Cup. A drive straight down the middle was probably a doddle for him.

Weston-Super-Mare is a very small ground, but on a hot summer's day it offers traditional seaside county cricket at its best. The pavilion, its one permanent building, is enhanced by temporary stands, tents, deckchairs, folding chairs, small caravans for press and scorers, and colourful advertising boards. There is not much space at the boundary's edge, so the ground appears full, and the fact that spectators are so close to the field of play gives a very intimate feel to the place.

I have no doubt that my old mate Botham has an affection for Clarence Park, for it was there in 1985 that he hit ten sixes on his way to 134, and it was there, too, that Vic Marks, in his tenth season with the county, finally scored his maiden hundred for them in 1984.

A Tiverton man, who played for England, Vic was better known as an off-spin bowler. He was coached as a boy by Ernest Steele, who had a spell as groundsman at Barnsley Cricket Club and also Barnsley Football Club.

Somerset also play at Bath, a lovely city of honey-coloured stone. The Recreation Ground is a natural amphitheatre which is also the home of Bath Rugby Club, whose pitch is used as a car park during county matches. Wooded hills, the River Avon and the abbey combine to provide yet another fine setting for a June cricket festival, when enthusiasts can also take advantage of the famous spa waters.

The Recreation Ground's low-lying position close to the river has meant that Bath has always had the reputation of producing a damp pitch which has assisted bowlers and made batting a bit of a lottery at times.

It was hardly surprising that Bertie Buse, the Somerset all-rounder, should choose the Recreation Ground in his home city to stage his benefit match in 1953. The pitch, however, left a good deal to be desired, and poor old Bertie ended up in an acute state of depression. An hour before the end of play on the first day, Somerset had slumped to a stunning defeat by an innings and 24 runs at the hands of Lancashire – and by taking 6 for 41 in Lancashire's only innings, Bertie himself had contributed to the early finish!

One former Somerset player who went on to join me on the first-class umpires' list was Bill Alley, the extrovert Australian who, in 1961, created the county's record for most runs in a season, 2,761, which still stands today. His total of 3,109 – most from leg-hits – made him the most prolific batsman in the country that year, with no less than ten hundreds included in his total.

What makes it even more remarkable is that he was at least forty-two years old at the time. I say at least, because I reckon he was even older. Bill always claimed that he did not have a birth certificate, and I am sure he lied about his age. I tackled him about it more than once, but he never let on how old he really was. What is known is that he came to England to play as a professional for Colne in the Lancashire League. After several successful seasons with them he moved to Blackpool in the Northern League, and just about re-wrote all the record books. For example, in 1953, he totalled 1,345 runs at an amazing average of 149.44. In that year he hit three unbeaten centuries of 144, 126 and 105. The following year he made four centuries, again all not out; in 1955 he topped the ton seven times, including six not-outs; and in 1956 had five more three-figure innings, three of them unbeaten.

Northern League bowlers were mightily relieved when he joined Somerset in 1957, but the runs continued to flow – taking his career total to nearly 20,000.

A left-hand batsman, he was also a good bowler, taking 768 first-class wickets, and there were few better close-to-the-wicket fielders, as those who fell victim to his 293 catches, mostly at gully, will testify.

Bill umpired at Test match level, and not many players dared tangle with him; before he came over to this country, he had been a very good welterweight boxer, with an unbeaten record in twenty-eight professional bouts.

In 1961 Bill shared a record sixth-wicket stand of 265 against Northamptonshire with another good all-rounder, Ken Palmer, who also served on the Test match panel, along with his brother, Roy, who opened the bowling for Somerset.

Peter Wight was another Somerset player to join me on umpiring duty, and I well remember one particular game he played against Yorkshire at Taunton in 1962. Peter never fancied facing Freddie Trueman – well, who did? Peter simply could not get any runs at all against Fiery, who used to knock him over as soon as he came in, either clean bowled, lbw, caught behind, or snapped up at slip. I don't think he ever got into double figures. However, on this occasion, Yorkshire captain Vic Wilson ordered Fred to return home after leaving him out of the side for being late in reporting to the ground, and Peter celebrated by scoring a big double hundred!

Johnny Lawrence was a Yorkshireman who played all his

career at Somerset, but he did develop an excellent indoor school 'back home' at Rothwell, near Leeds, where Geoff Boycott, Jack Birkenshaw, Don Wilson, myself and quite a few others used to practise. The specially designed pitch there used to take spin, and that is where we learned to play spin bowling.

Johnny had a caravan that he used to tow to all the Somerset games. When Jack Birkenshaw was a lad, he used to spend his holidays down there with Johnny and the family. He took the opportunity of bowling to all the great Somerset players in the nets, and learned an awful lot. Jack always used to say that there was only one county he wanted to play for, and that was Yorkshire. Failing that, it would be Somerset. How he ended up at Leicestershire, therefore, is a mystery to me.

Lawrence bowled leg-spinners and googlies and was scorned by Yorkshire, who never believed in playing that type of bowler. They argued that a slow left-armer did a better job, because he not only left the bat, but had more control. Johnny exploded that theory every time he played against his home county. He would bowl them out for fun.

Harold Stephenson was a fine wicketkeeper who wrote his name in the record books, claiming 1,007 dismissals in a career which ran from 1948 to 1964, including eighty-three in one season.

Roy Virgin was with Somerset for many years and scored a lot of runs for them, although not on one highly embarrassing occasion when, halfway to the middle, he realised that he had forgotten his bat. Red faced, he turned round and went back to the pavilion to fetch it. Eventually he joined his partner, took guard, shouldered arms to the first ball, and had his off-stump knocked over. Why on earth did he bother to go back for the bat?

The decision to sign forty-year-old Brian Close from Yorkshire in 1971 really provided the spark which was to ignite Somerset and turn them into a trophy-winning side. It was said that Closey disliked one-day cricket, he was rumoured to be less than fully fit, and he had a reputation for bluntness. Not, maybe, the type of man to fit in easily in rural Somerset.

However, he missed very few games before retiring in 1977. He proved inspirational with his fearless batting and fielding, instilled discipline into the side, and injected a new determination and will to succeed.

The only problem with Closey was that nothing was ever his fault. If he failed at anything, it was always as a result of some outside influence over which he had no control.

Once, at Trent Bridge, he went out to bat in a bid to avert a Barry Stead hat-trick. The scoreboard read 42 for 3. As he came out, he had a quick word with the outgoing batsman, Richard Cooper. There was a hush as Stead came in, with nine men huddled round the bat. Ever the one to take the bull by the horns, Closey aimed an almighty swipe at the hat-trick ball. It was bold, brave, and not as daft as it looked, because there was only one man, Nirmal Nanan, in the outfield. Unluckily for Closey, although he made good contact, the ball seemed to be attracted like a magnet to Nanan's hands and the fielder took the catch. The ground erupted.

All was quiet, however, in the Somerset dressing room as the players waited for the inevitable explosion when Closey stormed in. Sure enough, he hurled his bat to the floor, glared at the unfortunate Cooper, and snarled, 'Bloody hell, lad, you said it were swinging, but you never said it were seaming an' all.'

Another time, at Worcester, Closey struggled to get the ball off the square while Peter Roebuck was going like an express train at the other end. After a few overs Closey strode down the pitch to have a word with his partner, who thought he was about to be congratulated by his captain on the magnificent way he was dealing with the Worcestershire attack.

Muttered Closey, 'Can you try explaining how it is that they're bowling so many good balls to me and all t' bloody crap to thee?'

There was a similar episode when Closey was batting with Brian Rose. It was early in the game and Closey was taking most of the strike, with Rose a virtual spectator. After an over or two, Rose went up to Closey and asked him what the ball was doing. Was it swinging? Was it moving off the seam? Was it doing anything through the air? Said Closey, 'It's shifting all over t' bloody place, lad. Coorse, I'll be all reight, but you might struggle.'

Roebuck, incidentally, was a fine cricketer. At one time I thought he might have captained England, but he never even played for his country. These days he is a top-class writer for one of the quality dailies in England during the summer, and for the Australian press in the winter.

Closey was full of words of wisdom, as demonstrated when Somerset were playing Nottinghamshire at Bath. After the fall of an early wicket, the great Garfield Sobers strode out to bat. Tom Cartwright, who had taken stacks of wickets for Somerset, was bowling at the time, and he and Closey between them had more than fifty years of experience. The younger Somerset players were keen to earwig as the two got together for a consultation, wondering what magical tactical ploy they were about to conjure up to get Sobers out.

'Reight, Tom,' said Closey. 'Just remember, this lad's a left-hander.' And with that he strolled off to take up his fielding position.

He was also the proverbial bull in the china shop. I remember him being presented with a sponsored car, posing for the cameras holding the keys, getting in, driving off – and running straight into a lorry.

What I particularly liked about Closey was the way he led from the front. He never asked any of his players to do anything that he himself was not prepared to do.

I was umpiring a match between Somerset and the Australians at Bath when Closey was fielding in a typically suicidal position at silly point. The batsman stepped into a full toss and hit it so hard that it would have ended up on the other side of the city had it not struck Closey. He never flinched. He said nothing. Did nothing. He did not even bend down to rub his leg where the ball had thudded into him.

I went up to him, concerned. 'Are you all right, Closey?' I asked.

'Aye, nowt to worry about, lad,' he replied. 'Let's get on wi' t' bloody game.'

Later in the day, when he thought no one was looking, I caught him rolling up his trouser leg to survey the damage. I tell you, without a word of a lie, that a raw joint in a butcher's shop window was nothing compared to Closey's leg where the ball had hit him, but he did not go off the field for treatment, or even call for treatment on it. That was Brian.

He seemed indestructible. He once walked through a glass door and escaped without a scratch.

He retired in 1977, but returned to Somerset eight years later to play in a friendly, and it was still the same old Closey. Nothing had changed. He was still the boss man, chin jutting out, muttering and chuntering all the time.

Viv Richards skied the last ball of the innings, and it made its way towards Closey on the boundary edge. He ran round in circles, trying to get in position, but the fifty-four-year-old had neither the legs nor the judgment of his younger days, and the ball thudded to the turf a fair way from where Closey was waiting with cupped hands. Players wanted to laugh, it looked so funny, but laugh they dare not, although some found it hard to suppress the odd giggle as they trooped off.

It was just like old times in the dressing room. Total silence as they waited for Closey to say something. There was no outburst this time, but after a few moments he looked up and exclaimed, 'Nowt's changed, has it? It's still a funny old game, is this. I got into t' reight position, you know, but bloody ball fell too quickly.'

That was Closey all over. What a man. What a player. What a captain. I have nothing but admiration for him. Maybe one or two players were a bit scared of him, but they all respected him. He'd never let them down. Always backed them. Somerset have a lot to thank him for.

Success, however, was to elude him. Not until Brian Rose took over as captain and built on the good foundation that Close had left, did Somerset embark on their run of one-day trophies. In his first season, 1978, Rose led his side to a thrilling finale which saw them in the final of the Gillette Cup and with the prospect of also winning the John Player League. They failed to win either, but the following year they did carry off both those titles. Further success in the Benson and Hedges and Gillette/NatWest were to follow under Rose's excellent leadership.

Another Rose also bloomed for Somerset. He was all-rounder Graham, no relation to the skipper. He was a magnificent striker of the ball, and he deserved one-day international honours. He broke the record for the quickest NatWest Cup century, scored off only 36 balls against Devon at Torquay, Somerset totalling 413, which was also a competition record.

In one Sunday League match he scored an unbeaten 148 against Glamorgan at Neath, and at the close did a quick-march to the pavilion, before charging up the steps for his third rub-down of the day. Graham claimed he needed three or four massages to keep him supple, although the Somerset lads claimed that it was only because the new physio was a woman. I wouldn't know about that.

The big-hitting bonanza continued with a vengeance with the arrival of Ian Botham and Viv Richards. One match in particular that I remember was at Taunton when both of them were in full flight together. It was Earle and Wellard all over again, only more so. The big crowd had never seen anything quite like it.

The Taunton press box is situated right in the firing line at long-on, and Viv and Both had a bet as to who could land a ball right inside. Well, they both succeeded. There was glass everywhere as the windows were smashed. They needed danger money, did those press lads, or helmets, at least. One of them ducked to avoid one mighty six which winged its way towards him, and when he got back up he saw that the ball had landed in his egg sandwich.

It was exciting stuff, but despite the spectators always being well entertained when these two were at the crease, success in the county championship continued to prove elusive.

The 1985 season was typical. In the first three champion-ship matches at Taunton, Both scored 90 off 77 balls, 112 (including a century off 76 balls) and 149 off 106 balls, yet all three games were lost. In the third of those matches Richards made 186, and the next time Somerset played at Taunton the West Indian made the highest score by a Somerset player – 322 off 258 balls. Beefy went on to establish a new record of sixes for the season, made the three fastest hundreds of the year, and averaged 100 in the championship. Yet, unbelievably, Somerset still finished bottom of the county championship table.

Beefy could never resist a challenge, and when he was chatting over a pint or four with Lancashire tail-ender Paul Allott prior to a match at Taunton, he was persuaded to bowl his opponent a ball he could smash for six, hopefully straight out of the ground, and, even better, into the River Tone.

Naturally, though, Both wanted a payback. 'Fine by me,' he agreed, 'providing I can clean bowl you with the next delivery.' So the deal was struck.

Next morning Both kept his part of the bargain. He bowled a long hop, Walter – Allott's nickname – flung his bat with rare gusto, and the ball disappeared over the pavilion and into the river for six. I'll bet that river has some tales to tell: a lot of cricket balls must have been fished out of there.

Walter clearly forgot the rest of the script, however. He did a Barnacle Boycott impression and scratched around for the best part of an hour before an increasingly angry Botham managed finally to get one past his bat to flatten the stumps. Walter then had the barefaced cheek to help scuttle Somerset's second innings, the home team collapsing hopelessly to 119 all out after being set a modest target of 140 to win in well over 200 minutes.

Walter thanked Both many times over for the six-hit gift, although, according to the great man himself, never did have the decency to apologise for not allowing himself to be bowled next ball – or giving the Somerset all-rounder a similar delivery to get off the mark on a future occasion.

What more can you say about Both? Forget about some of the bad press he has had. Not only has he been one of England's greatest cricketers – somewhere along the line he would do something to win you a Test match – his influence in the dressing rooms has also been immense. He would certainly be the first name on my team sheet. On top of that, he has done some magnificent work for charity on those marathon walks of his.

All I can say is, thanks for the happy memories, Beefy. It was a real pleasure being around at the same time as you.

You need bowlers as well as big hitters, of course, to be successful, even in one-day cricket, and Somerset had one of the best at that time in Joel Garner.

I remember Joel playing his first match for Somerset against Australia in May, 1977. He was on trial at the time. Greg Chappell, who also played for Somerset for a couple of seasons and was the first player to score a century in the John Player League, made 90-odd before lunch at Bath, but did not last long after the resumption. He was bowled by Garner for 113 and the big West Indian went on to finish with 4 for 66 in 20 overs, eight of which were maidens. In the second innings Chappell was caught by Garner off the bowling of Botham, having made 39, and Somerset beat the Aussies by seven wickets. Believe me, that takes some doing by a county side.

After the match Brian Close told the Somerset boys, 'If this fella Garner signs for us we'll win the championship.' Well, they didn't quite manage that, but 'Big Bird' – all 6ft 8ins of him – did play a key role in their subsequent one-day triumphs.

Off-spinner Brian Langford also did his part, and he bowled himself into the record books against Essex at Yeovil in the first year of the John Player League, when every one of his allotted eight overs was a maiden, thus creating a record that can only be equalled.

Tom Cartwright was another fine all-rounder, and he proved a formidable force in combination with the wicketkeeping skills of Derek Taylor, a big mate of mine, who used to stand up to him. In one match I turned down an lbw appeal by Tom and thought no more about it until I went to the toilet during the lunch interval. Who should be there but Tom and Derek, doing what comes naturally and chatting about the morning's play. They didn't notice me.

'Here, Derek,' said Tom, 'what did you think about that lbw appeal that Dickie turned down?'

Replied Derek, 'It was plumb. No doubt about it.'

Did I give them some stick. 'I heard that,' I said. 'Right, I'm here now. Tell me that to my face.' I've continued to give them stick every time I've seen them since, although sadly I don't get much opportunity with Derek these days, as he lives in Australia.

Kerry O'Keefe made the trip the other way, coming over here from Down Under to bowl his leg-breaks and googlies. He was unfortunate to have Brian Close as his captain, because Closey had the typical Yorkshire attitude of believing that such a bowler was an extravagance.

Other overseas stars have included Jimmy Cook (South Africa), who came close to breaking Bill Alley's record runs in a season, finishing just short of 3,000; Sunil Gavaskar (India), Martin Crowe (New Zealand) and Mushtaq Mohammad (Pakistan).

When Mushy arrived, he was told to report for practice at a certain time, but failed to turn up. Nobody knew where he was, so they sent out a search party. He was eventually found in the local Asda. He had never been in a supermarket before and he was having a whale of a time. There he was, with his trolley, throwing everything in – including a cartload of curries.

233

Gavaskar scored a lot of runs for Somerset, but he did not have too happy a time of it when I umpired with Ken Palmer at Taunton in July, 1980. He made only 17 and 6 in the two innings against Kent, yet Somerset won by six wickets, largely due to an unlikely ninth-wicket stand of 179 – only four short of the county record – between tailenders Nigel Popplewell and Dennis Breakwell. They made 135 not out and 73 not out respectively in the first innings to rescue their side from 197 for 8 to 376 for 8.

Co-holders of that record ninth-wicket partnership of 183 are Chris Tavaré, who captained the side for three years between 1990 and 1992, and Neil Mallender. There is no way, however, that Tavaré can be included among the list of big-hitting crowd-pleasers who have graced the Somerset scene through the years.

Journalist Martin Johnson one revealed that he used to carry a box of pigeons by way of insurance, just in case the telephone lines went down. One day, he said, it backfired on him. He was strapping an account of a six-hour Tavaré innings on to the pigeon's back when he realised that the poor bird had fallen into a deep coma. By the time he managed to revive it, the last edition of his paper had long gone.

Martin was only half joking. Many's the time I've had to shake myself when Chris has been batting. I've been standing there at square leg and felt myself nodding off, and have had to pinch myself to keep focused. 'Come on, Dickie, lad, don't fall asleep on the job. What will Lord's think? Get a grip of yourself.' It was hard work keeping my eyes open, and I would even put some matchsticks in my pocket. The poor pigeon had my sympathy.

One of the most talented of the current crop of young players at Somerset is Marcus Trescothick, a left-handed batsman with bags of potential. He went off the rails a bit at one time, and put weight on through eating too much junk food. The powers that be had a long chat with him, told him to sort himself out, and he has done. These days he is vice-captain, which could bring the best out of the boy. He is certainly captaincy material, as he proved when he skippered England Under-19s against the West Indies, and on tours of South Africa and Sri Lanka.

Marcus's career has mirrored that of Anthony McGrath, of Yorkshire. Both broke all records as schoolboys, and everyone said that if they progressed in the right way they would soon be in the full England team.

Another who has not quite fulfilled his early promise is Mark Lathwell, although he has played twice for England at full Test level. He suffered through too many coaches telling him how he should play, instead of leaving him to get on with it and develop his own style. He is the type of batsman who knows his limitations, and should have been left alone. He is twenty-seven now and has long since passed the 'promising youngster' stage.

Marcus is known as 'Banger', because of all the sausages he eats. He has always maintained that 'the size of the lunches at most

grounds cannot possibly sustain you all day in the field.' Mind you, at 6ft 3ins he's a big lad. Takes some filling.

Having been tutored by Dennis Lillee and Jeff Thomson in Madras, where the two great Australians coach the Indian fast bowlers, Matthew Bulbeck is one who could come through at full international level. He played for England Under-19s in 1998 and had previous experience with England Under-15s in the West Indies, and Somerset Under-16s in South Africa.

Andy Caddick has taken a lot of wickets in the county championship, and he looked very impressive when I umpired him against Northants at Taunton towards the end of my final season, taking 5 for 70 and 4 for 45 in that game. However, for some reason he cannot seem to reproduce those kinds of figures on a regular basis when he plays for England. On his county form, he would be an automatic choice, but he has so far lacked the vital consistency at Test level.

Finally, before I leave the county, one painful and one amusing reflection of my delightful days in Somerset.

In 1986 I arrived for the third day's play in the match between Somerset and Worcestershire at Weston-Super-Mare. As I parked my car, my left leg locked completely – the result of a back problem. I could not get out of the car, and my fellow umpire John Hampshire was fetched to lift me out. There was no way I could umpire. I could hardly move, let alone stand.

Somerset man, Alan Whitehead, was called to stand in for me. He lived at Wells, which was not too far away. Alan is a fine umpire, and a bit of a character, as I'm sure he will not mind me saying. He tosses a coin to decide which end we stand, and in thirty years with him I never won the toss once. I always challenged him to show me both sides of the coin, but he never would. 'Don't you trust me, Dickie?' he would complain. I've always been convinced it was a double header, and now I've retired I'm determined to find out.

So, back to Taunton. Picture the scene. The third day of a county game. The cockerel had decreed that the weather would be favourable, and the crowd was enjoying some typically entertaining cricket in the sun.

At the fall of one wicket in the afternoon the fielders stood around waiting for the next batsman to appear. Instead, to their amazement, a woman with a parasol and a large picnic basket came down the pavilion steps, walked straight across the field and into the crowd at the opposite end of the ground.

The mystery was later solved. It was discovered that the same woman had brought her husband's tea on the previous two days, crossing the ground while the official interval was in progress. She did not know that tea was taken at a different time on the third day!

The Oval

SURREY

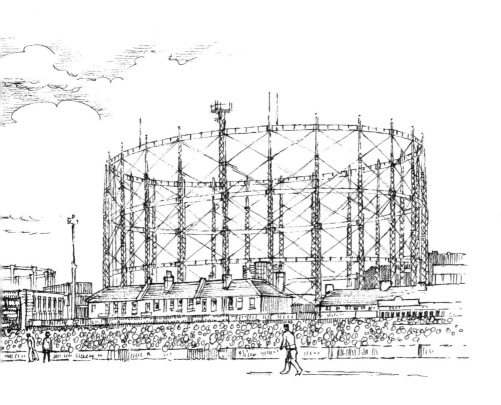

14

IT IS remarkable how many county grounds are identified by certain individual features. With the Oval it is the gas holders.

I found myself perched right on top of one of them during an England v. West Indies Test – although not physically. We were out there in the middle when the players called my attention to a large blow-up of myself displayed on a gas-holder advert extolling the virtues of cooking chicken by gas. Next thing everybody was staring up at it. Not just the players, but the other umpire, the crowd – and those watching on television, as the cameras zoomed in. Of course, the lads had a dig at me. 'Bet you're earning a fortune from that, Dickie.' I knew nothing about it, however, and I never got a ha'penny for it. Not even a boiled egg.

Alf Gover, the great Surrey fast bowler, was also to be seen 'cooking with gas' as soon as he resolved which end he should bowl from. He preferred to work downwind, so his first job on a morning was to find out which direction the wind was blowing, which he discovered by the smell either of the local breweries or the gas holders!

I once managed to lose my fellow umpire, Barrie Leadbeater, at the Oval. All the doors there have security keypads, and, believe me, there are a lot of doors. After lunch in a one-day game between Surrey and Gloucestershire, I came out of the umpires' dressing room, through door after door, punching keypad after keypad, immersed in my own thoughts, but believing that Ledders was following on behind.

As I eventually strode out on to the pitch, one of the players shouted to me, 'Hey, Dickie, where's your mate?' I looked round. No Ledders.

'Goodness knows where he's got to,' I replied. 'You'll have to hold on a minute while I try to find him.' I shouted, 'Ledders!' at the top of my voice, by which time the crowd had cottoned on to what had happened.

I eventually discovered Ledders back in the umpires' room, banging on the door. He was locked in. How he managed that, I'll never know. He's a lovely man, and a good umpire, but he can be dozy at times.

The Oval itself is an enormous ground, with excellent facilities. There have been many alterations and improvements down the years, and it is now a magnificent Test match arena. The pitches there have always been excellent, and the Test strips have been some of the best in the world. This is due in no small measure to Harry Brind, now retired, who went on to become inspector of pitches for the England and Wales Cricket Board. His son has now taken over as head groundsman with a tremendous staff of hard-working lads who have carried on the good work.

Another feature of the Oval are the Hobbs Gates, in honour of that great Surrey and England cricketer Jack Hobbs, one of the best batsmen of all time. He played for thirty years and produced an aggregate of 61,237 runs – a total that has never been bettered. A quite remarkable record, it included 197 hundreds and was accumulated at an average of 50.65.

Despite such individual brilliance, however, Surrey enjoyed only one county championship success during Hobbs's career, in 1914, an astonishing statistic when you consider that they have won the title fifteen times outright – more than any county except Yorkshire – plus one shared with Lancashire in 1950.

Their triumphs came during two dominant spells, at the turn of the century (1890, 1891, 1892, 1894, 1895, 1899 and 1914) and in the 'fifties (1952, 1953, 1954, 1955, 1956, 1957 and 1958). Their latest success was in 1971.

They have not done so well in the limited-overs game, their only victories being in the NatWest Trophy in 1982, the Benson and Hedges in 1974 and 1997, and the Sunday League in 1996.

Percy Fender was a magnificent player in the early part of the century. He captained the side for twelve years, and was acknowledged as one of the most astute and boldest skippers in the game, who led from the front. When Surrey wanted runs, Percy would get them. When Surrey wanted wickets, Percy would oblige with his leg-breaks.

The fastest hundred in first-class cricket, made in thirty-five minutes at Northampton in 1920, flowed from the Fender bat. It was technically equalled more than sixty years later by Lancashire's Steve O'Shaughnessy, but Fender still holds it morally, since the young Lancastrian took at least eight more balls than his predecessor, and his achievement was cheapened by the fact that Leicestershire were just tossing the ball up at the time trying to buy a declaration.

After that Old Trafford encounter the two joint record-holders were introduced to each other, Fender then ninety-one years old.

Fender also held a world bowling record for forty-five years, having taken six wickets for one run in eleven balls against Middlesex at Lord's in 1927. That record was broken by another Surrey spinner, Pat Pocock, at Eastbourne, in 1972, when he claimed six Sussex wickets in nine balls, and seven in eleven balls.

I have already mentioned the quality of the pitches at the Oval through the years, but going right back into history they were maybe just too good. The groundsmen got into the habit of preparing them so that they were as faultless as possible for batting, which was all very well, but it proved difficult to get results when the odds were so heavily weighted in favour of the batsmen.

One of the most famous of these perfectionist groundsmen was 'Bosser' Martin, who was quite brilliant at his job, but went to extremes in wanting to prepare what he considered to be the ultimate in pitches.

In 1938 'Bosser' produced a Test pitch that was an absolute dream to bat on, but must have been a nightmare for the bowlers. Playing against Australia, England scored 903 in a timeless Test dominated by Len Hutton, who batted for more than thirteen hours to accumulate 364.

Donald Bradman had to be helped off after injuring his ankle when he turned it over in an enormous hole dug by Bill O'Reilly. In those days they did not fill in the footholds like they do now. Walter Hammond would only declare when he knew Bradman would not be fit to bat.

Incredibly, 'Bosser' was disappointed because England did not reach a thousand. As far as he was concerned, that would have been the ultimate accolade. A landmark total.

The man who led Surrey to five of their seven successive championships in the 'fifties – a feat that has never been repeated – was Stuart Surridge, not only a great captain but also a good quick bowler and brilliant close-to-the-wicket fielder. Yorkshire ended that record sequence, taking the title in 1959, and Surrey's Alec Bedser sent a lovely telegram congratulating us on our tremendous achievement.

It was Alec who clean bowled me in both innings – for 6 and 23 – when I first played against Surrey for Leicestershire at Grace Road in 1960. He was a great bowler of inswingers and brilliant leg-cutters, and bowled for his country. Twin brother Eric was not bad, either. Eric was a good off-spinner, could bat a bit as well, and if he was around today he would probably also play for England.

As for Jim Laker and Tony Lock, what a marvellous spin combination they were, working in tandem, both for Surrey and England.

Laker, of course, was the man who made Test history by taking nineteen wickets against the Australians at Old Trafford in 1956. In the ensuing years, at least 100,000 people assured Jim personally that they had been there to see him achieve the historic feat. He used to say, 'If they did, a hell of a lot of them must have got in without paying.'

It is not so commonly known that Jim also took all ten Australian wickets in an innings when Surrey became the first county to beat the tourists for forty-four years, during that same summer.

Laker also went on tour with England on several occasions, and he once told me of the time when he was in the West Indies and heard that Fred Trueman would be sharing a room with Tony Lock. Said Jim to Fred, 'Hard luck, Fiery, you've certainly drawn the short straw this time.'

'How's tha mean?' queried Fred, flummoxed.

'You'll find out soon enough,' observed Jim mysteriously.

In the middle of the night Locky suddenly shot up in bed, arms stretched out in front of him, and let out a tremendous roar of 'How's that!' before sinking back under the bedclothes and continuing his sound sleep.

Poor Fred, of course, was by now fully awake, wondering what the hell was happening. He was just about nodding off again some time later when Locky sat bolt upright for a second time, gave a round of applause and yelled, 'Well done, great catch,' before resuming his slumbers.

By now a bleary-eyed, cursing Mr Trueman knew full well what Laker had meant.

Locky was a magnificent bowler. He was also one of those players who would dive under a bus to get a caught and bowled. I don't think I have ever seen a better fielder off his own bowling.

One catch at the Oval stands out in my memory. Locky was bowling to Len Hutton, who drove him on the outside, not too far off the ground and with a lot of power. Locky somehow managed to check his follow-through, change direction, take off, and hold a quite superb catch with his right hand – he was, of course, a left-hander. Trueman always said it was the best caught and bowled he had ever seen.

Another, in Pretoria in 1956, was at least its equal, however. Ken Funston was doing his level best to hold together a South African XI innings which was on the verge of total collapse. Tony made one ball turn and lift quite alarmingly, and Ken, on the back foot, played a textbook defensive shot, dropping his wrists and playing the ball with soft hands so that the cushioning effect would allow it to drop only a foot or so in front of him.

What happened next, as they say in *A Question of Sport*, was unbelievable. Locky continued on his follow-through for a few more paces, took a flying dive, completed the last couple of yards skidding along the pitch on his forearm, before grabbing the ball with both hands an inch or so off the ground.

No one had ever seen anything quite like it, and there was a stunned silence around the ground for a second or so before the applause began to ring out, even from the partisan home crowd, for such a superb piece of fielding.

Tony paid a price for it, however, sustaining horrific grazes from wrist to elbow and he was soon covered in blood, from his extremely painful injuries. Throughout the rest of his career he always played with the sleeves of his shirt very firmly buttoned at the wrist. It was not, as the cynics believed, a ploy to hide an alleged kink in his arm action, something which resulted in his being called for throwing on more than one occasion.

Locky was called in Kingston, Jamaica, during a Test match between England and the West Indies, in 1953–4, and he was shattered by it. When he was not keeping Fiery awake with his bedtime ramblings, he was clearly extremely upset, both physically and mentally. Fred told me he had still been white and shaking when he turned in that night. After he was called by a number of different umpires, Locky eventually reverted to his earlier style of slow-flighted deliveries.

It was in that same Kingston Test that he produced one of the great balls of his career to dismiss the great George Headley – 'The Black Bradman' – who averaged more than 60 in Tests, one of only four players to do so. It was Locky's quicker ball which dumbfounded the West Indian, who just stood there, a look of total bewilderment on his face. Rather like Mike Gatting after he had been done by that famous delivery from Shane Warne.

Playing for Nottinghamshire at the same time as Laker and Lock were performing their magic for Surrey and England, was a lovable rascal by the name of Charlie Harris, who produced one of his madcap moments in a county championship game between the two sides. One of the Surrey fast bowlers was racing in at full pelt when Charlie stepped away from the crease and held up his hand. The bowler screeched to a halt, grass sods flying everywhere as he slammed on the brakes in mid-run, and all hell was let loose.

Charlie apologised. 'Sorry about that,' he said, 'but you have an extra fielder in the gully.'

When the Surrey fielders and umpires went to investigate,

Left Feels like more rain – and the wind is getting up as well. Time to bring them off?

ve The New Road boating lake. A typical scene at Worcestershire's county ground
n heavy winter rain causes the backwaters feeding the River Severn to overflow their
s. The umpires' room is below those steps!

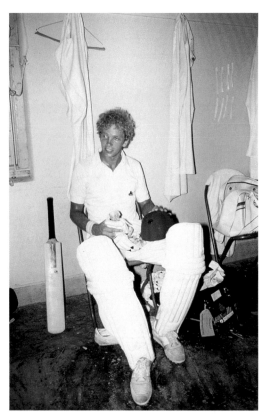

Above left The golden boy himself. A young David Gower, stylish of Leicestershire and England, whose dress sense, however, is ofte anything but stylish.

Above right I have th perfect view of yet another of those grace strokes which made Gower such a pleasur watch.

Left Middlesex and England spin bowler I Edmonds, a bit of a re who often got on the wrong side of captains managers and England selectors.

_e_ Chris Cowdrey (Kent) whose first
.et for England in Test cricket caused
ather Colin to drive the wrong way up
e-way street.

Above Obviously Colin eventually saw the
funny side of it. Fortunately so did the
policeman who stopped him.

_e_ Lord Cowdrey of Tonbridge, as he became, caught in more serious pose in the
idour of the famous Long Room at Lord's.

Above They say an elephant never forgets, and neither will anyone who witnessed Ian Botham's marathon 'Hannibal Walk' for charity. What a man!

Above An artist with both wicketkeeping gloves and paintbrush, Jack Russell, of Gloucestershire and England, puts the finishing touches to one of his canvases. He has painted one of me giving him out against India at Lord's in June 1996 – my final decisi in Test cricket.

ove left Derek Randall
(Nottinghamshire and
England), one of the best
fielders I have ever seen,
demonstrates his agility by
performing a cartwheel
to entertain the paying
customers. I don't think
even he made a catch
from that position.

ove right Derek Pringle,
with his trademark gold
stud in his ear, who was
selected to play for
England while still a
Cambridge undergraduate.

ght Botham again, this
time in more familiar
surroundings, going
through a loosening-up
exercise with Somerset
colleague Viv Richards at
Weston-Super-Mare.

Above left 'Lord' Ted Dexter, a good captain both Sussex and Engla although some said he had more theories tha Darwin and Einstein together.

Above right Three wis men. England selector Alan Smith, Micky Stewart and Peter May putting their heads together.

Left The familiar gas holder at the Oval, dwarfed in the camera angle by that great We Indian fast bowler Cur Ambrose.

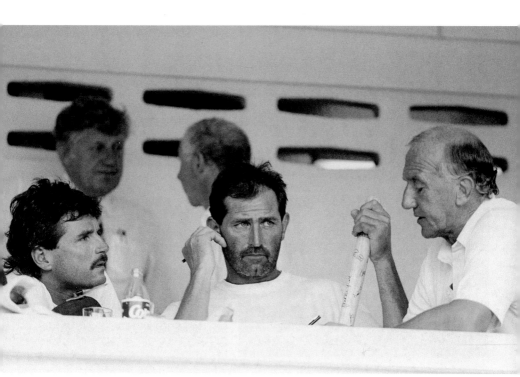

ve We have a problem: Allan Lamb, Graham Gooch and Micky Stewart looking
dedly gloomy after England had been bowled out for 46 in the third Test in Trinidad
993–4.

ve Happier times for Stewart, celebrating with his son, Alec, after victory over
stan.

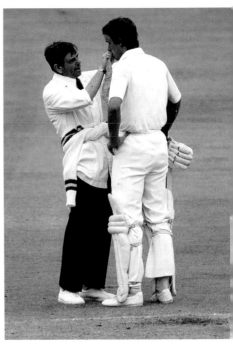

Above 'Hissing Syd' Lawrence, of Gloucestershire and England. I always knew when he was coming in from my end because I could hear him hissing.

Above Removing a speck of dirt from Chris Tavaré's eye. Sadly, it did not help the Kent, Somerset and England opener score any quicker.

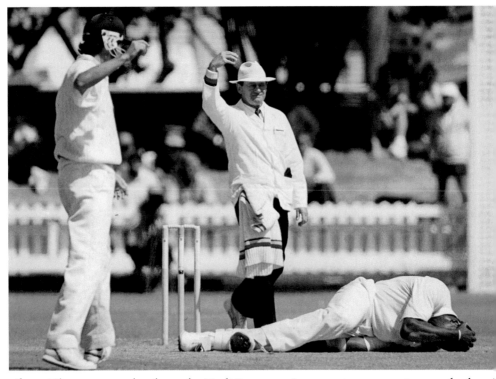

Above The moment that brought 'Syd' Lawrence's career to a premature end when knee collapsed under him in a Test match in Wellington, New Zealand.

they found Charlie's false teeth grinning up at them in roughly the place where gully would stand.

On another occasion Charlie sent a dolly catch into the air and three Surrey fielders plus the wicketkeeper set off, all with an equal chance of catching it. Charlie joined them, shouted, 'Mine,' and as everybody stopped to leave it to him, the ball fell gently to the ground. It was the sort of thing you might expect on a village green, but not on a Test ground. However, you would not put anything past Charlie.

During Surridge's reign as captain Surrey played 170 matches, won 101, drew 42 and lost only 27 – a remarkable record. It was a hard act to follow when Peter May succeeded him. May had already captained England for two seasons, and under his leadership Surrey remained at the top for two more years before finally relinquishing the crown to Yorkshire after a great fight right down to the wire.

May eventually captained England forty-one times, and went on to become Chairman of Selectors and President of Surrey. Sadly he died so tragically in his early sixties, and it was a very great loss to cricket. For me he was the best English batsman since the war, and a very able administrator.

Another Surrey player who died comparatively young was Ken Barrington, a fine batsman, brilliant slip fielder, and lovely man. He had a massive heart attack while in the West Indies as coach of the England team.

Micky Stewart led the side for ten years from 1963, and he took them to another championship success in 1971. Although there was some good bowling from Geoff Arnold, later to become coach, Pat Pocock and Intikhab Alam, the attack was never as potent as it had been in the great days of Laker and Lock, the Bedser twins, and Peter Loader, and Surrey failed to follow up that isolated triumph.

John Edrich was next in line for the captain's role, and during his spell, in July 1975, at Edgbaston, he produced the finest Test innings I have ever seen. His 34 runs came in an England total of 101 all out on the second day of the first Test between England and Australia on a rain-affected pitch on which Dennis Lillee and Max Walker, who were virtually unplayable in the conditions, took five wickets each.

It was also a Test which cost Mike Denness the captaincy. He chose to field after winning the toss, and after Australia had scored 359, a thunderstorm broke at five minutes to three on the second day. England were doomed from that moment. The decision about the toss had been supported by most of the England team because the first morning had been dull and grey. The local weather forecast mentioned the possibility of rain later, but that was ignored, leaving England to pay the ultimate penalty. They lost by an innings and 85 runs, with 20 wickets going down in 120.5 overs.

Graham Gooch bagged a pair on his Test debut in that same game, caught twice by Rodney Marsh, who took four other catches in the match.

My abiding memory of that match was the superb defensive innings played by the little Surrey left-hander in dreadful batting conditions exploited to the full by Lillee – especially after I had advised him, perhaps unwisely, to 'pitch 'em up'. Edrich batted for 165 minutes and dealt with a moving and lifting ball in a way that impressed me more than any other innings I have seen at such close quarters. People will probably say I must be crackers picking an innings of only 34 above all the great hundreds I have witnessed, but I will never forget how Edrich played on that occasion. England lost in four days. Without him they would have lost in three.

Edrich made his Surrey debut in 1958 and scored two separate hundreds in his first game as opener the following year – the first of four occasions on which he achieved that feat. He went on to score 39,790 first-class runs, including 103 hundreds.

His career-best was a remarkable 310 not out against New Zealand at Headingley in 1965, in which he demonstrated his ability to punish every loose delivery. He played and missed an awful lot in that marathon innings, yet he hit five sixes and fifty-two fours – the most in any Test innings. He told me later, 'Do you know, Dickie, I stopped playing and missing once I got past 200.'

Three players who were to develop into top-class bowlers, came up through the Surrey ranks together – Robin Jackman, Geoff Arnold and Bob Willis. As young professionals, they were once faced with a long drive to Swansea for an away fixture after a day spent playing golf. Willis, along with cricket bags, golf tackle and overnight gear, was somehow squeezed into the back of Robin's mini-van, and off they went. Suddenly there was an ear-piercing scream from Willis, who had developed cramp in his right thigh. Because his leg was wedged under all the bags, he could not move to relieve it.

Jackman had to pull over on to the hard shoulder of the M4, and he and Arnold then hauled Willis, face distorted with pain, on to the grass verge, still writhing in agony until circulation was finally restored.

Said Robin, 'We didn't half get some funny looks from other motorists. They must have wondered what on earth was happening. Yet no one stopped to ask what was wrong, or if they could do anything to help. As for the rest of the journey, I could hardly see. I was constantly wiping away tears of laughter.'

As for poor old Bob, he never did see the funny side of it. He complained that if Jackman had transported them in a Robin Reliant, it could hardly have been any more uncomfortable than the back of the mini-van.

Some years later, when Robin took his thousandth wicket for Surrey, his wife told their five-year-old daughter, Deborah, about the milestone dismissal, and she was thrilled. 'Oh, good,' she said, 'that means we must have won, then.'

Graham Roope was a talented batsman around the same time. He played for England, but could also have made a career as a top-class professional goalkeeper, as he demonstrated with some outstanding slip catches.

Arnold Long, meantime, maintained Surrey's long line of excellent wicketkeepers – Arthur McIntyre was another – and established a record at Hove in 1964 when he held eleven catches against Sussex, a county he later joined.

Roger Knight was appointed captain in 1978, and led his side to four successive Lord's finals between 1979 and 1982, although they managed to win only one, beating Warwickshire to carry off the NatWest Trophy in 1982.

It was in that same season, at Guildford, that Surrey were involved in the highest-scoring match – nearly 1,400 runs were put on the board – against Glamorgan, with four individual hundreds being completed. Surrey eventually won, which was consolation for Knight, whose car had taken a direct hit from one of the many sixes. Quite a few tiles on surrounding houses had also been dislodged.

Wicketkeeper Jack Richards claimed ten dismissals in a match against Sussex at the same ground, but his finest hour came when he played for England in a remarkable Boxing Day session at the MCG in Australia and reduced the Melbourne crowd to a stunned silence with five outstanding catches.

Ian Botham told me that the dismissal of Craig McDermott was one of the greatest catches ever taken off his bowling. Both was cursing himself for bowling a bad delivery as McDermott top-edged an intended hook. When Both looked up, he saw Richards streaking off towards long-leg in pursuit of the ball, which had gone many a mile into the air in that general direction. Chris Broad and Gladstone Small were also heading in from deep square-leg and fine-leg, and it looked as though there might be a very painful three-man collision. Amazingly, Richards scampered on regardless, dived full length and clutched the ball triumphantly inches above the grass.

It was one of a handful of catches that had Aussie skipper Allan Border and his lads shaking their heads in disbelief.

On that same Australian tour Richards hit a magnificent century as he and David Gower put on 207 for the sixth wicket. It was rated as fine a ton as had ever been scored by an England wicketkeeper in an Ashes Test. He did it under a lot of pressure, too. He knew that it was make or break for him, having waited a long time for his chance, and with Paul Downton, David Bairstow and Bruce French waiting in the wings.

It was a good tour for Jack on the whole, which makes it all the more surprising that this man, who liked his cricket when it was hard and challenging, hardly played for England after that. He was pretty low when he got back home to find that he had been relegated from number one to number three in the England wicketkeeping pecking order. Ian Greig, who was Surrey captain at the time, had the difficult task of picking him up again.

Just before they played Kent, Greig had a long chat with Jack, but was not too sure that it had done any good. Greig won the toss, decided to bat first, and quickly realised that he had dropped a king-sized clanger. In no time at all Surrey were 56 for 4 and in the toils. He thought to himself, 'We're in a right mess here, and Jack's in next. He's in no state of mind to cope with something like this.'

However, Jack went in and made 172 not out in a breathtaking knock, putting on 262 with Keith Medlycott to break

Surrey's seventh-wicket partnership record, which had stood for sixty-six years.

Unfortunately that day was also the start of the football season, so Jack received little credit in the press for his outstanding knock. It was football, football, football.

The way Richards responded after such a huge disappointment summed up his attitude, and the character of the man.

Jack had been deputy wicketkeeper to Bob Taylor on an earlier tour of India, where he found himself in a bungalow on a guesthouse complex with Taylor and Bob Willis. They were reading in the dingy lounge one evening when they heard a squeaking. They looked round nervously and saw a huge rat. Never did those three cricketers move so fast. Derek Underwood had told them scary stories about Roddy the Rat, but they had not believed him. Now they did.

One of the characters of the 1980s was Monte Lynch, whose pre-match preparation comprised ten minutes patting his Michael Jackson perm into place, another ten minutes arranging all his gold jewellery, and a final check to make sure that his sprayed-on white jeans were spotless.

He even had a Monte Lynch identity medallion hung round his neck, and one day a short ball from Clive Rice hit him smack on it, leaving an imprint on his chest. He sought sympathy from his team-mates, but none was forthcoming. They said it was the height of vanity for a player to have his name engraved on his body!

Monte was a real big-hitter, although the ball did not always go where he intended. One of the most common sounds in the Surrey dressing room when he was batting was Alan Butcher yelling, 'Lynch, you bloody idio . . . Oh, great shot, man!'

Pat Pocock, who had one year as captain and took 1,399 wickets in 485 matches during my years as a player and umpire, once decided to try to improve his batting by wearing glasses. Colleagues thought that was at least a step in the right direction, as they had been suggesting for years that he needed them. Pocock went out to bat against Middlesex in his new glasses, knowing full well that he would have to endure a good deal of leg-pulling.

Fred Titmus was bowling for Middlesex, and being deaf in one ear, failed to hear the titters and jibes aimed at 'Percy' Pocock. As he turned to bowl the first ball at the new batsman, he stopped in full stride, staring in amazement. 'Good grief, Percy,' he exclaimed, 'what on earth are you wearing those for?'

Replied Percy, with heavy sarcasm, 'To hear the ball better, of course.'

Titmus eventually recovered his composure sufficiently to bowl the first ball to Pocock, and it beat his defensive push to hit the stumps. As Percy began the long walk Titmus remarked, 'Well, I must say, you didn't hear that one very well, did you?'

Pocock went out with the England team to face the West Indies in 1983–4, and was nominated for the nightwatchman's role, should either of the openers fail against that formidable pace attack of Holding, Garner and Marshall.

Chris Broad had managed to scrape four when Garner dismissed him.

Back in the dressing room they looked round for Percy, but he was nowhere to be seen. A frantic search began, and they eventually found the reluctant nightwatchman in the washroom cleaning his teeth. When they asked him what the hell he thought he was playing at he replied, 'Just freshening up my mouth in case Bernie Thomas [the physio] has to give me the kiss of life.'

In recent years there have been two sets of cricketing brothers who have made their mark with the county – Martin and Darren Bicknell, and Adam and Ben Hollioake.

Darren, a left-hand opening batsman, was unlucky not to be given a chance to play for England at one stage when he was going really well. He has since had a back problem and had to have major surgery, but he was fit to return for the 1999 season. Brother Martin is a very good fast bowler.

The Hollioake brothers have both played for England, and are fine young cricketers who have not yet quite fulfilled their exciting potential, although I am sure they will in time. Ben in particular has a great deal of natural talent, while Adam has proved himself a very good captain.

The famous Surrey father-and-son combination of Micky and Alec Stewart have both captained the side, and both played for England, Alec as captain.

I am not convinced that you can open the innings, keep wicket and captain a side, as Alec has tried to do for England, nor can you captain a side from behind the stumps. As a wicketkeeper, there are so many different things to consider and concentrate on.

In any case, I am a big believer in picking your best wicketkeeper, whether he can or cannot bat. A top-class wicketkeeper will take crucial catches which less specialised players would miss, and Alec is not in the top bracket. He is certainly not in the class of Alan Knott, Bob Taylor, Ian Healy, Rodney Marsh, Wasim Bari or Jimmy Binks.

There is no more demanding job in cricket than keeping wicket, simply because of the constant involvement. There is no place to hide, and even if runs are not being scored, the man behind the stumps is likely to be concerned with every delivery. It is a specialist position and people are often guilty of forgetting that. Alec Stewart should just concentrate on his batting.

Finally, a lovely story which I heard while speaking at a

dinner in Surrey, which concerned Berkhamsted CC. One day they were playing Chesham, and the Berkhamsted captain, who had never scored a century in his life, was 98 not out. His team needed 18 to win and there were still a few wickets in hand, with plenty of time left. He found himself with a new partner, a young lad called Jamie Brook, who was making his first appearance for the club. Brook promptly smashed three sixes to win the match, robbing his despairing captain of his long-awaited century. The youngster was dropped for the next match and never played for the team again!

Arundel

SUSSEX

15

O N RECEIVING my umpiring fixtures for the season, I would always check to see how many times I was standing in Sussex. I consider it to be one of the most beautiful of all the counties, with delightfully situated grounds.

Hove, with its attractive seaside setting, is the headquarters of Sussex CCC, and I certainly would not mind being a young hopeful with the prospect of playing cricket there for twenty years or so. The only drawback is that it can be quite breezy there, not to say chilly, and when the cold wind whips inland off the sea, spectators soon wrap themselves up in anoraks, scarves and gloves. I have had my thermal long johns on a fair few times at Hove, I can tell you.

The wind helps the fast bowlers from that end, and when Imran Khan, John Snow and Garth le Roux strutted their stuff, they could be very, very quick on that pitch.

Of Sussex's legendary figures, Maurice Tate is immortalised in the gates of the Hove ground, which are named after him; there is the George Cox memorial garden, recalling how he took nearly 2,000 wickets and still played for the county aged fifty-four; and the Arthur Gilligan Stand celebrates the memory of Tate's captain and bowling partner.

In 1984 Viv Richards became the first man to hit the ball right over that stand, which is twenty-six feet high. The shot carried straight out of the ground, and went so far it could have bounced all the way into the sea.

The Hove scoreboard stands in memory of Ranjitsinhji, who was one of the finest batsmen of his era, dominating the Sussex record books and playing for England, despite the fact that at Cambridge he failed to win a Blue until his fourth year. It seemed that he would never make the first-class grade, but he had the financial clout to pay for the professional services of some of the leading bowlers of his day, who tossed them down for hours on end in the nets until at last he began to bat with greater promise. That promise was fulfilled with fourteen double hundreds in a Sussex career spanning 1895 to 1920, including a five-year spell as captain. His nephew, Duleepsinhji, later scored 7,791 runs in three seasons for the county, including 333 against Northamptonshire in one day at Hove.

Arundel is another picturesque, essentially English ground, and I love the story of a match there when an Arundel team, led by the Duke of Norfolk, played Sussex Martlets. The Duke

was at the non-striker's end when his partner decided that it was high time to give His Grace a share of the batting. Playing the ball into the covers, he yelled, 'Come one,' and set off for what should have been a comfortable single. The Duke responded, but stumbled halfway down the track and was still trying desperately to disentangle himself when the stumps were broken and a cry of 'How's that' went up from the Martlets fielders.

Poor Mr Meadows, the umpire, did not know quite what to do. He also happened to be the Duke's butler, and caught between loyalty and truth, he displayed a large slice of Jeeves-style diplomacy by announcing, 'His Grace is not in.'

Although Eastbourne's famous Saffrons ground is a fair distance from the sea, it is still first and foremost a bucket-and-spade place and has therefore been extremely popular with club sides touring during the late summer holiday season.

My abiding memory of this lovely ground is not a particularly happy one. I went there as a player with Leicestershire, and Alan Oakman bowled us out twice.

Our captain, Maurice Hallam, had come up with the idea of inserting the opposition whenever he won the toss. For the life of me I could not see what possible advantage could be gained from it, because in those days once you had started the game the pitch was left open to the elements. If you won the toss, you batted first, and this was an ideal toss to win. Surely even Maurice would elect to bat. But, no. He put Sussex in. They must have thought all their birthdays had come at once.

They batted all day on the Saturday, scoring well over 300. Sunday was a rest day, and it rained from morning until night. On Monday the sun had got its hat on again, so we were left with a dreadful sticky dog, and were rolled over for a very low score. We were asked to follow on. And we were rolled over again, to be stuffed by an innings and plenty inside two days.

Oakman, a good all-rounder and brilliant close-to-the-wicket fielder, did us with his off-spin, and every time we meet we still talk about that match at Eastbourne. He'll say, 'Whatever possessed Maurice Hallam to put us in, Dickie?'

'Beats me,' I reply. 'Beats me.'

Oaky also played for England, and caught a few at short-leg for Jim Laker when the Surrey off-spinner took those nineteen wickets in a match against the Australians at Old Trafford.

The Central Ground at Hastings was used by the county until 1986, giving the impression that first-class cricket in Sussex is a completely seaside affair. Horsham provides the contrast, however, with a typical village green setting. The church spire is a very prominent feature, and from the churchyard you can approach the ground over a little bridge which spans a brook babbling along its merry way. Delightful.

All the Sussex grounds have one thing in common, however: the outsize coloured eggs which are positioned round the boundary. These are an advertising stunt by the Stonegate County Eggs Company, who used to offer £3,000 to any batsman who could hit one full-toss. The figure was promptly reduced to £1,000 after Paul Parker did so at Eastbourne in 1986.

Sussex County Cricket Club was formed in 1839, and probably the oldest opening bowler to have played in first-class cricket was William Lillywhite, who played for them against England in July, 1853, when he was sixty-one years old. It is reported that he had 'a tidy spell of eleven overs from which twenty-three runs were scored'.

Going back even further in time, it is recorded that the first match at Rottingdean Cricket Club, where many Sussex players now stage their benefit matches, was played on 28 June, 1758, on a hill above the village. On one occasion a batsman held up play for twenty minutes while he waited for a sailing ship to pass beyond the bowler's arm.

Around the middle of the nineteenth century, some players were rolling the Rottingdean pitch when the one-ton roller escaped their grasp and careered full pelt down the hill into another field. Unable to get it back up again, they decided to transfer their ground to where the roller had come to rest. And that is where, tradition has it, Rottingdean play today.

There is a saying in Yorkshire that 'you get nowt for being second', and Sussex have had to live with the harsh truth of that throughout their history. Although they have been runners-up in the county championship on no less than seven occasions – in 1902, 1903, 1932, 1933, 1934, 1953 and 1981 – they have never won the title.

They were, however, the first winners of the Gillette Cup when Ted Dexter led them to victory at Lord's in 1963, and they were successful again a year later. They also won the 60-overs competition in 1978 and 1986. They have topped the Sunday League once, in 1982, the same year that they reached the semi-final of the Benson and Hedges Cup, which is their best performance in a competition that has now been scrapped.

During my time as a player and umpire, Ken Suttle scored the most runs for Sussex, a total of 24,134 in 466 matches. He batted at three and was a good left-hander. He was always shuffling about in the crease, which is why he became known as 'Shuffler' Suttle.

Ian Thomson was the chap who took most wickets in that time – 1,136 in 297 matches – including mine on numerous occasions. In fact, he was responsible for providing me with a record I could well have done without. I bagged two ducks between tea and close of play on the first day of a match – and that will surely take some beating. Sussex batted first and scored well over 300 runs before their captain, Ted Dexter, declared. We went in after tea. I was out for nought and the entire team was soon back in the dressing room, bowled out for little more than 30. We had to follow on, and there was just time for one over before close of play. Guess who opened? That one over was still enough to see the back of me, another big fat nought by my name, caught Doggart bowled Thomson, exactly as I had been in the first innings.

Thomson was a splendid bowler, his inswingers and leg-cutters being particularly productive. I did eventually master him, however, and got stacks of runs off him later on. At least, that is what I tell him when he brings up the subject.

Two other players who spring to mind from the 1950s are Jim Parks and Robin Marlar.

Parks was a good batsman, especially against off-spin. One of the best, in fact. He also kept wicket, and when his county captain, Ted Dexter, was in charge of the England team, Parks was preferred to Yorkshire's Jimmy Binks. Although Binks was the better wicketkeeper, Parks was the better batsman, and Ted always gave his man the nod because of that.

Marlar was one of those frustrating players who always found it difficult to arrive anywhere on time. He was once due to appear in a benefit match, and it was not until play had been in progress for an hour or so that Robin's car was seen on the horizon, half lost in a cloud of dust. It came to a screeching halt and out stepped Marlar, resplendent in his cricketing flannels, but with his white shirt hanging out untidily.

Behind him bounded a huge Newfoundland dog, which ran on to the pitch after its master, toing and froing all over the place. Robin apologised to all and sundry before turning to shout a commanding 'Sit!' The dog duly sat, but only until the next ball was bowled. Then it was off again, patrolling the third-man region. This prompted an apprehensive cover point to move closer to extra cover, a little further away from the cavorting canine.

Marlar also captained Sussex, and it has been somewhat unfairly suggested that while players followed David 'The Rev' Sheppard out of faith, and 'Lord Ted' Dexter out of loyalty, they followed Marlar out of sheer curiosity.

Sheppard was selected to tour Australia in 1962–3, which came as a bit of a surprise, since his ecclesiastical duties had prevented him from playing much cricket prior to this, even at county level. His lack of time at the crease was one problem, his lack of fielding practice another.

When Sheppard made a mess of yet another slip catch attempt, Freddie Trueman glowered at him, eyebrows twitching. 'You might 'ave yer eyes shut when yer prayin', Vicar, but I do wish you'd keep 'em open when I'm bowling.'

Sheppard did take one blinding catch on the boundary in the match against Victoria, when Test opener Bill Lawry pulled a shot to leg. Mightily relieved at finally finding one that stuck, David hurled the ball high in the air in triumph. Unfortunately he had failed to hear the umpire call 'no-ball', and Lawry and his partner pinched an extra run while David was busy celebrating the catch that never was.

Later in the tour he came up with an authentic catch, which prompted Trueman to remark, 'Let's face it, fellas, when the Rev puts his hands together, he should have a better chance than most of us.'

Trueman continued to tease Sheppard throughout that tour, and when a team party was attended by the Bishop of Perth, the Yorkshireman dug his clerical colleague in the ribs and muttered, out of the corner of his mouth, 'Watch it, David, 'ere comes senior professional.'

Throughout my career I have been on the receiving end of

many frivolous appeals for all kinds of dismissals. One of my fellow umpires in the Mod-Dec Devon League in the 1950s had a devastating response: in his coat he concealed a device which, when activated, gave out shrieks of hysterical laughter which could be heard all round the ground. I did toy with the idea of borrowing the contraption when I became an umpire myself, but thought better of it. Lord's would possibly not have approved.

I was not too keen on another idea put into operation by the Northchapel Cricket Club in Sussex around about that same time. When visiting umpires arrived at the ground, they were presented with rabbit droppings instead of pebbles for counting the balls in an over. They were told, 'Our Northchapel umpires always count with them. They swear by them. They are nice and handy because, although they are hard, they are nowhere near as heavy as pebbles.'

That fine England bowler John Snow – he who gave the pigeons crumbs of comfort when he spread bits of bread all over the ground during a Test match between England and the West Indies when I umpired at Trent Bridge in 1976 – was involved in another memorable prank in a county championship game, between Leicestershire and Sussex at Leicester.

It was cold and it was raining on and off, although not heavily enough to justify abandoning the game. The spectators, however, gradually drifted away, so that eventually the only people left watching were the scorers and officials. After yet another stoppage Snow went out to resume his over. He took out of his pocket a bright red soap cricket ball that he had bought at the local Woolworth's, and craftily swapped it for the real thing. His first delivery was the perfect bouncer. The soap ball skidded on the damp grass and Peter Marner, the batsman, got into position for a fierce hook, which he completed with impeccable timing. The ball shattered into fragments.

The Sussex scorer, Len Chandler, placed an asterisk beside the dot in his book, and at the bottom of the page, he elaborated briefly, 'Ball exploded.' Len has been with Sussex for donkey's years and is a very good scorer, as well as having a sense of humour.

Brothers James and John Langridge both gave tremendous service to the county. James scored nearly 29,000 runs and John more than 34,000. No other Sussex batsman has ever approached those totals. James also took more wickets than any other bowler apart from George Cox, Maurice Tate and Albert Relf, while John caught more catches than any other fielder, wicketkeepers excluded. John umpired with me in later years, and I was not surprised at his ability to snap them up at slip, when I saw his hands at close quarters. They were like buckets.

Ted Dexter, who captained the side from 1960 to 1965, was a great player. In full flight he was poetry in motion as a batsman. He was just as good off both back and front foot, and all in all was one of the best players I have seen. Because of his exciting batting, a lot of people forgot about the quality of his bowling. He hit the deck hard and picked up a lot of useful wickets at county and Test match level. He was a good captain both for Sussex and England, although it used to be said of him that he had 'more theories than Darwin and Einstein put together'.

It looked as though Ted's career might be over in 1965, when he retired after breaking his leg. He was persuaded to make a comeback three years later, and in his first innings he scored 203 against Kent at Hastings. It was his only double hundred for Sussex, and was a remarkable innings, not only for its power and size, but also for the pace at which he accumulated those runs, the second hundred coming up in only 103 minutes. He was subsequently selected for the last two Tests of that season.

Coincidentally, Tony Greig scored the only double hundred of his career at Hastings. Going in at 24 for 3 against Warwickshire, he hit 226 in just over four hours. His end came when, having scored four sixes in a row off P. J. Lewington, he gave similar treatment to a fifth ball, only to see it fall just short of the boundary and into the waiting hands of Dennis Amiss.

Greig had shown his potential in his first match for Sussex as a twenty-year-old, when he made 156 to save his side from defeat by Lancashire. The South African-born all-rounder, who also did a very good job as England captain, and is now a cricket commentator for Australian television, took the bowling honours when Sussex beat Kent by ten wickets in 1972. He claimed 11 for 46 in the match, as Sussex bowled out their big rivals for 54 and 199.

The following year Kent gained their revenge, winning by the huge margin of an innings and 161 after scoring 282 on the only dry day of the game. Sussex, caught on a brute of a pitch, were skittled for 67 and 54. On the third day it was impossible to start play until four o'clock, and that was due only to the assistance of the fire brigade, with keen help from Kent players and supporters, who combined to mop up the saturated pitch. Twenty overs later Derek Underwood had taken eight wickets for nine runs.

It was another example of what a decisive role could be played by the weather in those days of uncovered pitches. No one could play Underwood in conditions as helpful to him as those. He must really have enjoyed his visits to Sussex. In 1964, in only his second season with Kent, he took 9 for 28, and twenty years later, again at Hastings, he scored the first and only century of his career. I eventually gave him out lbw. He still reminds me of that to this day. Out lbw to Dickie Bird on the unlucky Nelson. What a way to go!

The Nawab of Pataudi was another Sussex captain who also

played for India. He tragically lost the sight of one eye in a car accident, however, and was never the same player again.

At a Sussex v. Yorkshire match at Hove in the 'sixties, Richard Hutton was bowling to a young Peter Graves, who kept playing and missing. An exasperated Hutton, who was renowned for his dry wit, remonstrated with his adversary. 'Excuse me, young man,' he queried, 'pray tell me what you are in the side for? Can you bowl?'

'Not really,' Graves replied.

'Well, maybe you are in the side for your fielding, then?' Hutton persisted.

'Not really,' repeated Graves.

'Well, it beats me,' exclaimed Hutton, 'because you can't bloody well bat.'

As a matter of fact, Peter could bat a bit. He developed into an elegant left-hander who went close to a Test call. As for his fielding, he was one of the best close to the wicket. Sadly, however, his career was hampered by illness and injury.

When Mike Griffith, son of former Test and County Cricket Board Secretary Billy, captained Sussex in the late 'sixties and early 'seventies, he selected John Barclay to play when the latter was only sixteen and a half years old. He was so young, that Griffith thought he had better check with the lad's mother to see if it was all right for him to travel to Swansea for the game against Glamorgan.

Griffith obviously had an eye for talent, because Barclay blossomed and eventually became captain of the side himself in 1981, although he had a trial run during the 1980 season when he deputised for Arnold Long. It was a spell which almost ruined his captaincy credentials for good.

When Sussex entertained Middlesex at Hove, it was the sort of pitch that made captaincy a hazardous occupation, and Barclay had to decide whether to bat or whether to bowl. It might be a good thing to put the opposition in: the pitch could get better and better, because, after all, groundsman Peter Eaton was renowned for preparing some of the best tracks in the country. It could turn out to be another belter. On the other hand, there was a tinge of green to be seen, plus a sea breeze, and no doubt there would be movement in the air and off the pitch at least until lunchtime.

Barclay was faced with a dreadful dilemma on that first day, and no doubt his opposite number, Mike Brearley, could sympathise, although he had faced such situations many times before.

John secretly hoped that he would lose the toss, leaving Brearley to make the difficult decision, but he called right. The choice was his. He elected to put Middlesex in – and by the end of the day they had scored 360 for 4 in 100 overs.

After play he had a drink with Brearley and commented on 'what a jolly good day's cricket' it had been, despite the fact that his team had been on the receiving end. That was typical of John, a lovely, Christian man.

However, he was not quite so chirpy the following morning when the chairman carpeted him. 'Tell me, young man – if you can – why you keep putting the opposition in on such friendly pitches. We are being caned all over the county. Look at the last match, Surrey were inserted. They scored 301 for 4 declared and 251 for 3 declared. What did we get? I'll tell you. We got 152 and 255 all out, that's what. So, come on, explain yourself.'

Barclay thought that his chances of ever captaining Sussex on a regular basis had been blown away, but then came one of those dramatic twists of fate which make cricket such a fascinating game. Sussex having been made to follow on, some fool in the Middlesex office ordered a dozen bottles of champagne to be put on ice, because a win would have sealed the championship for them. That did it. Kepler Wessels, the fine South African left-hander, scored 254 for Sussex in a knock of magnificent defiance, and the game ended in a draw.

Imran Khan used to regard Barclay as the typical eccentric Englishman, and with good reason. In those days Imran's philosophy was to enjoy life to the full, both on and off the field, and he was none too pleased one night to find himself sharing a room with Barclay in a boring hotel at the back of beyond.

Imran popped into the room quite early on in the evening and was surprised to find John already tucked up in bed. 'Are you sick?' he asked anxiously.

'Oh, no,' replied John. 'Just trying to get maximum rest for the morning. I want to be fresh to face Clive Rice and Richard Hadlee.'

'Fair enough,' said Imran, 'but you do realise it's not yet nine o'clock?'

Left with little else to do, Imran switched on the telly, after promising to keep the volume right down so as not to disturb his room-mate, and settled down to watch the film *Marathon Man*.

Imran told me, 'John kept tossing and turning, obviously struggling to come to terms with Hadlee's outswingers and Rice's bouncers. Finally he sat up and started to watch the film, hoping it might take his mind off the horrors of the Nottinghamshire attack.

'Before long he was in there with Dustin Hoffman, dodging the baddies and the bullets. He ducked under the sheets when Hoffman was tortured, and the more tense the film became, the more he covered his head. When there was a lull in the action he tried to get to sleep, but he couldn't manage it. He had to see the ending. He got really excited, like a big kid.'

Barclay said he needed something for a headache. It must have been all the excitement, he thought. He muttered something about it being a big mistake to have watched the film.

By then Imran had decided that next time there was a decent film on the box, he would go to watch it in someone else's room.

Imran finally nodded off to sleep himself, only to be woken by the sound of the radio, and the kettle being filled. He leaped out of bed, thinking that he must have overslept, but when he drew back the curtains he was amazed to find that it was still quite dark. He looked at his watch. It was five a.m.

Imran was still trying to figure out what on earth was happening, when Barclay declared that Imran was to blame for his headache and sleepless night. Had he not been made to watch *Marathon Man* he would have been fresh as a daisy to take up the challenge later in the day. He then headed towards the door saying that he needed a walk along the river to restore his peace of mind. At five o'clock in the morning?

Needless to say, it was the last time they roomed together. Imran discovered that he was not the only one who had found it difficult to live with Barclay's sleeping habits. No wonder the entire team was delighted when he was eventually made captain and given a single room of his own.

Barclay was an Old Etonian, as you can probably tell by his remark following another difficult decision he had to make in a county match, when Gehan Mendis was batting for Sussex. Barclay declared with Mendis on 97 not out and chasing his fifth century in six innings. Said Barclay, 'Oh, I do hope he doesn't think I'm a swine and a cad.'

His nickname was 'Trout', which had nothing to do with his love of fishing, as some people thought: he was actually christened John Robert Troutbeck Barclay. Surrey off-spinner Pat Pocock probably landed the biggest 'Trout' of his life when Barclay took the bait and was caught at short leg for 99 in the ninety-ninth over of one match. For John it was a case of the one that got away.

In the first championship match of the 1984 season at Worcester, John was in a panic because they were still trying to complete the overs at seven thirty, and he had a dinner engagement twenty miles away at seven forty-five. When he finally left at eight fifteen, he was still in his flannels, with his dinner suit tucked underneath his arm, ready for a quick change somewhere along the way.

Someone asked him, when he reached the age of thirty-two, whether he should consider retiring at the end of his benefit season in order to make way for a younger man. He said the question made him feel a little bit like the chap who read his obituary in *The Times* and was compelled to write to the editor, stating that the report of his death had been grossly exaggerated.

John was an excellent leader of men, and could have captained England. These days he coaches at Arundel's indoor school and does a magnificent job with kids from all over the place. Cricket needs characters like him, but, sadly, they are fast disappearing from the scene.

Paul Parker played just one Test for England against Australia at the Oval in 1981, at which I was umpire. Unfortunately he did not get many runs and that was the last we saw of him on the international scene.

As a schoolboy waiting to go in to bat, Paul used to practise hitting the ball against the pavilion wall. One day he edged a shot through the pavilion window. It was a big window, and there was glass all over the place. He escaped immediate retribution, because just then a wicket fell and he was next man in. Sadly, all that practice failed to make perfect. He met the first delivery with a beautiful straight defensive bat, right out of the textbook. However, the ball had not read the script. It nipped back, missed the bat and rapped the batsman on the pad. Although he was well forward, there was a loud appeal, and the umpire, not being Dickie Bird, gave him out lbw, bowled Armstrong, for a first-ball duck.

Rather shamefaced, Paul returned to the pavilion, where he was offered a certain amount of sympathy – along with a dustpan and brush to sweep up all the glass from the broken window.

He batted rather better, I remember, when Sussex thrashed the Northamptonshire bowling to all parts of the ground at Hove in 1980. Paul made a rapid 122 as Sussex rattled up nearly 500 runs in next to no time. There was also a century from Northants' Tim Lamb, although that came off Tim's own bowling!

Jack Jennings, the Northants physio, who also played football for Middlesbrough, always saw the best in everything, and as he greeted the bedraggled players at the dressing room door he sympathised, 'Never mind about all that stick, lads. Just think. It could have been worse. We could have got behind with the over rate.'

The scorer, Jack Mercer, known to generations of players for his cricketing yarns, conjuring tricks, convenient bouts of deafness and dry sense of humour, summed up the Eastbourne fiasco in typical fashion. Emerging rather later than usual from the scorebox, he apologised to Jim Watts on his arrival in the dressing room. 'Sorry I'm late, captain, but I was weighed down by the bowling figures.'

Once at Eastbourne, I was umpiring the match against Durham with Pasty Harris. During the tea interval I told him to shove a new ball in his pocket. We had our tea, went out into the middle, and I said to him, 'Got the new ball?'

His eyes glazed over. 'Oh, hell, no. I've forgotten the damned thing.'

'Well, you'd better nip back and fetch it, then,' I scolded him.

Unfortunately the door to the umpires' room had been locked and he could not find the attendant, who had the key.

'What are we going to do, Dickie?' the players asked.

'What can we do?' I replied. 'We'll just have to wait here until he finds him. We might as well make ourselves comfortable while we do.' So we all sat down out there in the middle.

Eventually Pasty arrived with the ball after finally discovering where the attendant had been hiding himself. I could not believe the attendant had disappeared so suddenly and completely. He had been all over me during the interval, making my tea, putting sugar in, stirring it, cleaning my boots – I even thought he might offer to go to the toilet with me to wipe my bottom, he was so fussy and so concerned about my welfare. Could we find him when we really needed him, though!

Edgbaston, Birmingham

WARWICKSHIRE

16

THE pitch at Edgbaston used to be one of the best in the world. Then they brought in the Brumbrella, and with it came disease. There was a deterioration in quality, and only now is the pitch getting back to something like its previous high standards.

So what on earth is this dreaded Brumbrella, which brought such serious repercussions? It is a remarkable contraption that has proved invaluable in protecting the entire playing area from the weather. The groundstaff just wheel it out flat, press a button, blow it up, and it forms a massive tent which covers every inch of grass. It is a wonderful thing, and they have lost very little play due to rain at Edgbaston since its introduction.

The disease was an unforeseen problem, but Bert Flack, who went on to become Inspector of Pitches for the Test and County Cricket Board, worked at it until he got to the bottom of it.

Steve Rouse, who played in Warwickshire's last county championship-winning side, took over from Flack and continued the remedial treatment until the disease was finally cured.

Edgbaston is undoubtedly one of the top Test grounds in the world. It has excellent visibility for players, umpires and spectators alike, and the facilities are right out of the top drawer

– dressing rooms, physio rooms, gym, showers, baths, indoor practice area, are all up there with the best. It may not be the most picturesque ground, but it is still a magnificent place to play cricket.

One of the features of the ground is a small archway in the boundary wall, designated the 'Sydney Barnes wicket-gate', which is traditionally the point where Barnes entered the ground on 20 August, 1894, to play in his first county match, and where his ashes now rest. He served Warwickshire, Lancashire and England, yet spent most of his career with Staffordshire in the Minor Counties League.

The club room displays many mementoes of Warwickshire cricket, perhaps the strangest being a pair of M. J. K. Smith's spectacles, which he wore throughout the 1959 season. Mike was identified by those glasses, and he certainly needed them.

When I was with Yorkshire, as soon as Mike walked to the crease we would give the ball to Freddie Trueman. We had discovered that you had to get him out early, or the odds were that he would go on to make a big hundred. And Fred was the ideal man for the job. It seemed that M. J. K. needed more time than most to focus fully, probably something to do with his eyesight.

When Mike did get set, there were few better batsmen. He was a fine player all round the wicket and a prolific run-scorer, his career total of just short of 40,000 being a Warwickshire record until it was broken by Dennis Amiss.

There were no helmets in those days, and no contact lenses, either, so to go out there and stand up to fast bowlers such as Fiery Fred was incredibly brave. Had the ball struck his glasses, it could have been very, very serious.

Yet Mike captained both county and country, and is now Chairman of Cricket at Warwickshire. His son, Neil, an off-spin bowler/batsman, has so far followed in his father's footsteps by becoming captain of Warwickshire. Will it be England next, I wonder?

If the 1973 Test against the West Indies was the most eventful I have umpired at Edgbaston – Arthur Fagg walked out in the middle of the game after becoming incensed with the behaviour of Rohan Kanhai – another Test, this time against India in 1986, provided me with my funniest experience at the ground.

It was the Saturday afternoon, and play was being televised, when suddenly a young bird, dressed only in panties and bra, jumped over the advertising boards in front of the press box, and ran towards the much older Bird in the middle. I didn't know quite where to look. Chased by stewards, she ran past me and over to my colleague Barrie Meyer, at the bowler's end.

She then took one of the bails off the top of the stumps and put it down her panties. Being a bachelor, I had never seen anything like it. What were we going to do? I certainly didn't fancy retrieving it.

Barrie, however, took a hand. He calmly reached inside the young lady's nether garment, plucked out the missing bail, and nonchalantly placed it back where it belonged.

By this time a female special constable had arrived on the scene to arrest the scantily clad interloper and escort her to the waiting police van.

It's funny, but ever since, I've always wondered if she managed to get bail!

Edgbaston was also the scene of that record-breaking 501 not out by West Indian Brian Lara against Durham in 1994, when Warwickshire ran up their highest ever total of 810 for 4 declared. During that season they claimed one of their five championship successes, retaining the title the following year. Their other triumphs came in 1911, 1951 and 1972.

They have also won the Gillette/NatWest five times – in 1966, 1968, 1989, 1993 and 1995, with just one success in the Benson and Hedges Cup in 1994. They have claimed the Sunday League crown in 1980, 1994 and 1997.

In the period after the Second World War, one of their star performers was spin-bowler Eric Hollies, who wrote his name into the history books by bowling Don Bradman for nought, second ball, in the great man's last Test, to prevent him from finishing with an average of 100.

Hollies became the butt of the Aussie crowd's cutting humour during the tour by Freddie Brown's England side in 1951. No matter how hard he tried on the boundary edge, the ball kept eluding his outstretched hand and desperate boot. Throughout a long, hot afternoon, he chased until he could hardly breathe, flung himself about, and finished limp and sweat stained. As he stood there, panting and red faced, a wag in the crowd shouted, 'What's the matter, Hollies, don't they bury their dead in Birmingham?'

'No, they don't,' replied Eric with feeling. 'They stuff 'em and ship 'em out to become Australians.'

Typically, that won him a lot of friends – the Aussies love a gutsy character.

In the 1950s, one of my Yorkshire colleagues was Eddie Legard, a Barnsley lad who had played with me at Shaw Lane for our home-town club in the Yorkshire League. We progressed into the Yorkshire second team together, but when Eddie realised that he stood little chance of making it into the first team because of Jimmy Binks, he decided to move to Warwickshire. Unfortunately he found himself in a similar situation as understudy to Alan Smith. It was a great pity, because Eddie was a very good wicketkeeper.

We were such good friends that I was best man at his wedding, and, naturally, the photographer wanted to record the happy scene with the usual series of pictures, including one with Eddie, his bride Marie, and the handsome best man. Just as the photo was about to be taken, Don Wilson, another Yorkshire second team player of that time, pushed me to one side and took my place. So, ever since, looking at those wedding snaps, everyone assumes Don was the best man and not me.

When I moved to Leicestershire, I played a game against Warwickshire when Alan Smith was keeping wicket to Bob Barber, a leg-spin and googly bowler. Maurice Hallam was on strike at the other end, and he went down the pitch to one ball, failed to pick the googly and missed it completely. Similarly fooled, Smith, who was rather knock-kneed, allowed the ball to go through the large space below his knees for four byes. I couldn't help but laugh.

It did not prevent Smith from being a top-class wicketkeeper, though, and he played for England. When Deryck Murray was signed, Smith switched to bowling, having always fancied himself as a genuine medium-pacer. To be fair, he was not a bad one, despite his bizarre whirling action, all arms and legs, which made him look rather like an octopus running in to bowl.

Alan took over the captaincy of Warwickshire from Mike

Smith – no relation – and led them to the championship in 1972. He later became Chief Executive at the club, and then Chief Executive of the Test and County Cricket Board.

A combination of the ground's development, the county's success, and increased attendances, brought Test cricket back to Edgbaston in 1957 after a twenty-eight-year absence, and the first match proved a memorable one.

'Collie' Smith, so tragically killed two years later in a car accident at the age of twenty-six, scored 161 in his first Test for the West Indies against England, and in the home team's reply, captain Peter May and Colin Cowdrey scored 285 not out and 154 respectively to put on 411 – England's highest partnership for any wicket, and a Test record for the fourth. At the same time, 'Sonny' Ramadhin, who had taken seven wickets for the West Indies in the first innings, achieved his own endurance record of ninety-eight overs, the most ever bowled in a first-class innings.

Warwickshire occasionally play at Nuneaton, a ground that holds particularly happy memories for all-rounder Tom Cartwright, who made 210 there in 1962, the highest score of his career, and two years later demonstrated his bowling skills by taking 4 for 3 and 5 for 37 as Nottinghamshire were skittled for 34 and 57.

Journalist and broadcaster Michael Parkinson is another of my old Barnsley Cricket Club colleagues, and through the years he has managed to wangle a game on every Test ground in England, apart from Trent Bridge and Old Trafford. He boasts that he is the only player to have opened an innings at Lord's with Elton John. Moreover, he says, there can be few people on this planet who can say they caught John Edrich, of Surrey and England, off the bowling of American singer Andy Williams, who, at the time, had a number one hit.

Parky's Edgbaston experience, however, was not so successful. Asked to play in a benefit match for Warwickshire's opening batsman John Jameson, he was in Vic Lewis's showbiz side, whose bowling was being thrashed mercilessly to all parts of the ground. Parky's one success was to dismiss that magnificent batsman Alvin Kallicharran.

He described his lethal delivery thus: 'Kalli proved that he was susceptible to my slower ball, which bounced twice before hitting the wicket.'

Otherwise there was very little for Parky to enthuse about. His three overs cost him just short of forty runs, and one hit by Jameson went so high that he never saw it come back down.

When it was Parky's turn to bat, he opened the innings with the then manager of the England team, Micky Stewart. Bob Willis, who had just returned from injury, decided to take the opportunity of a full-scale work-out. In his excitement he must have forgotten who he was bowling to, and fired down a bouncer which Parky never saw. The next was a yorker, again invisible to the Parky eye, which smashed into his middle stump, sending it many a mile towards the pavilion, as if pointing the way for my mate's departure.

Willis was cock-a-hoop. You would never have thought that he had bowled a mere hack-cum-chat-show-host. It was as if he had just dismissed Garfield Sobers.

As for Parky, he was a little miffed that no one invited him to play in any more benefit matches, just to write articles for the brochures. Perhaps it was just as well: as a writer, no one does it better.

Vic Lewis, who captained that showbiz side, was a top agent for the likes of Barbra Streisand, Nat King Cole and Frank Sinatra, and he loved his cricket. In another benefit match at Edgbaston, Alvin Kallicharran hit one skywards towards mid-wicket, and he and Geoff Humpage had already run one before the ball started its descent towards Vic.

Vic was not exactly the most nimble of fielders, and there

was an unwritten rule that the nearest colleague would cover for him. Consequently there was a general shout of, 'Hold on, Vic, we're coming,' from the cavalry. They could not come soon enough for the former bandleader, whose arms were flapping about as though he was still waving his baton, and his legs were performing the strangest of contortions. But too late. The ball landed on Clive Lloyd's hat, which just happened to be perched on Vic's head. The next thing, he was lying flat out on the deck, gazing heavenwards with unseeing eyes.

Back in the middle Kalli and Humpage laughed their socks off, and the big crowd had collapsed in mirth, tears rolling down their collective cheeks.

It wasn't funny for Vic, though: a cartoon-style bump came up on his head, and incredibly Clive's hat seemed to be elevated a few inches as the bump swiftly grew in size. All he could say was, 'Why are they all laughing? I was nowhere near it.'

When his turn came to bat, Vic received a snorter in the thigh from Willis. That felled him, too. Another bruise, but one of which he could be proud. Next morning he dropped his trousers to show all and sundry the black, blue and purple mark of honour. 'Bob Willis did that,' he proclaimed proudly. We were sure that he actually touched up the bruise for several nights, and he dined out on that story for weeks afterwards.

Vic was keen as mustard, as you will have gathered, and he also insisted on looking the part. He used to borrow Clive Lloyd's hat, Bob Willis's boots, Garfield Sobers' bat – and Mike Brearley's box!

That particular match was in aid of Rohan Kanhai, who shared in the greatest single county event of recent years at Edgbaston when he and John Jameson set a then world record of 465 for the second wicket in 1974, Jameson making 240 not out and Kanhai 213 not out.

Kanhai was one of several talented West Indians who

have played for Warwickshire, including Lance Gibbs, Alvin Kallicharran, Deryck Murray, Brian Lara, and Barbadian-born England player Gladstone Small.

Small was a great servant for Warwickshire and England, but had not always been a fast bowler. At school he used to bowl off-spinners, changing to the quicker stuff after someone whistled a couple of bouncers around his ears. He felt a desire to get some of his own back, so he deserted his usual style and fired a six-ball broadside as fast as he could. He enjoyed it so much, that it was pace rather than guile from then on.

Gladstone was always one of the biggest sleepers in the game. At every opportunity he nodded off. If Warwickshire were batting, you could guarantee that he would sneak off to the physio's couch for a kip. Sometimes, after a good meal, he had to sleepwalk the last few yards just to get there. Team-mates would have to wake him up when it was his turn to bat, and he would have a job keeping his eyes open while he sat there waiting with his pads on to take next knock. No worries at all. I could never do that when I played. I was a bag of nerves.

Everybody in cricket, it seems, has a nickname. Mine is Dickie, for obvious reasons, and nearly everybody calls me that now, although my real name is Harold Dennis. Ian Botham has a few – Both, Beefy and Guy the Gorilla. Gladstone Small is Gladys. Or at least he was until he was playing in a match against Beefy, who heard several of the Warwickshire fielders use the name Manos.

Beefy had not heard that one before, and he was intrigued. 'What's this Manos thing, Gladys?' he enquired in between overs.

'Oh, it's nothing, Both,' said Gladys, looking a trifle embarrassed.

After the day's play Beefy had another go, but still Gladys

tried to wriggle out of any explanation. 'I tell you it's nothing. It's totally irrelevant. Now let it drop, will you.'

Both is never one to let anything drop once he gets the bit between his teeth, and eventually Gladys cracked under pressure. He told his interrogator the story on the understanding that Both would not spread it around.

Apparently, while Gladys had been touring with England in Australia, his colleagues had noticed a chicken-processing factory just outside Adelaide called Manos, which used the advertising slogan, 'Top quality chicken. No waste. No claws. No neck.'

You need to have seen Gladstone to appreciate the humour of it, and Beefy certainly saw the funny side. So did he keep it quiet? Did he heck. Poor old Manos has been getting it in the neck ever since.

Gladys always reckoned that batsmen were pampered, that the laws of the game were weighted in their favour. He once told me, 'We know from bitter experience that 2 for 75 off 30 overs on a flat pitch beats a boring fifty any time. But no one comes near the bowler with a microphone in that situation. Still, we don't mind being the real-ale cricketers rather than the champagne Charlies.'

Another of those hard done by bowlers was Jack Bannister, who took a record-breaking 10 for 41 against the Combined Services at Edgbaston in 1959 – in the same week that I created my own personal best of 181 not out for Yorkshire. As you probably know by now, I was dropped for the next game. I doubt Jack was.

Birmingham City manager Trevor Francis has always been a big Warwickshire supporter. In his playing days with City, he was never away from the Edgbaston ground in the summer, and one year he was asked to play in a benefit match. Trevor fancied himself as a fast bowler, but possibly tried to send one down a little too quickly, and strained his achilles tendon.

Freddie Goodwin, who was City boss at the time, was not amused. The injury caused Francis to miss the opening games of the new football season. Cricket was immediately banned, and it was diplomatic not to mention such a dirty word within hearing distance of the manager, who was himself a good cricketer, having played for Lancashire, as well as giving good service as a footballer with Manchester United.

Francis, incidentally, has travelled the country following cricket, and says there is no better place to watch than Edgbaston.

Another footballer/cricketer was Jimmy Cumbes, who played cricket for four counties, including Warwickshire, in a career spanning twenty-two years, as well as serving a number of football clubs as goalkeeper. He was asked hundreds of times which sport he preferred, and his stock answer was, 'Football in the winter, cricket in the summer.'

In Jimmy's day it was still possible to combine the two sports, and there were times, during the seasons' overlap, when football training in the morning would be followed by cricket nets in the afternoon. Chris Balderstone actually played in a first-class cricket match for Leicestershire before dashing off to play in a Second Division football match with Doncaster Rovers that same night.

Cumbes had the distinction of sharing in a county championship triumph for Worcestershire in 1974 and then walking out at Wembley in front of nearly 100,000 people to pick up a League Cup winner's medal with Aston Villa six months later.

Three days after that final, Villa played Sheffield United in an FA Cup tie at Villa Park, winning 4–1, and who should be at left-back for United but Worcestershire dressing room buddy Ted Hemsley.

Jimmy was keeping goal against Carlisle United at Brunton Park when the home team were awarded a penalty. He found himself facing another cricketing colleague, the aforementioned Chris Balderstone. Jim grinned at Chris and said that Chris would need his cricket bat to whack the ball past him. He'd never do it with his boot. The psychology worked. Chris was so fired up that he hammered the ball harder than he had ever done before. It nearly snapped the crossbar in two, and Jimmy survived.

The dual sportsman is a thing of the past, although the ability is still there. I have seen several footballers who could have been fine professional cricketers with a bit of coaching – Steve Ogrizovic (Coventry City), Andy Goram (ex-Rangers and Scotland), Nigel Spink (Aston Villa), Gary Pallister (Middlesbrough) and Clayton Blackmore, who joined my club Barnsley towards the end of the 1998–9 season, to name just a few.

Dennis Amiss played for Warwickshire until 1987, breaking every club record along the way. He was a real run-machine, scoring 43,423 in his career. Dennis much preferred batting to fielding, and if a batsman nicked the ball in his direction in the slips, he would let out a cry of anguish at the prospect of trying to catch it. If he could have just batted and been excused fielding, he would probably still be playing today instead of becoming a pipe and slippers man.

It was his suggestion that protective helmets should be brought into the game and people claimed that emphasised his uneasiness against fast bowling. Yet the best two innings of his Test career were both against the fearsome West Indies attack.

I umpired the Test at the Oval when the West Indies had worked out that they could do Dennis every time if they attacked his leg stump, because he had a habit of falling over as he tried to deal with that particular delivery. He proved them wrong by scoring more than 200.

His other magnificent knock came at Kingston in February 1974. There were seven Warwickshire players in that Test – Amiss, Willis and Jameson in the England side, and Kanhai, Kallicharran, Gibbs and Murray in the West Indian ranks.

With England in the toils, Amiss lost Jameson, caught for 38, and was joined just before tea by Frank Hayes. It was vital that England did not lose any more wickets before the break, so what did Amiss do? He ran Hayes out for a duck. He was distraught.

He said afterwards, 'I felt I had even more responsibility then. It was my fault we had lost Frank. I made a huge effort to try to put that mistake out of my mind and concentrated on making amends by playing a long innings.'

Amiss batted through the last nine and a half hours to score an unbeaten 262 and ensure a draw which rescued England from going 2–0 down in the series. England subsequently squared it by winning the final Test in Trinidad.

Asif Din was on the groundstaff at Lord's when Warwickshire signed him, and it proved to be a wise move, because he scored a lot of runs for them. Although he was born in Uganda, Asif went to school in Birmingham, so it was fitting that he should play for the county whose headquarters were based in the city.

Asif's nickname, naturally enough, was Gunga, and all he eats is Indian food. One night he took fast bowler Bob Cottam for an Indian meal in Manchester. Bob managed only three balls next day before he had to make a beeline for the smallest room, where he spent most of the morning. Bob was not too clever for the next twenty-four hours, and it was so bad he was frightened to sneeze.

Asif is a deeply religious man, as all-rounder Paul Smith discovered when the two of them shared a room at Hove in 1984. One morning Paul noticed that Asif's bed had not been slept in. There was no sign of him anywhere, but Paul heard a strange wailing sound coming from the next room. Concerned that his colleague sounded to be in some pain, he gently opened the door, and there was Asif on his prayer mat.

Prior to the NatWest final against Sussex at Lord's in 1993, it looked as though Asif's days with Warwickshire were numbered. He was called into the office and told that he was not being retained for the following season. He immediately went out and scored a magnificent 104 to lead Warwickshire to a match-winning 322. First thing Monday morning he was called into the office again, where a two-year contract was waiting for him!

Warwickshire were involved in another thrilling final, which I umpired. It was almost pitch black by the time Neil Smith, the off-spin bowler who is also renowned for his big-hitting, slammed a six in the last over to beat Middlesex.

Andy Lloyd, who captained the county between 1988 and 1992, was a good left-hand batsman who was delighted to receive an England call-up against the West Indies. In his first Test, on his home ground at Edgbaston, he ducked into a ball from Malcolm Marshall that did not get up as much as he thought it would, and was struck a terrible blow. He took

no further part in the match – and was never selected again.

When Warwickshire played Notts at Trent Bridge one year, someone broke into the dressing room and stole sixteen bats, four of which belonged to Andy. Why he needed four, I'll never know. He bumped into Chris Broad in the car park that morning, and, as they both used a Fearnley bat, Andy asked if Chris had a spare he could borrow. He had, but it needed a little knocking in. Lloydy certainly knocked it in: that day, not having scored too many runs previously, he hit the Notts attack for more than a hundred. Afterwards he refused to let Chris have his bat back.

Lloydy was once sitting in the Knights of St John pub at Lord's, enjoying a chat with several of his colleagues and a chap who was obviously known to the older players, but not to him. He was an Australian, by the sound of it, he drank well, and he spoke in familiar terms of great players such as Bradman and Harvey. During a lull in the conversation, the Aussie asked Lloydy what he would like to drink and went to fetch it.

Whispered Lloydy to one of his team-mates, 'Who is that chap?'

'You prat,' came the reply. 'You mean to tell me you don't honestly know? That's only one of the all-time greats of the game. That's Keith Miller.'

Lloydy sat even more quietly after that, listening in awe to the tales the legend had to tell.

Geoff Humpage, the Warwickshire wicketkeeper, stood in as captain on a number of occasions, and he reckons that he is the only county skipper ever to be thrown out of a Wimpy Bar. When Warwickshire were playing Oxford University at the Parks, he and four colleagues popped in to the local Wimpy for a quick evening snack. The tables were built strictly for four, but Geoff pulled up a high chair to accommodate spinner 'Diddy' Smith. The waitress, however, was a bit of a dragon, and insisted that they all leave immediately. Obviously she had no sense of humour, but then, few south of Birmingham do.

Humpage's exceptional feats in 1984 earned him one of *Wisden*'s Five Cricketers of the Year awards. He scored 1,891 first-class runs – a total exceeded only twice in the history of cricket by full-time wicketkeepers, Leslie Ames of Kent, and Jim Parks of Sussex – and also snapped up sixty-six victims behind the stumps. He bettered that latter total the following season, when he created a Warwickshire record of eighty victims in a summer, beating Jack Smart's seventy-nine in 1932.

Geoff was also to the fore in that remarkable championship match I umpired when Warwickshire met Lancashire at Southport in 1982, when he and Alvin Kallicharran scored 254 and 230 not out respectively in a magnificent fourth-wicket stand of 470.

Nor will I ever forget his terrific unbeaten 141 against Yorkshire at Edgbaston in 1983, when Warwickshire were set 299 to win, comfortably the highest total of a low-scoring match on a dodgy pitch. With his side tottering at 136 for 6 and then 180 for 8, Humpage hit no less than 134 of the last 166 runs scored from the bat, to clinch an astonishing victory.

Tim Munton was once rejected as a county player, although he went on to play for England, for which he has Bob Willis and an unknown admirer to thank. When showing promise with his home club of Melton Mowbray, Tim was invited for trials with Leicestershire, but he failed to impress, and believed the chance of a professional career had passed him by.

However, he was nominated for a country-wide course for fast bowlers, run by Willis. Tim went on the course, Bob saw him, and promptly snapped him up for Warwickshire. He subsequently took stacks of wickets and was called up by England.

Tim was touring Pakistan with England 'A' when the whole squad was evacuated to Sri Lanka, away from the threat being

posed by Saddam Hussein. Sri Lanka was a comparative paradise, but it was forty degrees, and paradise proved more like
hell for Tim. He took a thirty-yard run when he first arrived,
and before long it had been reduced to three. As he walked off
the field, dehydrated, at the end of one session he declared, 'I
am seeing those big pink elephants, boys.' It is so important
to drink plenty of liquid in that heat and humidity, as I have
discovered to my cost.

Tim enjoyed the tour of the West Indies rather more,
although even there he discovered that the deadly fast bowling
was only just a little less life-threatening than Saddam Hussein's
bouncers.

Tim personifies the Warwickshire attitude of playing the
game as hard and as competitively as possible, but off the field
you could not wish to meet a nicer man. The only occasion
when he did become really grumpy was when he discovered
that someone had tampered with one of his bats. Maybe he
does bat at number eleven, but does that mean he should be
denied a love-affair with his favourite piece of willow? After
all, he holds the record, in partnership with Ashley Giles, for
the tenth-wicket stand of 141, scored against Worcestershire
at Worcester in 1996. Giles, a slow left-armer, also played for
England. He bats right down the order, but is a good player to
have in that position, and it is just possible, without delving
into the record books to find out, that Ashley might well have
scored 140 of those runs. No doubt Tim will be in touch if it
was any different.

Tim was appointed captain in 1997, but sadly never played
because he developed a serious back injury. By the time he was
fit again, Brian Lara had taken over the captaincy.

David Brown was another fine bowler for Warwickshire and
England, and a real gentleman to boot. He went on to become
manager. His big relaxation is the horses, and he was forever

handing out dressing room tips. Small, Lloyd, Norman Gifford and Willis in particular all used to enjoy a bet, so they were first in the queue for some advice. However, I heard Gladys complain one day, 'How is it, with all these straight-from-the-horse's-mouth tips, that I never win anything?'

It was David who contacted me about a Newmarket stable who wanted to name a horse after me. I said I had no objections, and was thrilled one day while I was umpiring a county match to hear over the Tannoy that Dickie Bird, ridden by Pat Eddery, had won a race. It caused quite a bit of merriment among the players and spectators, but I've never heard of it since. Can anyone enlighten me? Is it still running? Or has it, like its namesake, gracefully retired?

Worcester

WORCESTERSHIRE

17

IT IS not often you find a cricket field that can also be used as a boating lake, so I suppose you could say that Worcestershire's New Road ground is pretty unique in that respect. I have seen photographs of schoolboys sailing on the flooded ground in the 1950s. Such an image will not surprise those who know New Road well, because virtually every year the backwaters feeding the River Severn from all sides of the ground overflow their banks and spill over on to the cricket area.

The water very often advances right up the pavilion steps and into the dressing rooms. The umpires' room is on a lower level, so it can be waist high in there. The buildings on the boundary edge, including the scoreboard, are actually built on stilts to avoid the worst of the flooding. A plate in the pavilion records the record water level in 1947. Groundsman Roy McLaren must feel a bit like King Canute at times, trying to hold the waters back. It makes his job very difficult, and he is expected to walk on water in his efforts to prepare the square for the curtain-raiser of the season. However, having had all that water on it, the grass is always lush, adding to the lovely appearance of the ground.

If you were to ask cricket lovers to nominate the most beautiful county ground, many would go for Worcester, with good reason. My choice would be Queen's Park, Chesterfield, but New Road certainly runs it close. These are, without doubt, the most picturesque grounds in the world along with Newlands in South Africa.

The view from the pavilion at both grounds is very similar. At Derbyshire you look through the trees on a sunny summer's day to the crooked spire beyond, and at Worcester you look through the trees to the cathedral and the River Severn. When the flowers at New Road are in full bloom, it really is a marvellous sight. It is a wonderful place to play and watch cricket, and the facilities are excellent.

The pitch has a history of uneven bounce, but we were faced with a greater problem one day when one of the players, practising on the outfield prior to the start of play, hit the ball on to the pitch while the groundsman was still rolling it. Before anyone realised what was happening, the ball had been rolled into the ground, just on a length. We had to bring the pitch forward and make fresh markings, the whole bagatelle.

Another feature at Worcester is the space reserved in the car park for the tea ladies. One anxious reporter, having arrived late at the ground for an important fixture, was looking for somewhere to park when the attendant told him, 'Sorry, sir, I'm afraid you can't come in, there are no spaces left.'

'Yes, there are,' replied the reporter, pointing to several vacant spots.

'Oh, but those are reserved for the tea ladies, sir,' said the attendant.

'You surely don't need all that space for them,' complained the increasingly frustrated hack.

'Oh, but we do, sir,' replied the attendant. 'And I'll tell you this for nothing: it's a lot more important that we get our tea than you get anything in the paper, young man.'

I have had a lot of fun with Jimmy Cumbes at his various clubs through the years, and Worcestershire proved no exception.

I was umpiring a match at which he was bowling to Wayne Larkins, of Northamptonshire, who mistimed a shot. The ball looped off his bat in the air towards Jim, who was following up. It was the simplest catch you could ever wish to see. A real dolly. A little baby could have caught it. Just as it lobbed into his hands, I said, 'Good luck, Jim.'

The ball hit him right on the end of his little finger and then fell to the ground.

'Oh, bad luck, Jim,' I sympathised. 'I didn't put you off, did I?'

I dare not tell you what he replied. Or what he said later when it was discovered that his little finger was broken!

It must have been like waiting for a number 47 bus as Worcestershire hung around ninety-nine years for their first championship success. For, after they had enjoyed one victory, along came another in next to no time. The breakthrough came in 1964, and it was a dream come true for the smallest county. The fairytale continued when they retained the title a year later, Don Kenyon captain on both occasions.

Norman Gifford led them to a further championship triumph in 1974, helped by the rain at Bournemouth in the last week of the season, which ruined the chances of Hampshire, who, needing only three more points, suffered five successive days without play.

Under Phil Neale, Worcestershire enjoyed their most successful period, with two more championship wins in 1988 and 1989, Sunday League victories coming in 1971, 1987 and 1988, a Benson and Hedges Cup win in 1991, and a NatWest Trophy triumph in 1994.

Neale was not only a good player, but also very good at man-management, and he should have had international recognition. He was another who combined football and cricket, playing for Lincoln City, and, to his irritation, he was sometimes confused with Phil Neale of Liverpool FC.

When commentating on a Wolves v. Spurs game, John Motson suggested that Tony Galvin was the only player in league football to have a degree in Russian. He was wrong: Neale also had one.

Graham Taylor, the former Aston Villa and England manager, who is now doing a very good job back at Watford, is a close friend of Phil, who helped Taylor get on the waiting list for the MCC. He has worked out that he should finally make it by the time he is seventy-three!

It was Phil's idea to enlist England fast bowler Graham Dilley and all-rounder Ian Botham to play for Worcestershire. He had heard that they were both unhappy at Kent and Somerset respectively, and signed them up to give impetus to his own team's prospects.

Dilley, however, found his new captain to be a rather annoying character. For a start, Dilley complained that no one else thought there was more bounce and seam from the scoreboard end. And when nobody wanted to sit in Neal Radford's passenger seat or room with Steven 'Bumpy' Rhodes, Neale suggested that Dilley did.

Dilley was also aggrieved that while he had to keep half an eye on his waistline, Neale could pile up the calories without it having the slightest effect – he could still slip into twenty-eight-inch trousers – and while Graham threw himself around getting covered in mud and grass stains, the skipper always seemed to look spick and span. As one who liked to get from A to B as quickly as possible, Graham was also irritated to find that Phil stuck to the speed limit, stopped for a Mars bar and still got back to the hotel before him.

Graham could add to that. 'There are those of us who prefer to bat first, and we are fed up with him because he never wins the toss.'

Phil won a few other things, though.

There were several other dual sportsmen before Phil, in the 'fifties and 'sixties, including Jimmy Cumbes (Aston Villa, West Brom and Tranmere), Jim Standen (Arsenal) and Ted Hemsley (Sheffield United). Later on, commercial manager Jim Osborne kept goal for West Brom.

If Ted Hemsley had stuck to cricket, instead of combining it with football, he might have played for England. He was an excellent all-rounder and shared Worcestershire's sixth-wicket record partnership of 227 with Dipak Patel against Oxford until it was broken by Graeme Hick and Steven Rhodes, who put on 265 against Somerset at Taunton in 1988.

Norman Gifford captained the county for a while, enjoying a fair bit of success. Although he played for England, his appearances were limited, because as a slow left-armer he had the misfortune to be plying his trade at the same time as Derek Underwood. When Ray Illingworth was the England captain, he selected Gifford if the pitch was good. If it looked as though it would take spin, he went for Underwood.

I remember Norman once bowling from Kevin Lyons' end against Sussex at Hove. He kept appealing for lbw, and Kevin kept turning him down. 'Not out . . . not out . . . not out,' he repeated, almost as if the record had got stuck. Norman continued yelling at him whenever ball struck pad. It went on over after over. Then Norman went up, along with every other fielder, and there was a massive appeal. Lyons shook his head again. Not out. Whereupon Norman raced across to me at square leg and said, 'I want a second opinion. What do you think, Dickie?'

I replied, 'Nay, Norman owd lad, 'ow the 'ell can I tell from 'ere?'

Two of the best umpires of all time, Frank Chester and Syd Buller, both played for Worcestershire, and Chester looked at one time as though he would be a very good player for England. Sadly, with a great future in prospect, he lost his right arm in the war and his playing career came to a premature end. *Wisden* once wrote of him, 'Probably no cricketer at eighteen has shown such promise since the days of W. G. Grace.' It was a tragedy that he was lost to cricket as a player, although he retained his love for the game and went on to become a very fine umpire.

Buller was another of the greats. He played with Hunslet Nelson in the Leeds League before joining Worcestershire, and was always fiercely proud of his Yorkshire background. It was an honour for me to stand at Test matches with him, and it was a great blow when he died during the tea interval while umpiring a match at Edgbaston.

Wicketkeeper Hugo Yarnold also became a first-class umpire, and I stood with him quite a few times, including a match at Northampton when I took both ends for a while because he was not well. I kept telling him to go home, but he said, 'I'm all right, lad.' He kept doing a stint, then having to go off again.

At the end of the match I said, 'Look, Hugo, I don't think

you should drive back to Worcester. Go back on the train. Please.'

He replied, 'Don't worry about me, I'll be all right.'

Hugo got into his car, and I never saw him again. He drove under a lorry on his way home and was killed.

He was a sad loss to cricket, and I can see him there now, telling me the story of when he used to keep wicket for the great Roly Jenkins. While Roly bowled his leg-spin and googlies, Hugo used to offer a torrent of advice to any young player who had the misfortune to be batting.

'Don't go down the wicket to this one, stay where you are. That's it, lad, well played.'

Next over, as Jenkins rolled in Hugo would be at it again. 'On your back foot to that one. Oh, well done, lad. That's the way to play.' Then came the killer ball. 'Right, lad, that's the one, down the pitch. Off you go.'

The youngster would go down the pitch, miss it, and the scoreboard would read 'Stumped Yarnold bowled Jenkins.'

West Indian Vanburn Holder, one of the current crop of first-class umpires and a lovely man, is also a former Worcestershire player. I have always had a great time when I've umpired with him, because he is good fun. His only drawback is that he smokes a pipe, and whenever he was standing with me I would always insist, 'No pipe-smoking in my dressing room, if you please, Mr Holder.' And he would go outside. Lunch and tea. For a puff.

Vanny is 6ft 6ins with bandy legs, a combination which made him a natural target for Fred Trueman whenever Yorkshire played Worcestershire. Fred would pop into the dressing room before the start of play and say to the big West Indian, 'Nar then, Vanny me owd lad. Good to see thee again. Ar tha gooin' on?' Then he would look him up and down and say, 'Does tha know, if thy legs were straight tha'd be over seven feet tall.'

Over the years Worcestershire have produced some fine opening bowlers, and two who spring immediately to mind are Jack Flavell and Len Coldwell, who both played for England. Dennis Amiss was facing the two of them in one match and was considering going on the front foot to Flavell, who had taken the new ball. Jack noticed this and let him have a bouncer. Dennis said it was one of the best he had ever received. It passed so close to his nose that he swore he could see the maker's name, Duke, on the ball.

One cricketer I have always admired is Basil D'Oliveira, a Cape Coloured. It took guts and willpower for him to come from the slums of Cape Town to play in the Central Lancashire League with Middleton and work his way up to serve Worcestershire and England with such distinction, and showed the character of the man. Apartheid dogged his career, but he came through it, which was a marvellous achievement.

Bas talked a lot of sense. A stickler for the right kind of coaching, I worry that we tend to over-coach sometimes, preventing young players from developing natural ability and flair. It came as a breath of fresh air, therefore, to find myself having a chat with Bas on the terracing at Worcester early one beautiful morning, and listening to his words of wisdom on the subject.

He told me that the most important things about coaching are balance and enjoyment. A player needs balance to hit the ball, balance to bowl straight, balance to pick up the ball when fielding.

He went on, 'Coaching in any sport can be of enormous benefit, provided it is correctly and intelligently used. Incorrect or over-coaching can be ruinous, and cricketers can so easily be diverted from the whole essence of the game, which is taking wickets, scoring runs, and enjoying it.'

Bas told me that once, while he was coaching in South Africa, he was approached by a headmaster who had been watching him take a net. He felt that Bas should have stopped a young boy, who kept hitting the ball in the air.

Said Bas, 'I had to agree with him to a certain extent, Dickie, but I also told him to watch the boy's face each time he hit the ball, which was quite often. The smiling enjoyment said it all.'

I have never forgotten that conversation. Bas's words should be included in every coaching manual: never has more sense been spoken on the subject. Great players are not made by coaching alone. As Bas said, it is down to natural skill, basic fundamentals and personal qualities. However, there is no substitute for hard work, and all the best players have worked very hard at their game.

Bas himself was a natural, and I don't believe he was ever coached. He simply worked hard at improving his God-given talent, and he practised and practised, believing in his own ability. He had great mental strength.

His son, Damian, also played for Worcestershire, and is now doing a great job looking after the young lads in the second eleven.

New Zealander Glenn Turner, one of the best players I have seen, was with Worcestershire many years. He captained his county and his country and scored a mountain of runs. The outstanding innings of his career came at Worcester against Warwickshire in 1982, when he reached his hundredth hundred before lunch and went on to score 311 in the day.

Around that time, Glenn claimed he had found a method of playing fast bowling – by stepping away from his stumps and, with a good eye and a good arm, attacking the ball. He had tried this against Bob Willis on a couple of previous occasions, with some success, so it was no surprise when, on that Saturday morning, on a white, flat pitch in

May, he decided to employ these tactics against Bob once again.

After fifteen minutes he had forty runs on the board. At the end of one over during that early onslaught, Dennis Amiss jokingly suggested to Glenn that he did not have a prayer of getting a big score, playing like that. He would soon get his come-uppance. How wrong he was. It was a superb innings, even though it was against a weakened Warwickshire attack, and to score 300 in a day was unbelievable.

Rodney Cass was a very good wicketkeeper/batsman from Yorkshire. He made cricket bats by trade, and he knew how to use them, too.

If you ask Rodney what his most embarrassing moment was, he will probably recall one particular county match when he was left running round in circles and getting nowhere.

When a ball is skied near the stumps, it is always down to the wicketkeeper to go for it, because, as the only one wearing gloves, he has a better chance of taking the catch. This one went up many a mile in the air, and Cass, as you would expect, yelled, 'My ball!'

Everybody stood back for him to take the catch. You have never seen such a performance. First he whipped off his cap, ran round in a circle, then took off one of his gloves and threw it to the ground. Having done that, he realised it could be a bit

awkward catching the ball with only one glove, so he threw the other down as well, leaving only his inner hand protectors on. He might just as well have had bare hands, which defeated the whole object of his going for the catch, rather than one of the close-to-the-wicket fielders. Rodney went through another 360 degrees and ended up diving full length without so much as getting a touch on the ball.

Whenever that fine bowler John Inchmore popped into the dressing room to choose the new ball before the start of a game – he preferred the slightly smaller one, for the grip – I used to say to him, 'Whatever you do, Inches, don't open from my end, 'cos you're a nightmare, lad.'

And he was. It was a fulltime job keeping an eye on his front foot. I used to no-ball him and no-ball him until I was fed up to the back teeth with no-balling him. He was one of those bowlers who are always close, and he tended to overstep the mark just slightly, making life very difficult for the umpire.

I used to say to him, 'Come back, Inches,' which he needed to do quite literally. He took no notice, though, and next ball it would be just the same.

I also used to warn him about running on to the pitch. 'Get wider, man,' I would tell him. 'Come back, Inches . . . get wider, Inches.' There were times when he hardly knew whether he was coming or going.

I couldn't let him get away with it, though: give an inch and he'd take a yard.

Inches' moment of glory with the bat came against Essex at the county ground in August, 1974 – and I was there to see it at close hand. Replying to Essex's opening knock of 264, Worcestershire were 59 for 2, with Glenn Turner having retired hurt for thirty when Inches went out as the nightwatchman.

After seeing the final few overs through, he went out next morning, and although he kept hitting across the line, he also kept connecting, mainly through mid-wicket. Before you could blink he had 50 on the board, then 75. And finally up came the hundred. Not even he could believe it. He had given it an almighty thrash, and it had come off.

He and New Zealander John Parker, who made 140, put on 226 for the third wicket, Inches eventually being run out after scoring 113 – his first and only century. He never remotely approached such a score again.

Worcestershire went on to win by ten wickets, with Inches also taking 3 for 52 in the first innings. I have to admit that I turned down one or two lbw shouts from him that day: 'You're a big mate of mine, Inches, but it's still not out when you hit those pads unless it's plumb.'

Inches was a great character. I once read a description of him that said he was built like an Olympic weightlifter, and that was just about right. A big, big fella, and a smashing bloke.

Worcestershire also play at Kidderminster, a very nice, neat club ground with a pitch that is one of the best in the country to bat on. It is full of runs, which makes Neal Radford's performance against Nottinghamshire in July, 1987, all the more remarkable.

On that batsman's paradise, the medium-pacer took 8 for 55 in 16.1 overs as the wickets tumbled like skittles. Bowling from my colleague Barrie Meyer's end, he had four of his first five victims lbw, and at one point I thought Neal would go right through the card with such decisions, although he didn't get any from me.

Radford's comb and mirror were in constant use that day. He always used to have his hairdressing equipment in his back pocket, so that he could keep his locks neat and tidy. After every over he used to stroll back to the third man boundary, take out the mirror, have a good look, and then carefully comb his hair back into place. He did the same before he went out to bat.

Richard Hadlee was the only batsman to show any real resistance that day as Notts were bowled out for 167, the great New Zealand all-rounder making 84 before falling to Richard Illingworth.

Tim Curtis scored 110 in Worcestershire's opening knock of 349 and the home team won by ten wickets. It was a good knock by Curtis, but not a particularly entertaining one. Like Chris Tavaré, Curtis scored a lot of runs, but very, very slowly.

Graeme Hick has always remained a complete mystery to me. In county cricket and the one-day game he simply butchers attacks. Tears them apart. When he gets into the Test match arena against world-class bowlers, however, he cannot seem to reproduce that kind of form.

My theory is that when he comes up against the very best attacks, he falls down because the positioning of his feet is all wrong. I have always maintained that the most important aspect of batting is position and movement of feet. Get your feet in the right position and you get in line with the ball. Graeme's feet are not properly positioned, and that throws his head and eyes off line.

Despite that, he has a hundred centuries to his credit in first-class cricket, including 405 not out against Somerset at Taunton. You can't achieve a record like that without being a very, very good player.

Graeme is an incredibly nice lad, and I've prayed for him to do well. It is a tragedy that he has never quite made it at Test match level, but maybe there is still time.

Worcestershire wicketkeeper, Steven 'Bumpy' Rhodes, was once playing against Nottinghamshire at Trent Bridge and Eddie Hemmings was bowling to him, with Derek Randall so close in that he was virtually standing on the batsman's toes. Rhodes played forward. Randall thought he heard a bat-pad, caught

modern, as depicted by the new stands and futuristic media centre at Lord's . . .

and the traditional, as spectators settle down in deckchairs during Canterbury week.

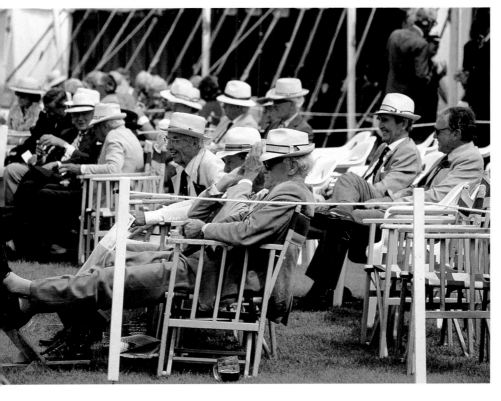

Above England captains past and present: Michael Atherton of Lancashire and Nasser Hussain (Essex) going out to bat together.

Above Fitness fanatic Robin Smith, of Hampshire and England, puts Michael Atherton through his obviously painful pa

Below Worcestershire's Graeme Hick butchers county attacks but so often fails again world-class bowlers in the Test arena. Could it be because the positioning of his feet all wrong, and he gets found out by the best attacks?

ve Adam Hol016ake holds aloft the Texaco Trophy in 1997, watched by Mark
am, Darren Gough, Alec Stewart, Ben Holoioake and Graham Thorpe.

w Corks a-popping in celebration for Phil Tufnell of Middlesex – with the inevitable
rette – and Somerset's Andy Caddick after they had bowled Australia out at the
l in 1997. But these two, like Hick and the Holoioake brothers, have never cemented
r Test places.

Above Lancashire's Neil Fairbrother, a one-
day specialist who has never quite made
the transition to Test cricket.

Left Yorkshire captain David Byas, who
done a wonderful job for his county and
must have been in the thoughts of the
England selectors from time to time.
Nearly everyone else has.

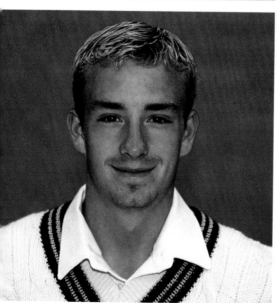

Above Matthew Bulbeck, an emerging left-
arm over-the-wicket bowler from
Somerset.

Right Darren Thomas, a young Glamorgan
all-rounder who is attracting a lot of
attention.

ve Andrew Flintoff, a promising
castrian all-rounder who was selected
England's World Cup squad in the
mer of 1999.

w Another young player, Marcus
cothick, who let himself go at one
e, eating too much junk food and
etting about fitness. But now the
erset batsman has pulled himself
ther and looks a fine prospect.

Above Northamptonshire's gifted 21-year-
old David Sales, who scored a 300 and a
200 for his county in the 1999 season. I
made a point of telling him that if he sorted
himself out and buckled down to his cricket
he would go on to play for England.

Below What more can you say about
Yorkshire paceman Darren Gough? He has
brought a breath of fresh air to the
England team, and it is a great pity that
injuries continue to dog his footsteps.

Left American thriller wr[iter]
Stephen King, who came
over to watch me umpire [a]
game at Trent Bridge but
had to return home witho[ut]
seeing a ball bowled. Nee[d I]
say it rained? Another hor[ror]
story.

Right Racehorse Dickie B[ird]
ridden by Pat Eddery. It w[on]
the race, but nobody has s[een]
it since. Is it still running?

Below left Come on then,
man, talk to me. Don't jus[t]
sit there. I've got to admit [your]
face is familiar, but I can't
place it.

Below right With the
Duchess of Kent after
receiving my Honorary
Doctor's Degree in Law a[t]
Leeds University. Don't I
look smart!

Above right Off you go, Birdy! My old Barnsley Cricket Club colleague Michael Parkinson – whatever happened to him? – points to the exit door.

Above left Who did that? Don't you know this is my last match? Not very nice, is it, go hitting me on the knee like that? A painful farewell appearance in the match betw Yorkshire and Warwickshire on my home ground of Headingley.

Above Where's my hanky? The tears flow again as the England and Indian teams line to clap me on to the field for my final Test at Lord's in June, 1996.

the ball, and let out a massive appeal. The umpire said not out. Next ball the same thing happened. This time there was no appeal. Randall was frightened to ask again because he had made such a big song and dance on the previous delivery. Next thing he knew Bumpy was walking off. As he did so, he patted Randall on the head, a great show of sportsmanship.

In February, 1995 Bumpy was invited by Allan Lamb and Ian Botham to a *Question of Sport* recording. Lamby had recently decided to give up drink, but he was finding it hard because he and Both were touring with their show, *Beef and Lamb in a Stew* at the time, and after the cameras had stopped rolling, he could only watch with a glass of orange in his hand as the other guests downed the harder stuff.

Bumpy had arranged to be driven down to Worcester, while Lamb and Beefy were due to travel to Swansea, but he was persuaded to join the other two in their chauffeur-driven car instead. They would drop him off on the way.

Beefy decided to take 'a few' bottles of red wine with them.

311

Non-drinker Lamb was plonked in the passenger seat next to the driver, leaving Beefy and Bumpy in the back to consume all the drinks. When they arrived at Bumpy's house at two thirty in the morning, Beefy wanted to wake up his wife, Judy, but Steven thought that this was perhaps not too clever an idea, so he talked Beefy out of it. Instead, with the river again in flood, he convinced the keen angler that he had seen salmon rising – and the big fella went off to see for himself. Goodness knows what time they eventually arrived in Swansea!

Rhodes and Richard Illingworth spent so much time together, that Barrie Meyer christened them Bill and Ben. Two Yorkies, one a slow left-arm bowler, the other a wicketkeeper. They were forever whispering to each other, walking down the pitch for a confab. What about doing this? Or that? Or maybe the other?

The physio at Worcester for many years, Les Pink, was also physio for the West Indies, and during a pre-match practice on a tour of India he was crossing the outfield in Madras when my old mate Vanburn Holder playfully directed a ball from his bat towards Pinky. As he prepared to take the catch, he was mowed down by what he thought at first was a Centurion tank. It was, in fact, merely Gordon Greenidge.

Poor old Pinky was down and out – of breath, at least. He heard West Indies manager Gerry Alexander shout, 'Leave him, leave him,' and thought to himself, 'That shows how much he cares.' The four or five thousand Indian spectators, who had already gathered in the stadium for the day's play, thoroughly enjoyed the entertaining sideshow.

It was far less entertaining for Pinky, especially when he discovered that he had broken two ribs. Greenidge, however, consoled him by saying that because he had knocked him out of the way and taken the catch himself, he had prevented Pinky from bruising his fingers.

Another of Pinky's stories concerned an unnamed Test player, who, at the end of an illustrious career, was called to the dressing room to receive an award. Four of his colleagues carried in the treatment table, saying, 'We're giving you this, mate. You've spent so much bloody time on it, we felt you'd be lost without it.'

One of my favourite New Road tales goes back to 1952, during a stoppage for rain in the game against the Indian tourists. Brian Johnston attempted a live interview with the visiting manager, who was a splendid chap, but, as Jonners quickly discovered, did not have too good a grasp of English. After assuring his interviewer that his team had seven very good batsmen and seven very good bowlers, the manager was asked if he was a selector as well.

'No,' he replied, 'I'm a Christian.'

Headingley, Leeds

YORKSHIRE

18

HEADINGLEY will always have a special place in my affections. It is my home ground; it is where I first played county cricket; it is where I umpired my first Test; and it is where I umpired my final first-class game. There have been many other magical moments for me there, and some very funny ones, too.

Headingley is full of history. The home of legends. All the greatest players have appeared at the ground, and on Test match days the atmosphere is second to none.

There are prettier grounds, and no one could describe Headingley as beautiful. There is nothing fancy or pretentious about Yorkshire's county ground, which is perhaps a reflection of the county itself. That fact that it is plain and functional is part of the attraction, though. It is a place to watch cricket – nothing more, nothing less – and most of the Yorkshire crowd are very knowledgeable about the game.

Having said all that, improvements are being made, and the spacious dressing rooms are quite magnificent. I have been in the Manchester United dressing rooms at Old Trafford, and they do not hold a candle to Headingley. There is also a gymnasium, physio facilities, a first aid room, and a doctor's surgery.

The only drawback about the umpire's room is that it is

round the back, so that you cannot see what is happening when you are off the field. Judging bad light can also be tricky, as it is so gloomy where we are!

I was always terrified of bringing the players off for bad light at Headingley, because the crowd would give me dreadful stick. I used to insist on playing on in the dark, in case they lynched me for taking the players off. Before every game on my home ground I would get down on my hands and knees and offer a prayer: 'From rain and bad light Good Lord deliver me today.'

As a spectator at Headingley, I have heard the crowd yell, 'Send for Dickie Bird, all is forgiven,' when the umpires have brought the players off for bad light. For the most part I have enjoyed the banter with the spectators, and it is all done in good humour, although I did very nearly lose my rag in the 'burst drains' episode in a Test match between England and the West Indies, when I was blamed for bringing the teams off because of a waterlogged pitch. I snapped, 'You can't blame me for this. It's not an umpire you need here, it's a plumber.'

It is said that the ball swings about more at Headingley than anywhere else, although strangely it has not done so quite as much in the last few years, since they cut down the trees at the Kirkstall Lane End.

There has always been something in the pitch for the seamers at Headingley, but not many spinners bowl out teams there. Current captain David Byas is keen for all Yorkshire matches to be played at headquarters, feeling that the conditions suit his attack of Gough, Hutchison, Hamilton, Hoggard, Sidebottom and White. He regards Headingley as a good twelfth man, and reckons that his side has a better chance of winning the championship if they concentrate on playing all home matches there.

A championship success is certainly overdue: although

Yorkshire have won the title thirty times, including a shared triumph in 1949, it is now thirty years since Brian Close led them to their last success in 1968.

The legendary Lord Hawke was the captain for the first eight championship wins in 1893, 1896, 1898, 1900, 1901, 1902, 1905 and 1908. Brian Sellers also enjoyed tremendous success, leading the county to six more titles in 1933, 1935, 1937, 1938, 1939 and 1946. Brian Close had four top finishes to his credit in 1963, 1966, 1967 and 1968, and Geoff Wilson had a hat-trick of triumphs in 1922, 1923 and 1924 in his only three years as captain.

The other wins came in 1912 (Sir A. W. White), 1919 (D. C. F. Burton), 1925 (A. W. Lupton), 1931 and 1932 (F. E. Greenwood), 1949 – joint (N. W. D. Yardley), 1959 (J. R. Burnet) and 1960 and 1962 (V. Wilson).

In limited-overs cricket Yorkshire have won the Gillette Cup in 1965 and 1969, the Benson and Hedges Cup in 1987, and the Sunday League in 1983.

Lord Hawke was probably more renowned for his aristocratic attitude than his playing ability, and that immortal all-rounder Wilfred Rhodes used to say of him, 'Oh, aye, very nice man, Lord Hawke. Very good captain, too. Did as he was told. We used to tell him to go to mid-on and mid-off while we professionals got close in for a bit of a natter.'

There is no doubt, however, that Lord Hawke was a fine captain who built self-respect into the side and earned the loyalty of all his players. He was a great influence on the development of the game, not just in Yorkshire, but countrywide.

Wilf Rhodes took 4,187 wickets and scored 39,802 runs in a memorable career which included Test appearances. Opening against the Australians once, he took a lot of stick from the Aussies, who tried to psych him out. After he had scored a century, one of their bowlers went up to him and said, 'I don't

318

know how you score a bloody run, Wilf, you've only got one stroke.'

Wilf looked him straight in the eye and replied, 'Aye, well, that's all I need to get a hundred against thee.'

Wilf must go down as Yorkshire's greatest all-round cricketer, but George Hirst was a magnificent player in the early part of the century, and he later became an excellent coach. It was George who discovered Len Hutton and Freddie Trueman, among others. He said he could not teach Len anything, and described Fred as a 'diamond'.

In one remarkable season George scored 2,385 runs and took 208 wickets, and I don't think anyone has come near that. When asked if he thought anyone would ever beat it, he replied, 'I don't know, but if he does he'll be bloody tired.'

Emmott Robinson arrived on the scene a little later, another in a long line of fine all-round cricketers who went on to become first-class umpires. Robinson was obsessed with beating Lancashire, and one morning, arriving early for a Roses match, he went into the deserted Yorkshire dressing room, knelt on a cushion and prayed something like this: 'Dear Lord above, I know thou art the greatest judge of any cricket match. If it be thy will for Yorkshire to win, they will do so. If it be thy will for Lancashire to win, they will do so. If it be thy will for rain or bad light to bring about a draw, then that is how it will be. But, dear Lord, if thou wilt just keep out of it for the next seventy-two hours, we'll knock the bloody hell out them.'

Robinson was a contemporary of the great Maurice Leyland, of Yorkshire and England, who turned to coaching in later years. Maurice loved to have a bit of banter, particularly with the 'old enemy'. In one Roses match in the 1930s, with the Old Trafford gates locked by eleven o'clock, and a capacity shirt-sleeved crowd enjoying some thrilling cricket, one of the Lancashire batsmen hoisted a delivery from Bill Bowes high into the sky towards Maurice. The crowd fell silent as the ball winged its way ever closer to the fielder, who had taken up a perfect position. There was a burst of raucous laughter and ironic cheering as Maurice spilled it.

Amidst all the noise one voice was heard to say, 'Nay, I could have caught that in my mouth.'

Quick as a flash Maurice turned and snapped, 'Aye, and if my mouth was as big as thine, so could I.'

In another Roses battle, this time at Headingley, George Macaulay, a magnificent off-spin bowler, was walking from the field having taken 12 for 52 in the match to spearhead a great Yorkshire victory. Strangely, he was looking far from cheerful about it.

Maurice put his arm round him and asked, 'What's up, George lad? Why look so miserable? You should be as happy as a sandboy.'

George replied, 'Ah, well, you see, Maurice, I was just thinking. If only I could bowl against them on that pitch every time.'

After the war, although county championship success was sparse by Yorkshire standards, there were still players of great individual skill. If Percy Holmes and Herbert Sutcliffe had been the outstanding pre-war batsmen, then Len Hutton was undoubtedly the outstanding batsman in the world of his time until his retirement in 1955, compiling eighty-five Yorkshire centuries and scoring nearly 25,000 runs, as well as performing memorable feats for England.

Len once asked Keith Miller to introduce him to Ray Lindwall. Although the two had been in opposition, they had never met off the pitch. Miller assured Hutton that Lindwall thought the world of him and encouraged him to go over for a chat. Hutton returned moments later looking rather crestfallen. Said Miller, 'What did he say, then, Len?'

Replied Len, 'He said he was sick of the sight of me batting against him and told me to bugger off.'

'See,' rejoined Miller, 'I told you he admired you.'

I remember Len coming into my dressing room in later years and asking me, 'Can that lot out there play, Dickie? Can they really play?'

'Oh aye,' I replied, 'but not as good as thee.'

In the 1950s two eighteen-year-olds emerged who were to become legends in their own right – Brian Close and Fred Trueman.

The two of them were involved in an incident against Gloucestershire. Fred bowled a rare long hop to Martin Young, who pulled the ball with great ferocity straight at Closey, who was, as usual, fielding in a suicidal close-to-the-wicket position and did not have time to take the appropriate evasive action. The ball hit him on the head and deflected into the hands of slip. Closey did not even rub the spot where the ball had landed with such sickening force, although a bruise the size of an ostrich egg appeared frighteningly quickly.

At close of play a spectator, concerned for Closey's welfare, went over to him and asked if he was all right. 'Aye, nowt to worry about. Nowt at all,' said Closey.

'But just think, Brian,' said the man. 'What if the ball had hit you between the eyes?'

'Well, that would have been a different kettle of fish,' admitted Brian. 'Most likely catch would have gone to cover.'

Little wonder that the great comedian, Eric Morecambe, who was a cricket fanatic, once said, 'I can always tell it is the start of the English cricket season by the sound of ball thudding against Close.'

Closey was the kind of chap who maybe lacked a bit of patience as a player, and as a captain. He wanted to get at the opposition and hammer them, and his very high standards were not always easy to live up to.

After one particularly poor morning in the field, he gave his team a dressing-down at the lunch interval. 'There are three things we need to do,' he barked. 'First, you bowlers. Get your act together. Cut out all the damn rubbish you've been sending down all morning. Second – and this concerns everybody – you've got to smarten up the fielding. We've been giving runs away for charity. It's not good enough.'

There was a pause while everyone waited for Closey to continue with his rallying call, but he fell silent.

'Come on, then, skip,' said wicketkeeper Jimmy Binks. 'What's the third thing?'

'Oh, I don't know,' snapped Closey. 'You think of something.'

Committeeman Sid Fielden was eyewitness to another Close pep talk in more recent times, when the sixty-seven-year-old Brian was captaining Yorkshire's Academy team of teenagers in a game at Headingley.

Closey said to him, 'Come in here, Sid. You're the PR man, so I want you to listen to my talk.'

Sid was surprised, but accepted the invitation, and the talk, he tells me, went something like this.

'I've won the toss and we're fielding. Now remember, cricket matches are won and lost in the field. I want no kissing and cuddling, none of this 'ere shouting "bowlin'" or "well bowled" when the ball goes by the off-stump. That's not well bowled, that's a wasted delivery. And when we get a wicket, I want none of this Indian war-dancing and palm-slapping. Next thing, do you all know what a maiden is?'

There was a silence.

'Come on, speak up. What's a maiden?'

One of the more daring youngsters ventured, 'It's when we bowl six balls and the batsman doesn't score, Mr Close.'

'Rubbish,' said Closey. 'It's when we bowl six balls, all on the stumps, batter has to play them all, and he still doesn't score. That's a maiden. Then we clap. Got it?'

Picking up a helmet with a cage in front of it, he then asked, 'And what's this thing?'

'A helmet, Mr Close.'

'And what's it for?'

'It's for t' short-leg fielder, Mr Close.'

'Aye, well, am fielding at short-leg today, so we shan't be needing that,' he said, and tossed the helmet contemptuously to one side.

The father of one of these young cricketers told of a conversation he had with his son, who complained that Close swore an awful lot.

'What does he say?' asked his father.

'Oh, he only ever says bloody,' replied the son, 'but he never stops saying it.'

After a thoughtful pause the young man then asked, 'Dad, was Mr Close a good player?'

'Wash your mouth out, lad,' snapped his dad. 'He scored 22,650 runs for Yorkshire, including thirty-three centuries; took 967 wickets; and he's one of only five players in the world to take more than eight hundred catches.'

The young man was, as the hymn puts it, 'Lost in wonder, love and praise'.

He then turned to his mother and said, 'Oh, by the way, Mr Close says I've got to ask you to sew up my pockets, though goodness knows why.'

Closey also had a habit of blaming anybody and anything for his dismissals, other than himself. He once said of a ball from Vanburn Holder, which had him caught and bowled, that he had it covered for everything except bad bounce. On another occasion he stormed into the dressing room after lasting only two balls, to find the other players hiding behind newspapers, pretending to be asleep, or contemplating their navels, all in anticipation of another furious outburst. With those beetle brows of his twitching, Closey flung his bat across the room and sat down, fuming. There was a silence of calm before the storm, then he thundered, 'That bloody twelfth man gave me chewing gum of t' wrong bloody flavour.'

Young Master Trueman made his mark in his first Test series in 1952 when the Indians visited Headingley. He destroyed their batting with some fearsome fast bowling, and at one time the visitors had four men back in the pavilion without a single run having been scored in their second innings as Fred set about them.

Twenty-two years later, the manager of the 1974 touring party was Lt. Col. Hemu Adhikari, who had been one of Fred's victims in that series. They met in the bar at Old Trafford during a Test there, and Fred put out his hand and said, 'Hello, Colonel, I'm pleased to see you've got your colour back.'

On one tour of Australia, Fred's opening gambit was to go over to the umpire and say, 'Good morning, sunshine.' One day Fred kept shouting for lbws, and the umpire kept turning him down. He had a go for a few caught behinds. Not out. Was that a slip catch? Didn't carry. And so it went on. As they walked off the field, Fred was feeling sunny no longer and played hell with the umpire.

Eventually it was England's turn to bat, and towards the end of their innings Fred arrived at the crease. The first ball rapped him on the pads. His friend the umpire had his finger in the air like a shot. 'That's out,' he confirmed. As a disconsolate Trueman walked past, the umpire smiled sweetly and said, 'All the best, sunshine.'

Fred was forced to take some of his own medicine in 1963 when he faced the formidable West Indian pace attack of Wes Hall and Charlie Griffith, backed up by Garfield Sobers and

Lester King, in a Yorkshire match at Sheffield's Bramall Lane. Needing to avoid an innings defeat, Yorkshire were 75 for 5 just after lunch on the last day, and Fred was told to hold up his end as long as possible, while everybody else prayed for rain.

Griffith disappeared into the distance to begin his run-up, then came thundering down in the well-worn footmarks, increasing speed with each menacing step. Just as he reached his delivery stride, however, Fred moved away from the crease and held up his hand. Griffith nearly did himself a mischief jamming on his brakes as Fred apologised, 'Sorry about that, Charlie, but I'm going to have to ask for the sightscreen to be moved. I could hardly see a bloody thing.'

The sightscreen at Bramall Lane in those days was fastened down, and it needed the entire groundstaff to carry out the necessary adjustments, which naturally took quite a while.

Finally, the action resumed, and the West Indians decided to get their own back on Fred by crowding him, with close-to-the-wicket fielders in catching positions. Griffith began the long, weary walk back to his mark on the other side of the city and set off again at full pelt. Nearer and nearer he roared, and he was just about to let fly when Fred stepped away again.

'Now what the hell's the matter?' demanded my old umpiring colleague Tommy Spencer.

'I still can't see,' complained Fred. 'It's this damn lot round the bat. They're blocking out all the light. If they don't move back, I'm going to have to make an official appeal for bad light.'

It was a good try, but a few minutes later it was all over. Yorkshire, having lost five wickets for nine runs in just seventeen minutes, had been comprehensively defeated.

Playing in a Test match in searing heat, Fred was once asked by his captain to have another bowl. He had hardly recovered from his previous unproductive stint, and was not too keen on another in those temperatures on an unresponsive pitch, but his captain pleaded, 'Come on, Fred. England expects.'

'Aye,' sighed Fred. 'That's bloody trouble. England's always expecting. No wonder they call her the mother country.'

Fred was travelling home from Headingley one day when he was overtaken by a traffic policeman, who pulled him over to the kerb. The bobby stuck his head through the window and asked for Fred's driving licence. He looked at the driver. 'Nar then, Mr Trueman,' he said, 'I'm afraid you were driving a lot faster than you bowl.'

To which an indignant Fred replied, 'Tell thee summat, sunshine. Tha wouldn't 'ave caught me if I had been.'

David Bairstow emerged in the 1970s as an excellent wicket-keeper with a bubbling personality. He was also very determined to pursue his cricketing career, as he showed when he was due to make his Yorkshire debut at the age of eighteen. He sat his A-level exams at six o'clock in the morning, in order that he could play in the county match later that day. He showed no signs of being over-awed – or tired – with a good performance behind the sticks.

David was no mean batsman, either, as Notts' Basharat Hassan will testify. In a match at Trent Bridge, umpire Ken Palmer had been forced to leave the field through injury, and Basharat, who later became a first-class umpire himself, took his place at square leg. Bob White, the off-spinner, was bowling to Bairstow, who blasted 'Knocker' with a full-blooded lap shot straight to Basharat, striking him an almighty blow. He went down in agony, just as if he had been pole-axed, and had to be carried off. He ended up lying on the adjoining couch to Palmer in the physio's room!

Yorkshire were playing Somerset at Bath in a Sunday League game when Bairstow and Tony Nicholson came together as the last pair, with their side needing just five runs for victory. Ian

Botham was bowling at the time, and the two batsmen had a confab in the middle of the pitch. Said Bluey to Nick, 'I have to get the strike, so whatever happens to the first ball Beefy bowls at you, I'll set off running from the non-striker's end. You run as hard as you can, and hopefully we'll be okay. Just so long as we both know what we're doing.'

'Right,' said Nick. 'Got it. Whatever happens, I run.'

So Nick faced up to the young Both. The first ball whistled past the batsman's off-stump through to wicketkeeper Jim Parks, standing back. Off went Bairstow like a greyhound, only to realise with alarm, halfway down the track, that Nick was making no attempt to move. Bluey slammed on the brakes, turned, and made a mad scramble to get back. Nick, meanwhile, had suddenly decided to run after all, charged out of his crease, and had progressed only a few yards down the pitch when Parks broke his wicket to give Somerset victory.

As the two batsmen made their way disconsolately through the celebrating Somerset supporters, Bairstow demanded of his partner, 'What the hell did you think you were doing?'

'Sorry, Blue,' replied Nick. 'I forgot what we'd agreed.'

Bairstow also played for England, and he found himself seated next to Australian wicketkeeper Rodney Marsh at a luncheon in Victoria. It was quite a warm day, so they both took off their jackets. When it was time to go, Marshy got to his feet, and was surprised to find two members of the England touring party very kindly holding his jacket for him, butler-style. He slipped one arm into his jacket, then the other. As his two 'assistants' let go, Marshy stumbled to the ground, as if drunk, much to the merriment of all and sundry.

It transpired that Bluey had placed silver cutlery in every pocket of the jacket, so that it weighed an absolute ton, and as soon as the two English lads released it, the sheer weight caused Marshy to crash face down on to the floor.

Five years later, in a floodlit one-dayer at Sydney, England were on the receiving end, and the Aussie crowd was already celebrating the prospect of another victory when Yorkshire all-rounder Graham Stevenson strode to the crease to join county colleague Bairstow. It was a similar situation to the one years earlier when one Yorkshireman had famously said to another, 'We'll get these in singles.' This time Bluey was rather more blunt. He said to Stevo, 'We can p*** this lot, old son.' And they did.

Stevenson had great natural ability, and some people said that at eighteen he was more talented than Botham. He went on a scholarship to Australia, and all the Aussies said then that if they had to make a choice between Stevenson and Botham, they would go for Stevo. He was a powerful lad, with a good eye and great timing. He was a fine hitter of the ball, and an excellent new-ball bowler. He should have played longer, and achieved more, than he did.

Towards the end of the 1974 season Yorkshire played Kent at Scarborough, and Tony Nicholson found himself having to toil away with no reward as Colin Cowdrey caressed his way to a century in that classic style of his. Barrie Leadbeater, who later joined me on the first-class umpires' list, was at first slip that day, and, as a player with a very fine technique himself, appreciated the quality of Cowdrey's batting.

'Oh, good shot, Colin,' he would exclaim as yet another beautifully timed shot accelerated on its way to the boundary over the fast outfield.

Finally, Nick could stand it no longer. 'If I hear you say "well played" once more, Ledders, I'll kick you up the backside, and that's a promise.'

'Sorry,' said Ledders, 'but you've got to admit it's simply marvellous to watch.'

'Marvellous?' retorted Nick. 'Let me tell thee I'd just as soon walk all the way back to Leeds with a nail in my shoe than have to put up with yon for another bloody minute.'

It is a tragedy that Nick and Bluey both died at a comparatively early age, and I was also sad to hear that Stevo had fallen upon hard times. There was so much talent there. I have wonderful memories of all three of them.

Yorkshire still play the odd game at Scarborough, a super ground where their visits attract big gates. It is best known for the cricket festival, when various trophies are played for by Yorkshire and visiting guest teams. The cliffs overlooking the glorious North Bay are close at hand on one side of the ground, although not visible to the spectators, but there is a marvellous view of the North Yorkshire Moors on the opposite side.

Despite the ever-present threat of the sea mist, and the fact that the pitch takes spin, there have been many instances of quick scoring and massive hitting at Scarborough. It was there that Jack Hobbs made 266 not out in the Gentleman v. Players match of 1925. C. I. Thornton, playing for the Gentlemen of England against I Zingari, scored 107 in twenty-nine hits – eight sixes and twelve fours – with one mighty strike ending up in Trafalgar Square. Herbert Sutcliffe and Maurice Leyland scored 102 off six consecutive overs in the Essex match of 1932, and twenty years on, Peter May, playing for the MCC, made 174 and 100 not out off the Yorkshire bowling.

It is a ground loved by all Yorkshire cricket followers – and enjoyed by holidaymakers, who turn up in their hundreds with their picnic lunches and swell the crowds. Festival week is what cricket should be all about.

Bill Bowes, one of the best bowlers Yorkshire and England have ever had, covered cricket for the *Yorkshire Evening Post* when he retired from playing. He was faced with the usual problems of telephoning his reports from the ground to the sports desk back in Leeds, and during one Scarborough Festival week he sent the following item: 'After a quiet spell, Parfitt went down the wicket to Illingworth and edged him over the slips and into the deep for three.'

Unfortunately, the young lady on copy-taking duty that day had no interest whatsoever in cricket, and she typed out, 'After a quiet spell, Parfitt went down the wicket to Illingworth and edged him over the cliffs and into the deepest parts of the sea.'

The press box at Bradford Park Avenue used to be situated at the front at one end, the windows below it opening out on to the rows of members' seats, so that the public could hear quite a lot of what was going on in the media circus. Bill told me about the time when Yorkshire were making very little progress against Warwickshire, who had been to the forefront in signing a number of overseas stars, and the game had reached a bit of a stalemate. It was going nowhere, and slowly at that.

Bill's regular copy-taker, Lillian – he called her Lilly for short – had nipped out for a call of nature when Bill phoned to file a lack-of-progress report, and her deputy was not *au fait* with the cricketing terminology. The poor girl struggled to follow what Bill was saying, and constantly interrupted him for an explanation.

Finally, even this usually mild-mannered man exploded, 'Oh, for heaven's sake, put Lilly on.'

Someone from the members' area immediately shouted, 'Good heavens, don't tell me they've signed him an' all.'

As a fast bowler himself, Bill would have been equally amused to hear Brian Johnston describing the occasion when a little Dachshund ran on to the pitch at Headingley. Said Jonners, 'He's a splendid little chap, wagging his tail like mad. I can tell he's a fast bowler because he has four short legs and his balls swing both ways.'

Bradford Park Avenue has one particular memory for me, for

it was there in May, 1959, that I made my highest score of 181 not out against Glamorgan.

In the mid-1970s Yorkshire stopped playing at Sheffield's Bramall Lane. Having been the first home of county cricket, it was also the home of Sheffield United Football Club, and it was sad when the owners decided to convert the site into a purely football arena for United's First Division side. I loved playing at Bramall Lane and I loved umpiring there, too.

In my days as a young player just making my way, I used to practise in the old shed at Bramall Lane where the football car park is now situated. There was no heating, and it was always bitterly cold there in the winter. The pitch was concrete, and I can still feel my hands jarring as I recall how the bat struck on that surface. I went back there later on with Yorkshire Seconds, with those two excellent coaches Maurice Leyland and Arthur Mitchell.

There used to be a big clock on the pavilion at Bramall Lane, and players would have bets on who could hit it. Memory plays strange tricks at times, but I seem to remember Keith Miller might have won his bet one day.

Sheffield continued to stage county cricket at Abbeydale Park, which is a much more picturesque ground but without the atmosphere of its predecessor, and now county matches are no longer played there either.

Harrogate is another ground where matches were always well supported, but that has sadly also fallen by the wayside. A pity, because it was always a good pitch for getting a result. Every match I have umpired there has reached a positive conclusion, and if you look back into the record books you will find that Yorkshire had a lot of wins on that ground.

Geoff Boycott was the dominant batsman during my time as a player and umpire. He scored 30,570 runs in 414 matches, and was involved in some stirring deeds at international level.

He also figured in a good deal of controversy on and off the pitch.

Sid Fielden has always supported Geoff, and he backed him when he heard about Geoff's troubles in France in 1998, when he was alleged to have struck a woman companion. Said Sid, 'One of Geoffrey's great strengths as a batsman was that he knew which ball to leave alone. It's a pity he did not always apply the same principle to women. But I have never believed he was guilty of this offence.'

Sid told Boycs to his face, 'You're about as good a judge of women as you were of a short single.'

There was one match when Boycs was hit on the pad and someone shouted, 'That's lbw.'

'Never in this world,' retorted Boycs. 'Dickie wouldn't have given that.'

'That's because Dickie never gives thee out,' interjected another fielder.

Sid claims that on the only two occasions I did give Boycs out, between 1970 and 1986, I rang him up afterwards to apologise.

I was once told that to make the best Yorkshire pudding you had to have a very slow batter – and Boycs springs immediately to mind.

I was umpiring a John Player League match at Fartown, Huddersfield, when Boycs lost two of his contact lenses in a matter of seconds. He told me, 'We'll have to find them, I haven't got any more.'

'What's this "we" business?' I asked. However, seeing Boycs go down on his hands and knees in search of the missing lenses, I got down on my hands and knees alongside him. The crowd must have thought we were holding a Sunday afternoon prayer meeting.

After a couple of minutes' fruitless exploration I said to

Boycs, 'Right, then, Geoffrey, that's it. We can't waste any more time. We've got forty overs to get through before ten past four. What are you going to to do?'

'But I can't see properly, Dickie.'

'In that case,' I told him, 'you'd better beggar off and send the next man in.'

So off he went, dragging his bat behind him. Retired blind.

The crowd cheered, and I heard someone shout, 'Good old Dickie. He was putting us all to sleep.'

For someone who batted so slowly, Boycs was a bit of a speed merchant when it came to driving. He was once on his way through Chesterfield *en route* for London when his passenger, David Bairstow, warned him, 'Look out, Boycs. Police.' Geoff slammed on the brakes and eased his way past two other carloads of Yorkshire players who had been pulled up. They couldn't believe they had copped it while Stirling Moss had escaped.

He did pick up one or two speeding tickets, but usually found himself let off, including one occasion immediately prior to his making his hundredth century against the Australians at Headingley in 1977.

Geoff once asked Sid Fielden if he would take him to the West Yorkshire Police Driving School at Crofton, near Wakefield, as he was keen to try out the 'skid pan'. He allowed his partner, Anne Wyatt, to go first, and watched with Sid from the upstairs office window. It was hair-raising. Even for Geoffrey.

The instructor turned to Boycs and said, 'Right, now it's your turn.'

Boycs looked at him quizzically for a moment, and then replied, 'I don't think I'll bother. I'm playing for England next week.'

Let no one doubt that Geoff was a great batsman, though.

If I needed anyone to bat for my life it would be him.

A group of old-timers were once marvelling at another flawless Boycott century, this time at Bradford Park Avenue. 'But I reckon that our Geoffrey must be t' best batsman in t' world,' said one. 'Just look at yon shot through mid-wicket. Magnificent.'

'Aye,' said another. 'There are times when you think he'll never get out. He's so good I reckon he could go on batting 'till he's fifty.'

'Could be,' said a third member of the Boycott appreciation society. 'But time'll come when even he'll have to bow to Anno Domini.'

'Tha talks rubbish,' said the chap in the next seat. 'Anyone knows them Italians can't laik cricket. So how's one of them going to get best batsman in t' world out?'

Boycs played his early cricket with me at Shaw Lane, home of Barnsley Cricket Club, and another Yorkshire captain, Martyn Moxon, also made a name for himself there in the Yorkshire League before going on to win fame with the county and England. I always thought Martyn was too nice a bloke to be captain: as a captain you have to be ruthless at times, which doesn't win you too many friends. You simply cannot satisfy everyone, and that is what Martyn tried to do. These days he coaches the youngsters, and he is the ideal man for the job.

The current Yorkshire captain is David Byas. David is a farmer, and when he played his first match for the county second team, he had to deliver eight or nine calves to another farm immediately prior to making his way to the ground for the fixture. He arrived for the game with about thirty seconds to spare – still in his farmer's muck. Thankfully, however, there were no ducks to follow. Not that day, anyway.

At the county's annual meeting in Leeds in 1999 there was an item on the agenda with regard to cutting the committee from twenty-four members to twelve. Sid Fielden, who is also a Methodist lay preacher, argued that it should be left as it was. Barbara White, however, a Yorkshire member from Taunton, argued, 'Why is it you want twenty-four? Jesus had only twelve apostles, and they managed to make decisions which had great repercussions for all mankind. What was good enough for Jesus should be good enough for the Yorkshire committee, and you, as a preacher of the Gospel, should realise that better than anyone.'

Yorkshire have some good young lads coming through, among them Matthew Wood, who is a tremendous prospect. Cricket is in his blood. His father played for Emley Cricket Club, near Huddersfield, his mother made the teas, and his sister was scorer.

Matthew is also a very dedicated fan of Emley Football Club, and when they had a good run in the FA Cup a couple of years ago, he flew back from New Zealand, where he was coaching, to watch a tie with Lincoln City – and then took the next flight back to New Zealand. Now there's loyalty and dedication for you. If he shows that kind of attitude for Yorkshire he should go far.

No doubt Matthew's father is very proud of his lad, because all good Yorkshiremen and true nurse an ambition for their sons to play cricket for the county. Father-to-be Leslie Taylor was such a man.

The Taylors were living in Bermuda, 3,500 miles from the Broad Acres, but Mrs Taylor was persuaded to travel back to Yorkshire in plenty of time for the birth. However, to her husband's consternation, she was visiting her sister in Oldham, Lancashire, when she went into labour – three weeks early.

Mrs Taylor immediately called for a taxi and said to the driver, 'Get me to Yorkshire, quick as you can!' With her sister gripping her tightly by the hand, she made the thirty-mile dash to Leeds, where, an hour later, her son Duncan was born.

Asked about the fuss, Mrs Taylor reflected, 'Oh, I'm getting quite used to it all by now. I did the same thing fifteen months ago. But then we had a daughter!'

Lord Roy Mason, of Barnsley, who has always been a good friend of mine, is not too sure whether my Jaguar XJ8 is a joy or a pain. He claims that I only use it when I have a car-sitter – or when it can be seen from a window. It is true to say that I have managed to acquire the services of his protection officers: on our frequent outings to functions and meals together, I ask them to guard my car as well. It's not likely to get scratched when they are around.

You cannot always believe what Roy says, though. He has told people that I travel so slowly on the motorways – so much so that lorry drivers wave to me as they pass – simply to cut down on petrol consumption because the damn thing costs so much to run. As if I would!

Sometimes I leave the car at home, and take the train, for example, when spending a few days down in Torquay with my good friends John and Pat Perry at the Livermead Cliff Hotel. I am treated like royalty on the train. Reserved carriage, table set for tea, with tablecloth and all the best crockery. Mind you, the guard does happen to be a cricket buff.

I once embarrassed His Lordship when he took me for a meal in the House of Lords' restaurant on the occasion of my one hundredth international at Lord's cricket ground. My steak from the serve-yourself hot table was delicious, so I went back and got another! Lord Mason always did say that I could eat for England. 'You've got an appetite more like a horse than a Bird,' he teases me.

Incidentally, I had just bought my new Jag when Yorkshire Television came over to my cottage to interview me. They asked me to drive it to the top of my lane while the cameras rolled.

Who should come down the main road at the end of the lane but Yorkshire and England fast bowler Darren Gough, another Barnsley lad. He drew up, stuck his head out of the window and called out a greeting.

The camera crew said to him, 'When are you going to get a car like this, Goughie?'

He replied, 'When I become a best-selling umpire.'

The Parks, Oxford

UNIVERSITIES

19

A NY mention of Fenner's conjures up a lovely picture in
my mind's eye . . . of bangers and mash! Strange, isn't
it, how certain mundane things stay locked in the memory.
This traditional dish is always served at Fenner's on one of the
three lunch-times during matches, and everyone looks forward
to that particular culinary delight at a place where the food is
always very good.

Fenner's has always been one of the best pitches in the
world, and a lovely place to play cricket. Many Cambridge
undergraduates have begun to blossom there before going on to
make a name for themselves at county and international level.

There is no doubting the quality of the pitch, so lovingly
tended for many years by that master of his craft, Cyril Coote,
who produced magnificent tracks of good, even bounce that
were a delight, particularly for the batsmen, and it is little
wonder that many top quality players emerged from Cambridge
University, having honed their batting skills at Fenner's.

Peter May, Michael Brearley, Ted Dexter, David Sheppard
and Michael Atherton all went on to captain England after
playing for Cambridge, while Majid Khan became captain of
Pakistan after completing his studies there.

Cyril, a lovely fellow, also acted as a father figure and adviser
to countless undergraduates through the years, and I once asked

him to tell me who, in his opinion, was the best player he had seen at Cambridge. He thought for a moment, then replied, 'Majid Khan. After him, Peter May. I have seen no one to touch those two.'

It was on Parker's Piece, the open common adjacent to Fenner's, that Tom Hayward and Jack Hobbs both learned their cricket. There can be as many as eight or nine matches being played on these Cambridge pitches at any one time, and the story goes that Hubert Doggart, who had a voice like a foghorn, once sent back his partner at Fenner's, with the result that two batsmen were run out on Parker's Piece.

That was similar to the time I was umpiring a county match and called 'no-ball' in my usual no-nonsense fashion. A chap down the road, playing in a village match, heard the shout, took an almighty swipe, and was clean bowled.

Doggart, incidentally, once shared a second-wicket stand of 429 with John Dewes against Essex at Fenner's in 1949 – only 26 short of the then world record.

During the days of Wilfred Rhodes, one of the greatest all-round cricketers the world has ever seen, Yorkshire paid a visit to Fenner's, and the legend was bowling to a young University freshman. To the amazement of everyone, the batsman proceeded to knock Rhodes all over the field and went in at lunch on 99 not out.

While they were having lunch, one of the Cambridge players said to the batsman, 'I can't believe what you've just done. You do know, don't you, who it is that you've just been thrashing around Fenner's?'

The young man replied, 'No, I've no idea. Who is it?'

'That,' said his team-mate, 'just happens to be the great Wilfred Rhodes.'

The batsman was still reeling from that piece of information when he resumed his innings at the start of the afternoon

session, needing just one more for his century. Now knowing who the bowler was, he was a bag of nerves. He was
shaking all over. Couldn't keep the bat still. And was out
first ball.

In 1982 Derek Pringle was selected to play for England while
still a Cambridge undergraduate. It caused quite a stir at the
time, but I applauded the England selectors for that decision.
Unless you give youngsters a chance, you will never know
how they will fare at a higher level. My motto has always
been that if they are good enough to play for England, they
are old enough.

There was some debate about the selection of the team
on a later occasion, and I remember a delightful quote in
The Times newspaper which read, 'The only change England
might propose would be to replace Derek Pringle, who remains
troubled by no balls.'

A year after Pringle's elevation to international status there
was another notable achievement by Robin Boyd-Moss, who
went on to play for Northamptonshire. He became the first
player to score a century in each innings of a University match.

While normally I enjoyed my visits to the University grounds,
two occasions caused me quite a bit of upset.

After one game at Fenner's I was preparing to travel up to
Leicester, where I was due to stand at a county match the
following day. I had packed all my gear and was just about to
put it in the boot of the car ready for the trip north, when Chris
Balderstone, who had been umpiring with me, came across to
wish me all the best. We had a brief chat, then set off on our
separate ways.

I arrived in Leicester at about eleven thirty that night, opened
the boot of the car to get out my overnight things, and stared
at the empty space. No bag. No gear. Nothing. Suddenly it
dawned on me what must have happened. I had shut the boot

after talking to Chris, without first putting my tackle in. It must still be standing in splendid isolation in the Fenner's car park.

I was umpiring at Grace Road first thing next morning, and there I was with no gear. The only thing I could think of was to drive back home to Barnsley, pick up a spare set of umpiring clothes and get back to Leicester as quickly as I could. People will tell you I am not exactly Michael Schumacher, not even on the M1, so it was nearly three thirty a.m. when I eventually arrived back at my Leicester hotel.

Meanwhile, Mr Johns, who looks after the cricketers at Fenner's, had rung Leicestershire County Cricket Club to tell them that one of the groundstaff lads had found my bags in the car park, and that he himself would drive up to Grace Road at the crack of dawn to make sure that it was available for me in time for the game.

'Tell Dickie not to worry,' he said. I did not know all this, however, and I worried all night long. It was incredibly frustrating therefore to arrive at the ground next morning to find that I had not one, but two sets of clothes.

On another occasion I had been staying, as usual, with the Oxford scorer while umpiring a match at the Parks. The first two days had gone without a hitch, but when I woke up on the third and final day I discovered, to my horror, that my car had been vandalised overnight.

It was amazing, however, how so much damage was repaired in so little time. A quick telephone call brought immediate help, and by the time I came off the field at close of play, my car had been miraculously restored to something like its old self, and I was able to drive it up to Nottingham, where I was due to umpire a county championship game at Trent Bridge.

I booked into a hotel on arrival, had a good night's sleep, went out to my car after breakfast – and found that it had been vandalised again, in much the same way. The steering column had been ripped away, windows smashed, seats slashed, radio stolen. It was a terrible mess, and this time it took three days to repair.

I slumped into a chair in the hotel foyer, in a state of shock, and buried my head in my hands. One fellow was obviously concerned about me, and he tapped me on the shoulder and said sympathetically, 'Are you all right, Dickie? You don't look too clever.'

I looked up. 'You're right,' I said. 'I'm feeling pretty sick, to tell the truth. I've just had my car smashed up for the second time in two days. I had it repaired in Oxford yesterday, but now someone's given it a right old going-over and it's in a worse mess than ever.'

The chap went out into the car park to survey the damage for himself. When he came back he was as white as a sheet. 'I don't believe it,' he whispered hoarsely, completely distraught.

'Told you it was bad, didn't I?' I said.

'It's not that,' he muttered, almost in a daze.

'Whatever's the matter, then, man?' I asked.

He gave me an agonised look. 'Your car may have been vandalised, but I was parked right next to you, and some bugger's pinched mine!'

The Parks at Oxford is yet another very picturesque ground, and in June, July and August, when all the flowers and trees are in full bloom, it is quite wonderful. In April and May, however, you would be hard pressed to find a chillier ground in the whole of England.

Like Cambridge, Oxford have produced some great players who have gone on to represent their countries as captains – Donald Carr, Colin Cowdrey, M. J. K. Smith, the Nawab of Pataudi, Imran Khan and Alan Melville, of South Africa.

Whatever you do, do not mention the Parks to Geoffrey Boycott, however: it is the only first-class ground where he has failed to score a hundred. He was determined to put that right in his last year in county cricket when he captained Yorkshire in a match there. Yorkshire batted first, but to his consternation Boycs was quickly on his way back to the pavilion, a long, long way from recording his first Parks century. He strode angrily from the square and went straight into the nets, where he practised for the rest of the day.

The following day Oxford were bowled out cheaply and Yorkshire were in a position to enforce the follow-on, but Boycs had other ideas. He so badly wanted that elusive hundred, that he decided to bat again. Sadly, my old mate was rolled over again early doors and he never did make that Oxford ton.

Stories abound about the old days, and I once read an incredible account of a game Oxford played against the MCC in 1877 – just before my time – which produced the lowest single-innings score in a first-class game. Oxford were bowled out for a mere twelve runs. Only three men troubled the scorer, and the Oxford captain did not appear at all. By the time he rolled up the innings had ended.

To be fair, Oxford tried to make a game of it. Despite a badly depleted attack, they bowled out the MCC for 124, with Tilecote, who was normally the wicketkeeper, turning his arm over to such good effect that he finished with 8 for 51. He did not fare quite so well with the bat: he opened the innings and was one of five University men to bag a pair as MCC bowled out their hosts for 35 in the second innings to win by an innings and 77 runs. Visiting bowler Frederick Morley recorded match figures of 13 wickets for 14 runs from 33.1 overs, including an astonishing 27 maidens.

Tim Lamb, who is now doing an excellent job as Chief Executive of the England and Wales Cricket Board, was another player to have limited success with the bat in more recent times.

He admits that in two seasons of cricket for Oxford University, he reached double figures only twice.

He does, however, remember preventing a premature Yorkshire victory at the Parks by batting out the last over of the second day, but even that proved to have a hollow ring about it. Tim discovered later that the last-over bowler was under instructions not to get him out: the Yorkshire players had arranged a party in Oxford that night, and no way did they want an early trip back to the Broad Acres.

In view of what was almost an allergy to batting, it was hard to fathom why Tim should be on the receiving end of four bouncers from John Snow in a match at Hove, despite the fact that the Oxford man had, more by pure good luck than management, hung around to share a forty-odd partnership with Martin Vernon. As Tim later told me, one good yorker would have seen him off.

Fortunately the pitch was hard and fast and he was able to see the ball clearly and quickly enough to allow it to whistle over his head, but wicketkeeper J. T. Murray was having chickens in the pavilion, fearing for his colleague's safety. He leaned out of the window, gesticulating in frenzied fashion to the umpires that something should be done about Snowy before poor old Lamb was slaughtered.

Tony Pawson, who went on to play for Kent and later became the world fly-fishing champion, as well as the *Observer*'s angling correspondent, claims that he and his father have the distinction of being the only father and son to captain Oxford to an innings victory in a Varsity match.

Tony's father must also be the only person to play in a Varsity match and not know he was on the winning side. Thinking the game had been rained off, he sneaked away to the wilds of Scotland for the unexpected bonus of an extra fishing trip. He returned a month later to discover that play had resumed after all, and Oxford had managed to win without him.

Earlier in that same game, Pawson Senior featured in an unseemly incident when Cambridge's opening batsman, R. A. Young, who fancied himself a bit, having played at international level, snicked a delivery into his pads. The ball lodged there and wicketkeeper Pawson darted round from behind the stumps and started delving into the batsman's pads with his gloves, believing that Young would be out if he got the ball before it fell to the ground.

An angry Young tried to fight him off by bashing him on the back with his bat, but Pawson eventually emerged, bruised, battered but triumphant, holding the ball aloft. The whole Oxford team appealed with him, to no avail. Not out was the only verdict.

The bowler on that occasion was H. A. Gilbert, who came very close to England selection. His nickname was 'Barmy', more because of his behaviour as a fly-fisherman than as a cricketer. Tony told me that 'Barmy' once left a wedding in full morning dress, grabbed a rod and plunged straight into the River Wye. Shortly afterwards, a grey topper could be seen bobbing along in the current, having been displaced in the excitement of hooking a big salmon.

White cap and bails? Top hat and tails, more like.

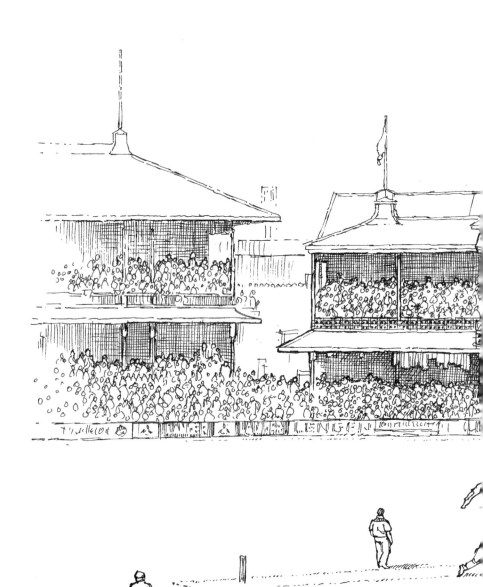

Sydney Cricket Ground, Australia

AUSTRALIA AND
NEW ZEALAND

20

I F I had to put my head on the block and select a favourite
Australian ground, it would have to be Sydney. Adelaide
beats it for beauty, in a picture postcard setting, and Melbourne
is bigger, but taking everything into consideration, the SCG
reigns supreme. It is, quite simply, a magnificent stadium.

Although situated away from the centre of Sydney, it is nevertheless in a built-up area. The ground itself has everything you
could wish for in terms of top-class facilities. There is an excellent
pitch, marvellous stands, spacious dressing rooms, superb practice
facilities, a 65,000 capacity, with plans to increase that.

The famous hill has long gone, to be replaced by an impressive new stand, and maybe just a little of the unique character
of the place has disappeared with it. No doubt the crowd in
that area still hurl the same abuse as they always did when they
congregated on that big grass mound, but it has somehow lost
its cutting edge.

Melbourne is a massive ground. One stand alone holds
49,000, and the total capacity is 110,000. When it is full,
it is an awesome sight. Once again the facilities leave little
to be desired, and a big bonus is that the roads in and out
of Melbourne are so good that there are never any traffic
problems getting to the ground. In any case, the stadium is
only five minutes' walk from the centre of the city.

The MCG shares a curious phenomenon with Sydney. Stand in the middle of either ground when everyone has gone, and you can hear a distinct humming sound. I've tried the experiment myself, and it is strange. It may be something to do with the way the stands tower so high on all four sides, but the atmospherics produce a definitely ghostly sound that resembles the humming of the old telegraph wires.

Melbourne has featured in some of the great moments of Australian cricket. It was there that they played the first Test against England in 1876–7, winning by 45 runs; it was there that South Africa slumped to the lowest total ever scored against the Aussies – 36 in 1931–2; it was there that Sir Donald Bradman and Jack Fingleton shared a record sixth-wicket stand of 346 against England in 1936–7; and it was there that Arthur Mailey recorded the best single-innings bowling figures for Australia against England of 9 for 121 in 1920–1.

Mailey was a splendid chap who did not mind having a laugh at his own expense. When he retired from playing he became a cricket correspondent, and ended up running a butcher's shop near Sydney. Very shortly after he opened up, a sign appeared in the shop window which read, 'I used to bowl tripe. Then I wrote tripe. Now I'm selling it.'

Adelaide is a lovely spot. It resembles New Road, Worcester, in many ways, particularly with the cathedral in the background, and I am a little sad that I have never had the pleasure of umpiring there. Likewise Brisbane, where development is still taking place, with another 100,000 capacity in the pipeline.

The WACA ground at Perth is a beautiful arena, and the floodlights they use for the day–night internationals are the best in the world. It is almost like playing in daylight even when it is dark.

It was during the England tour of 1991 that Allan Lamb

decided to go on one of his customary long runs. After three kilometres he turned to go back to the hotel, and he had covered barely a hundred metres of the return trip when he suddenly pulled up lame with a hamstring problem. He could hardly walk, never mind run, so there he was, stranded.

In the end he had to hail a cab, and you can imagine the mirth of his team-mates when he arrived back at the hotel, to be helped out of the cab by a kindly driver. Someone suggested that the next time he attempted a training run, it might be as well if he took along a cab-charge voucher.

Australia's final Test ground is Hobart, in Tasmania, which is very pleasant, right alongside a river and not too far from the sea. It is not as big a stadium as the others, but still maintains the high standard of facilities you find on all Australian grounds.

Although such a small island, Tasmania has produced some very fine cricketers, including David Boon, who has a wonderful Test record. David has toured all over the world, which means that he has spent a lot of time away from his family. After he had departed for yet another long spell abroad his daughter turned to her mother and asked, 'Has Daddy gone to heaven, Mummy?'

Not quite that far. David had only gone to England, but the next best thing, I suppose.

Ricky Ponting, who is currently making a name for himself, and Jamie Cox, who announced his arrival on the English scene by scoring 172 against Yorkshire in his first game as captain of Somerset at the start of the 1999 season, also hail from Tasmania.

Keith Miller was one of the great Australian characters before and after the war. I remember him once putting a Rugby ball on the centre spot at the Rugby ground at Headingley and kicking it straight between the posts. It was a massive kick, and he did it in his cricket boots.

Keith lived in Sydney and captained New South Wales. He was a bit forgetful at times, and one day the umpire called him over and said, 'Excuse me, Mr Miller, but I think you'll find that you've got twelve men on the field.'

Miller turned to his men, pointed at one of them at random, and barked, 'You, bugger off. The rest, scatter.'

On another occasion the team was all set to take the field when Keith was asked, 'Where's old so-and-so?'

'No idea,' said Keith. 'Is he supposed to be playing?'

'Yes,' came the reply. 'And you were supposed to be giving him a lift.'

One day a player too many, another one short. Typical Miller, but what a player. He was the best all-rounder Australia have produced.

Alan Davidson, who was around at the time of Neil Harvey and co., was no mean performer with bat and ball, either. One day he bemoaned the fact to me that nobody seemed to swing the ball like they did in the old days. Believe me, Alan could swing it in and also swing it away late, which was why he got so many wickets.

He explained to me how he did it. He said it was because he always had his thumb on the seam of the ball. He told me, 'It's like the kangaroo's tail, Dickie. That controls the way the kangaroo goes. It's the same with a cricket ball. The seam controls the way it goes.'

So there you have it. The theory of the kangaroo's tail. And if you can follow it, no doubt there will be bowlers all over the world going out and putting it to the test the minute they read this.

Talking of kangaroos, the last time I was in Australia I was told a tale about an MCC member who made the trip Down Under in the winter of 1980–81. In between the cricket, he decided to hire a car, fitted with steel bars above the bumper to avoid serious damage on impact with a jay-walking kangaroo, and pay a visit to the bush.

He toured for several days without incident, but then suddenly a kangaroo bounded out in front of the car, which was doing sixty miles an hour. There was an almighty thud and the poor old roo bounced off the steel bars and lay lifeless on the track.

For a keepsake of the incident the driver decided to take a photograph, and, helped by his companion, dressed the helpless roo in an MCC tie, cap and blazer. However, while the fellow was checking the light meter on his camera, the roo revived and ran off, still sporting the MCC regalia.

And, do you know, I'm sure I once saw it on the hill at Sydney.

That great English batsman, Denis Compton, heroically confronted the equally great Ray Lindwall and Miller on numerous occasions, and he once went out to face them despite having had five stitches inserted in a cut over his eyebrow. There were no helmets in those days, but he later said he would not have worn one had they been available, because it would have been an insult to his manhood. With all that Brylcreem he advertised, the darn thing would probably have slipped off anyway.

Lindwall was particularly fast, but there have been some pretty quick bowlers plying their trade in club cricket in Australia, and one such player once delivered what can only be described as a real scorcher. The batsman's trousers burst into flames when the ball hit him on the thigh. He had apparently left a box of matches in his pocket. I suppose that is what is known as a strike bowler.

Another match saw one prison team playing against another, and the umpire, himself a convict, gave the opening batsman out in the first over. The batsman, however, refused to walk.

He claimed that a convicted criminal such as the umpire could not possibly make a reliable decision.

My old mate Geoff Boycott will not forget one Christmas in Australia in a hurry. On the England tour of 1965–6 one of the matches against South Australia was played during the festive period, and England were made to toil in the field for two days in uncomfortably hot weather. Eventually they bowled the home side out and took their turn at the crease on Christmas Eve.

Boycs opened the innings and was out first ball. And the name of the youngster who took such a prize scalp in that heat? 'Jack' Frost.

Brothers Ian and Greg Chappell have both captained Australia, and I rate the former as one of the best I have seen. I had a long chat with him in Melbourne when I visited Australia in the winter of 1998–9, and we got to talking about retirement. I told him I had thought long and hard about the right time to call it a day, and asked him how he had come to his decision.

He replied, 'It came to me in a Test match at Adelaide. I found myself clock-watching. It was something I had never done before – I had always enjoyed my cricket so much. But from ten thirty a.m. onwards on that day, I kept looking at the clock. I must have glanced at it seven or eight times and it was still showing only five past eleven. I knew then it was time to go.'

Greg once got five ducks on the trot for Australia. He was in such good nick in the nets, and felt in great form, but along came a handful of ducks. He batted in another Test at Melbourne and unbelievably made it six of the worst as he failed to trouble the scorer yet again. As he walked off, someone threw a duck on to the field. A real one!

If Lindwall and Miller were the dynamic duo of the immediate pre-war and post-war years, then Dennis Lillee and Jeff

Thomson struck fear into the hearts of batsmen everywhere in more recent times. However, one of their most memorable partnerships came not with the ball, but with the bat.

I was umpiring the World Cup final of 1975 between Australia and the West Indies at Lord's, and when Lillee and Tommo came together for the last wicket, the Aussies still needed 59 to win. Hardly surprisingly, not even the rest of the team fancied their chances, and had already started packing their bags when their attention was drawn to the fact that the two tail-enders were slowly but surely whittling away the runs.

They stopped their packing and went back to the window of the dressing room to watch. Maybe they still had a chance after all. The runs continued to flow, and by this time it was 'Sir Dennis Lillee' out there. The tension was almost unbearable as the Australians got to within twenty runs of victory, then Lillee lofted one into the covers and Roy Fredericks took the catch.

The crowd ran on to the ground like a plague of locusts and Lillee turned to make his way back to the pavilion, disappointed but thinking to himself, 'Oh, well, we've at least given them a real run for their money.' Then he noticed Fredericks shy the ball at the stumps and wondered what the hell was going on. The ball missed its target and sped on its way, with West Indian fielders chasing frantically after it. Only then did he realise that my colleague, Tommy Spencer, had signalled a no-ball. The game was still very much alive.

The ball had by this time disappeared among thousands of onrushing spectators, wildly celebrating West Indians who thought it was all over.

Lillee screamed at a bewildered Tommo, 'Come on, run. Run. We can run all twenty and win the game.'

It was at this point that Lillee's version of what happened

differs slightly from mine, which appeared in my autobiography. Dennis recalled it as follows, 'I was still yelling at Tommo to run as I charged down the pitch to join him at the other end, but he wouldn't budge. He told me to get back and not be so bloody stupid, because one of those West Indians could hide the ball in his pocket and run us out.'

According to the laws we had to award four runs and call 'dead ball', and shortly afterwards Thomson became the fifth run-out victim of the innings, to leave the West Indies victors after all by 17 runs.

Len Pascoe was another fine fast bowler, but he always operated in the shadow of Lillee and Thomson. He and Dennis were good friends, and during one Test they decided to have a night out in London with their old adversary, Ian Botham.

They had a few drinks before going on to a hotel, and as they entered the foyer, they saw a dummy in the corner with an absolutely gorgeous wig perched on its head. Botham immediately whipped it off and placed it on Lillee. 'Suits you down to the ground,' he chuckled. 'Much better than the old one.'

Len was not amused. 'What the hell do you think you're playing at? Put it back where it belongs. You'll get us all into trouble.'

Both retorted, 'You keep quiet, Pinocchio. Speak when you're spoken to.'

Lennie, it has to be said, has a nose that is somewhat larger than average, and he was livid at this reference to his proboscis. Like an elephant, however, he did not forget.

The Test match continued next day, and Lennie was all fired up when Both strode in to take the crease. He peppered him with everything. Assaulted him, even. Hit him in the ribcage, on the shoulder, hands, helmet. Bang, crash, wallop. All over. 'I don't know what the hell's the matter with your mate,' Both said to Lillee. 'I must have upset him. Was it something I said, do you think?'

'Who nose?' replied Dennis.

It has always been accepted policy to sign bats for players' benefits, helping a fellow cricketer, and the job always has to be done right. Lennie and Doug Walters were doing the honours in the pavilion one day, and Doug was distraught to find that Lennie had signed the bat upside down.

He scolded him, 'Lennie, you bloody idiot, you've signed this one the wrong way up.'

An abashed Pascoe replied, 'Jeez, Dougie, how did you know it was me?'

Dean Jones was a magnificent Test player, averaging the high forties at that level, and he was probably one of the best one-day players I have seen as well. He did a lot for Derbyshire when he came to England to play for them and led them to second place in the county championship. Amazingly he was sacked the following season.

He had a field day against the West Indies in one match. He was in tip-top form and enjoying the rare experience of simply murdering the famed pace attack. In the first innings he was all set, it seemed, for a massive score, until he made the biggest mistake of his cricketing life. He stepped back from the crease, held up his hand, and brought Curtly Ambrose to a juddering halt as he was about to explode into his delivery stride.

'Excuse me,' said Jonah, 'but would you mind removing that white sweat band on your wrist? It's distracting me.'

Ambrose went spare. He whipped the offending item off, threw it angrily to the ground, marched menacingly back to his mark and tore in like a madman. Before the Jones boy and his Aussie team-mates knew what had hit them, Curtly had taken five wickets for one run.

358

Said a shell-shocked Jones, 'I wish I'd kept my bloody mouth shut.'

The retirement of Australian captain Mark Taylor in 1999 was a sad loss to the game. Not only was he a great leader of men, he was one of cricket's gentlemen, and a credit to the game. However, he decided to go out at the top, at the height of his career, and people will therefore remember him at his best. I can understand why he decided to go when he did: I felt exactly the same when I made the decision to quit the international scene.

Mark was 334 not out overnight in a Test match in Peshawar, Pakistan, in the 1998–9 series, thus equalling Sir Donald Bradman's record score, and people asked me if I thought he would retire on the overnight total or bat on the following morning in order to beat Bradman's record.

I said, 'Knowing Mark as I do, he will declare for the good of the team, because he will feel that he needs as much time as possible to bowl Pakistan out.'

I was proved right. Mark did declare and thus forfeited the opportunity to make history for himself. That was the kind of player he was. He always put the team first.

I have always said that the four greatest captains I have ever seen are Ray Illingworth, Ian Chappell, Michael Brearley and Richie Benaud. I have no hesitation now in adding Taylor to that elite quartet.

Merv Hughes was another in the long line of fearsome Australian fast bowlers, and he was never short of a word or three.

I helped Ally McCoist's team win a round of *A Question of Sport* on BBC television in April 1999 and Andy Goram, who was also on the panel, told me of the time he came up against Merv.

Andy was playing for Scotland against the Australians at

cricket – he was a very good cricketer as well as a top-class goalkeeper for Scotland and Rangers. Merv, true to form, let Andy have a few bouncers, just to soften him up. Andy was left ducking, diving and weaving all over the place. One vicious delivery flew straight towards his head, and how it missed him no one knows. In taking evasive action Andy went down full length on the ground, goalkeeper style, his bat going one way and his gloves the other.

Merv, oozing sympathy, went down the pitch, looked pityingly at Goram and grunted, 'Stick to bloody football, sonny.'

Javed Miandad, of Pakistan, also found himself out-manoeuvred by Merv during a Test match in which there was considerable needling. Merv had a go at Miandad, who jabbered back nineteen to the dozen, eventually snarling, 'Oh, get back to your mark, you bus conductor.'

Merv bridled. The old moustache started quivering. His nostrils flared. He stomped back muttering dark curses under his breath. He tore in like a man possessed for the next delivery and clean bowled Miandad. As the Pakistani tucked his bat under his arm and took off his helmet to make his way back to the pavilion, Merv quipped, 'By the way, sunshine, here's your bus ticket.'

One of Merv's colleagues was larger-than-life wicketkeeper Rodney Marsh, who was never one to admit being second best to anybody.

Rodney became involved in a dispute between team-mates in the aftermath of that controversial underarm game against New Zealand. Doug Walters claimed that if he had been batting for New Zealand, he would have hit the contentious delivery for six.

Border pooh-poohed the idea. 'That's impossible,' he said. 'How can you do that when the ball is rolling along the ground? You're talking rubbish, man.'

Dougie insisted, however, and the result was a ten-dollar wager. So the next day, with Rodney Marsh acting as referee and umpire rolled into one, the three of them gathered at the SCG, Border with the ball, Walters with the bat, and Marsh wearing his umpiring hat.

Border sent down the perfect underarm delivery, all along the ground. Walters came charging down the track, flicked the ball up with his boot, and as it ballooned into the air, he smacked it with perfect timing into the blue beyond and out of the ground.

Border protested, but to no avail. Even a belated lbw appeal was turned down by Marsh because Walters was too far down the pitch.

Whenever Australia played at the WACA ground at Perth, Greek restaurateur Nick Lekias used to supply a huge seafood platter for the players at the end of the match, delicious six-inch king prawns being the *pièce de résistance*.

After one match between Australia and New Zealand, Marsh and the opposition opening batsman John Wright found themselves sitting next to each other.

Wright is nicknamed 'Shake' because of the way he just chucks everything into his bag and then shakes it about until the contents settle sufficiently to enable him to operate the zip fastener. On this occasion Wrighty apparently confused his rival's wicketkeeping gloves with the rubbish bin. Not all that surprising, really, as there was little difference in the state of them.

The two teams had to travel to Sydney next day to play in the first of the Benson and Hedges Series Cup finals later that week. The temperature was over a hundred, and prawns being much more at home in water than in smelly, sweaty, steaming wicketkeeping gloves, by the time Marshy dragged his cricket bag into the SCG dressing room for practice two

361

days later, people were really beginning to turn up their noses at him.

After going through several tins of talcum powder, Marshy finally decided that he was not the problem, and set about trying to locate the source of the dreadful smell. When he realised what had happened, he sent a message to the New Zealand dressing room threatening retribution.

Wrighty walked to the middle to open the New Zealand innings in the first final and immediately apologised to Marshy. He almost got down on both knees. Marshy ignored him, however.

The Aussies won the first game and off they all went to Melbourne, by which time Wrighty was obviously more concerned about what Marsh was going to do to him than about his batting, which was great from the Australian point of view, because he was a very fine batsman. Although the smell in the gloves was finally beginning to wear off by now, still Marsh would not accept another Wright apology.

Australia ran up a huge total, and when Wright was caught by Marsh off Hogg for a duck, the cup was as good as in Australian hands. As John left the field, head bowed, Marshy shouted, 'You can relax now, Wrighty. Apology accepted.' The damage had been done. Vengeance was Marshy's.

Touring Australia one year, Wrighty woke up in his hotel room one night to the sound of a cricket whistling. He could not get to sleep because of it, so he tried to find the darn thing. He searched high and low, to no avail. He went out on to the balcony, but no joy there either. Still the whistling went on. He eventually traced the noise to his briefcase. Inside was the culprit – not a cricket after all, but his watch alarm going off.

Wrighty once had his nose broken by a ball from Sri Lankan Rumesh Ratnayake in the second Test at Wellington in 1983, and when he arrived at Auckland to play in the one-day international, he withdrew from the side because the injury was still bothering him. Looking out of the pavilion window he saw a big banner which read, 'John nose the right thing to do.'

The Test grounds at Auckland and Christchurch in New Zealand are both Rugby stadiums where the All Blacks play their matches in the winter. Come the spring the squares are transformed for the cricket season and the groundsmen there produce some magnificent pitches. It really is a work of art. I am told that the marvellous re-growth of the grass is due to the volcanic nature of the soil.

Wellington is the windy city. It blows an absolute gale there. I umpired a Women's World Cup match at the ground in 1982, when not even the weighted bails would stay put. In fact, when England's Sue Goatman and New Zealand's Barbara Bevege tossed up, the coin was blown almost to the boundary.

New Zealand legend Richard Hadlee was a magnificent all-round cricketer, but it was as a bowler that he really made his mark. He dominates the New Zealand record books: best bowling performance, R. J. Hadlee, 9 for 52 v. Australia at Brisbane, 1985–6; best match bowling, R. J. Hadlee, 15 for 123 v. Australia at Brisbane 1985–6; most wickets in a series, 33, R. J. Hadlee v. Australia 1985–6; most wickets in a career, R. J. Hadlee, 431 (86 matches at an average of 22.29).

He also figures in the batting records, sharing the highest sixth-wicket partnership of an undefeated 246 with Jeff Crowe against Sri Lanka at Colombo in 1986–7, and the record seventh-wicket stand of 186 with W. K. Lees against Pakistan in Karachi ten years earlier.

One British national newspaper described the 1986 New Zealand attack as having Richard Hadlee at one end and the Ilford Second XI at the other. Game for a laugh, the New

Zealanders had T-shirts inscribed 'Ilford Second XI' and wore them for the rest of the tour.

. Hadlee captained the New Zealand side on a handful of occasions, usually when the regular skipper and vice-captain wanted a game off. Being in charge often lifted his own performance because he wanted to lead by example.

On one tour of England he was asked to captain the side against Worcestershire. It was a damp green-top and conditions suggested that the team winning the toss would be well advised to bowl. Hadlee decided to bat, however, feeling that the pitch would deteriorate over three days, with cracks in the pitch becoming wider and the bounce more unpredictable.

Richard usually batted at number eleven when taking on the extra duties as skipper, but on this occasion he promoted himself to number nine as New Zealand crashed to 38 for 6 and 71 for 7. He made 68, and, with Martin Crowe chipping in with a half-century, total collapse was averted.

The top-order batsmen were up in arms because their tour average had taken a battering as early wickets went down like ninepins. Someone suggested that Hadlee should never captain the side again – or, at least, if he did he should consult his team-mates before deciding whether to bat or bowl.

One player asked, 'What did you call it?'

'Heads,' replied Hadlee.

'Why?'

'I always call heads. There are two sides to a coin, heads and tails. Like having two ends. One to think with, the other to sit on. As I have always been taught to think with my head, that's the way I call.'

'Well,' came the reply, 'if you had sat on your arse first, you would have thought more about bowling on a pitch like that.'

Hadlee had the last laugh, however: Worcestershire were bowled out for 200, New Zealand scored runs quickly in their second innings, bowled the home team out for a second time and won with half a day to spare as the pitch, as Hadlee had predicted, deteriorated badly.

Hadlee experienced one of the most embarrassing moments of his distinguished career when bowling in a Test at Lord's. In his early days he used to bowl off a longer run, and before getting into his approach, he did a bit of a hop, skip and jump to find his rhythm. As he did so on this occasion, he tripped over his size twelve boots and ended up flat on his face, much to the amusement of the 28,000 spectators and his team-mates. Not to mention two English batsmen and the umpires.

Hadlee, incidentally, came close to equalling Jim Laker's 1956 Test wicket haul of all ten in an innings. In 1985–6, against Australia at Brisbane, the New Zealand all-rounder, who later became Sir Richard, finished with 9 for 52. After taking the first eight wickets, he pocketed a skied catch from Geoff Lawson's bat off the bowling of Vaughan Brown to rob himself of the chance of a record-equalling all-ten performance.

Some years ago in New Zealand I watched a fifteen-year-old boy play. I said at the time that he would go on to play for his country and break batting records – it was obvious, even at that tender age, that the lad had great talent. His name was Martin Crowe, and he fulfilled my predictions about his future.

Crowe scored more runs than anyone else for New Zealand – a total of 5,444 in 77 matches at an average of 45.36 – and he holds the record for the highest individual innings – 299 against Sri Lanka at Wellington in 1990–91. He must have had mixed emotions that day: elation at achieving such a feat, and frustration at getting out one short of his triple hundred.

Crowe was one of the best players I have ever seen, and it was a tragedy that a knee injury should curtail his career. I am sure he would have gone on to break many more records if he had been able to continue for a couple more years.

Another fine batsman, Glenn Turner, holds the record for the most runs in a series, scoring 672 at an average of 96.00 against the West Indies in 1971–2.

New Zealand have never been one of the strongest cricketing nations, but they have always retained an ability to laugh at themselves. With his team in desperate straits on one tour of England, captain Ken Rutherford was asked by a journalist if he found it personally distressing to be captain of the New Zealand ship.

Rutherford looked at him, smiled, cupped a hand to his ear and said, 'Sorry, I didn't quite catch that. Did you say ship – or shit?'

It was a perfect example of how a little bit of light-hearted repartee can deflect criticism and lift the mood at a time of crisis. It was also a lesson to others who, in such a situation, have become sullen and decidedly grumpy.

I am not sure, however, of the reaction of Middlesex and England cricketer Denis Compton to an incident during the New Zealand tour of 1949. In those days play often started at eleven thirty, and the story goes that Compton was feeling a little anxious when he was held up in the traffic at Marble Arch shortly before eleven o'clock on the second day, because he was the next man due to bat.

A motorist in the next car was listening to the match on the radio when he noticed Compton alongside. Winding the window down he queried, 'Excuse me, Denis, but shouldn't you be at the Oval?'

'Yes,' said Compton, 'I'm on my way now.'

'Well, you'd better get a move on,' said the other driver, as he turned up the car radio so that Compton could hear. 'It's an eleven o'clock start today.'

With that, Compton, to his horror, heard the commentator say, 'Denis Compton is the next batsman and he will be coming down those pavilion steps any moment now.'

It seems strange, but in all my globe-trotting experiences, the only two occasions when my baggage has gone astray involved trips Down Under.

The first time was when I arrived in New Zealand to find the carousel at the airport going merrily round and round with no sign of my personal belongings. I was left with no clothes except those I stood up in. Ian Botham offered to lend me some of his, but I'm nowhere near as beefy as he is, and they were far too large for my slim, trim figure. I had to make do with what I was wearing, despite everything being creased and sweat-stained after a twenty-nine-hour flight, and go out and buy a new toothbrush and shaving gear. Thank goodness the bags arrived the following day, or I might have had to fork out for a complete new wardrobe.

Then, in the winter of 1998–9, having paid a visit to the Test series between Australia and England, I put my baggage on board at Sydney for the trip home. First-class priority, change of flights at Singapore, then on to Heathrow, and shuttle to Manchester. Not a problem. Or so I thought.

When I arrived in Manchester, no bags. I later discovered that they had been left on the tarmac at Heathrow. All those thousands of miles travelling to the other side of the world and back again, and my luggage gets lost between London and Manchester.

St Vincent

WEST INDIES

21

PITCHES in the West Indies have changed a lot. They used to be full of pace and bounce, yet always good for a big score once the batsman had established himself, as is clearly illustrated by the triple hundreds achieved by top-class Test players.

Five of those mammoth scores particularly come to mind; Brian Lara made 375 at St John's against England in 1993–4; Gary Sobers amassed 365 not out when playing against Pakistan at Kingston in 1957–8; Frank Worrell was also unbeaten on 308 when Barbados played Trinidad at Bridgetown in 1943–4; and Jeffrey Stollmeyer knocked up 324 at Port-of-Spain in the Trinidad v. British Guiana match of 1946–7. Hanif Mohammad, the brilliant Pakistani opener, compiled 337 against the West Indies at Bridgetown in 1957–8.

Over the years, however, the pitches throughout the islands have become slower and lower, although in Jamaica a couple of years ago they had to abandon a Test match because of uneven bounce, with the ball flying dangerously all over the place.

The outfield is generally rougher than in England, being very bare, with little grass on it, but facilities generally are good at all the grounds, and the West Indies is a lovely place to play cricket. No thermal days there, although the rain can still be a problem at times.

The Bourda is the principal ground in Guyana; Queen's Park at Port-of-Spain is the major Trinidad ground; Sabina Park is the main venue in Kingston, Jamaica; Antigua stages Tests at the Recreation Ground; but my favourite is the beautiful Kensington Oval, Barbados.

It was there that the first Test in the West Indies was played against England in January, 1930, although the West Indians had made their Test debut two years earlier in England, when they were defeated at Lord's.

The first West Indian batsmen to capture the imagination were the famous 'W' trio of Walcott, Weekes and Worrell. They took English cricket by storm, and Worrell and Weekes still hold the record partnership for the third wicket, scoring 338 against England at Port-of-Spain in 1953–4.

Jim Laker, that great England off-spin bowler, regarded Everton de Courcy Weekes as the greatest of the three, but was always curious as to how he had come by his first name. One day he plucked up courage to ask him.

'Ah, well, you see,' explained the West Indian, 'my dad was a football nutter. At the time I was born, Everton were the cock of the walk in the English First Division, so he decided to call me after that team.'

'It's a bloody good job,' reflected Laker, 'that he wasn't a fan of West Bromwich Albion.'

Over the years the West Indies became feared for their awesome pace attack, with a battery of four fast bowlers bombarding terrified batsmen over after over after over, but prior to that they revelled in the magnificent off-spin artistry of Sonny Ramadhin, who took a lot of wickets at Test level.

Like England's Tony Lock, Ramadhin always used to bowl with his sleeves buttoned at the cuffs. It was alleged that he had a suspect action, and it was not as noticeable if he had his sleeves rolled right down.

On his retirement from the international arena Ramadhin played for Lincolnshire in the Minor Counties League, and one day he was bowling to Geoff Cope, of Yorkshire Seconds. Cope kept playing the ball negatively with his pad, and Ramadhin eventually lost his rag.

'Come on, man,' he fumed. 'Don't you know what that thing in your hand is for? It's to hit the damn ball.'

Ramadhin continued to give Cope some earache on the subject, and it reached the stage where the Yorkshireman decided to try to get a word in edgeways. He strode down the pitch and declared, 'Tell thee summat, Sonny. I'll use my bat if you'll roll up your sleeve.'

Denis Compton was one of the West Indies' great adversaries in the 'forties and 'fifties, and he was once batting against them in a Test in England partnered by John Warr, who was only too well aware of his colleague's debonair, not to say suicidal, approach to the art of running between the wickets. Denis admitted himself on his retirement that he had probably been the worst in the world for running people out. Worse, even, than Geoff Boycott, which almost beggars belief.

Warr's worst fears were realised when Compton hit the ball, called for a single and set off, giving his partner no time to query the decision, and as they crossed in the middle Denis remarked breezily, 'Best of luck, John.' It did no good. JJ was run out by a mile.

Garfield Sobers was the dominant figure in West Indies cricket during the 'fifties and 'sixties. Quite simply he was the greatest all-rounder I have ever had the pleasure of seeing. He was three cricketers rolled into one. Great batsman, marvellous left-arm over-the-wicket bowler – swung in, swung it away – and a brilliant fielder.

After all these years he still has a share in four West Indian batting records: 446 for the second wicket with Conrad Hunte against Pakistan at Kingston in 1957–8; 399 for the fourth wicket with Frank Worrell against England at Bridgetown in 1959–60; 265 for the fifth wicket with Seymour Nurse against England at Leeds in 1966; and in that same year an unbeaten 274 with David Holford against England at Lord's.

It was during that 1966 tour of England that the West Indian officials became fed up with the practical jokes played by members of the party, and decided to put an end to it. Larking about was fine in small doses, but the players had gone too far, and enough was enough. Manager Jeffrey Stollmeyer called all the players together to thrash the matter out in a team meeting.

Fast bowler Charlie Griffith arrived late and so did not know what on earth they were talking about as he sat down to listen to the debate, but his ears pricked up when he heard Sobers say, 'That's it, then. There has been far too much leg-pulling, and it has got to stop.'

Charlie was most indignant. 'No more leg-pulling?' he exclaimed. 'So how am I going to get any runs? That's the only shot I've got.'

Griffith's 'partner-in-crime' was Wes Hall. These two formed a formidable opening attack, and often had the England batsmen in a stew. However, the boot was very firmly on the other foot in a game at Port-of-Spain during the England tour of the Caribbean in 1967–8. The West Indies had been forced to follow on 205 behind, and when David Brown claimed three wickets in the final over before tea on the last day, it left the home team tottering on 180 for 8 and in grave danger of losing by an innings.

Hall emerged to partner Sobers, who was doing his magnificent best to hold the innings together. The two of them survived until stumps were drawn, batting out time to save the Test. As they were leaving the field a reporter asked Hall if he had ever been worried about the situation he had found himself in.

'Not personally,' he replied, 'but I did wonder if the chap at the other end could hold out.'

Griffith was the West Indian hero in a Test at Headingley when he claimed 6 for 36 in 21 superb overs, to send England packing for 174 in reply to the visitors' opening knock of 397. The next morning, Hall was opening the mail when he came across a letter which was addressed to 'The West Indies Opening Bowlers, c/o Headingley Cricket Ground, Leeds'.

Curious, he pulled out a scribbled note which read, 'Why don't you go back home, you big black ugly baboon.'

He called across to Griffith, 'Hey, Charlie, there's a letter for you.'

Since then England have had to suffer the onslaught of other fast bowling greats such as Andy Roberts, Michael Holding, Malcolm Marshall, Joel Garner, Colin Croft, Courtney Walsh and Curtly Ambrose.

I included Roberts and Holding in my World Squad in my autobiography. Roberts was a fearsome bowler, very quick and with so much control, while 'Whispering Death' was the nickname given to Holding, because of the menacingly quiet way he would glide up to the stumps before rocketing the ball towards the batsman at a frightening pace.

Holding figured in the side-splitting comment from Brian Johnston during one *Test Match Special* broadcast, when the delightful Jonners greeted World Service listeners with the news that, 'England are fifty-two for three; the bowler's Holding, the batsman's Willey.'

It was Holding who bowled Bob Willis to end the last Test of the 1976 series, prompting a celebratory litter-throwing spree of empty Bacardi bottles as thousands of triumphant West Indian supporters invaded the pitch. I recorded the fact

ve 'Whispering Death' Michael ding, the fearsome West Indian pace ler, who played county cricket for cashire and Derbyshire. He was given nickname because of the menacingly et way he used to glide up to the stumps re exploding into his delivery stride.

Above West Indian Brian Lara stands in front of the Edgbaston scoreboard showing his record-breaking 501 not out against Durham in 1994, when Warwickshire ran up their highest ever total of 810 for four on the way to winning the county championship.

ve Spot the white man. That's me, right in the middle of the West Indian squad r to a Test match in Barbados in the winter of 1997–8. The photograph now has e of place in the Club Rockley Hotel, where it was taken.

Above left What a combination! West Indian Gordon Greenidge and South African Barry Richards stride out to open the innings for Hampshire at Southampton.

Above right Michael Procter, who, along with West Indian Malcolm Marshall of Hampshire, was the best overseas professional I have ever seen playing in England. The South African gave everything for Gloucestershire County Cricket Club.

Left The apartheid issue a thing of the past as Peter Kirsten (South Africa) enjoys a laugh and a joke with Alvin Kallicharran (West Indies).

e Ali Bacher, who led the talks to get
h Africa back into international cricket
has done a fabulous job for his country
ayer and administrator, pictured in the
pany of Clive Lloyd of the West Indies,
has similarly made the transition from
player and captain to influential
ager.

Above Northamptonshire captain Allan
Lamb trying to determine if Curtly
Ambrose is fit enough to continue bowling
during a Lord's final. Nigel Felton, David
Ripley and Kevin Curran look on with
interest.

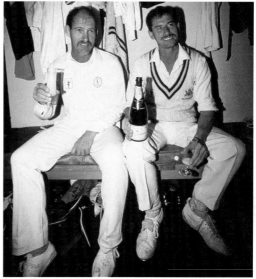

Above Clive Rice and Richard Hadlee, who
brought the combined talents of South
Africa and New Zealand to transform a
very ordinary Nottinghamshire outfit into a
championship-winning side.

Left Martin Crowe, arguably New
Zealand's greatest ever batsman.

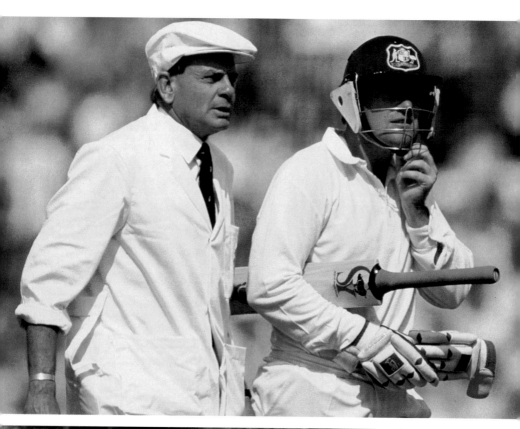

Above Here I am walking off the field w Australian captain Mar Taylor. In 1998–9 he equalled Sir Donald Bradman's Australian record Test score of 33 and then declared overnight to give his si more time to bowl out Pakistan.

Left Aussie pace duo Dennis Lillee and Jeff Thomson, who struck fear into the hearts of batsmen everywhere b produced one of their most memorable partnerships with the bat in the World Cup final of 1975.

ve Australian Rodney Marsh, whose
ketkeeping gloves were used as a rubbish
by New Zealand opener John Wright,
ch to the latter's eventual regret.

it The Chappell brothers, Greg and
who have both captained Australia.

ve Merv Hughes, one of cricket's great characters, goes down on his hands and knees
ackle a stray dog, which was much more scared of Merv than Merv was of it – with
d reason. Not many dared tangle with the Australian bowler, as Pakistan's Javed
ndad found to his cost.

Left Imran Khan, the ladies'
pin-up, who was a great Pakista[n]
captain as well as dominating h[is]
country's bowling records.

Right Aravinda de Silva, Sri
Lanka's most prolific batsman [and]
a wonderful player to watch in [full]
flow.

Far right Muttiah Muralithara[n]
whose action has often been
questioned, is undoubtedly Sri
Lanka's most exciting bowler.

Below left Two more Pakistanis
who have captained their coun[try]
– and there have been a lot of
them in recent years – Wasim
Akram and Javed Miandad.

Below right India's Sachin
Tendulkar, who I believe is the
best player in the world right n[ow]
and will go on to break all reco[rds]

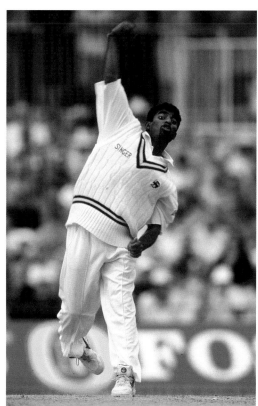

Above Tendulkar again. Fancying a spell of bowling this time?

Right South African paceman Allan Donald, still going strong after taking more than 240 Test wickets.

Above Magnificent Australian bowler Shane Warne, whose famous action gives him superb control of leg-spin, flipper and googly.

in my autobiography that one chap pushed fifty pounds into my hands, saying, 'Give that to Michael Holding.' However, I invested it in the Halifax building society instead. Since the book was published I have received angry letters from church people demanding that I pass that fifty pounds on to Holding – plus all the interest that has built up over the last twenty-three years!

England batsman David Steele always said that nobody enjoyed batting against the really quick bowlers, but some were better at it than others, and David blamed the introduction of the protective helmet for a decline in technique against the quicks.

He told me, 'I do feel, watching the modern game, that some players do a lot of ducking and diving and generally hiding behind the helmet. They know that if they do get hit on the head, the helmet will protect them. The technique for playing short-pitched deliveries has therefore all but disappeared.'

He is absolutely right. There is no substitute for watching the ball. Keeping an eye on it. That way you get inside its flight, and you don't get hit. I was never a good player, but one thing I always did was get my head in line with the ball so that I could just move inside it and watch it as it went past.

David also mourns the passing of the great England quick bowlers. We once had Trueman and Statham in tandem, but that was a long time ago. Where are their like now? We just don't seem to breed them any more. David says he found that very frustrating when he played for England. He had to stand there and take the flak, knowing full well that England were in no position to give it back.

As Brian Close said to David during the 1976 series, 'They've got cannon, we've got pea-shooters.'

Phil Tufnell, the Middlesex and England slow left-arm bowler, echoed those sentiments in a way when speaking at a benefit dinner. He rose to make his speech and started off by saying, 'Don't worry, I won't be on my feet long – just about as long as when I go out to face Curtly Ambrose in a Test match.' Ninety seconds later he sat down.

While the fast bowlers continued to flourish in the West Indies, Viv Richards emerged as a dominant force with the bat, and he still holds the records for most runs in a series (829 against England in 1976) and most runs in a career (8,540 in 121 matches at an average of 50.23). Only the record for the highest individual innings eludes him, that being held by Brian Lara, with his 375 against a hapless England at St John's in 1993–4.

Viv was always the pride and joy of his fellow Antiguans, right from his schooldays. He could do absolutely nothing wrong in their eyes. They were devastated, therefore, when, playing for Antigua against their greatest rivals, St Kitts, in the Leeward Islands tournament of 1969, the eighteen-year-old they had come to hero worship was out for a fourth-ball duck.

Viv was even less happy. He had been given out to a bat–pad catch, and was convinced that he had not touched the ball. He made his feelings known as he stalked off in high dudgeon.

Sensing an injustice, the partisan crowd staged a massive protest. The chant went up, 'We want Viv, we want Viv, we want Viv,' followed by 'No Viv, no play, no Viv, no play.'

This prompted a hastily convened conference of officials, and Viv was stunned when he was told that it had been decided to allow him to resume his innings as there appeared to have been some mistake.

Viv strode back out, to the accompaniment of wild cheering, determined to repay the crowd with some scintillating calypso-style stroke-play. A few balls later he was back in the pavilion.

Stumped. A long way out of his crease, no room for argument this time. And another duck to his name.

Still, he mused, there was always the second innings. He could make up for all the disappointment and frustration then. But guess what? He was out for his third duck of the match. A unique record he would prefer to have done without.

Later in his career, during a tour of England, when Clive Lloyd was captain of the side, Viv came up against an up-and-coming fast bowler from Wales who was determined to make the England selectors sit up and take notice by claiming the scalp of the master batsman.

When Viv's turn came to bat, the young man could hardly wait to get at him, and his first ball, predictably, was a bouncer. A good one, too. So good that Viv had to sway out of the way to avoid being hit on the head. The lad's dander was really up now, and the next ball was a perfect outswinger which nicked the outside edge of Viv's bat and was a whisker away from being snapped up in the slips.

The Welshman glared cockily down the pitch at Richards and exclaimed, 'Look yer, boyo, don't you know what a cricket ball looks like? It's red and round and it weighs five and a half ounces.'

Viv said nothing, but just stared back at the young pup then twirled his bat in that businesslike way of his, surveyed the field placings, and settled down to face the next ball. It was just a fraction over-pitched and Viv was on to it like a flash. He timed his shot to perfection and the ball soared into the air until it became only a speck as it cleared the boundary by some distance, exited the ground still climbing skywards and eventually landed with a mighty splash in the river which flowed alongside.

Richards sauntered down the pitch with just a hint of arrogance, tapping imaginary blemishes in the surface as he went.

When he got threequarters of the way down, he interrupted his gardening for a moment, looked up at the startled bowler, and told him, 'Look you, boyo. You know what it's like. Red, round and weighs five and a half ounces. So bloody well go and find it.'

Alvin Kallicharran was another fine West Indian batsman, and also captained his country. He was a magnificent stroke-maker, despite his very small stature, which caused him a bit of a problem during the tour of New Zealand in 1979–80. On entering his hotel room, he was amazed to find that he had to climb a small ladder in order to get into his bed.

Tired out after all the travelling from one venue to the next, he was distraught. 'Just look at that,' he fumed. 'They could at least have the decency to provide a lift.'

Back in dear old England, I had the privilege of umpiring a one-day international featuring the West Indies at the Oval. On arriving at the ground, the security man told me to leave my car keys with him and he would park my vehicle for me away from the ground at a nearby grammar school, along with all the players' cars.

They kept the news from me while I umpired, but I discovered, to my horror, on leaving the field at the end of the day's play, that the security man had reversed my car into a lamp-post, ripping it all down the side as he did so. To make matters worse, it was a Bank Holiday weekend, and there was no way I could get the car repaired. They had to hire a car for me to get to my next fixture at Tunbridge Wells, and I drove round in it for the next four weeks, which was how long it took to get my BMW roadworthy again.

Two matches I umpired in the West Indies during 1992–3 also stand out in my memory.

The first was at Queen's Park, Port-of-Spain, where Steve Bucknor and I combined to produce a world record of seventeen lbw decisions, six of which came from me. It was a very difficult pitch, on which the batsmen had great trouble getting the ball away, and the reason for the large number of lbws was that the ball kept very low.

Mind you, there were some great bowlers operating as well – Wasim Akram and Waqar Younis for Pakistan, Curtly Ambrose, Ian Bishop, Courtney Walsh and Carl Hooper for the West Indies.

That Port-of-Spain Test was delayed by one day because of allegations that some of the Pakistan players had been taking drugs. I was at home, bags packed, passport to hand, waiting for the call and wondering if my journey was going to be necessary. For a while it seemed that the Test series might be cancelled, but luckily, for the good of the game, it went ahead.

The home team were on top for most of the game and eventually won by 204 runs, thanks, in no small measure, to some exceptional batting in such tricky conditions by Desmond Haynes and Brian Lara, who was just beginning to make his mark at international level.

Haynes batted right the way throughout the West Indies' second innings for an unbeaten 143, while Lara showed his outstanding potential with 96 in that third-wicket stand of 169. To give you some idea of just how well these two batted, the last seven batsmen failed to reach double figures.

Port-of-Spain, incidentally, is Lara's home. It is also where Manchester United and England striker Dwight Yorke comes from, and the two men are very close friends. So much so that Lara dearly wanted to go to watch Yorke in the European Champions League final between United and Bayern Munich at the Nou Camp Stadium in Barcelona at the end of May, 1999. The West Indies' manager, Clive Lloyd, would not give him permission to go, however, which was quite understandable in view of the fact that the West Indies were in the middle of a World Cup in England at the time. Yorke did, however, drive on the drinks buggy at Old Trafford during that World Cup competition.

I witnessed another magnificent knock of 125 from Haynes as he continued to enjoy a marvellous series in the next Test at the Kensington Oval, Bridgetown, where the West Indies strolled to a ten-wicket victory, some in-depth batting being complemented by top-class bowling, particularly from Courtney Walsh, who had match figures of 7 for 107 in 42 overs.

Then it was on to another memorable match at the Antiguan Recreation Ground at St John's. This time it was Carl Hooper who produced the batting goods with a glorious 178 not out, as the West Indies rattled up 438 in their opening knock, with Inzamam-ul-Haq restoring a little Pakistan pride as he made 123 out of his side's reply of 326.

The West Indians, however, were still in a very strong position at 153 for 4 in their second innings, when rain came to the visitors' rescue. The ground was soon awash. The Bird-man had struck again. There was no more play and the match was drawn.

In some ways it was a pity that the rain could not have come earlier. It would have saved me a lot of pain. During the Pakistan innings I was standing at square leg keeping a keen eye on the batsmen as they scampered for a quick single, when I felt an excruciating pain right at the base of my spine. I thought I had been shot. The pain travelled all the way down my leg and I collapsed in agony.

It turned out that Keith Arthurton, one of the hardest throwers in world cricket, had hurled the ball in from a position just behind me and had made a slight error in the missile's intended flight path.

The physio dashed on, had a quick look, and ordered, 'Right, Dickie, on your feet and drop your trousers.'

I looked at him aghast. 'I can't do that. Not in front of all these people.'

'Please yourself,' came the brusque reply, 'but I'm warning you, if you don't let me spray the area, then you're going to end up in even more pain. The bruise will be so bad that you won't be able to walk. You will have a very serious problem.'

There was, it seemed, nothing else for it, so I reluctantly unfastened my belt and allowed my trousers to fall to my ankles, revealing brightly coloured underpants and the Bird lunch-box in all their combined glory.

'Right-oh, then,' I told him, 'get on with it,' adding in my most Methodist ministerial fashion, 'Let us spray.'

CHARMS CUP   CHARMS CUP   PAHUNMARINE EMPIRA

Cuttack, India

INDIA, PAKISTAN AND SRI LANKA

22

IT WAS at the National Stadium in Karachi during the 1994–5 series that Pakistan and Australia combined to provide me with the best Test match I have ever umpired. It had everything: magnificent batting, bowling and fielding, and a thrilling climax as the home team staged a dramatic fight-back to win by one wicket.

With the pitch taking spin – the ball was virtually turning square – and Shane Warne operating at one end, Pakistan's last pair were at the crease with 57 still needed to win, and Australia thought they had the game in the bag. The players said to me, 'Dickie, it's all over. We've won it.'

However, Inzamam-ul-Haq and last man Mushtaq Ahmed knocked off the runs to clinch an amazing victory which left the Aussies stunned. Inzamam made an undefeated 58 and Mushtaq gave him terrific support with 20 not out.

Warne took 3 for 61 in the first innings and 5 for 89 in the second, while Pakistan relied on their tried and trusted pace duo of Wasim Akram and Waqar Younis, these two claiming fifteen victims between them in the match.

It was not an easy pitch to umpire on, because players hovered round the bat like vultures throughout, and there was some huge appealing, with fielders and bowlers running down the pitch yelling at me and my colleague Khizar Hayat every time there was a remote possibility of a wicket. The noise from the crowd did not help either.

I took a great deal of satisfaction from that match. Not only was it the greatest Test I have ever taken part in, it was also one of my best as an umpire. In fact, I subsequently received a letter from David Richards, Chief Executive of the ICC, which I treasure to this day. It said, 'Congratulations on some magnificent umpiring. I thought you would like to know you got ten out of ten from both captains.' That really did make my day.

The first home Test match played by Pakistan was at the Dacca Stadium in 1954–5, when it was in what was at that time known as East Pakistan and is now Bangladesh, and there was an extraordinary incident at that ground when New Zealand toured there in 1969–70.

One of the problems, in both Pakistan and India, is that spectators are a fruity lot, inclined to hurl all manner of it at players unfortunate enough to be stationed on the boundary edge. Kiwi opener Bruce Murray, known as 'Bags' because of his initials, was down on the third-man boundary, and he must have felt as though his head was the target on a coconut shy.

Finally, he could stand it no longer and complained to his captain, Graham Dowling, who threatened to stop the game if anything else was thrown at Murray. Not long afterwards, an expertly aimed banana, travelling at a fair old lick, flew over the fence and became, quite literally, a pain in the neck for poor old Bags.

He bent down, picked up the missile and ran towards the middle, brandishing it in the air. At the same time, the bowler, Dayle Hadlee – brother of Richard – set off on his run, quite oblivious of what was happening, and he failed to hear Dowling's shout to abort the delivery. He let Asif Iqbal have a short riser which was fended into the vacant gully area. Or, at least, it was vacant before Bags, on his fruit and veg delivery run from the boundary, arrived just in time to take a peach of a diving catch, coming up with the ball in one hand and the banana in the other.

He was not, however, the apple of the umpire's eye, and he must have felt a bit of a lemon when the official called dead ball.

That great Pakistani batsman, Hanif Mohammad, proved his mental toughness when winning a war of words with Freddie Trueman during one series against England. Hanif was getting Fred's goat with his dead-bat tactics, and Fiery, becoming more frustrated by the minute, finally exploded, 'If you don't bloody well get out of the way, I'll knock you right over.'

Hanif stared straight down the pitch at the red-faced Trueman. 'If you mean you will knock me over with your fists, Mr Trueman, then I am very frightened. But if you mean with the ball, I would love you to bowl me another. I am very much liking it.'

It is Hanif who holds the record for the highest individual innings for Pakistan, of 337 against the West Indies at Bridgetown in 1957–8, and he also made 499 for Karachi in a match against Bahawalpur at Karachi the following year.

Hanif was one of fifteen Pakistan captains during my time as a player and umpire, but that tells only half the story. They actually changed captains thirty-two times in that period, with Javed Miandad and Imran Khan replacing each other on ten occasions. Wasim Bari, Asif Iqbal, Waqar Younis, Ramiz Raja, Saeed Anwar, Aamir Sohail, Rashid Latif and Moin Khan all captained the side for only six Tests or less.

While I was umpiring in the World Cup in Pakistan in 1986–7, one of my colleagues gave Javed Miandad out lbw. If there was one thing you never did in Pakistan, it was to give Javed Miandad out lbw. It was simply not on. The story goes that when that umpire went to heaven, he was met at the Pearly Gates by Saint Peter, who asked him, 'Have you ever done anything wrong?'

The umpire thought for a moment, then replied, 'Well, I do remember once giving Javed Miandad out in a World Cup match in Pakistan, but that was a long time in the past.'

'No, it wasn't,' said Saint Peter. 'It happened just three minutes ago.'

Imran Khan, of course, was a great cricketer and a great captain, and I will always remember his quote after the 1992 World Cup final in Melbourne. He said, 'Bits-and-pieces players can take you so far, but you win big one-day games by picking specialist players, such as leg-spinners and out-and-out quick bowlers, who prove that the best way of saving runs is taking wickets.'

It was a sideways smack at the modern trend for stacking sides with all-rounders, and I have to agree with Imran. He was spot-on.

Imran dominates the Pakistan bowling records, with the best match figures of 14 for 116 against Sri Lanka at Lahore in 1981–2; most wickets in a series (40 against India in 1982–3); and most wickets in a career (362 in 88 matches at an average of 22.81). The only record he does not hold is for the best single-innings bowling, which goes to that magnificent spinner Abdul Qadir, with 9 for 56 against England at Lahore in 1987–8.

One of the most eccentric actions in Test cricket belonged to Pakistan bowler Asif Masood, once called, in error, Massif Arsood by Brian Johnston. I've umpired Tests when he has been bowling, and could not better the description of John Arlott, who said that, when going forward, Asif 'looked like Groucho Marx chasing a pretty waitress'.

England captain Mike Brearley was far from amused when

he was given out on a caught-behind appeal in Lahore, another Pakistan Test match venue. He was convinced that the ball had flicked his pad strap and had gone nowhere near his bat. His sense of injustice was heightened by the fact that he had scored only four, after sweating it out for a day and a half in the field while the home team ran up a big total.

His feelings were only partially appeased later in the day when he received a message from a sympathetic liaison officer which read, 'Dear Mr Brearley, the umpire asks me to tell you that he is very sorry, but he felt his arm going up and could not stop it.'

Karachi wicketkeeper Abdul Aziz was the victim of a particularly vicious off-break while batting in the final of the 1959 Quaid-e-Azam trophy. He collapsed and died at the crease while awaiting the next delivery, but despite the tragedy, the game went on. The scorer, however, was obviously left in a bit of a quandary as to how he should record the event in the scorebook. Eventually he solved the problem by writing as follows: 'First innings, Abdul Aziz, retired hurt 0; second innings, Abdul Aziz, did not bat – dead.'

There have been nineteen venues for Test cricket in India, but the oldest and most senior ground is Eden Gardens, Calcutta, where India first played England in 1933–4. It is a massive place, capable of accommodating 120,000 spectators, making it the biggest stadium in the world. I have umpired there in front of such a crowd in the World Cup finals, and it is not easy, believe me.

Sometimes the Indian crowd over-reacts, and there was such an incident in 1999 when their idol, Sachin Tendulkar, was adjudged to have been run out. Fans threw fireworks and bombed the ground with cabbages, oranges, bananas, bottles, and whatever else they could lay their hands on, and it was impossible to continue. Officials had to clear the ground of well over 100,000 people, joining thousands more outside listening to the match on their transistor radios. That was typical of the fanaticism of both Indians and Pakistanis when it comes to cricket.

Another thing you have to watch out for at Calcutta is the smog. Sometimes the pollution becomes so bad that a peculiar kind of mist develops, a bit like the sea frets we experience back home at Scarborough. It is possible for play to continue at ground level while those in the top tiers of the mighty stands cannot see a thing. It is an amazing sight.

I love India, and the people. They are quite wonderful. Emotion may get the better of them at times, but that is because they care so much about the game. I never had any problem with them, and I enjoyed every minute of my visits there. They were marvellous experiences.

In Sachin Tendulkar I believe India have the greatest player in the world at the moment. If he keeps fit and well, I am certain he will go on to break all records. He did not enjoy much success as captain, and I would not place that responsibility on him again. I would just let him go out there and concentrate on what he does best: scoring runs. Sir Donald Bradman thinks very highly of Tendulkar and paid him the ultimate compliment when he said, 'In many ways he reminds me of myself.'

For the time being, all the Indian batting records remain in the talented hands of Sunil Gavaskar, who scored the highest individual innings (236 not out against the West Indies at Madras in 1983–4); most runs in a series (774, also against the West Indies, in 1970–71); and most runs in a career (10,122 in 125 matches at an average of 51.12).

The fact that he created two of those records facing the formidable West Indies pace attack tells you just how great a batsman he was. When Michael Holding, Malcolm Marshall, Andy Roberts, Joel Garner, Curtly Ambrose, Courtney Walsh and Colin Croft were at the height of their powers, the little Indian scored thirteen centuries against them. The nearest anyone can come to that is fellow countryman Dilip Vengsarkar, Australia's Doug Walters, and our own Sir Colin Cowdrey, with six each, which is why I rate Gavaskar as one of the finest opening batsmen of my era.

One of the problems about umpiring in India is that, because the pitches take more spin than anywhere else, you find that the slower bowlers operate most of the time, with fielders clustered close to the bat, and with the deafening background noise from the crowd, it is very difficult to pick up bat–pad decisions and those little nicks for caught behind.

During one match at Bangalore, when the Australians were batting, Ray Jordon was given out to a bat–pad catch from the last ball before tea. All the way back to the pavilion he shook his head and muttered, 'I didn't touch the bloody ball. I was nowhere near it.' All through the tea interval he informed all within earshot, 'No bloody way did I hit that ball. I was never out in this wide world.'

Finally, someone suggested that if he felt so strongly about it, he ought to take his complaint to the top, so he went to see the umpire who had given him out, as a matter of courtesy. 'There is no bloody way I hit that ball,' he insisted.

The umpire looked at him, then smiled a knowing smile. 'Ah, well now, Mr Jordon, if you did not hit the ball, I can tell you that you were welly much lbw.'

On a visit to Edgbaston in 1986, India made a marvellous start to a Test match, with Graham Gooch and Bill Athey dismissed in the first over, and it was left to David Gower and Mark Benson to try to rebuild the England innings.

Play had been going on for about fifty minutes, by which time England had moved to 30 without further loss, when one of the BBC radio commentators – I think it was Brian Johnston – said,

'I can tell listeners at home that, after a disastrous start, England are righting the ship.'

Reception must have been a little below standard that day, because immediately the BBC switchboard was jammed by calls from irate listeners demanding to know how a commentator could have the nerve to say that England was 'right in the shit'.

Jonners, of course, was not only the master of the *faux pas*, he also built up a wonderful rapport with his listeners, one of whom once asked if he knew who the ice-cream man was in the Bible. Jonners had to admit defeat, and no one in the commentary box could help him out. He was amused to discover that the answer was 'Walls of Jericho'.

When Jonners returned from a holiday that September, he found a second letter on the subject from another listener, who said he had thoroughly enjoyed the ice-cream story, but what about 'Lyons of Judah'?

Freddie Trueman bowled Jonners the perfect bouncer during another *Test Match Special* broadcast. Returning for a new spell of commentary, Jonners remarked casually to Fred, 'Just seen an old friend of yours.'

'Oh aye,' said Fred, puffing away furiously at that famous pipe. 'And who might that be?'

'The Bishop of Liverpool,' said Jonners.

A conversation then developed about Fred touring Australia with the Rev, and as commentary resumed, Jonners mentioned three other people he had met while strolling round the ground during his break.

Fred grew more and more narked by this and finally asked, 'Right then, Jonners, old son, who's that chap darn there in t' green beret and brown shirt?'

Jonners looked. 'No idea,' he replied. 'Why do you ask?'

'Well,' rejoined Fred, 'I thowt you'd be bound to know. You know every other bugger in t' ground.'

Sri Lanka were elevated to Test match status as recently as 1981–2, and seven different grounds have been used for Test matches – the Saravanamuttu Stadium, Sinhalese Sports Club, Colombo CC, and the Premadasa Stadium, all in Colombo, plus grounds at Kandy, Moratuwa, and Galle.

All the Asian grounds are very similar in style, but the grass is much greener in Sri Lanka than in India and Pakistan, because they get more rain. The result is that there is not much pace in the pitches and they are good to bat on, as is demonstrated by the fact that in 1997–8 Sri Lanka ran up a massive 952 for 6 declared against India at the Premadasa Stadium, Sanath Jayasuriya making 340, the highest ever individual innings by a Sri Lankan. That was seen as ample revenge for the 676 for 7 amassed by the Indians at Kanpur the previous year.

Muttiah Muralitharan, whose action has often been questioned, is the country's most exciting bowler, and he rocked England at the Oval in 1998 by taking 9 for 65 in an innings, and 16 for 220 in the match. At the start of 1999 he had already taken 203 wickets in forty-two matches at an average of 26.90, and obviously there is much more still to come from him.

Aravinda de Silva is Sri Lanka's most prodigious batsman, with more than five thousand career runs, and he really is a wonderful player to watch in full flow.

My umpiring colleague, David Constant, found himself in a most unusual situation when standing at a one-day international between England and Sri Lanka at the Oval. Allan Lamb drove the ball for three on the off-side, and just about made his ground. It was very close, and the Sri Lankans appealed confidently for a run-out. Conny shook his head. Not out. Lamby nodded his approval of the decision, but the Sri Lankans were obviously upset. They were convinced the batsman had not quite made his ground.

Lamb, of course, was born in South Africa. The same applied

to the batsman at the other end, Robin Smith. And Conny's umpiring partner that day was John Holder, of Barbados. As the mutterings from the Sri Lankans continued, Lamby turned to Constant and smiled. 'I think you ought to have danger money, Conny. Do you realise you're the only Englishman out here?'

Paarl, South Africa

SOUTH AFRICA
AND ZIMBABWE

23

O NE of my big regrets in cricket is that I never had the opportunity to umpire a Test match in South Africa. I stood at the Test at Lord's after they had been readmitted to the international arena in 1995, but I never had the thrill of umpiring at one of the beautiful grounds in South Africa itself. I spent many winters there coaching, however, prior to the Gleneagles Agreement, and I have some lovely memories of that country.

The stadiums at Johannesburg and Durban are marvellous, with excellent facilities, while Newlands is one of the most picturesque Test grounds in the world. With Cape Town and the imposing Table Mountain in the background, it is a most glorious sight, and possibly beats even the best England can offer for its breathtaking loveliness.

Newlands is the home ground of Allan Lamb, and it is a well-known fact that when he was a young man playing for Western Province, he was a bit of a prankster. Nothing has changed there, then.

Lamby's captain in those days was Eddie Barlow, who became so irritated with Lamby's antics in one game, that as a punishment he had him operating on the third-man boundary – at both ends. That is a very long walk on any ground, and before long Lamby decided he had had quite enough. After all, he was a fit young man. He did not need all that exercise.

He caught sight of a man with a bike on the boundary edge, standing quite near Brian Davison, who played for Rhodesia, as it then was, and happened to be watching the game. Lamby called out to him, 'Hey, Brian, ask that chap if I can borrow his bike, will you?'

'What the hell do you need a bike for, Lamby?' came the reply.

'You'll see,' rejoined Lamb. 'Just get on with it and ask the fellow, there's a good chap.'

At the end of that over, bike duly borrowed, Lamby cycled from one third-man position right across the pitch to the other boundary at the opposite end of the ground. Having completed his journey, to wild applause from the crowd, he dismounted, put the bike down, and waited in anticipation of the biggest rollocking of his life from Barlow.

Even Barlow saw the funny side of it, though. 'Okay, Lamby,' he said, 'you've made your point. Forget about third man.'

Willie Watson once did exactly the same to me when I was with Leicestershire. He had me traipsing across from one side of the ground to the other all day long. I must have walked miles and miles at Trent Bridge that day. I still can't for the life of me think what I had done to upset him. I wish I had found a bike that day – I wouldn't have thought twice about taking Lord Tebbit's famous advice.

Lamby, of course, settled in England and went on to become a great batsman for his adopted country. Two more South African youngsters accompanied him in those early days, Garth le Roux and Peter Kirsten, both of whom have played for their country.

All three players gained experience in the Huddersfield League, Lamby joining Holmfirth, who had a very small ground with a river running alongside. He soon worked out how to send the ball sailing into the water; in fact, he got it off to such a fine art that the club was in danger of running out of cricket balls. Eventually the committee decided that it would be cheaper to employ a boatman to patrol the river with a big net every time Lamby was playing, rather than fork out for dozens of new balls. Le Roux, who was with Lascelles Hall, often had to bowl against Lamby at Holmfirth – and he used to end up in the river with the rest of them.

Durban was the scene for one of the most bizarre last innings in any Test match anywhere, in March, 1939, when England were set 696 to win on a perfect pitch. There was no need for any of the batsmen to hurry or take risks, because it was a timeless Test.

Len Hutton made 55, Paul Gibb 120, Eddie Paynter 75, Walter Hammond 140, Bill Edrich a magnificent 219, and on day ten, those two men of Kent, Bryan Valentine and Leslie Ames, were still there, playing superbly, with the total on 654 for 5, only 42 runs away from an amazing victory.

As they walked out after the tea break, dark clouds had begun to gather, but Valentine remarked, 'Not to worry, we'll knock these off before the rain comes.' However, halfway through the second over, the storm broke and the pitch was soon under water as the rain came down like stairrods.

With the good ship *Athlone Castle* approaching Cape Town to take the England team home, the game had to be abandoned as a draw. Even then, the players only just made it to the boat in time. The gangplank was just about to be pulled up when they arrived at the docks. Ten days. Only forty-two to win. Five wickets left. So near, and yet so far. It must have been heartbreaking for the England party.

Johannesburg was the setting for another remarkable chapter in the history of Test cricket. When I read an account of the game between South Africa and New Zealand, who had yet to taste international victory, at Christmas, 1953, it moved me to tears.

Late on Christmas Eve, back in New Zealand, the railway express linking Wellington and Auckland had plunged into a swollen river. One hundred and fifty people died in the country's worst railway disaster, and the Christmas presents scattered among the wreckage made it seem all the more dreadful.

The New Zealand cricketers were grief-stricken when they heard the news in Johannesburg, and more so when it was discovered that the fiancée of their fast bowler, Bob Blair, was among those who had been killed. Blair was immediately withdrawn from the match, and, although play continued, the New Zealand lads were obviously distraught as they faced up to a furious Boxing Day blitz from fast bowler Neil Adcock, on a pitch tailor-made for him.

Worse was to come, however. Bert Sutcliffe was dealt a sickening blow on the head and had to retire; Lawrie Miller had to leave the field after being on the receiving end of another brute of a delivery; and wickets began to tumble with monotonous regularity.

In desperate trouble, New Zealand called on the injured Miller to return to the crease, still clearly in some distress. Then, at the fall of the next wicket, Sutcliffe, head swathed in bandages and the blood still seeping through, slowly but doggedly made his way back out to the middle.

It was delaying the inevitable, and when Miller was out, the fielders began to make their way towards the pavilion, assuming that the innings was over.

Suddenly a white-clad figure emerged from the pavilion and into the bright sunlight. It was Blair. The crowd gasped. If ever there was a hush in the close, this was it. You could have heard a pin drop. When Blair joined Sutcliffe in the middle, the two men embraced, then got on with the job, putting on 38 in ten minutes for the last wicket.

It was a bold, brave, defiant gesture, and when the end of the innings came, they made their way from the field arm in arm, the crowd giving them a standing ovation all the way back to the pavilion. It was said there was not a dry eye in the New Zealand dressing room. Nor, I suspect, among the spectators outside.

On their tour of South Africa in 1993–4, Australia really got the wind up when playing Orange Free State at Bloemfontein. Or, at least, my old friend Merv Hughes did. He was just accelerating into his delivery stride as he bowled to South African captain Hansie Cronje, when he broke wind. It was just like a pistol shot. Cronje fell about laughing, tears rolling down his cheeks, and before long everyone else had joined in. The game was held up for several minutes before order was eventually restored.

Cronje, however, recovered his composure completely. He went on to make a career-best score of 251.

Hansie is still leading by example, and I remember him and Jonty Rhodes sharing a record-breaking fifth-wicket partnership of 184 against England at Lord's in 1998.

For the highest individual Test innings by a South African, you have to turn to Graeme Pollock, who made 274 against the Australians at Durban in 1969–70. Pollock also holds the record with Eddie Barlow for a third-wicket stand of 341 they shared against Australia at Adelaide in 1963–4.

Most South African bowling honours have gone to Hughie Tayfield, who holds the records for the best bowling (9 for 113 v. England at Johannesburg in 1956–7); the best match bowling (13 for 165 v. Australia at Melbourne in 1952–3); and most wickets in a series (37 v. England in 1956–7).

Tayfield cannot match Allan Donald, however, for most wickets in a career. At the end of January 1999 the great fast bowler had already taken his tally to 260 in 52 matches at an average of 21.64, and was still going strong.

Perhaps the most remarkable of all the characters in South African cricket history was Major R. M. Poore, who was around when they played their first Test in 1888–9, which resulted in defeat by England at Port Elizabeth.

A brilliant all-round games player, the Major played most of his cricket in England, and in the 1889 season he averaged 116 for Hampshire, hitting seven centuries, including 301 against Somerset.

He continued to play a good deal of relatively minor cricket in England in the twilight of his career, and when asked by some enthusiastic undergraduates during a match at the Parks in the late 1920s how on earth a batsman should deal with the frighteningly fast and fearsome Nottinghamshire and England quick bowler Harold Larwood, he replied, 'Charge him, sir. Charge him. Fix yer bayonets and charge him.'

On sunny days he used to play wearing a broad-brimmed hat,

and on one occasion he was fielding at mid-off during an MCC match in the West Country while Middlesex leg-spinner Jim Powell went through the local opposition like a dose of salts. One batsman, in particular, did not have the foggiest idea how to tell Powell's leg-break from his googly, and Major-General Poore – he had been promoted by this time – turned to George Fenner in the covers, cupped his hands and boomed, 'Depend upon it, Fenner, we shall have a catch directly.'

No sooner had the words left his lips than the batsman tried a tremendous heave, finally managed to make some sort of contact, and the ball flew high into the wide blue yonder in the general direction of extra cover. The very model of a Major-General had a bit of problem at this point: he could not see the ball because of his hat's broad brim. He began to run round on the spot, rather like a dog chasing its tail, but like the dog, he could never catch it. In exasperation he called out, 'It's no good, Fenner. I've lost the beggar.'

To which Fenner replied, 'Hardly surprising, General. Mid-off caught it ten seconds ago.'

One of the heroes of more recent times is undoubtedly Ali Bacher, who has done a fabulous job for South African cricket. It was he who led the talks to get South Africa back into international cricket, and his country owes him a lot. He was also a very good cricketer, and captained South Africa when they had a great side, one of the best I have ever seen. It would have been a magnificent contest between them and the great West Indian and Australian teams – a triangular series to savour.

Even the best of players, and the most organised and dedicated of officials, can be reduced to jabbering wrecks when it comes to running between the wickets, however, and Bacher was no exception. He was once playing in a club match for Balfour Park, and he and Arnie Wilson were at the crease. The latter hit the ball into the covers and both batsmen started off for a quick single. Halfway down the track Wilson suddenly had a change of mind. He called, 'No,' and turned to go back. Bacher was so taken by surprise that he just kept on running, so that both of them were heading for the same end.

The ball was immediately thrown to the end where the bowler was standing over the stumps, but he was so startled by the sight of the two batsmen scampering towards him at full pelt, that he broke the wicket without having the ball in his hand. The batsmen then split up. Wilson headed for the wicketkeeper's end, Bacher stayed put.

When communication between the wicketkeeper and bowler broke down, Bacher and Wilson were again tempted out of their respected creases. Further cries of 'Yes', and 'No', 'Wait' and 'Sorry' were heard, and by the time order and a little sanity had been restored, both batsmen were still not out, both had run more than a hundred yards, both sets of stumps were flat on the ground, and not a run had been scored.

My old Yorkshire mentors, Arthur Mitchell and Maurice Leyland, hit the headlines when South Africa played a Test match at Headingley in 1935. Leyland was due to play for England, but he took ill, and a message was sent for Mitchell to take his place. He was in the garden of his home in Baildon when the call came, and in typically matter-of-fact fashion he said he would be along 'once I've got missen tidied up a bit.'

Arriving at the ground, he scored a half-century in both innings, figured in an opening stand of 128 with Denis Smith, of Derbyshire, and fielded magnificently throughout. What a way to mark his first home Test match! But he played in only two more Tests.

I have said many times that I rated Barry Richards as the greatest batsman I have seen, and it is a tragedy that he was unable to play more than a handful of games for his country. Mind you, fellow South African Basil D'Oliveira must have wished Richards had been on international duty, rather than playing for Hampshire, the day Brian Johnston told BBC radio listeners, 'Welcome to Worcester, where Barry Richards has just hit one of D'Oliveira's balls clean out of the ground.'

And, of course, it was that master of the microphone, John Arlott, who came out with the immortal phrase when England captain George Mann hit South African left-arm spinner Tufty Mann for six. 'That was,' said Arlott, 'a perfect example of Mann's inhumanity to Mann.'

In 1995 I was caught up in the infamous 'ball tampering' affair when England met South Africa at Lord's. BBC television pictures showed Michael Atherton take something out of his pocket and apparently sprinkle it on the ball before vigorously polishing the other side of the ball on his flannels.

Neither I nor my colleague Steve Randell knew anything about the incident until after close of play, however.

Countless callers had rung in to say what they had seen on the television, and the management got a message out to Graham Gooch on the pitch to tell Atherton not to talk to anyone when he came off at tea, as there was some ball-tampering trouble in the air.

Now, it has to be remembered that, at tea, South Africa were approaching a 300-run lead with only two second-innings wickets down, and Gooch, after relaying the message to his skipper, sent one back to the management. 'It must be their ball, then, because ours is doing bugger all.'

The England captain made a statement afterwards admitting that he had put his hand in his pocket to collect some dust he had scooped up to dry the ball, not to tamper with it, just to dry it. When match referee Peter Burge asked him if he had any substance in his pocket, Atherton had said 'No,' thinking of iron filings, Vaseline or Lypsyl. He had never thought there would be so much fuss about a bit of dust.

Later, on reflection, Atherton said, 'We all make mistakes.

Mine were magnified. I never thought of making it a resignation issue. I just wanted to let the dust settle.'

I had to smile when he said that, whether it was intentional or not.

Zimbabwe have only just been accepted into international cricket, and I had the privilege of umpiring their first Test match against India at Harare in 1992–3, when I became the first independent umpire under the auspices of the International Cricket Council.

I was a little surprised to find the Harare Test ground no more than a modest sports club stadium, and just as surprised to discover that it boasts one of the best pitches in the world. The setting is quite beautiful, too. As for facilities, they are improving all the time, although they still erect miniature temporary stands for Test matches.

Zimbabwe captain Dave Houghton made a big mistake in that game by not persevering with spinner John Traicos, who took five wickets as India replied to the home team's big total of 456, of which Houghton himself had made 121. His decision handed the initiative back to the visitors, and Manjrekar (104) and Kapil Dev (60) steered their side to a respectable 307 all out, having been in dire straits at 101 for 5 at one stage. The game eventually petered out into a draw.

My abiding memory of my first visit to Harare, however, was being mugged in the town centre at half past midday on a Saturday and having my wallet stolen, along with the two hundred pounds stashed inside it.

From there I flew on to Bulawayo, for the Test with New Zealand. The area was experiencing one of its worst droughts in living memory, but cometh the hour cometh the rain-man, and as soon as I stepped down from the plane on to the airport tarmac, the heavens opened. The Messiah had arrived, bringing the rain with him.

The problem then, of course, was that the heavy rain affected the pitch at the Bulawayo Athletic Club, and there was a delay before play could commence. Despite an unbeaten 101 by opening batsman Kevin Arnott in the second innings, there was not enough time left to reach a result and the game ended in another draw.

A few days later it was back to Harare for the second game against New Zealand, and I probably made more runs there than in my entire cricketing career. The diarrhoea became so bad that I eventually had to retire from the proceedings altogether towards the end of the day, leaving a third umpire, Ian Robinson, to deputise for me.

Typical of me. I avoided the Delhi belly in Delhi itself, but caught it in Harare.

STATISTICS
SECTION

Compiled by Vic Isaacs

FIRST-CLASS COUNTIES

(Records up to and including the end of the 1998 County season)

DERBYSHIRE

Derbyshire started as a first-class county in 1882, and in their long history have won the County Championship on just one occasion when A.W. Richardson led them to success in 1936. They were runners-up in 1996. They were the first winners of the NatWest Trophy in 1981, won the Sunday League in 1990 and the Benson and Hedges Cup in 1993.

Dickie Bird's years 1956–98

Dickie's first County Championship match as a player was against Derbyshire at Headingley, scoring 10 and 5. His best score against them was 78 for Leicestershire at Ashby-de-la-Zouch. Kim Barnett's playing career with Derbyshire has run parallel with Dickie's umpiring career. Kim Barnett has been the most prolific Derbyshire run machine during these years, with Harold Rhodes taking the wicket prize with 984.

Derbyshire have had fourteen captains in the last forty-three years:
D.B. Carr (1955–62), C. Lee (1963–64), D.C. Morgan (1965–69),
I.R. Buxton (1970–72), J.B. Bolus (1973–75), R.W. Taylor (1975–76),
E.J. Barlow (1976–78), D.S. Steele (1979), G. Miller (1979–81),
B. Wood (1981–83), K.J. Barnett (1983–95), D.M. Jones (1996),
P.A.J. DeFreitas (1997), D.G. Cork (1998).

First-Class Records

Team

Highest total by Derbyshire: 645 v. Hampshire at Derby 1898
Highest total against Derbyshire: 662 by Yorkshire at Chesterfield 1898
Lowest total by Derbyshire: 16 v. Nottinghamshire at Trent Bridge 1879
Lowest total against Derbyshire: 23 by Hampshire at Burton-on-Trent 1958

Batting

Highest individual innings: 274 G.A. Davidson v. Lancashire at Old Trafford 1896
Most runs in a season: 2,165 D.B. Carr 1959
Most runs in career: 23,854 K.J. Barnett 1970–98

Best partnership for each wicket:

1st   322   H. Storer and J. Bowden v. Essex at Derby 1929
2nd   417   K.J. Barnett and T.A. Tweats v. Yorkshire at Derby 1997
3rd   316*   A.S. Rollins and K.J. Barnett v. Leicestershire at Leicester 1997
4th   328   P. Vaulkhard and D. Smith v. Nottinghamshire at Trent Bridge 1946
5th   302*   J.E. Morris and D.G. Cork v. Gloucestershire at Cheltenham 1993
6th   212   G.M. Lee and T.S. Worthington v. Essex at Chesterfield 1932
7th   241*   G.H. Pope and A.E.G. Rhodes v. Hampshire at Portsmouth 1948
8th   198   K.M. Krikken and D.G. Cork v. Lancashire at Old Trafford 1996
9th   283   A. Warren and J. Chapman v. Warwickshire at Blackwell 1910
10th   132   A. Hill and M. Jean-Jacques v. Yorkshire at Sheffield 1986

Bowling

Best bowling in an innings for Derbyshire: 10–40 W. Bestwick v. Glamorgan at Cardiff 1921
Best bowling in a match for Derbyshire: 17–103 W. Mycroft v. Hampshire at Southampton 1876

Most wickets in a season: 168 T.B. Mitchell 1935

Most wickets in career: 1,670 H.L. Jackson 1947–63

DURHAM

Durham started as a first-class county in 1992, the eighteenth side to join the County Championship. However, they have a long and distinguished history as a Minor County, having been formed in 1882. Their highest position to date in the Championship is fourteenth in 1998. In 1973 as a Minor County, Durham defeated Yorkshire by 5 wickets in the first round of the Gillette Cup, in 1985 they beat Derbyshire, and reached the quarter-finals in 1992. They failed to qualify for the knock-out stages in the Benson and Hedges Cup. In the Sunday League their highest position is seventh in 1993.

Dickie Bird's years 1956–98

In the short time Durham have been a first-class county, their leading run scorer has been John Morris with 4,878 in 85 matches, their leading wicket taker Simon Brown with 383 in 107 matches. Dickie first visited Durham in a County Championship match on 2 June 1992 when he officiated in the game against Somerset at Darlington. He visited the new Chester-le-Street ground later that same year when the Pakistanis became the first touring side to play there.

Durham have had four captains since achieving first-class status: D.A. Graveney (1992–93), P. Bainbridge (1994), M.A. Roseberry (1995–96) and D.C. Boon (1997–98).

First-Class Records

Team

Highest total by Durham: 625–6dec v. Derbyshire at Chesterfield 1994

Highest total against Durham: 810–4dec by Warwickshire at Birmingham 1994

411

Lowest total by Durham: 67 v. Middlesex at Lord's 1996

Lowest total against Durham: 73 by Oxford University at Oxford 1994

Batting

Highest individual innings: 210* J.J.B. Lewis v. Oxford University at Oxford 1997

Most runs in a season: 1,536 W. Larkins 1992

Most runs in career: 4,278 W. Larkins 1992–95

Best partnership for each wicket:

1st   334* S. Hutton and M.A. Roseberry v. Oxford University at Oxford 1996

2nd 206 W. Larkins and D.M. Jones v. Glamorgan at Cardiff 1992

3rd   205 G. Fowler and S. Hutton v. Yorkshire at Leeds 1993

4th   204 J.J.B. Lewis and J. Boiling v. Derbyshire at Chester-le-Street 1997

5th   185 P.W.G. Parker and J.A. Daley v. Warwickshire at Darlington 1993

6th   193 D.C. Boon and P.D. Collingwood v. Warwickshire at Birmingham 1998

7th   110 P.D. Collingwood and M.J. Foster v. Nottinghamshire at Nottingham 1998

8th   134 A.C. Cummins and D.A. Graveney v. Warwickshire at Birmingham 1994

9th   127 D.G.C. Ligertwood and S.J.E. Brown v. Surrey at Stockton-on-Tees 1996

10th 103 M.M. Betts and D.M. Cox v. Sussex at Hove 1996

Bowling

Best bowling in an innings for Durham: 9–64 M.M. Betts v. Northants at Northampton 1997

Best bowling in a match for Durham: 14–177 A. Walker v. Essex at Chelmsford 1995

Most wickets in a season: 77 S.J.E. Brown 1996

Most wickets in career: 376 S.J.E. Brown 1992–97

ESSEX

Although formed in 1876, Essex took 103 years to record their first County Championship success when Keith Fletcher led them to the top honour in 1979. They won again, also under Fletcher, in 1983 and 1984, and under Graham Gooch in 1986, 1991 and 1992. They have had some success in the limited-overs game, winning the Benson and Hedges Cup in 1979 and 1998, the NatWest Trophy in 1985 and 1997 and the Sunday League in 1981, 1984 and 1985.

Dickie Bird's years 1956–98

Dickie's first match as a player against Essex was in 1959 at Sheffield. He was stumped off Greensmith for 10 in the first innings, and bowled by the same bowler second time around for 0. Graham Gooch was by far the leading batsman for Essex during Dickie's years with 30,701 in 391 matches; John Lever with 1,473 wickets in 443 matches held the bowling honours.

During the same period, Essex have had six captains. D.J. Insole (1951–60), T.E. Bailey (1961–66), B. Taylor (1967–73), K.W.R. Fletcher (1974–85 and 1988), G.A. Gooch (1986–87 and 1989–94), P.J. Prichard (1995–98).

First-Class Records

Team

Highest total by Essex:	761–6dec v. Leicestershire at Chelmsford 1990
Highest total against Essex:	803–4dec by Kent at Brentwood 1934
Lowest total by Essex:	30 v. Yorkshire at Leyton 1901
Lowest total against Essex:	14 by Surrey at Chelmsford 1983

Batting

Highest individual innings:	343* P.A. Perrin v. Derbyshire at Chesterfield 1904
Most runs in a season:	2,559 G.A. Gooch 1984
Most runs in career:	30,701 G.A. Gooch 1973–97

Best partnership for each wicket:

1st 316 G.A. Gooch and P.J. Prichard v. Kent at Chelmsford 1994
2nd 403 G.A. Gooch and P.J. Prichard v. Leicestershire at Chelmsford 1990

3rd   347* M.E. Waugh and N. Hussain v. Lancashire at Ilford 1992
4th   314   Salim Malik and N. Hussain v. Surrey at The Oval 1991
5th   316   N. Hussain and M.A. Garnham v. Leicestershire at Leicester
             1991
       ⎡ 206 J.W.H.T. Douglas and J. O'Connor v. Gloucestershire at Cheltenham
6th   ⎨   1923
       ⎣ 206 B.R. Knight and R.A.G. Luckin v. Middlesex at Brentwood 1962
7th   261   J.W.H.T. Douglas and J. Freeman v. Lancashire at Leyton 1914
8th   263   D.R. Wilcox and R.M. Taylor v. Warwickshire at Southend-on-
             Sea 1946
9th   251   J.W.H.T. Douglas and S.N. Hare v. Derbyshire at Leyton 1921
10th   218   F.H. Vigar and T.P.B. Smith v. Derbyshire at Chesterfield 1947

Bowling

Best bowling in an innings for Essex: 10–32 H. Pickett v. Leicestershire at
                                         Leyton 1895
Best bowling in a match for Essex: 17–119 W. Mead v. Hampshire at
                                         Southampton 1895
Most wickets in a season: 172 T.P.B. Smith 1947
Most wickets in career: 1,610 T.P.B. Smith 1929–51

GLAMORGAN

The Welsh county were formed in 1888, and have won the coveted County Championship three times since the Second World War – in 1948 under Wilf Wooller, in 1969 with Tony Lewis as captain, and most recently in 1997 under Matthew Maynard. In the limited-overs game their only success is the Sunday League title in 1993. They have reached just one final at Lord's, the Gillette Cup in 1977, losing by 5 wickets to Middlesex. Their best performance in the Benson and Hedges Cup is a semi-final place in 1988.

Dickie Bird's years 1956–98

Dickie's first County Championship match as a player against Glamorgan was in 1958 for Yorkshire scoring 23 and 30 at Swansea.

414

His highest first-class score of 181* was scored at Bradford against the county in 1959. Alan Jones was by far the most prolific run scorer for Glamorgan with 33,883 in 608 matches. Their leading wicket taker was Don Shepherd with 1,767 in 486 matches.

There have been thirteen captains at the Welsh county since 1956. W. Wooller (1947–60), O.S. Wheatley (1961–66), A.R. Lewis (1967–72), Majid Khan (1973–76), A. Jones (1977–78), R.N.S. Hobbs (1979), M.A. Nash (1980–81), Javed Miandad (1982), M.W.W. Selvey (1983–84), R.C. Ontong (1985–86), H. Morris (1987–89 and 1993–95), A.R. Butcher (1990–92), M.P. Maynard (1996–98).

First-Class Records

Team

Highest total by Glamorgan:	597–8dec v. Durham at Cardiff 1997
Highest total against Glamorgan:	712 by Northamptonshire at Northampton 1998
Lowest total by Glamorgan:	22 v. Lancashire at Liverpool 1924
Lowest total against Glamorgan:	33 by Leicestershire at Ebbw Vale 1965

Batting

Highest individual innings:	287* D.E. Davies v. Gloucestershire at Newport 1939
Most runs in a season:	2,276 H. Morris 1990
Most runs in career:	34,056 A. Jones 1957–83

Best partnership for each wicket:

1st	330	A. Jones and R.C. Fredericks v. Northamptonshire at Swansea 1972
2nd	249	S.P. James and H. Morris v. Oxford University at Oxford 1987
3rd	313	D.E. Davies and W.E. Jones v. Essex at Brentwood 1948
4th	425*	A. Dale and I.V.A. Richards v. Middlesex at Cardiff 1993
5th	264	M. Robinson and S.W. Montgomery v. Hampshire at Bournemouth 1949
6th	230	W.E. Jones and B.L. Muncer v. Worcestershire at Worcester 1953
7th	211	P.A. Cottey and O.D. Gibson v. Leicestershire at Swansea 1996
8th	202	D. Davies and J.J. Hills v. Sussex at Eastbourne 1928

9th 203* J.J. Hills and J.C. Clay v. Worcestershire at Swansea 1929
10th 143 T. Davies and S.A.B. Daniels v. Gloucestershire at Swansea 1982

Bowling

Best bowling in an innings for Glamorgan: 10–51 J. Mercer v.
                                           Worcestershire at Worcester 1936
Best bowling in a match for Glamorgan: 17–212 J.C. Clay v.
                                        Worcestershire at Swansea 1937
Most wickets in a season: 176 J.C. Clay 1937
Most wickets in career: 2,174 D.J. Shepherd 1950–72

GLOUCESTERSHIRE

Gloucestershire County Cricket Club first saw the light of day in 1871, but so far they have not won the County Championship, coming a tantalising second on six occasions, 1930, 1931, 1947, 1959, 1969 and 1986. In 1988 they came second in the Sunday League, but they have won both Cups, the Benson and Hedges in 1977 and the Gillette Cup in 1973.

Dickie Bird's years 1956–98

As a player, Dickie first met up with Gloucestershire in 1959 when at Headingley he scored 20 in the first innings. Ron Nicholls scored the most runs during Dickie's years for the West Country side with 23,053 in 502 matches, with Jim Mortimore taking 1,458 wickets in 507 matches. Before the advent of floodlit cricket, Dickie umpired the famous televised semi-final of the Gillette Cup between Gloucestershire and Lancashire at Old Trafford in 1971, which lasted until 8.50 p.m.

Gloucestershire have had fourteen captains in Dickie's time: G.M. Emmett (1955–58), T.W. Graveney (1959–60), C.T.M. Pugh (1961–62), J.K.R. Graveney (1963–64), J.B. Mortimore (1965–67), C.A. Milton (1968), A.S. Brown (1969–76), M.J. Procter (1977–81),

D.A. Graveney (1982–88), C.W.J. Athey (1989), A.J. Wright (1990–93), C.A. Walsh (1993–94 and 1996), R.C. Russell (1995), M.W. Alleyne (1997–98).

First-Class Records

Team

Highest total by Gloucestershire:	653–6dec v. Glamorgan at Bristol 1928
Highest total against Gloucestershire:	774–7dec by Australians at Bristol 1948
Lowest total by Gloucestershire:	17 v. Australians at Cheltenham 1896
Lowest total against Gloucestershire:	12 by Northamptonshire at Gloucester 1907

Batting

Highest individual innings:	318* W.G. Grace v. Yorkshire at Cheltenham 1876
Most runs in a season:	2,860 W.R. Hammond 1933
Most runs in career:	33,664 W.R. Hammond 1920–51

Best partnership for each wicket:

1st 395 D.M. Young and R.B. Nicholls v. Oxford University at Oxford 1962

2nd 256 C.T.M. Pugh and T.W. Graveney v. Derbyshire at Chesterfield 1960

3rd 336 W.R. Hammond and B.H. Lyon v. Leicestershire at Leicester 1933

4th 321 W.R. Hammond and W.L. Neale v. Leicestershire at Gloucester 1937

5th 261 W.G. Grace and W.O. Moberley v. Yorkshire at Cheltenham 1876

6th 320 G.L. Jessop and J.H. Board v. Sussex at Hove 1903

7th 248 W.G. Grace and E.L. Thomas v. Sussex at Hove 1896

8th 239 W.R. Hammond and A.E. Wilson v. Lancashire at Bristol 1938

9th 193 W.G. Grace and S.A.P. Kitcat v. Sussex at Bristol 1896

10th 131 W.R. Gouldsworthy and J.G. Bessant v. Somerset at Bristol 1923

Bowling

Best bowling in an innings for Gloucestershire:	10–40 E.G. Dennett v. Essex at Bristol 1906
Best bowling in a match for Gloucestershire:	17–56 C.W.L. Parker v. Essex at Gloucester 1925

Most wickets in a season: 222 T.W.J. Goddard 1937
                                    and 1947
Most wickets in career: 3,170 C.W.L. Parker
                                    1903–35

HAMPSHIRE

Formed in 1863 and entering the Championship in 1895, Hampshire first won the competition under the flamboyant Colin Ingleby-Mackenzie in 1961. Twelve years later Richard Gilliat led an unbeaten side. Hampshire took a long time to reach a Lord's final with a string of semi-final defeats, but they finally won the Benson and Hedges Cup in 1988 and again in 1992. In between they lifted the NatWest Trophy in 1991. They have won the Sunday League three times, in 1975, 1978 and 1986.

Dickie Bird's years 1956–98

The late Mervyn Burden was Dickie's antagonist in 1958, dismissing him twice in his first meeting with Hampshire but not before he had scored 19 and 47. The swashbuckling Roy Marshall led the batting honours with 28,243 in 470 matches, and the niggling Derek Shackleton led the bowlers with 1,797 in 376 matches.

Hampshire have had just nine captains in this period: E.D.R. Eagar (1946–57), A.C.D. Ingleby-Mackenzie (1958–65), R.E. Marshall (1966–70), R.M.C. Gilliat (1971–78), G.R. Stephenson (1979), N.E.J. Pocock (1980–84), M.C.J. Nicholas (1985–95), J.P. Stephenson (1996–97) and R.A. Smith (1998).

First-Class Records

Team

Highest total by Hampshire: 672–7dec v. Somerset at Taunton 1899

Highest total against Hampshire: 742 by Surrey at The Oval 1909
Lowest total by Hampshire: 15 v. Warwickshire at Birmingham 1922
Lowest total against Hampshire: 23 by Yorkshire at Middlesbrough 1965

Batting

Highest individual innings: 316 R.H. Moore v. Warwickshire at Bournemouth 1937
Most runs in a season: 2,854 C.P. Mead 1928
Most runs in career: 48,892 C.P. Mead 1905–36

Best partnership for each wicket:

1st 347 V.P. Terry and C.L. Smith v. Warwickshire at Birmingham 1987
2nd 321 G. Brown and E.I.M. Barrett v. Gloucestershire at Southampton 1920
3rd 344 C.P. Mead and G. Brown v. Yorkshire at Portsmouth 1927
4th 263 R.E. Marshall and D.A. Livingstone v. Middlesex at Lord's 1970
5th 235 G. Hill and D.F. Walker v. Sussex at Portsmouth 1937
6th 411 R.M. Poore and E.G. Wynyard v. Somerset at Taunton 1899
7th 325 G. Brown and C.H. Abercrombie v. Essex at Leyton 1913
8th 227 K.D. James and T.M. Tremlett v. Somerset at Taunton 1985
9th 230 D.A. Livingstone and A.T. Castell v. Surrey at Southampton 1962
10th 192 H.A.W. Bowell and W.H. Livsey v. Worcestershire at Bournemouth 1921

Bowling

Best bowling in an innings for Hampshire: 9–25 R.M.H. Cottam v. Lancashire at Manchester 1965
Best bowling in a match for Hampshire: 16–88 J.A. Newman v. Somerset at Weston-Super-Mare 1927
Most wickets in a season: 190 A.S. Kennedy 1922
Most wickets in career: 2,669 D. Shackleton 1948–69

KENT

Formed as a county club in 1859, Kent were crowned County Champions for the first time in 1906, followed by success in 1909, 1910 and 1913. It took another fifty-seven years before Colin Cowdrey led them to the top spot in 1970. They shared the honours with Middlesex in 1977 and won it outright in 1978. Kent have had good success in the limited-overs format, winning the Gillette Cup in 1967 and 1974, and the Benson and Hedges Cup in 1973, 1976 and 1978. The Sunday League was won in 1972, 1973, 1976 and 1995.

Dickie Bird's years 1956–98

It took until the end of the 1960 season before Dickie first met Kent, when at Dover he recorded scores of 43 and 5. Since the start of Dickie Bird's cricketing career, Colin Cowdrey has dominated the batting with 20,459 runs in 339 matches, and 'deadly' Derek Underwood took some 1,951 wickets in that time.

Kent have had nine captains during this period: D.V.P. Wright (1954–56), M.C. Cowdrey (1957–71), M.H. Denness (1972–76), Asif Iqbal (1977 and 1981–82), A.G.E. Ealham (1978–80), C.J. Tavaré (1983–84), C.S. Cowdrey (1985–90), M.R. Benson (1991–95) and S.A. Marsh (1996–98).

First-Class Records

Team

Highest total by Kent:	803–4dec v. Essex at Brentwood 1934
Highest total against Kent:	676 by Australians at Canterbury 1921
Lowest total by Kent:	18 v. Sussex at Gravesend 1867
Lowest total against Kent:	16 by Warwickshire at Tonbridge 1913

Batting

Highest individual innings:	332 W.H. Ashdown v. Essex at Brentwood 1934
Most runs in a season:	2,894 F.E. Woolley 1928
Most runs in career:	47,868 F.E. Woolley 1906–38

Best partnership for each wicket:

1st 300 N.R. Taylor and M.R. Benson v. Derbyshire at Canterbury 1991
2nd 366 S.G. Hinks and N.R. Taylor v. Middlesex at Canterbury 1990
3rd 321* A. Hearne and J.R. Mason v. Nottinghamshire at Nottingham 1899

420

4th 368 P.A. de Silva and G.R. Cowdrey v. Derbyshire at Maidstone 1995
5th 277 F.E. Woolley and L.E.G. Ames v. New Zealand at Canterbury 1931
6th 315 P.A. de Silva and M.A. Ealham v. Nottinghamshire at Nottingham 1995
7th 248 A.P. Day and E. Humphreys v. Somerset at Taunton 1908
8th 157 A.L. Hilder and A.C. Wright v. Essex at Gravesend 1924
9th 171 M.A. Ealham and P.A. Strang v. Nottinghamshire at Nottingham 1997
10th 235 F.E. Woolley and A. Fielder v. Worcestershire at Stourbridge 1909

Bowling

Best bowling in an innings for Kent: 10–30 C. Blythe v. Northamptonshire at Northampton 1907

Best bowling in a match for Kent: 17–48 C. Blythe v. Northamptonshire at Northampton 1907

Most wickets in a season: 262 A.P. Freeman 1933

Most wickets in career: 3,340 A.P. Freeman 1914–36

LANCASHIRE

Lancashire, formed in 1864, have won the County Championship on seven occasions, all before the Second World War. Their Championship successes were in 1897, 1904, 1926, 1927, 1928, 1930 and 1934. As a limited-overs team they have dominated much of the format winning the Gillette Cup/NatWest Trophy in 1970, 1971, 1972, 1975, 1990, 1996 and 1998. They won the Benson and Hedges Cup in 1984, 1990, 1995 and 1996. Their Sunday League successes came in the inaugural year 1969, 1971, 1989 and, completing a limited-overs double, in 1998.

Dickie Bird's years 1956–98

Dickie never played in a Roses match for Yorkshire and first met Lancashire at Grace Road in 1960 when he scored 1 before retiring hurt and being absent in the second innings. David Lloyd has scored the most runs for the northern county in Dickie's years with 17,877 in 378 matches, and the great Brian Statham with 1,321 wickets in 305 takes the bowling spoils.

Lancashire have had fourteen captains during this period: C. Washbrook (1954–59), R.W. Barber (1960–61), J.F. Blackledge (1962), K.J. Grieves (1963–64), J.B. Statham (1965–67), J.D. Bond (1968–72), D. Lloyd (1973–77), F.C. Hayes (1978–80), C.H. Lloyd (1981–83 and 1986), J. Abrahams (1984–85), D.P. Hughes (1987–91), N.H. Fairbrother (1992–93), M. Watkinson (1994–97) and Wasim Akram (1998).

First-Class Records

Team

Highest total by Lancashire:	863 v. Surrey at The Oval 1990
Highest total against Lancashire:	707–9dec by Surrey at The Oval 1990
Lowest total by Lancashire:	25 v. Derbyshire at Manchester 1871
Lowest total against Lancashire:	22 by Glamorgan at Liverpool 1924

Batting

Highest individual innings:	424 A.C. MacLaren v. Somerset at Taunton 1895
Most runs in a season:	2,633 J.T. Tyldesley 1901
Most runs in career:	34,222 G.E. Tyldesley 1909–36

Best partnership for each wicket:

1st 368 A.C. MacLaren and R.H. Spooner v. Gloucestershire at Liverpool 1903
2nd 371 F.B. Watson and G.E. Tyldesley v. Surrey at Manchester 1928
3rd 364 M.A. Atherton and N.H. Fairbrother v. Surrey at The Oval 1990
4th 358 S.P. Titchard and G.D. Lloyd v. Essex at Chelmsford 1996
5th 249 B. Wood and A. Kennedy v. Warwickshire at Birmingham 1975
6th 278 J. Iddon and H.R.W. Butterworth v. Sussex at Manchester 1932
7th 248 G.D. Lloyd and I.D. Austin v. Yorkshire at Leeds 1997
8th 158 J. Lyon and R.M. Ratcliffe v. Warwickshire at Manchester 1979
9th 142 L.O.S. Poidevin and A. Kermode v. Sussex at Eastbourne 1907
10th 173 J. Briggs and R. Pilling v. Surrey at Liverpool 1885

STATISTICS SECTION

Bowling

Best bowling in an innings for Lancashire: 10–46 W. Hickton v. Hampshire at Manchester 1870

Best bowling in a match for Lancashire: 17–91 H. Dean v. Yorkshire at Liverpool 1913

Most wickets in a season: 198 E.A. McDonald 1925

Most wickets in career: 1,816 J.B. Statham 1950–68

LEICESTERSHIRE

Leicestershire, Dickie's second county as a player, were formed in 1879, but it was not until another Yorkshireman, Ray Illingworth, led them to success in 1975 that they recorded their first Championship win. They have dominated the scene more recently with success in 1996 and 1998. Their one-day success is primarily in the Benson and Hedges Cup with victories in 1972, 1975 and 1985. They won the Sunday League in 1974 and 1977, but their only appearance to date in the 60-overs format final was in 1992 when they lost to Northamptonshire by 8 wickets.

Dickie Bird's years 1956–98

Dickie never played against Leicestershire for Yorkshire, before joining them in 1960 for five seasons. Maurice Hallam has been the county's leading run maker in Dickie's years with 20,277 in 399 matches, and Terry Spencer with 1,090 wickets in 404 matches dominated the bowling.

Leicestershire have had thirteen captains during Dickie's spell: C.H. Palmer (1950–57), W. Watson (1958–61), D. Kirby (1962), M.R. Hallam (1963–65 and 1968), G.A.R. Lock (1966–67), R. Illingworth (1969–78), K. Higgs (1979), B.F. Davison (1980), R.W. Tolchard (1981–83), D.I. Gower (1984–86 and 1988–89), P. Willey (1987), N.E. Briers (1990–95), J.J. Whitaker (1996–98).

423

First-Class Records

Team

Highest total by Leicestershire:	701–4dec v. Worcestershire at Worcester 1906
Highest total against Leicestershire:	761–6dec by Essex at Chelmsford 1990
Lowest total by Leicestershire:	25 v. Kent at Leicester 1912
Lowest total against Leicestershire:	24 by Glamorgan at Leicester 1971 24 by Oxford University at Oxford 1985

Batting

Highest individual innings:	261 P.V. Simmons v. Northamptonshire at Leicester 1994
Most runs in a season:	2,446 L.G. Berry 1937
Most runs in career:	30,143 L.G. Berry 1924–51

Best partnership for each wicket:

1st 390 B. Dudleston and J.F. Steele v. Derbyshire at Leicester 1979
2nd 289* J.C. Balderstone and D.I. Gower v. Essex at Leicester 1981
3rd 316* W. Watson and A. Wharton v. Somerset at Taunton 1961
4th 290* P. Willey and T.J. Boon v. Warwickshire at Leicester 1984
5th 322 B.F. Smith and P.V. Simmons v. Nottinghamshire at Worksop 1998
6th 284 P.V. Simmons and P.A. Nixon v. Durham at Chester-le-Street 1996
7th 219* J.D.R. Benson and P. Whitticase v. Hampshire at Bournemouth 1991
8th 172 P.A. Nixon and D.J. Millns v. Lancashire at Manchester 1996
9th 160 W.W. Odell and R.T. Crawford v. Worcestershire at Leicester 1902
10th 228 R. Illingworth and K. Higgs v. Northamptonshire at Leicester 1977

Bowling

Best bowling in an innings for Leicestershire:	10–18 G. Geary v. Glamorgan at Pontypridd 1929
Best bowling in a match for Leicestershire:	16–96 G. Geary v. Glamorgan at Pontypridd 1929
Most wickets in a season:	170 J.E. Walsh 1948
Most wickets in career:	2,130 W.E. Astill 1906–39

MIDDLESEX

Formed in 1864, Middlesex, who play the majority of their cricket at the MCC ground at Lord's, have had some success spread over a span of years. They won the County Championship in 1903, 1920, 1921, 1947, 1976, 1980, 1982, 1985, 1990 and 1993. They have won the Gillette Cup/NatWest Trophy four times in 1977, 1980, 1984 and 1988, and the Benson and Hedges Cup in 1983 and 1986, with just one Sunday League success in 1992.

Dickie Bird's years 1956–98

It was not until 1964 that Dickie made his first visit to Middlesex, retiring hurt for 5 in the first innings and being caught and bowled by Drybrough for 12 in the second. Mike Gatting has dominated the batting in those years with 28,411 in 412 matches in a career that has run parallel with Dickie's umpiring years. Fred Titmus with 1,940 wickets in 548 matches was the bowling star.

Middlesex have had nine captains in that time: W.J. Edrich (1953–57), J.J. Warr (1958–60), P.I. Bedford (1961–62), C.D. Drybrough (1963–64), F.J. Titmus (1965–68), P.H. Parfitt (1968–70), J.M. Brearley (1971–82), M.W. Gatting (1983–97) and M.R. Ramprakash (1997–98).

First-Class Records

Team
Highest total by Middlesex: 642–3 dec v. Hampshire at Southampton 1923
Highest total against Middlesex: 665 by West Indians at Lord's 1939
Lowest total by Middlesex: 20 v. MCC at Lord's 1864
Lowest total against Middlesex: 31 by Gloucestershire at Bristol 1924

Batting

Highest individual innings: 331 J.D.B. Robertson v. Worcestershire at Worcester 1949

Most runs in a season: 2,669 E.H. Hendren 1923

Most runs in career: 40,302 E.H. Hendren 1907–37

Best partnership for each wicket:

1st   372   M.W. Gatting and J.L. Langer v. Essex at Southgate 1998

2nd   380   F.A. Tarrant and J.W. Hearne v. Lancashire at Lord's 1914

3rd   424*   W.J. Edrich and D.C.S. Compton v. Somerset at Lord's 1948

4th   325   J.W. Hearne and E.H. Hendren v. Hampshire at Lord's 1919

5th   338   R.S. Lucas and T.C. O'Brien v. Sussex at Hove 1895

6th   270   J.D. Carr and P.N. Weekes v. Gloucestershire at Lord's 1994

7th   271*   E.H. Hendren and F.T. Mann v. Nottinghamshire at Nottingham 1925

8th   182*   M.H.C. Doll and H.R. Murrell v. Nottinghamshire at Lord's 1913

9th   160*   E.H. Hendren and T.J. Durston v. Essex at Leyton 1927

10th   230   R.W. Nicholls and W. Roche v. Kent at Lord's 1899

Bowling

Best bowling in an innings for Middlesex: 10–40 G.O.B. Allen v. Lancashire at Lord's 1929

Best bowling in a match for Middlesex: 16–114 G. Burton v. Yorkshire at Sheffield 1888 / 16–114 J.T. Hearne v. Lancashire at Manchester 1898

Most wickets in a season: 158 F.J. Titmus 1955

Most wickets in career: 2,361 F.J. Titmus 1949–82

NORTHAMPTONSHIRE

Formed in 1878, Northamptonshire joined the County Champion-ship scene in 1905, but so far have failed to receive a Championship pennant. They have been runners-up on four occasions, in 1912, 1957, 1965 and 1976. They have also had limited success in one-day cricket, winning the Gillette/NatWest Trophy twice in 1976 and

1992 and the Benson and Hedges Cup once in 1980. Their best Sunday League season was 1991 when they finished third.

Dickie Bird's years 1956–98

Dickie's first County Championship match as a player against Northamptonshire was in 1960 at Grace Road scoring 13 and 22*. Geoff Cook was Northamptonshire's leading run scorer in the period with 20,976 runs in 415 matches. Brian Crump with 807 wickets in 317 matches was the leading wicket taker.

Northamptonshire have had eleven captains in this time: D. Brookes (1954–57), R. Subba Row (1958–61), K.V. Andrew (1962–66), R.M. Prideaux (1967–70), P.J. Watts (1971–75 and 1978–80), R.T. Virgin (1975), Mushtaq Mohammad (1975–77), G. Cook (1981–88), A.J. Lamb (1989–95), R.J. Bailey (1996–97) and K.M. Curran (1998).

First-Class Records

Team

Highest total by Northamptonshire:	781–7dec v. Nottinghamshire at Northampton 1995
Highest total against Northamptonshire:	670–9dec by Sussex at Hove 1921
Lowest total by Northamptonshire:	12 v. Gloucestershire at Gloucester 1907
Lowest total against Northamptonshire:	33 by Lancashire at Northampton 1977

Batting

Highest individual innings:	322* M.B. Loye v. Glamorgan at Northampton 1998
Most runs in a season:	2,198 D. Brookes 1952
Most runs in career:	28,980 D. Brookes 1934–59

Best partnership for each wicket:

1st 372 R.R. Montgomerie and M.B. Loye v. Yorkshire at Northampton 1996
2nd 344 G. Cook and R.J. Boyd-Moss v. Lancashire at Northampton 1986

3rd 393 A. Fordham and A.J. Lamb v. Yorkshire at Leeds 1990
4th 370 R.T. Virgin and P. Willey v. Somerset at Northampton 1976
5th 401 M.B. Loye and D. Ripley v. Glamorgan at Northampton 1998
6th 376 R. Subba Row and A. Lightfoot v. Surrey at The Oval 1958
7th 229 W.W. Timms and F.A. Walden v. Warwickshire at Northampton 1926
8th 164 D. Ripley and N.G.B. Cook v. Lancashire at Manchester 1987
9th 156 R. Subba Row and S. Starkie v. Lancashire at Northampton 1955
10th 148 B.W. Bellamy and J.V. Murdin v. Glamorgan at Northampton 1925

Bowling

Best bowling in an innings for Northamptonshire:	10–127 V.W.C. Jupp v. Kent at Tunbridge Wells 1932
Best bowling in a match for Northamptonshire:	15–31 G.E. Tribe v. Yorkshire at Northampton 1958
Most wickets in a season:	175 G.E. Tribe 1955
Most wickets in career:	1,097 E.W. Clark 1922–47

NOTTINGHAMSHIRE

Formed in 1841, Nottinghamshire have had limited success in all the competitions. They have won the Championship four times in 1907, 1929, 1981 and 1987, the Gillette/NatWest Trophy in 1987, the Benson and Hedges Cup in 1989 and the Sunday League in 1991.

Dickie Bird's years 1956–98

In 1960 Dickie played his first county match against Nottinghamshire, scoring 18 and 0 at Loughborough. Tim Robinson, whose career runs parallel with Dickie's umpiring, has led the batsmen at Trent Bridge with 23,914 runs in 362 first-class matches. The popular Eddie Hemmings took the most wickets with 850 in 270 matches.

Nottinghamshire have had twelve captains since 1956: R.T. Simpson (1951–60), J.D. Clay (1961), A.J. Corran (1962), G. Millman

(1963–65), N.W. Hill (1966–67), G.St.A. Sobers (1968–71 and 1973), J.B. Bolus (1972), J.D. Bond (1974), M.J. Smedley (1975–79), C.E.B. Rice (1979–87), R.T. Robinson (1988–95), P. Johnson (1996–98).

First-Class Records

Team

Highest total by Nottinghamshire:	739–7dec v. Leicestershire at Nottingham 1903
Highest total against Nottinghamshire:	781–7dec by Northamptonshire at Northampton 1995
Lowest total by Nottinghamshire:	13 v. Yorkshire at Nottingham 1901
Lowest total against Nottinghamshire:	16 by Derbyshire at Nottingham 1879 16 by Surrey at The Oval 1880

Batting

Highest individual innings:	312* W.W. Keeton v. Middlesex at The Oval 1939
Most runs in a season:	2,620 W.W. Whysall 1929
Most runs in career:	31,592 G. Gunn 1902–32

Best partnership for each wicket:

1st	391	A.O. Jones and A. Shrewsbury v. Gloucestershire at Bristol 1899
2nd	398	A. Shrewsbury and W. Gunn v. Sussex at Nottingham 1890
3rd	369	W. Gunn and J.R. Gunn v. Leicestershire at Nottingham 1903
4th	361	A.O. Jones and J.R. Gunn v. Essex at Leyton 1905
5th	266	A. Shrewsbury and W. Gunn v. Sussex at Hove 1884
6th	303*	F.H. Winrow and P.F. Harvey v. Derbyshire at Nottingham 1947
7th	301	C.C. Lewis and B.N. French v. Durham at Chester-le-Street 1993
8th	220	G.F.H. Heane and R.Winrow v. Somerset at Nottingham 1935
9th	170	J.C. Adams and K.P. Evans v. Somerset at Taunton 1994
10th	152	E.B. Alletson and W. Riley v. Sussex at Hove 1911

Bowling

Best bowling in an innings for Nottinghamshire:	10–66 K. Smales v. Gloucestershire at Stroud 1956
Best bowling in a match for Nottinghamshire:	17–89 F.C. Matthews v. Northamptonshire at Nottingham 1923

Most wickets in a season:	181 B. Dooland 1954
Most wickets in career:	1,653 T.G. Wass 1896–1920

SURREY

Formed in 1845, Surrey are second only to Yorkshire with Championship successes, but their runs have come in two dominant spells – at the end of the last century (1890, 1891, 1892, 1894, 1895, 1899 and 1914) and in the fifties (1950 joint, 1952, 1953, 1954, 1955, 1956, 1957, 1958). More recently, Micky Stewart's side won in 1971. Their limited-overs success has been less prominent. They won the Gillette/NatWest Trophy in 1982, the Benson and Hedges Cup in 1974 and 1997 and had a solitary Sunday League success in 1996.

Dickie Bird's years 1956–98

Alec Bedser managed to bowl Dickie out for 6 and 23 when he first met Surrey in 1960 at Grace Road. Surrey's England opening batsman John Edrich has scored the most runs in Dickie's years with 29,116 in 408 matches, with Pat Pocock taking 1,399 wickets in 485 matches.

Surrey have had eleven captains since 1956: W.S. Surridge (1952–56), P.B.H. May (1957–62; although May was officially captain in 1960, A.V. Bedser filled the role due to May's illness), M.J. Stewart (1963–72), J.H. Edrich (1973–77), R.D.V. Knight (1978–83), G.P. Howarth (1984–85), P.I. Pocock (1986), I.A. Greig (1987–91), A.J. Stewart (1992–96) and A.J. Hollioake (1997–98).

First-Class Records

Team

Highest total by Surrey:	811 v. Somerset at The Oval 1899
Highest total against Surrey:	863 by Lancashire at The Oval 1990

430

Lowest total by Surrey: 14 v. Essex at Chelmsford 1983
Lowest total against Surrey: 16 by MCC at Lord's 1872

Batting
Highest individual innings: 357* R. Abel v. Somerset at The Oval 1899
Most runs in a season: 3,246 T.W. Hayward 1906
Most runs in career: 43,554 J.B. Hobbs 1905–34

Best partnership for each wicket:
1st 428 J.B. Hobbs and A. Sandham v. Oxford University at The Oval 1926
2nd 371 J.B. Hobbs and E.G. Hayes v. Hampshire at The Oval 1909
3rd 413 D.J. Bicknell and D.M. Ward v. Kent at Canterbury 1990
4th 448 R. Abel and T.W. Hayward v. Yorkshire at The Oval 1899
5th 308 J.N. Crawford and F.C. Holland v. Somerset at The Oval 1908
6th 298 A. Sandham and H.S. Harrison v. Sussex at The Oval 1913
7th 262 C.J. Richards and K.T. Medlycott v. Kent at The Oval 1987
8th 205 I.A. Greig and M.P. Bicknell v. Lancashire at The Oval 1990
9th 168 E.R.T. Holmes and E.W.J. Brooks v. Hampshire at The Oval 1936
10th 173 A. Ducat and A. Sandham v. Essex at Leyton 1921

Bowling
Best bowling in an innings for Surrey: 10–43 T. Rushby v. Somerset at Taunton 1921
Best bowling in a match for Surrey: 16–83 G.A.R. Lock v. Kent at Blackheath 1956
Most wickets in a season: 252 T. Richardson 1895
Most wickets in career: 1,775 T. Richardson 1892–1904

SUSSEX

Sussex County Cricket Club was formed in 1839, and they have managed to come second in the County Championship on seven occasions without ever crossing the threshold – 1902, 1903, 1932, 1933, 1934, 1953 and 1981. Sussex were the first winners of the Gillette Cup when Ted Dexter led them to success at Lord's in 1963 and 1964. They subsequently won the 60-overs trophy in 1978 and

1986. They have won the Sunday League just once, in 1982, when they also reached the Benson and Hedges Cup semi-final, their best performance in the competition.

Dickie Bird's years 1956–98

Dickie's first meeting with Sussex was at Hove in 1960, with not very successful scores of 1 and 6. Ken Suttle led the run stakes with 24,134 in 466 matches and Neil Thomson took 1,136 wickets in 297 matches.

Sussex have had thirteen captains in this time: R.G. Marlar (1955–59), E.R. Dexter (1960–65), Nawab of Pataudi jnr (1966), J.M. Parks (1967–68), M.G. Griffith (1968–72), A.W. Greig (1973–77), A. Long (1978–80), J.R.T. Barclay (1981–86), I.J. Gould (1987), P.W.G. Parker (1988–91), A.P. Wells (1992–96), P. Moores (1997) and C.J. Adams (1998).

First-Class Records

Team

Highest total by Sussex:	705–8dec v. Surrey at Hastings 1902
Highest total against Sussex:	726 by Nottinghamshire at Nottingham 1895
Lowest total by Sussex:	19 v. Surrey at Godalming 1830 19 v. Nottinghamshire at Hove 1873
Lowest total against Sussex:	18 by Kent at Gravesend 1867

Batting

Highest individual innings:	333 K.S. Duleepsinhji v. Northamptonshire at Hove 1930
Most runs in a season:	2,850 J.G. Langridge 1949
Most runs in career:	34,152 J.G. Langridge 1928–55

Best partnership for each wicket:

1st	490	E.H. Bowley and J.G. Langridge v. Middlesex at Hove 1933
2nd	385	E.H. Bowley and M.W. Tate v. Northamptonshire at Hove 1921
3rd	298	K.S. Ranjitsinhji and E.H. Killick v. Lancashire at Hove 1901
4th	326*	J. Langridge and G. Cox v. Yorkshire at Leeds 1949
5th	297	J.H. Parks and H.W. Parks v. Hampshire at Portsmouth 1937

6th   255   K.S. Duleepsinhji and M.W. Tate v. Northamptonshire at Hove
            1930
7th   344   K.S. Ranjitsinhji and W. Newham v. Essex at Leyton 1902
8th   229* C.L.A. Smith and G. Brann v. Kent at Hove 1902
9th   178   H.W. Parks and A.F. Wensley v. Derbyshire at Horsham 1930
10th 156   G.R. Cox and H.R. Butt v. Cambridge University at Cambridge
            1908

Bowling

Best bowling in an innings for Sussex: 10–48 C.H.G. Bland v. Kent at
                                         Tonbridge 1899
Best bowling in a match for Sussex: 17–106 G.R. Cox v. Warwickshire at
                                         Horsham 1926
Most wickets in a season: 198 M.W. Tate 1925
Most wickets in career: 2,211 M.W. Tate 1912–37

SOMERSET

Somerset County Cricket Club was formed in 1882, and as yet
have failed to win the County Championship, coming third on
five occasions (1892, 1958, 1963, 1966 and 1981). They won
the Gillette/NatWest Trophy in 1979 and 1983, and the Benson
and Hedges Cup in 1981 and 1982. Their one success in the Sunday
League came in 1979.

Dickie Bird's years 1956–98

Dickie first met Somerset in 1960, scoring 3 in the match at Grace
Road. Bill Alley, who was to become a prominent Test umpire,
was their leading run scorer with 16,667 runs in 350 matches, with
Bob Langford leading the bowling stakes with 1,339 wickets in 484
matches.

Somerset have had thirteen captains since 1956: M.F. Tremlett
(1956–59), H.W. Stephenson (1960–64), C.R.M. Atkinson
(1965–67), R.C. Kerslake (1968), B.A. Langford (1969–71),
D.B. Close (1972–77), B.C. Rose (1978–83), I.T. Botham

(1984–85), P.M. Roebuck (1986–88), V.J. Marks (1989), C.J. Tavaré (1990–93), A.N. Hayhurst (1994–96) and P.D. Bowler (1997–98).

First-Class Records

Team

Highest total by Somerset:	675–9dec v. Hampshire at Bath 1924
Highest total against Somerset:	811 by Surrey at The Oval 1899
Lowest total by Somerset:	25 v. Gloucestershire at Bristol 1947
Lowest total against Somerset:	22 by Gloucestershire at Bristol 1920

Batting

Highest individual innings:	322 I.V.A. Richards v. Warwickshire at Taunton 1985
Most runs in a season:	2,761 W.E. Alley 1961
Most runs in career:	21,142 H. Gimblett 1935–54

Best partnership for each wicket:

1st   346   H.T. Hewett and L.C.H. Palairet v. Yorkshire at Taunton 1892

2nd   290   J.C.W. MacBryan and M.D. Lyon v. Derbyshire at Buxton 1924

3rd   319   P.M. Roebuck and M.D. Crowe v. Leicestershire at Taunton 1984

4th   310   P.W. Denning and I.T. Botham v. Gloucestershire at Taunton 1980

5th   235   J.C. White and C.C.C. Case v. Gloucestershire at Taunton 1927

6th   265   W.E. Alley and K.E. Palmer v. Northamptonshire at Northampton 1961

7th   279   R.J. Harden and G.D. Rose v. Sussex at Taunton 1997

8th   172   I.V.A. Richards and I.T. Botham v. Leicestershire at Leicester 1983

9th   183   C.H.M. Greetham and H.W. Stephenson v. Leicestershire at Weston-Super-Mare 1963

         183   C.J. Tavaré and N.A. Mallender v. Sussex at Hove 1990

10th 143   J.J. Bridges and A.H.D. Gibbs v. Essex at Weston-Super-Mare 1919

Bowling

Best bowling in an innings for Somerset:	10–49 E.J. Tyler v. Surrey at Taunton 1895

434

Best bowling in a match for Somerset: 16–83 J.C. White v.
Worcestershire at Bath 1919

Most wickets in a season: 169 A.W. Wellard 1938
Most wickets in career: 2,166 J.C. White 1909–37

WARWICKSHIRE

Formed in 1882, Warwickshire have recorded five Championship successes, in 1911, 1951, 1972, 1994 and 1995. They won the Gillette/NatWest Trophy in 1966, 1968, 1989, 1993 and 1995, and have had just one success in the Benson and Hedges Cup, in 1994. They have won the Sunday League three times, in 1980, 1994 and 1997.

Dickie Bird's years 1956–98

Dickie's first encounter with Warwickshire was in 1958 when he scored 4 and 6 and was dismissed on both occasions by Bob Carter. Dennis Amiss with 34,145 runs was the Edgbaston side's most prolific run scorer, with 'mean' Tom Cartwright taking 1,058 wickets in 337 matches.

Warwickshire have had eleven captains since 1956: W.E. Hollies (1956), M.J.K. Smith (1957–67), A.C. Smith (1968–74), D.J. Brown (1975–77), J. Whitehouse (1978–79), R.G.D. Willis (1980–84), N. Gifford (1985–87), T.A. Lloyd (1988–92), D.A. Reeve (1993–96), T.A. Munton (1997 but failed to play owing to injury), B.C. Lara (1998).

First-Class Records

Team
Highest total by Warwickshire: 810–4dec v. Durham at Birmingham 1994
Highest total against Warwickshire: 887 by Yorkshire at Birmingham 1896
Lowest total by Warwickshire: 16 v. Kent at Tonbridge 1913
Lowest total against Warwickshire: 15 by Hampshire at Birmingham 1922

Batting

Highest individual innings: 501* B.C. Lara v. Durham at Birmingham 1994

Most runs in a season: 2,417 M.J.K. Smith 1959

Most runs in career: 35,146 D.L. Amiss 1960–87

Best partnership for each wicket:

1st   377* N.F. Horner and K. Ibadulla v. Surrey at The Oval 1960
2nd   465* J.A. Jameson and R.B. Kanhai v. Gloucestershire at Birmingham 1974
3rd   327 S.P. Kinneir and W.G. Quaife v. Lancashire at Birmingham 1901
4th   470 A.I. Kallicharran and G.W. Humpage v. Lancashire at Southport 1982
5th   322* B.C. Lara and K.J. Piper v. Durham at Birmingham 1994
6th   220 H.E. Dollery and J. Buckingham v. Derbyshire at Derby 1938
7th   250 H.E. Dollery and J.S. Ord v. Kent at Maidstone 1953
8th   228 A.J.W. Croom and R.E.S. Wyatt v. Worcestershire at Dudley 1925
9th   154 G.W. Stephens and A.J.W. Croom v. Derbyshire at Birmingham 1925
10th 141 A.F. Giles and T.A. Munton v. Worcestershire at Worcester 1996

Bowling

Best bowling in an innings for Warwickshire: 10–41 J.D. Bannister v. Combined Services at Birmingham 1959

Best bowling in a match for Warwickshire: 15–76 S. Hargreave v. Surrey at The Oval 1903

Most wickets in a season: 180 W.E. Hollies 1946

Most wickets in career: 2,201 W.E. Hollies 1932–57

WORCESTERSHIRE

Worcestershire County Cricket Club was formed in 1865 but it took ninety-nine years for them to win their first championship, which they did in 1964 followed by another success in 1965. Norman Gifford led them to further Championship success in 1974. Under

Phil Neale they had two more Championship successes, in 1988 and 1989. They won the Sunday League in 1971, 1987 and 1988, the Benson and Hedges Cup in 1991 and the NatWest Trophy in 1994.

Dickie Bird's years 1956–98

Dickie's first encounter with Worcestershire was at Grace Road in 1960, when he scored 5 and 15. His highest score against them was 46 at Worcester in 1963. Since 1956, New Zealander Glenn Turner has been the most prolific run getter with 22,298 in 284 matches. Norman Gifford took 1,613 wickets in 526 matches in the same period.

Worcestershire have had eight captains in the Dickie Bird era: P.E. Richardson (1956–58), D. Kenyon (1959–67), T.W. Graveney (1968–70), N. Gifford (1971–80), G.M. Turner (1981), P.A. Neale (1982–91), T.S. Curtis (1992–95), T.M. Moody (1995–98).

First-Class Records

Team

Highest total by Worcestershire:	670–7dec v. Somerset at Worcester 1995
Highest total against Worcestershire:	701–4dec by Leicestershire at Worcester 1906
Lowest total by Worcestershire:	24 v. Yorkshire at Huddersfield 1903
Lowest total against Worcestershire:	30 by Hampshire at Worcester 1903

Batting

Highest individual innings:	405* G.A. Hick v. Somerset at Taunton 1988
Most runs in a season:	2,654 H.H.I. Gibbons 1934
Most runs in career:	34,490 D. Kenyon 1946–67

Best partnership for each wicket:

1st   309   F.L. Bowley and H.K. Foster v. Derbyshire at Derby 1901
2nd   300   W.P.C. Weston and G.A. Hick v. Indians at Worcester 1996
3rd   438* G.A. Hick and T.M. Moody v. Hampshire at Southampton 1997

4th   281   J.A. Ormrod and Younis Ahmed v. Nottinghamshire at Nottingham 1979

5th   393   E.G. Arnold and W.B. Burns v. Warwickshire at Birmingham 1909

6th   265   G.A. Hick and S.J. Rhodes v. Somerset at Taunton 1988

7th   205   G.A. Hick and P.J. Newport v. Yorkshire at Worcester 1988

8th   184   S.J. Rhodes and S.R. Lampitt v. Derbyshire at Kidderminster 1991

9th   181   J.A. Cuffe and R.D. Burrows v. Gloucestershire at Worcester 1907

10th 119   W.B. Burns and G.A. Wilson v. Somerset at Worcester 1906

Bowling

Best bowling in an innings for Worcestershire:	9–23 C.F. Root v. Lancashire at Worcester 1931
Best bowling in a match for Worcestershire:	15–87 A.J. Conway v. Gloucestershire at Moreton-in-Marsh 1914
Most wickets in a season:	207 C.F. Root 1925
Most wickets in career:	2,143 R.T.D. Perks 1930–55

YORKSHIRE

Yorkshire was formed as a county club in 1863, and substantially re-organised in 1891. Their list of Championship wins is substantial They won in 1893, 1896, 1898, 1900, 1901, 1902, 1905 and 1908 under the captaincy of Lord Hawke; in 1912 under Sir A.W. White; 1919 under D.C.F. Burton; 1922, 1923 and 1924 under G. Wilson, in his only three years as captain; 1925 under A.W. Lupton; 1931 and 1932 under F.E. Greenwood, in his only two years as captain; 1933, 1935, 1937, 1938, 1939 and 1946 with A.B. Sellers as captain; 1949-joint under N.W.D. Yardley; 1959 under J.R. Burnet; 1960 and 1962 under J.V. Wilson; 1963, 1966, 1967 and 1968 under D.B. Close. In limited-overs cricket, Yorkshire won the Gillette Cup in 1965 and 1969, the Benson and Hedges Cup in 1987 and the Sunday League in 1983.

Dickie Bird's years 1956–98

Starting his playing career with Yorkshire, Dickie first played for them in an encounter with Scotland at Hull scoring 8 in his first first-class innings. In 1960, he played against Yorkshire at Grace Road. Geoff Boycott has dominated the Yorkshire batting scene during the period, scoring 30,570 runs in 414 matches. Ray Illingworth took 1,287 wickets in 407 matches.

Yorkshire have had twelve captains in this time: W.H.H. Sutcliffe (1956–57), J.R. Burnet (1958–59), J.V. Wilson (1960–62), D.B. Close (1963–70), G. Boycott (1971–78), J.H. Hampshire (1979–80), C.M. Old (1981–82), R. Illingworth (1982–83), D.L. Bairstow (1984–86), P. Carrick (1987–89), M.D. Moxon (1990–95) and D. Byas (1996–98).

First-Class Records

Team

Highest total by Yorkshire:	887 v. Warwickshire at Birmingham 1896
Highest total against Yorkshire:	681–7dec by Leicestershire at Bradford 1996
Lowest total by Yorkshire:	23 v. Hampshire at Middlesbrough 1965
Lowest total against Yorkshire:	13 by Nottinghamshire at Nottingham 1901

Batting

Highest individual innings:	341 G.H. Hirst v. Leicestershire at Leicester 1905
Most runs in a season:	2,883 H. Sutcliffe 1932
Most runs in career:	38,561 H. Sutcliffe 1919–45

Best partnership for each wicket:

1st	555	P. Holmes and H. Sutcliffe v. Essex at Leyton 1932
2nd	346	W. Barber and M. Leyland v. Middlesex at Sheffield 1932
3rd	323*	H. Sutcliffe and M. Leyland v. Glamorgan at Huddersfield 1928
4th	312	D. Denton and G.H. Hirst v. Hampshire at Southampton 1914
5th	340	E. Wainwright and G.H. Hirst v. Surrey at The Oval 1899
6th	276	M. Leyland and E. Robinson v. Glamorgan at Swansea 1926
7th	254	W. Rhodes and D.C.F. Burton v. Hampshire at Dewsbury 1919
8th	292	R. Peel and Lord Hawke v. Warwickshire at Birmingham 1896

9th 192 G.H. Hirst and S. Haigh v. Surrey at Bradford 1898
10th 149 G. Boycott and G.B. Stevenson v. Warwickshire at Birmingham
           1982

Bowling

Best bowling in an innings for Yorkshire: 10–10 H. Verity v.
                                           Nottinghamshire at Leeds 1932
Best bowling in a match for Yorkshire: 17–91 H. Verity v. Essex at
                                           Leyton 1933
Most wickets in a season: 240 W. Rhodes 1900
Most wickets in career: 3,608 W. Rhodes 1898–1930

MAJOR CRICKET-PLAYING COUNTRIES

(Test records up to and including 31 January 1999)

AUSTRALIA

Australia played in the very first Test match ever in 1876–77 when
they beat England by 45 runs in Melbourne.

Dickie Bird's years 1956–98

Australia have had fifteen captains in Dickie's era (listed alphabetically): R. Benaud, B.C. Booth, A.R. Border, G.S. Chappell,
I.M. Chappell, I.D. Craig, R.N. Harvey, K.J. Hughes, B.N. Jarman,

I.W. Johnson, W.M. Lawry, R.R. Lindwall, R.B. Simpson, M.A. Taylor, G.N. Yallop.

Test Match Records

Team

Highest total by Australia:	758–8dec v. West Indies at Kingston 1954–55
Highest total against Australia:	903–7dec by England at The Oval 1938
Lowest total by Australia:	36 v. Australia at Birmingham 1902
Lowest total against Australia:	36 by South Africa at Melbourne 1931–32

Batting

Highest individual innings:	334* M.A. Taylor v. Pakistan at Peshawar 1998–99 334 D.G. Bradman v. England at Leeds 1930
Most runs in a series:	974 D.G. Bradman v. England 1930
Most runs in career:	11,174 A.R. Border (156 matches, 50.56)

Best partnership for each wicket:

1st   382   W.M. Lawry and R.B. Simpson v. West Indies at Bridgetown 1964–65

2nd   451   W.H. Ponsford and D.G. Bradman v. England at The Oval 1934

3rd   295   C.C. MacDonald and R.N. Harvey v. West Indies at Kingston 1954–55

4th   388   W.H. Ponsford and D.G. Bradman v. England at Leeds 1934

5th   405   S.G. Barnes and D.G. Bradman v. England at Sydney 1946–47

6th   346   J.H.W. Fingleton and D.G. Bradman v. England at Melbourne 1936–37

7th   217   K.D. Walters and G.J. Gilmour v. New Zealand at Christchurch 1976–77

8th   243   R.J. Hartigan and C. Hill v. England at Adelaide 1907–08

9th   154   S.E. Gregory and J.M. Blackham v. England at Sydney 1894–95

10th   127   J.M. Taylor and A.A. Mailey v. England at Sydney 1924–25

Bowling

Best bowling in an innings for Australia:	9–121 A.A. Mailey v. England at Melbourne 1920–21
Best bowling in a match for Australia:	16–137 R.A.L. Massie v. England at Lord's 1972

Most wickets in a series: 44 C.V. Grimmett v. South Africa
                                    1935–36
Most wickets in career: 355 D.K. Lillee (70 matches,
                                    23.92)

ENGLAND

England played in the very first Test match ever when they visited
Australia in 1876–77, losing at Melbourne by 45 runs.

Dickie Bird's years 1956–98

England have had twenty-four captains in Dickie's era (listed alpha-
betically): M.A. Atherton, I.T. Botham, G. Boycott, J.M. Brearley,
D.B. Close, C.S. Cowdrey, M.C. Cowdrey, M.H. Denness, E.R. Dexter,
J.H. Edrich, J.E. Emburey, K.W.R. Fletcher, M.W. Gatting, G.A.
Gooch, D.I. Gower, T.W. Graveney, A.W. Greig, R. Illingworth,
A.J. Lamb, A.R. Lewis, P.B.H. May, M.J.K. Smith, A.J. Stewart,
R.G.D. Willis.

Test Match Records

Team

Highest total by England: 903–7dec v. Australia at The Oval 1938
Highest total against England: 729–6dec by Australia at Lord's 1930
Lowest total by England: 45 v. Australia at Sydney 1886–87
Lowest total against England: 26 by New Zealand at Auckland 1954–55

Batting

Highest individual innings: 364 L. Hutton v. Australia at The Oval 1938
Most runs in a series: 905 W.R. Hammond v. Australia 1928–29
Most runs in career: 8,900 G.A. Gooch (118 matches, 42.58)

Best partnership for each wicket:

1st   359   L. Hutton and C. Washbrook v. South Africa at Johannesburg
            1948–49
2nd   382   L. Hutton and M. Leyland v. Australia at The Oval 1938
3rd   370   W.J. Edrich and D.C.S. Compton v. South Africa at Lord's 1947

4th   411   P.B.H. May and M.C. Cowdrey v. West Indies at Birmingham 1957

5th   254   K.W.R. Fletcher and A.W. Greig v. India at Bombay 1972–73

6th   240   P.H. Parfitt and B.R. Knight v. New Zealand at Auckland 1962–63

7th   197   M.J.K. Smith and J.M. Parks v. West Indies at Port-of-Spain 1959–60

8th   246   L.E.G. Ames and G.O.B. Allen v. New Zealand at Lord's 1931

9th   163*   M.C. Cowdrey and A.C. Smith v. New Zealand at Wellington 1962–63

10th   130   R.E. Foster and W. Rhodes v. Australia at Sydney 1903–04

Bowling

Best bowling in an innings for England: 10–53 J.C. Laker v. Australia at Manchester 1956

Best bowling in a match for England: 19–90 J.C. Laker v. Australia at Manchester 1956

Most wickets in a series: 49 S.F. Barnes v. South Africa 1913–14

Most wickets in career: 383 I.T. Botham (102 matches, 28.40)

INDIA

India played their first Test match when they were defeated by England at Lord's in 1932.

Dickie Bird's years 1956–98

India have had twenty-one captains in Dickie's era (listed alphabetically): H.R. Adhikari, M. Azharuddin, B.S. Bedi, C.G. Borde, N.J. Contractor, D.K. Gaekwad, S.M. Gavaskar, Ghulam Ahmed, Kapil Dev, M.H. Mankad, Nawab of Pataudi jnr., G.S. Ramchand, Pankaj Roy, R.J. Shastri, K. Srikkanth, S.R. Tendulkar, P.R. Umrigar, D.B. Vengsarkar, S. Venkataraghavan, G.R. Viswanath, A.L. Wadekar.

Test Match Records

Team

Highest total by India: 676–7 v. Sri Lanka at Kanpur in 1986–87

443

Highest total against India: 952–6dec by Sri Lanka at Colombo (RPS) in 1997–98

Lowest total by India: 42 v. England at Lord's in 1974

Lowest total against India: 82 by Sri Lanka at Chandigarh in 1990–91

Batting

Highest individual innings: 236* S.M. Gavaskar v. West Indies at Madras 1983–84

Most runs in a series: 774 S.M. Gavaskar v. West Indies in 1970–71

Most runs in career: 10,122 S.M. Gavaskar (125 matches, 51.12)

Best partnership for each wicket:

1st   413   M.H. Mankad and Pankaj Roy v. New Zealand at Madras 1955–56

2nd   344* S.M. Gavaskar and D.B. Vengsarkar v. West Indies at Calcutta 1978–79

3rd   316   G.R. Viswanath and Yashpal Sharma v. England at Madras 1981–82

4th   256   S.C. Ganguly and S.R. Tendulkar v. Sri Lanka at Bombay 1997–98

5th   214   M. Azharuddin and R.J. Shastri v. England at Calcutta 1984–85

6th   298* D.B. Vengsarkar and R.J. Shastri v. Australia at Bombay 1986–87

7th   235   R.J. Shastri and S.M.H. Kirmani v. England at Bombay 1984–85

8th   161   M. Azharuddin and A. Kumble v. South Africa at Calcutta 1996–97

9th   149   P.G. Joshi and R.B. Desai v. Pakistan at Bombay 1960–61

10th   109   H.R. Adhikari and Ghulam Ahmed v. Pakistan at Delhi 1952–53

Bowling

Best bowling in an innings for India: 9–69 J.M. Patel v. Australia at Kanpur 1959–60

Best bowling in a match for India: 16–136 N.D. Hirwani v. West Indies at Madras 1987–88

Most wickets in a series: 35 B.S. Chandrasekhar v. England 1972–73

Most wickets in career: 434 Kapil Dev (131 matches, 29.64)

NEW ZEALAND

New Zealand played their first Test match when they were defeated by England at Christchurch in 1929–30.

Dickie Bird's years 1956–98

New Zealand have had nineteen captains in Dickie's era (listed alphabetically): M.G. Burgess, M.E. Chapple, J.V. Coney, B.E. Congdon, J.J. Crowe, M.D. Crowe, G.T. Dowling, S.P. Fleming, L.K. Germon, G.P. Howarth, A.H. Jones, J.F.M. Morrison, J.M. Parker, J.R. Reid, K.R. Rutherford, B.W. Sinclair, I.D.S. Smith, G.M. Turner, J.G. Wright.

Test Match Records

Team

Highest total by New Zealand:	671–4 v. Sri Lanka at Wellington 1990–91
Highest total against New Zealand:	660–5dec for West Indies at Wellington 1994–95
Lowest total by New Zealand:	26 v. England at Auckland 1954–55
Lowest total against New Zealand:	64 by England at Wellington 1977–78

Batting

Highest individual innings:	299 M.D. Crowe v. Sri Lanka at Wellington 1990–91
Most runs in a series:	672 G.M. Turner v. West Indies 1971–72
Most runs in career:	5,444 M.D. Crowe (77 matches, 45.36)

Best partnership for each wicket:

1st 387 G.M. Turner and T.W. Jarvis v. West Indies at Georgetown 1971–72
2nd 241 J.G. Wright and A.H. Jones v. England at Wellington 1991–92
3rd 467 A.H. Jones and M.D. Crowe v. Sri Lanka at Wellington 1990–91
4th 243 M.J. Horne and N.J. Astle v. Zimbabwe at Auckland 1997–98
5th 183 M.G. Burgess and R.W. Anderson v. Pakistan at Lahore 1976–77
6th 246* J.J. Crowe and R.J. Hadlee v. Sri Lanka at Colombo (CCC) 1986–87
7th 186 W.K. Lees and R.J. Hadlee v. Pakistan at Karachi 1976–77
8th 137 D.J. Nash and D.L. Vettori v. India at Wellington 1998–99
9th 136 I.D.S. Smith and M.C. Snedden v. India at Auckland 1989–90
10th 151 B.F. Hastings and R.O. Collinge v. Pakistan at Auckland 1972–73

Bowling

Best bowling in an innings for New Zealand:	9–52 R.J. Hadlee v. Australia at Brisbane 1985–86
Best bowling in a match for New Zealand:	15–123 R.J. Hadlee v. Australia at Brisbane 1985–86
Most wickets in a series:	33 R.J. Hadlee v. Australia 1985–86
Most wickets in career:	431 R.J. Hadlee (86 matches, 22.29)

PAKISTAN

Pakistan played their first Test match when they drew with India at Delhi in 1952–53.

Dickie Bird's years 1956–98

Pakistan have had twenty-two captains in Dickie's era (listed alphabetically): Aamir Sohail, Asif Iqbal, Fazal Mahmood, Hanif Mohammad, Imran Khan, Imtiaz Ahmed, Intikhab Alam, Javed Burki, Javed Miandad, A.H. Kardar, Majid Khan, Moin Khan, Mushtaq Mohammad, Ramiz Raja, Rashid Latif, Saeed Ahmed, Saeed Anwar, Salim Malik, Waqar Younis, Wasim Akram, Wasim Bari, Zaheer Abbas.

Test Match Records

Team

Highest total by Pakistan:	708 v. England at The Oval 1987
Highest total against Pakistan:	790–3dec for West Indies at Kingston 1957–58
Lowest total by Pakistan:	62 v. Australia at Perth 1981–82
Lowest total against Pakistan:	53 by West Indies at Faisalabad 1986–87

Batting

Highest individual innings:	337 Hanif Mohammad v. West Indies at Bridgetown 1957–58

Most runs in a series: 761 Mudassar Nazar v. India 1982–83

Most runs in career: 8,832 Javed Miandad (124 matches, 52.57)

Best partnership for each wicket:

1st   298   Aamir Sohail and Ijaz Ahmed v. West Indies at Karachi 1997–98

2nd   291   Zaheer Abbas and Mushtaq Mohammad v. England at Birmingham 1971

3rd   451   Mudassar Nazar and Javed Miandad v. India at Hyderabad 1982–83

4th   350   Mushtaq Mohammad and Asif Iqbal v. New Zealand at Dunedin 1972–73

5th   281   Javed Miandad and Asif Iqbal v. New Zealand at Lahore 1976–77

6th   217   Hanif Mohammad and Majid Khan v. New Zealand at Lahore 1964–65

7th   308   Waqar Hassan and Imtiaz Ahmed v. New Zealand at Lahore 1955–56

8th   313   Wasim Akram and Saqlain Mushtaq v. Zimbabwe at Sheikhupura 1996–97

9th   190   Asif Iqbal and Intikhab Alam v. England at The Oval 1967

10th   151   Azhar Mahmood and Mushtaq Ahmed v. South Africa at Rawalpindi 1997–98

Bowling

Best bowling in an innings for Pakistan: 9–56 Abdul Qadir v. England at Lahore 1987–88

Best bowling in a match for Pakistan: 14–116 Imran Khan v. Sri Lanka at Lahore 1981–82

Most wickets in a series: 40 Imran Khan v. India 1982–83

Most wickets in career: 362 Imran Khan (88 matches, 22.81)

SOUTH AFRICA

South Africa played their first Test match when they were defeated by England at Port Elizabeth in 1888–89.

Dickie Bird's years 1956–98

South Africa have had eight captains in Dickie's era (listed alphabetically): A. Bacher, W.J. Cronje, T.L. Goddard, G. Kirsten,

D.J. McGlew, P.L. Van der Merwe, C.B. Van Ryneveld, K.C. Wessels.

Test Match Records

Team

Highest total by South Africa: 622–9dec v. Australia at Durban 1969–70

Highest total against South Africa: 654–5 by England at Durban 1938–39

Lowest total by South Africa: 30 v. England at Port Elizabeth 1895–96
30 v. England at Birmingham 1924

Lowest total against South Africa: 66 by India at Durban 1996–97

Batting

Highest individual innings: 274 R.G. Pollock v. Australia at Durban 1969–70

Most runs in a series: 732 G.A. Faulkner v. Australia 1910–11

Most runs in career: 3,471 B. Mitchell (42 matches, 48.88)

Best partnership for each wicket:

1st 260 B. Mitchell and I.J. Siedle v. England at Cape Town 1930–31
2nd 238 G. Kirsten and J.H. Kallis v. England at Manchester 1998
3rd 341 E.J. Barlow and R.G. Pollock v. Australia at Adelaide 1963–64
4th 214 H.W. Taylor and H.G. Deane v. England at The Oval 1929
5th 184 W.J. Cronje and J.N. Rhodes v. England at Lord's 1998
6th 200 R.G. Pollock and H.R. Lance v. Australia at Durban 1969–70
7th 246 D.J. McGlew and A.R.A. Murray v. New Zealand at Wellington 1952–53
8th 147* B.M. McMillan and L. Klusener v. India at Cape Town 1996–97
9th 195 M.V. Boucher and P.L. Symcox v. Pakistan at Johannesburg 1997–98
10th 103 H.G. Owen-Smith and A.J. Bell v. England at Leeds 1929

Bowling

Best bowling in an innings for South Africa: 9–113 H.J. Tayfield v. England at Johannesburg 1956–57

Best bowling in a match for South Africa: 13–165 H.J. Tayfield v. Australia at Melbourne 1952–53

Most wickets in a series: 37 H.J. Tayfield v. England 1956–57

Most wickets in career: 260 A.A. Donald (52 matches, 21.64)

SRI LANKA

Sri Lanka played their first Test match when they were defeated by England at Colombo (PSS) in 1981–82.

Dickie Bird's years 1956–98

Sri Lanka have had six captains in Dickie's era (listed alphabetically): D.S. de Silva, P.A. de Silva, R.S. Madugalle, L.R.D. Mendis, A. Ranatunga, B. Warnapura.

Test Match Records

Team

Highest total by Sri Lanka: 952–6dec v. India at Colombo (RPS) 1997–98

Highest total against Sri Lanka: 676–7 by India at Kanpur 1986–87

Lowest total by Sri Lanka: 71 v. Pakistan at Kandy 1994–95

Lowest total against Sri Lanka: 102 by New Zealand at Colombo (SSC) 1996–97

Batting

Highest individual innings: 340 S.T. Jayasuriya v. India at Colombo (RPS) 1997–98

Most runs in career: 5,129 P.A. de Silva (74 matches, 43.10)

Best partnership for each wicket:

1st 159 S. Wettimuny and J.R. Ratnayeke v. India at Kanpur 1986–87

2nd 576 S.T. Jayasuriya and R.S. Mahanama v. India at Colombo (RPS) 1997–98

3rd 243 S.T. Jayasuriya and P.A. de Silva v. England at The Oval 1998

4th 240* A.P. Gurusinha and A. Ranatunga v. Pakistan at Colombo (PSS) 1985–86

5th 150 S. Wettimuny and L.R.D. Mendis v. England at Lord's 1984

6th 189* P.A. de Silva and A. Ranatunga v. Zimbabwe at Colombo (SSC) 1997–98

7th 144 P.A. de Silva and J.R. Ratnayeke v. Australia at Brisbane 1989–90

8th 76 P.A. de Silva and W.P.U.C.J. Vaas v. Pakistan at Colombo (SSC) 1996–97

9th   83   H.P. Tillekeratne and M. Muralitharan v. England at Colombo
            (SSC) 1992–93
10th   71   R.S. Kaluwitharana and M. Muralitharan v. New Zealand at
            Colombo (SSC) 1998–99

Bowling

Best bowling in an innings for Sri Lanka: 9–65 M. Muralitharan v. England
                                             at The Oval 1998
Best bowling in a match for Sri Lanka: 16–220 M. Muralitharan v.
                                             England at The Oval 1998
Most wickets in a series: 20 R.J. Ratnayake v. India
                                             1985–86
Most wickets in career: 203 M. Muralitharan (42
                                             matches, 26.90)

WEST INDIES

West Indies played their first Test match when they were defeated
by England at Lord's in 1928.

Dickie Bird's years 1956–98

West Indies have had fourteen captains in Dickie's era (listed
alphabetically): F.C.M. Alexander, J.D.C. Goddard, C.G. Greenidge,
D.L. Haynes, A.I. Kallicharran, R.B. Kanhai, B.C. Lara, C.H. Lloyd,
D.L. Murray, I.V.A. Richards, R.B. Richardson, G.St.A. Sobers,
C.A. Walsh, F.M.M. Worrell.

Test Match Records

Team

Highest total by West Indies: 790–3dec v. Pakistan at Kingston
                                    1957–58
Highest total against West Indies: 849 by England at Kingston 1929–30
Lowest total by West Indies: 53 v. Pakistan at Faisalabad 1986–87
Lowest total against West Indies: 46 by England at Port-of-Spain 1993–94

Batting

Highest individual innings: 375 B.C. Lara v. England at St John's 1993–94

Most runs in a series: 829 I.V.A. Richards v. England 1976

Most runs in career: 8,540 I.V.A. Richards (121 matches, 50.23)

Best partnership for each wicket:

1st 298 C.G. Greenidge and D.L. Haynes v. England at St John's 1989–90
2nd 446 C.C. Hunte and G.St.A. Sobers v. Pakistan at Kingston 1957–58
3rd 338 E.deC. Weekes and F.M.M. Worrell v. England at Port-of-Spain 1953–54
4th 399 G.St.A. Sobers and F.M.M. Worrell v. England at Bridgetown 1959–60
5th 265 S.M. Nurse and G.St.A. Sobers v. England at Leeds 1966
6th 274* G.St.A. Sobers and D.A.J. Holford v. England at Lord's 1966
7th 347 D.St.E. Atkinson and C.C. Depeiza v. Australia at Bridgetown 1954–55
8th 124 I.V.A. Richards and K.D. Boyce v. India at Delhi 1974–75
9th 161 C.H. Lloyd and A.M.E. Roberts v. India at Calcutta 1983–84
10th 106 C.L. Hooper and C.A. Walsh v. Pakistan at St John's 1992–93

Bowling

Best bowling in an innings for West Indies: 9–95 J.M. Noreiga v. India at Port-of-Spain 1970–71

Best bowling in a match for West Indies: 14–149 M.A. Holding v. England at The Oval 1976

Most wickets in a series: 35 M.D. Marshall v. England 1988

Most wickets in career: 397 C.A. Walsh (106 matches, 25.39)

ZIMBABWE

Zimbabwe played their first Test match when they drew with India at Harare in 1992–93.

Dickie Bird's years 1956–98

Zimbabwe have had three captains in Dickie's era (listed alphabetically): A.D.R. Campbell, A. Flower, D.L. Houghton.

Test Match Records

Team

Highest total by Zimbabwe:	544–4dec v. Pakistan at Harare 1994–95
Highest total against Zimbabwe:	553 for Pakistan at Sheikhupura 1996–97
Lowest total by Zimbabwe:	127 v. Sri Lanka at Colombo (RPS) 1996–97
Lowest total against Zimbabwe:	103 for Pakistan at Peshawar 1998–99

Batting

Highest individual innings:	266 D.L. Houghton v. Sri Lanka at Bulawayo 1994–95
Most runs in series:	466 D.L. Houghton v. Sri Lanka 1994–95
Most runs in career:	2,090 A. Flower (33 matches, 43.54)

Best partnership for each wicket:

1st   156   G.J. Rennie and G.W. Flower v. New Zealand at Harare 1997–98
2nd   135   M.H. Dekker and A.D.R. Campbell v. Pakistan at Rawalpindi 1993–94
3rd   194   A.D.R. Campbell and D.L. Houghton v. Sri Lanka at Harare 1994–95
4th   269   G.W. Flower and A. Flower v. Pakistan at Harare 1994–95
5th   277* M.W. Goodwin and A. Flower v. Pakistan at Bulawayo 1997–98
6th   165   D.L. Houghton and A. Flower v. India at Harare 1992–93
7th   131   G.W. Flower and P.A. Strang v. Pakistan at Sheikhupura 1996–97
8th   110   G.J. Whittall and B.C. Strang v. Pakistan at Harare 1997–98
9th   87   P.A. Strang and B.C. Strang v. Pakistan at Sheikhupura 1996–97
10th 42   H.H. Streak and A.C.I. Lock v. South Africa at Harare 1995–96

Bowling

Best bowling in an innings for Zimbabwe:	6–90 H.H. Streak v. Pakistan at Harare 1994–95

Best bowling in a match for Zimbabwe:	11–255 A.G. Huckle v. New Zealand at Bulawayo 1997–98
Most wickets in a series:	22 H.H. Streak v. Pakistan 1994–95
Most wickets in career:	106 H.H. Streak (26 matches, 24.83)

INDEX